If you're wondering why you need this new edition of *You Decide! Current Debates in American Politics*, here are 6 good reasons!

1. The Federalism chapter now covers **Arizona's new identity law** encouraging citizen identity checks by police and asks students to consider whether this law is state intrusion into national policy or permissible state action.

2. The Civil Rights chapter has been updated to include coverage of California's **Proposition 8** barring gay marriage posing the question: Is it a violation of equal rights protected by the Constitution, or a valid state law?

3. The chapter on Interest Groups tackles the issue of **corporations participating in election campaigns** and asks students to decide if this is constitutionally appropriate.

4. The Congress chapter looks at the **Senate filibuster** raising the question of its role in majority rule politics.

5. **Elena Kagan**'s nomination to the Supreme Court is debated in the Judiciary chapter.

6. A **new chapter on Budgetary Policy** has been added to the print edition of this text and examines attempts at reducing the federal budget deficit.

PEARSON

YOU DECIDE!
2011
Current Debates in American Politics

JOHN T. ROURKE
University of Connecticut

Longman

Boston Columbus Indianapolis New York San Francisco Upper Saddle River
Amsterdam Cape Town Dubai London Madrid Milan Munich Paris Montreal Toronto
Delhi Mexico City Sao Paulo Sydney Hong Kong Seoul Singapore Taipei Tokyo

23. EDUCATION POLICY

ASSIGNING STUDENTS TO SCHOOLS BASED ON RACE: JUSTIFIED *OR* UNACCEPTABLE?

Assigning Students to Schools Based on Race: Justified

ADVOCATE: National Education Association, et al.

SOURCE: Amicus Curiae brief to the U.S. Supreme Court in *Parents Involved in Community Schools v. Seattle School District No. 1* (2007)

Assigning Students to Schools Based on Race: Unacceptable

ADVOCATE: Asian American Legal Foundation

SOURCE: Amicus Curiae brief to the U.S. Supreme Court in *Parents Involved in Community Schools v. Seattle School District No. 1* (2007)

Also suitable for chapters on Constitution, Civil Rights

PREFACE

To the Students

This book is founded on two firm convictions. The first is that each of you who reads this book is profoundly affected by politics, probably in more ways than you know. The second "truth" is that it is important that everyone be attentive to and active in politics.

POLITICS AFFECTS YOU

The outcome of many of the 16 debates in this printed volume and the 7 supplemental debates on the Web will impact your life directly. If you are a woman, for example, the controversy over gender pay equity laws in **Debate 22** has and will help determine whether your pay will be equal to that of men doing the same work with the same experience. College-age students are most likely to be sent to and to die in wars. There has not been a military draft since the Vietnam War era, and U.S. casualties in wars have been relatively light since then. But in that war, 61 percent of the more than 58,000 Americans killed were between the ages of 17 and 21. Now, after many years, there is renewed talk about a draft—in part because the U.S. military is having trouble meeting its recruitment goals amid its now deescalating involvement in Iraq but escalating military role in Afghanistan, the focus of **Debate 17.**

On the domestic front, freedom of religion is one of Americans' most cherished rights and is protected by the First Amendment. But the application of the First Amendment is something of a double-edged sword. There is widespread agreement that people should have the right to whatever religious belief they may hold. What is controversial and presented in **Debate 3** is whether even such traditional references to God, such as the words "under God" in the Pledge of Allegiance, violate the separation of church and state principle in the First Amendment.

YOU CAN AND SHOULD AFFECT POLITICS

The second thing this volume strongly suggests is that you can and should take part in politics. One necessity to be involved is to know what is happening, and for that Americans necessarily rely heavily on the press. However, one of the traditional pillars of the news media—newspapers—are in huge financial trouble. There are also complaints that the most widely followed of the news media, television, is sacrificing solid news content for infotainment in order to hold its audience, and, by extension, its ad revenues. **Debate 7** takes up the implications of these media woes. If participation is good, then we should be wary of anything that limits participation. **Debate 6** addresses one limit, the almost complete ban on noncitizens voting. **Debate 10** also arguably involves a limitation on participation, given the argument by those who would abolish the Electoral College that it tends to suppress voting in the majority of states that are safe bets for one or the other presidential candidate. Whether they are for or against the candidate who clearly wins in their state, many people ask themselves: Why bother to vote? It may be, though, that more participation by all "persons" is desirable. **Debate 8** takes up the wisdom of the Supreme Court's ruling in *United Citizens v. FEC* (2010) that a law barring corporations from sponsoring independent "electioneering communications" close to elections violated the First Amendment free speech rights of corporations because they are considered legal "persons" with under Supreme Court decisions to the early 1800s.

POLITICS SHOULD NOT ALWAYS AFFECT YOU

It is true that politics affects us all and that we should try to affect politics, but it is also a cornerstone of democracy that many aspects of our lives should be shielded from political control. This principle is the basis of, among other things, the Bill of Rights. Many of the debates in this volume address the line between where the government can make policy and where it is violating our political and civil rights.

For example, **Debate 23** takes up how far the government can go to achieve racial integration in the country's schools. This debate focuses on the policy of the Seattle schools to try to achieve balance in the racial composition of the district's schools by sometimes busing students.

PAY ATTENTION TO THE POLICY PROCESS

Process may seem less interesting than policy to many people, but you do not have to study politics very long to learn that *who* decides something very often determines *what* the policy will be. Process does not always determine which policy is adopted, but it plays a large role. Therefore, there are a number of debates in this volume whose outcome does not directly affect a specific policy, but which could have a profound impact on the policy process. For example, **Debate 2**, on Federalism, debates how far in the federal system Arizona can go in passing laws affecting immigration, an area of regulation generally dominated by the national government. Federalism is also a key component of the dispute in **Debate 15** over whether states should be allowed to levy a sales tax on goods ordered from another state on the Internet or other form of remote commerce.

There is little doubt that the president is the most powerful actor in the political process, and **Debate 12** examines one aspect of that authority: the extent of the president's ability as commander in chief to unilaterally use U.S. military power. Yet another matter of process, the use of filibusters to defeat or force modification of legislation in the U.S. senate is the subject of **Debate 11**. Both sides agree that filibusters contravene the principle of majority rule but disagree on whether that is a good or bad thing.

WHO SERVES INFLUENCES POLICY

Policy is a reflection, in part, of who serves and the process by which they come to and remain in office. Debates 9 and 10 both focus on that issue. **Debate 9** takes up whether the huge victories scored by the Democratic Party in 2006 and again in 2008 reflect a long-term shift in voter sentiments that will leave the Republicans something of a political footnote for years to come. Then **Debate 10** takes up the complex procedure by which Americans elect their presidents and debates a plan to abolish the Electoral College and have the president be decided by a national popular vote.

The vast government bureaucracy is also part of the policy process. An ongoing issue concerns the degree to which career civil servants should be controlled in their statements and decisions by the president, as the elected head of the executive branch, or should be shielded from what some see as political interference. That matter is at the center of **Debate 13.**

It is also important to realize that the courts, especially the U.S. Supreme Court, are very much part of the policy process. That is evident in **Debate 14**, in which the advocates disagree on whether or not Elena Kagan, the most recent appointment to the Supreme Court, is qualified for that position and whether she will decide cases based on careful reading of the law and precedent, or will be strongly influenced by her liberal ideology. Along somewhat similar lines, **Debate 1** addresses the question of whether the meaning of the Constitution should be judged solely in terms of what those who wrote its provisions meant or more broadly in terms of contemporary circumstances and values.

STATE AND LOCAL GOVERNMENTS ARE IMPORTANT, TOO

The federal government is just one of the more than 80,000 different governments in the United States. Each of the state and local governments has the power to pass laws, establish regulations, and tax and spend. For example, state and local governments now collect over $1.2 trillion a year in taxes. About a quarter of this revenue comes from sales taxes, and **Debate 15** takes up whether to add to these receipts by allowing states to tax interstate commerce.

THERE ARE OFTEN MORE THAN TWO SIDES TO A QUESTION

Often public policy questions are put in terms of "pro and con," "favor or oppose," or some other such stark choice. This approach is sometimes called a Manichean approach, a reference to Manicheanism, a religion founded by the Persian prophet Mani (c. 216–276). It taught "dualism," the idea that the universe is divided into opposite, struggling, and equally powerful realities, light (good) and darkness (evil).

The view here is that many policy issues are more a matter of degree, and that the opinion of people is better represented as a place along a range of possibilities, rather than a black-or-white Manichean choice. Numerous issues are like that. For example, virtually all Americans favor doing something to begin to narrow the federal government's massive budget deficits and to eventually balance the budget. **Debate 16** presents something of a yes-no debate regarding whether to emphasize cutting spending or raising taxes, but the core of reforming the budget will be very complex. What do you spend less on, and how much. Taxes may be even more complex. Whose taxes should get increased and by how much? Should entirely new taxes, like a national sales tax, be instituted? Would it be advisable to end some tax breaks, like homeowners deducting their mortgage interest and real estate taxes from their income taxes? Another such issue that extends beyond a simple yes-no dichotomy is the question of how to judge President Obama's anti-terrorism efforts. He has be criticized by both the left and right about his policies, and **Debate 18** struggles, among other things, with how to balance the civil rights and liberties of Americans and, to a degree, alleged terrorists on the one hand, and the need to use normally unacceptable techniques ranging from torture to conducting wiretaps and other types of surveillance without a judicial warrant.

MANY ISSUES CANNOT BE DECIDED BY RATIONALITY ALONE

Values are an important aspect of many debates. For most Americans, the death penalty, the focus of **Debate 20**, is a matter of what is just or moral. Some people believe that no reason is great enough to execute someone. Other people believe with equal fervor that murderers and some other types of criminals forfeit their right to life, and justice is served by their execution. This does not mean that there are no objective, rational aspects to the death penalty debate, or that everyone is absolutely convinced one way or the other. Indeed, while a large majority of Americans favor the death penalty, surveys also show that people are troubled by a range of possible injustices, such as the relationship of wealth to the ability to mount a top-notch defense, the ability to execute people for crimes committed while a juvenile, and claims of racial injustice. What is just is also at the heart of **Debate 4**, which considers whether state laws barring same-sex marriages are a violation of equal rights under the U.S. Constitution.

The discussion in **Debate 5** about how well recent immigrants are melding into the larger American culture also has multiple aspects, including both facts and values. At the objective level, the question is the degree of the immigrants' acculturation. How much of their old culture have immigrants and their families kept, and how "Americanized" have they become, especially after an extended time and into the second and third generations? Irrespective of the answer, there is also a question of values. How much should these new-comers and their families become homogenized? **Debate 21**, on poverty, also includes both objective and subjective aspects. How objectively do we determine who is poor? You will see that the formula for measuring poverty is very controversial. There is also the question of what and how much to do about poverty. To a degree, your views probably depend in part on whether you think an individual's success in life is the product of that person's abilities and effort or the product of society.

All Americans want to reduce U.S. dependence on foreign energy sources. Increasing nuclear energy supplies is one way to do that, but as **Debate 19** shows, the rational debate on such matters as costs is joined by concerns about safety. That is not irrational, but safety is not easily measured because it is a matter of what degree of danger people are willing to tolerate.

SOME CONCLUDING THOUGHTS

The points with which we began are important enough to reiterate. Whether you care about politics or not, it affects you every day in many ways. As the legendary heavyweight boxer Joe Louis put it after knocking out Billy Conn, a more agile but less powerful opponent, in their 1941 championship fight, "You can run, but you can't hide."

Simply paying attention is a good start, but action is even better. Everyone should be politically active, at least to the level of voting. Doing so is in your self-interest because decisions made by the federal, state, and local governments in the U.S. political system provide each of us with both tangible benefits (such as roads and schools) and intangible benefits (such as civil liberties and security). Also, for good or ill, the government takes things away from each of us (such as taxes) and restricts our actions (such as speed limits). It is also the case in politics, as the old saying goes, that squeaky wheels get the grease. Those who participate actively are more likely to be influential. Those who do not, and young adults are by far the age group least likely to even vote, are consigned to grumbling impotently on the sideline.

As an absolute last thought (really!), let me encourage you to contact me with questions or comments. My e-mail address is john.rourke@uconn.edu. Compliments are always great, but if you disagree with anything I have written or my choice of topics and readings, or if you have a suggestion for the next edition, let me know.

To the Faculty

Having plied the podium, so to speak, for three decades, I have some well-formed ideas of what a good reader should do. It is from that perspective that I have organized this reader to work for the students who read it and the faculty members who adopt it for use in their classes. Below is what I look for in a reader and how I have constructed this one to meet those standards.

PROVOKE CLASS DISCUSSION

The classes I have enjoyed the most over the years have been the ones that have been the liveliest, with students participating enthusiastically in a give-and-take among themselves and with me. Many of the debates herein have been selected to engender such participation in your classes by focusing on hot-button topics that provoke heated debate even among those who are not heavily involved in politics and who do not have a lot of background on the topic. Debate 6 is just such a subject. Most of your students will almost certainly reject the idea of noncitizens voting out-of-hand. They will also have some trouble explaining logically why, though, and the process or "wrestling" with such a "weird" idea will get them going. Just a few of the other hot-button topics are use of the phrase "under God" in the Pledge of Allegiance (Debate 3), the death penalty (Debate 20), school busing (Debate 23), and gay marriage (Debate 4). I hope they rev up your classes as much as they have energized mine.

Another point about class discussion that I highlight in the preface section "To the Students" is that, while the debate titles imply two sides, many policy topics are not a Manichean choice between yes and no. Instead, I have tried to include many issues on which opinion ranges along a scale. From that perspective, I often urge students to try to formulate a policy that can gain majority support, if not a consensus. You will also find that many of the issues herein are multifaceted, and I try to point that out to the students. For instance, the debate about gun control is about more than weapons; it is also about how we interpret and apply the Constitution.

BE CURRENT

An important factor in engaging the students is being current. Debating Franklin Roosevelt's court-packing scheme has importance, but it is not as likely to interest students as debating the qualifications and decision standards of Justice Elena Kagan. Therefore, I vigorously update each edition. Even though *You Decide!* appears annually, almost a third of the topics in *You Decide! 2011* are wholly new or are revised from *You Decide! 2010*. Additionally, some of the introductory material, and especially the "Continuing Debate" sections of the issues are updated.

PROVIDE A GOOD RANGE OF TOPICS

I always look for a reader that "covers the waterfront" and have tried to put together this reader to do that. There are numerous debates on specific policy issues and others on process. All the major institutions are covered in one or more debates, and there are also debates touching on such "input" elements as parties, campaigns, interest groups, and the media. The primary focus of this book is on the national government, but federalism receives attention in Debate 2, and state and local government issues are taken up in Debate 15 on taxing interstate commerce. I have also included several debates that are at the intersection of domestic and foreign affairs, including Debate 18 (anti-terrorism policy) and Debate 17 (the U.S. presence in Afghanistan).

My sense of a good range of topics has meant balancing hot-button topics with others that, while they will draw less of an emotional response, are important to debate because they give insight about how the system works and how it might work differently. One example is Debate 11 on the use of filibusters in the Senate: Does their use subvert or protect democracy? In another example, Debate 4 relates to the hot-button topic of gay marriage. But as noted, its also touches on the issue of democracy and when, in a government that is supposed to respond to the public will, the courts are justified in overturning a law that was not just enacted, but done so by a majority of a state's people voting in a referendum. How does that square with democracy?

GIVE THE STUDENTS SOME BACKGROUND FOR THE READING

Readers that work well provide students with some background material that is located just before the reading. This debate volume follows that scheme. There is a two-page introduction to each debate that establishes the context of the debate. As part of this setup, each introduction provides the students with several "points to ponder" as they read the debates.

Moreover, the introductions do more than just address the topic per se. Instead, they try to connect it to the chapter for which it is designed. For example, the introduction to Debate 14 on Elena Kagan begins with a discussion of standards, such as precedence, for decision making and with the power of the judiciary in the American system.

PROVIDE FOLLOW-UP POSSIBILITIES

One of the rewards of our profession is seeing students get excited about a field that intrigues us, and the reader provides a "continuing debate" section after each of the two readings. This section has three parts. "What Is New" provides an update of what has occurred since the date(s) of the two articles. "Where to Find More" points students to places to explore the topic further. I have particularly emphasized resources that can be accessed on the Internet on the theory that students are more likely to pursue a topic if they can do so via computer than by walking to the library. Needless to say, however, I think libraries are great and students should have to use them, so there are also numerous references to books and academic journals. Finally, the continuing debate section has a "What More to Do" part. This segment presents topics for discussion, suggests projects, and advises how to get active on a topic.

FIT WITH THE COURSE

I favor readers that fit the course I am teaching. I prefer a book with readings that supplement all or most of the major topics on my syllabus and that also allows me to spread the reading out so that it is evenly distributed throughout the semester. To that end, this book is organized to parallel the outline of the major introduction to American politics texts in use today. For those who favor the foundations-politics-institutions-policy approach, the table of contents of this volume should match almost exactly with their text and syllabus. For those who use a foundations-institutions-politics-policy scheme, a little, but not much, adjustment will synchronize the debates herein with your plans. Moreover, to help with that, I have labeled each debate in the table of contents with the syllabus topic that fits with the debate. Additionally, for the 16 debates in the printed edition, I have indicated an alternative syllabus topic for each, and I have also made suggestions about how each of the seven debates on the Web might fit with various text chapters and syllabus topics.

FLEXIBILITY

While there is a fair amount of similarity in the organization of the major introduction to American politics texts, I suspect that the syllabi of faculty members are a good deal more individualistic. With that in mind, I have provided flexibility in the reader. First, there are 16 debates in the printed edition, each of which is related to a topic, but each of which has suggestions in the table of contents for alternative assignments. Then there are 7 additional readings on the Pearson Web site associated with *You Decide!* Each of these also has multiple uses and my suggestions about how to work each one into your syllabus. Thus, you can use all 23 debates or many fewer; you can substitute some on the Web for some in the printed edition; you can follow the order in the book fairly closely with most texts; or you can rearrange the order at will. As the Burger King slogan goes, "Have it Your Way!"

As a final note, let me solicit your feedback. Every text and reader that anticipates future editions should be a work in progress. *You Decide!* certainly is. Of course, I will be pleased to hear about the things you like, but I and the next edition of the text will surely benefit more from hearing how I could have done better and what topics (and/or readings) would be good in the next edition. Thanks!

CONSTITUTION

DECIDING ON THE CONSTITUTION'S MEANING:
Rely on the Original Authors *or* Interpret in Light of Modern Circumstances?

RELY ON THE ORIGINAL AUTHORS

ADVOCATE: Keith E. Whittington, William Nelson Cromwell Professor of Politics, Princeton University

SOURCE: "Originalism Within the Living Constitution," *Advance: The Journal of the American Constitution Society Issues Groups*, Fall 2007

INTERPRET IN LIGHT OF MODERN CIRCUMSTANCES

ADVOCATE: Erwin Chemerinsky, Alston & Bird Professor of Law and Political Science, Duke University

SOURCE: "Constitutional Interpretation for the Twenty-first Century," *Advance: The Journal of the American Constitution Society Issues Groups*, Fall 2007

Age is one remarkable characteristic of the U.S. Constitution. It is older than any other written constitution in the world. Moreover, it has survived for more than two centuries with relatively few written changes, having been amended only 27 times. Moreover, the first ten of these amendments, the Bill of Rights, were drafted in 1789, just two years after the Constitution itself had been written and ratified by the states. By contrast, the country which the Constitution governs and the world in which that country exists have undergone transformations that would leave any of the framers gaping is disbelief.

Brevity is the Constitution's second notable aspect. It is only 7,525 words, making it shorter than any of the 50 state constitutions. The few words with which the Constitution structures the American political system has made the document, as scholar Edwin Corwin has commented correctly, "an invitation to struggle" as judges and politicians clash over its meaning. For example, the Constitution designates the president as "commander in chief." But what does that mean, especially in light of the Constitution's delegation of the power to declare war to Congress? This remains an important controversy, as evident in Debate 12 of this volume.

The often vague wording of the Constitution has made the Supreme Court a more influential institution than the founders would have imagined. This has occurred for three reasons. One is that the Constitution designates itself as the "supreme law of the land." That means the Constitution overrides all other law in the United States.

Second, the Constitution gives the federal courts the right to decide case disputes arising under it. This includes disputes about what the Constitution's clauses mean and what language in the thousands of laws passed by Congress mean. As New York Governor (and later U.S. Supreme Court Chief Justice) Charles Evan Hughes put it in 1907, "We are under a Constitution, but the Constitution is what the judges say it is."

Third, the imprecision of the Constitution has strengthened the courts by giving them considerable latitude to decide cases under their power of "judicial review." This means the authority to decide whether laws passed by Congress and actions taken by the executive violate the Constitution and to strike them down if they do. According to the Supreme Court in *Marbury v. Madison* (1803), the "Constitution…confirms and strengthens the principle…" that law and actions "repugnant to the constitution [are] void."

Thus the Supreme Court at the apex of the judicial branch has the authority to hear and decide any case involving the Constitution, to decide what the wording of the Constitution means, and to void laws and actions that violate the intent of Constitution.

The question joined in this debate is how judges decide what the Constitution means. One school of thought called "originalism" or "strict constructionism" is represented by Professor Keith E. Whittington in the first reading. This approach holds that judges should interpret the Constitution by emphasizing its literal text and the original intent of its authors. This intent can be found by looking to the debates and the written commentary at the time of the Constitution and its amendments. The idea, Chief Justice Roger B. Taney wrote long ago in the *Scott v. Sandford* (1857), is that the Constitution should be read with "the same meaning and intent" it had "when it came from the hands of its framers."

The second school of thought contends that judges should consider the Constitution a "living document." This means interpreting it in light of contemporary circumstances. Critics of this approach call it "judicial activism," but advocates such as Erwin Chemerinsky in the second reading might call it "judicial progressivism" or "judicial modernism." Advocates of this approach would say that in deciding what is cruel and unusual punishment, the courts should be less concerned with what that meant in 1787 and more concerned with what modern standards are. From this perspective, Justice Oliver Wendell Holmes noted in *Missouri v. Holland* (1920), the Constitution should be interpreted "in light of our whole experience and not merely in light of what was said a hundred years ago."

POINTS TO PONDER

➤ Think about whether Americans and their courts should be bound in the first decade of the 21st century by what people meant in the last decade of the 18th century when deciding what the Constitution means.

➤ What does Whittington say about how originalists believe that judges should decide issues like abortion, about which the Constitution says nothing, or pornography on the Internet, which did not even exist in the 1789 when the First Amendment was written?

➤ What are the views of the two authors about whether originalism prevents judges from "legislating from the bench," that is, deciding what the constitution means according to their own policy views rather than the intent of the authors of the constitutional or statutory language?

Deciding the Constitution's Meaning: Rely on the Original Authors

KEITH E. WHITTINGTON

The argument that original meaning should guide constitutional interpretation is nearly as old as the Constitution itself. Before there were strict constructionists, before there were judicial activists, there were originalists. In those early days, few seriously objected to the notion that the Constitution should be read in accord with its original meaning, though there were plenty of debates over how best to ascertain that original meaning and what exactly was required to be faithful to the Constitution of the founding.

The modern originalism debates are different. The authority of the original meaning of the Constitution has been routinely challenged in basic ways. The claim that the Constitution should be understood differently—that it is a "living Constitution" that means something different today than it meant when it was adopted, for example—is now itself quite old. It is now thought that adherence to original meaning is one alternative among many, a choice that might be made or that might not. If originalism is not exactly on the defensive, it at least has to be defended.

For judges who wish to exercise the power of judicial review, adherence to the original meaning of the Constitution is the only choice that is justifiable. We might make use of the language of the Constitution to help make sense of and to express our highest political ideals and aspirations. We might borrow from the constitutional text to help remind us of our past political struggles or inspire us to take on new national projects. When judges attempt to set aside the policy decisions of our elected representatives, when they claim that their own constitutional judgments trump those of others, then they cannot rest such claims on mere political idealism couched in a loose constitutional rhetoric. Judges are only entitled to respect when asserting that a law is null and void when they can back up such assertions with a persuasive explanation of how the law violates the meaning of the Constitution as it was framed and ratified.

I. WHY ORIGINALISM?

There are several interrelated justifications for jurisprudence of originalism. Originalism is implicit in the design of a written constitution. The adoption of a written constitution is justified by the desire to fix certain principles and raise them over others as having special weight. The writing of a constitution allows the people to assemble and, in a moment of reflection and deliberation, adopt those specified principles. Originalism makes sense of the fact that it was this text and no other that was adopted and ratified, and it channels the judicial inquiry into discovering what was meant by those who adopted this text. A jurisprudence of originalism recognizes and emphasizes that the Constitution is a communication, an instruction, from an authorized lawgiver, the sovereign people, and that the task of the faithful interpreter is to discover what that instruction was and to apply it as the situation demands.

At heart, all of these justifications are concerned with explaining the basis on which judges can claim the authority to ignore the policies made by elected legislators. Government officials in the United States do not exercise force and power by divine right. Their authority for making legitimate laws that average citizens are expected to obey ultimately comes from their constitutional office. Government officials are chosen to make policy within the limited scope of their predefined legal authority. Legislators are elected to make laws that are intended to serve the public good and operate within constitutional limits. The president is elected to secure the national interest and to insure that those laws are implemented effectively. Judges are not elected for the general purpose of making good policy. Judges are selected to interpret and apply the law in the cases and controversies that arise before them.

The claim to exercise the power of judicial review, the claim to the authority to ignore an otherwise valid law, can only be inferred from the Constitution. The Constitution does not in so many words simply give judges the power to veto laws. The power of judicial review in a particular case is merely an inference from the judicial duty to apply the law—all the law—correctly and appropriately to the case at hand. As Chief Justice John Marshall explained over two centuries ago, if Congress were to instruct the judges that a citizen be convicted of treason on the testimony of only one witness when the Constitution requires two or that a citizen be held criminally liable for actions that were legal when they were committed, then judges would have no choice but to recognize that the superior law of the Constitution would have to govern the case, regardless of the instructions of Congress. A jurisprudence of originalism makes better sense of why John Marshall was correct than does any alternative. Once judges depart from originalism, once they are no longer guided by the original meaning of the Constitution in resolving the cases that come before them, then their very claim to the power of judicial review becomes open to question.

The point of issuing an instruction is to convey the meaning of those authorized to issue them to those obliged to obey them. As James Madison noted, the faithful interpreter must recur to "the sense in which the Constitution was accepted and ratified. In that sense alone it is the legitimate Constitution." It is only by recurring to the original meaning intended by those who created the Constitution that we can make sense of and maintain the notion that we seek to establish, in the words of the Federalist, "good government from reflection and choice." It is only by "carry[ing] ourselves back to the time when the constitution was adopted, recollect[ing] the spirit manifested in the debates," seeking the most "probable [meaning] in which it was passed," rather than by seeing what meaning "may be squeezed out of the text, or invented against it," that we can avoid rendering the Constitution a "blank paper by construction."

For some this may seem to be begging the question: Must even a faithful constitutional interpreter be committed to the language and intent of the founders? The short answer is yes. The implicit link between "language" and "intent" indicates the direction of the interpretive imperative. We readily recognize that we cannot be said to be interpreting the text if we disregard its language. But the language of the text does not emerge from the sea or drop from the sky; it was intentionally written by the authors of the text in order to communicate a message, to convey their thoughts to others. At a minimum, the choice of constitutional language reflects the intentions of the framers that a faithful interpreter is bound to respect. But language is a means, not an end in itself. We use language to convey meaning. We interpret language in order to understand that meaning. If we are free to ignore the meaning that the founders sought to convey in the text, then why are we not equally free to ignore the text itself? Why be bound by the words that they happened to write down if we are not bound by what they meant to say with those words? Why should the language of the Constitution, disassociated from any intended meaning, have any particular authority? If the authority of the Constitution lies in the fact that founders were specially authorized to give instruction, to create supreme law, then the meaning of the law that they laid down must be as authoritative as the particular words they used to convey that meaning.

II. WHAT IS ORIGINALISM?

By the original meaning of the Constitution, I am referring to the meaning that the constitutional text was understood to have at the time it was drafted and ratified. To adopt originalism does not mean that judges must hold a séance to call the spirit of James Madison to ask him what was on his mind in Philadelphia in the summer of 1787 or how he would deal with the tricky constitutional question that is raised by the case before the court. It does mean that judges should not feel free to pour their own political values and ideals into the Constitution. It means that the constant touchstone of constitutional law should be the purposes and values of those who had the authority to make the Constitution—not of those who are charged with governing under it and abiding by it.

One important point should be clarified. The commitment to originalism is not a commitment to the particular practices, plans and expectations of particular framers or of the founding generation. We are bound by the constitutional text that they adopted and by the principles embodied in that text. Their understandings about the practical implications of those principles and the particular applications that they expected to flow from them may be helpful to us as we try to figure out what exactly those constitutional principles were, but those early applications are rarely equivalent to the constitutional requirements themselves. The founders and early government officials who were members of or close to the founding generation may well have fully implemented the principles of the Constitution, but in many cases they did not. Some issues may simply not have arisen at an early date, or the circumstances with which they dealt may not have tested the limits or full extent of those constitutional principles. They may have self-consciously limited themselves, adopting policies that did not test or stretch the limits of the powers that they thought the government possessed or the rights to which they thought individuals were entitled. They could also be wrong about what their own principles required.

The members of the founding generation were as aware as anyone of the limits of human reason and of the temptations of political power. They drafted constitutions precisely because they knew that they and their successors would need constant reminders of the principles that they held dear and the foundational agreements that they had struck. As constitutional interpreters, we are required to reason from the principles that they laid down, not take their word for the particular applications that should be made of those principles. The task of constitutional interpretation requires wisdom, learning and discernment, but it also requires humility and discipline. The operative question for a faithful constitutional interpreter is not what would Madison do in such a situation, or even what did Madison do in such a situation, but what does the principle that Madison and his fellows wrote into the Constitution require in such a situation. Reference to the founders is indispensable to answering such a question, but it remains only a starting point.

This should also caution us against confusing a commitment to originalism with hostility to the full range of methods that judges normally employ to resolve legal problems. A jurisprudence of originalism is entirely consistent with traditional doctrinal analysis, engagement with constitutional text and structure, and attention to constitutional purposes and values. Originalism does not insist that judges eschew doctrinal analysis or that they refuse to draw inferences from the structure of the Construction and the government that it creates ("unwritten" though those structural implications might be). Originalism does insist that such interpretive aids be recognized as the tools that they are. Their value lies in their ability to help us in the process of discovering and applying the original meaning of the Constitution. They become inimical to originalism only when the interpreter forgets that they are mere tools, when the manipulation of precedent becomes an end in itself or when a focus on larger constitutional purposes leads us to ignore the specific ways in which the original Constitution was designed to achieve those purposes.

III. ORIGINALISM AND JUDICIAL ACTIVISM

It should be emphasized that the point of originalist constitutional interpretation is not to clear the way for current legislative majorities. Originalist arguments have frequently been marshaled to criticize what the Supreme Court has done, to show how the Court is guilty of "judicial activism" and of striking down laws without constitutional warrant. In that context, it makes sense to say that the Court was mistaken because it departed from original meaning and that a properly originalist Court would not have taken the same action, that an originalist Court would have upheld rather than struck down a particular statute, that an originalist Court would have left a particular policy choice up to the legislature. But we should not generalize from those particular cases. Originalist judges are not necessarily deferential judges. It may well be the case that the originalist Constitution has little of substance to say about some particular current political controversy. The Constitution may not require anything in particular in regards to euthanasia, abortion, homosexuality, or affirmative action. Deferring to the Constitution in such cases may simply mean holding them open for future political resolution, and the constitutional interpreter should be sensitive to that possibility. The judge should have the humility to recognize that the Constitution may not provide clear answers to all the questions asked of it, that elected officials have the right to make important policy choices without judicial intervention, and that the Constitution may not simply write the judge's own preferred policies into the fundamental law.

Nonetheless, it may also be the case that faithful constitutional interpretation requires turning aside the preferences of current legislative majorities. The Constitution enshrines popular, not legislative, sovereignty. It creates a republic with a limited government, not simply a majoritarian democracy. The goal of a jurisprudence of originalism is to get the Constitution right, to preserve the Constitution inviolable. It denies that judges are freewheeling arbiters of social justice, but it also denies that they are mere window dressing. As Chief Justice William Rehnquist once wrote, "The goal of constitutional adjudication is…to hold true the balance between that which the Constitution puts beyond the reach of the democratic process and that which it does not." The jurisprudence of originalism seeks to hold true that balance, whether that requires upholding the application of a statute in a particular case or striking it down. The issue for originalism is which laws should be struck down, not how many (something which, after all, also depends greatly on the behavior of legislators). Proponents of originalism merely open themselves up to charges of hypocrisy when they approve of instances of judicial review if they do not make plain that it is not deference to politicians that they seek but fidelity to the Constitution.

It is also sometimes contended that the value of originalism lies in its ability to limit the discretion of judges. Originalism, it has been argued, will prevent judges from legislating from the bench or imposing their own value judgments on society. There is something to this argument but it can be overstated. To be sure there was a time in which judges and scholars often thought that the very purpose of courts and the power of judicial review were simply to pursue social justice. Thankfully, such hubris is less common today. But here again, judicial discretion as such is not the issue. The issue is the role of the courts and how the power of judicial review is to be used. Individual judges may well feel little discretion about what they should do in a given case, even if their jurisprudential philosophy is one based on, say, theories of liberal egalitarianism or utilitarian pragmatism. Such judges are in error not because they feel free to do what they personally want in constitutional cases but because they misperceive the basis of their own power and the requirements of constitutional fidelity.

At the same time, proponents of originalism should not delude themselves or others as to the difficulty of the task of identifying and applying the original meaning of the Constitution. It is in no way "mechanical." Disagreement among individuals seeking in good faith to follow a jurisprudence of originalism is entirely possible. The judgment, intelligence, skill, and temperament of the individuals called upon to interpret the Constitution still matter. Judges must still resist the temptation to line up the constitutional founders to agree with their own personal views, just as they must resist the temptation to line up the precedents or the moral philosophies or the policy considerations. A jurisprudence of originalism will at least insure that judges are focused on the right discussion—what the Constitution of the founders requires relative to a given case—even though it cannot insure that everyone will reach the same or the correct conclusion once engaged in that discussion. It is one thing, however, for judges to be open to the criticism that they cut corners in their effort to discover the original meaning of the Constitution. It is quite another for them to be open to the criticism that they are imposing the wrong moral value judgments on the political process. A jurisprudence of originalism insists that judges should strive never to be guilty of the latter criticism, while endeavoring to avoid being guilty of the former.

IV. CONSTITUTIONAL SELF-GOVERNMENT

There are three ways to resolve current political disagreements. We can somehow work them out ourselves, through majority rule, bargaining and compromise, deliberation and debate, and the like. That is, we can make our decisions through normal politics. Alternatively, we can delegate the decision to somebody else. To some degree we almost always delegate anyway, by electing and hiring representatives to hash out the nation's business in the capital while we get on with the more important business of living our lives. But "we" could choose to delegate our controversial political decisions to an even greater degree, throwing the issue into the lap of a "blue-ribbon commission," some executive administrator, or even the courts, perhaps with little or no guidance as to how that issue ought to be resolved by this favored agent. We can simply divest political discretion to some third party and live with the results. We do sometimes use courts in this way. The Sherman Antitrust Act famously handed the problem of identifying monopolies and monopolistic behavior over to the courts, instructing them to do something but not leaving many clues as to what they were to do.

It is possible to use courts in that way, but we should be reluctant to conclude that constitutional judicial review was such a delegation of unfettered policy discretion. Statutory delegations such as those contained in the original Sherman Act are subject to legislative oversight and revision; judges exercise discretion, but only for now and only with implicit or explicit accountability to elected representatives. It is possible that the Constitution contains similar delegations to judges. The founders might have said the equivalent of "protect 'liberty,' whatever that is." Given the general design of the Constitution and the political assumptions on which it was based it would be surprising if they did so, or at least did so very often or in especially important ways. Those who would claim such an authority on the part of judges bear a very high burden not only to show that the founders did not give more substantive content to their constitutional language but also to show that when they left constitutional discretion to later generations that they entrusted that discretion to unelected and largely unaccountable judges rather than to the people and their representatives. Those who would give a freewheeling discretion to judges to develop and enforce "preferred freedoms," "fundamental values," or "active liberty," unconstrained by the value choices that were already made at the time of constitutional drafting, bear a heavy burden to show why it is that judges rather than legislators or citizens should have the ultimate authority to identify "our" favored values and most cherished liberties or what is to be done to best realize our national aspirations.

The other way to resolve our current disagreements is to abide by decisions that have already been made; that is, we can adhere to the existing law. Rather than revisit controversies ourselves or trust the discretion of someone else, we can simply defer to earlier judgments embodied in the law. Having made the decision to keep faith with the law, we may appoint someone to interpret and apply the law for us and keep things on even keel until we are ready to revisit the issue—perhaps recognizing that we ourselves may be too tempted to deviate from the law in particular instances or may be too prone to make unintended or unthoughtful mistakes in applying the law. We should recognize that the interpretive effort will require the exercise of some judgment, but we would, of course, expect the appointed interpreter not to exercise the discretion of a delegated decision-maker.

The issue is what standard should be used to resolve contemporary political controversies and who should have the authority to make the resolution. Contemporary political actors are displaced by any judicial decision. If judges offer an interpretation of the text in accord with the language and intent of the founders, then those contemporary political actors have only deferred their right to make the choice themselves and remake the law. If judges make constitutional law without offering an interpretation of the original Constitution, then we have simply replaced one relatively democratic set of contemporary policymakers with another much less democratic one. If judges interpret the originalist text, then the people retain their sovereign lawmaking authority to create, amend or replace the higher law. If judges do not, then the legislative power of the sovereign people would have been lost. The basic constitutional choices would be made by judges rather than by those who draft and ratify the constitutional text, whether those drafters and ratifiers did their work two hundred years ago or yesterday. As future Supreme Court justice James Iredell observed even as the federal Constitution was being drafted, there would be no point to assembling and writing a constitution if those charged with interpreting and adhering to it could ignore what was decided in those assemblies and instead chose to follow a different rule. The supreme power would no longer lie with those who write the Constitution but instead would lie with those who write the constitutional law.

We privilege the intentions of the founders out of respect for the role of the constitutional founder, not out of respect for any particular founder. It is commonplace that we distinguish between the office and the officeholder, between institutional and personal authority. We respect the actions of the president and the Congress out of regard for the offices, not out of regard for the individuals who hold those offices. Likewise, those who drafted and ratified our present Constitution occupied a political role. It is a role that we do and should respect, not least because it is a role that we could ourselves play. There is no question that the founding generation was uniquely situated at the historical birth of the new nation and uncommonly blessed with political talent and wisdom, but too much myth-making can also be subversive of consensual constitutional governance and should certainly form no part of our current justification for adhering to the inherited Constitution. We should respect the substance of the constitutional choices of the founding not because the founders were especially smart, because they necessarily got it right or because we happen to agree with them on the merits. Although the founders did create a remarkably flexible and successful constitutional system, there are any number of individuals in our own society who are smart, think they can get it right, or whose values others would likely endorse. If being smart or "right" was the sole lodestar for our judgments about constitutional meaning, then there would be plenty of aspirants who could claim that we should follow them rather than the founders. We should respect the substance of choices of the founders because only they spoke on the basis of the "solemn and authoritative act" of the people. We should respect their choices because we should take seriously the idea of constitutional deliberation and choice through democratic means, of constitutional foundings as conscious, real-time political events. We should act so as to preserve the possibility of constitutional self-governance.

Deciding on the Constitution's Meaning: Interpret in Light of Modern Circumstances

Erwin Chemerinsky

The goal is to develop an understanding of the Constitution for the 21st century. It makes no sense to find this by looking to the 18th century. Throughout American history, the Supreme Court has decided the meaning of the Constitution by looking to its text, its goals, its structure, precedent, historical practice, and contemporary needs and values. This is what constitutional law always has been about and always should be about. It is misguided and undesirable to search for a theory of constitutional interpretation that will yield determinate results, right and wrong answers, to most constitutional questions. No such theory exists or ever will exist.

Only a few Justices in American history have professed to follow an originalist philosophy and they are originalists only some of the time. For example, Justices [Antonin] Scalia and [Clarence] Thomas, the self-professed originalists on the Court, believe that the meaning of the Constitution was fixed when it was adopted and that constitutional interpretation is the process of finding and following this original meaning. But these Justices did not apply originalism in their Tenth and Eleventh Amendment decisions of the last decade. The Court's decisions prohibiting Congress from commandeering state governments and forcing them to adopt laws or regulations cannot be derived from the text of the Tenth Amendment or its intent or its historical meaning. Nor can originalism explain the Court's expansion of sovereign immunity to bar suits against states by their own citizens in federal courts or in state courts. Perhaps even more profoundly, these Justices pay no attention to originalism in condemning all affirmative action programs despite strong evidence that the original intent of the Fourteenth Amendment was very much to allow such efforts.

Moreover, it must be remembered that on many occasions, the Supreme Court has expressly rejected originalism. *In Home Building & Loan Ass'n v. Blaisdell* [1932], the Court declared:

> If by the statement that what the Constitution meant at the time of its adoption it means today, it is intended to say that the great clauses of the Constitution must be confined to the interpretation which the framers, with the conditions and outlook of their time, would have placed upon them, the statement carries its own refutation.

Most famously, in *Brown v. Board of Education*, Chief Justice Earl Warren, writing for the Court [in 1954], stated: "In approaching the problem, we cannot turn the clock back to 1868 when the [Fourteenth] Amendment was adopted, or even to 1896 when *Plessy v. Ferguson* was written."

For decades, prominent constitutional scholars have advanced devastating critiques of originalism. Yet, over the last few decades, originalism as a philosophy of constitutional interpretation seems to have gained legitimacy and even acceptance.

In this essay, I want to explore why this has happened. My thesis is that the appeal of originalism is that it offers a false promise of constraining judges and of limiting, if not eliminating, value choices by judges. Getting past originalism requires demonstrating that this truly is a false hope; no theory of constitutional interpretation can significantly reduce or eliminate judicial discretion. Progressives need to defend constitutional decision-making as it always has been practiced, by both liberals and conservatives: it is a product of judges considering a myriad of sources, including the Constitution's text, its goals, its structure, precedent, historical practice, and contemporary needs and values. No theory can offer determinacy in constitutional decision-making or avoid the reality that results depend on value choices made by judges in determining the meaning of the Constitution. A John Paul Stevens and an Antonin Scalia will disagree in most important constitutional cases, not because one is smarter or has a better approach to constitutional interpretation. They will come to different results because they have vastly different ideologies and values.

First, there is no doubt that the appeal of originalism is its promise of constraining judges. It is the allure of formalism, of decisions derived deductively from sources external to the judges. Originalists claim that decisions in constitutional cases would be based on seemingly objective sources and not on the ideology of the judges. Justice Scalia, for example, has advanced exactly this defense for his originalist philosophy and declared: "Originalism…establishes a historical criterion that is conceptually quite separate from the preferences of the judge himself." There is an understandable appeal to an approach to constitutional law which provides for decisions that have nothing to do with the identity or values of the individual judges.

Second, it is crucial to recognize and to expose this as a false promise. Originalism, no less than any theory of constitutional interpretation, still involves tremendous judicial discretion and decisions that are very much the result of value choices by the judges. There are many reasons for this. Balancing of competing interests is an inevitable part of constitutional law and inescapably involves judicial discretion, just as much for originalists as for non-originalists. Balancing competing interests is a persistent feature of constitutional decision-making. How should the President's interest in executive privilege and secrecy be balanced against the need for evidence at a criminal trial? How should a defendant's right to a fair trial be balanced against the freedom of the press? How should legitimate, important, and compelling government interests be determined in individual rights and equal protection cases? Levels of scrutiny are, after all, just a tool for arranging the weights in constitutional balancing. Moreover, constitutional law constantly asks, as does so much of law, what is reasonable. Under the Fourth Amendment, courts routinely focus on whether the actions of police officers are reasonable. Under the Takings Clause, courts determine whether there is a public purpose by examining whether the government acted out of a reasonable belief that its action would benefit the public. Such balancing is not an exclusively liberal exercise. In a recent case, Justice Scalia, writing for the Court, stressed that the application of the exclusionary rule depends on a weighing of its costs and benefits.

Moreover, originalism allows tremendous judicial discretion because the intent behind any constitutional provision can be stated at many different levels of abstraction. For example, who was the equal protection clause intended to protect? The intent could have been solely to protect African Americans; to protect all racial minorities; to shelter all groups that have been historically discriminated against; or to defend all individuals from arbitrary treatment by the government. Each of these potential answers is a reasonable way of describing the drafters' intent for the Fourteenth Amendment. Yet a judge must eventually choose among these answers, and a great deal depends on that choice. Whether sex discrimination or affirmative action violates equal protection depends entirely on the choice among levels of abstraction. Here, too, neither formalism nor originalism can provide a discretion-free answer.

Originalism also provides enormous discretion to judges in deciding the original intent. The theory focuses on the Framers, but so many people were involved in drafting and ratifying the Constitution and its amendments that it is possible to find historical quotations supporting either side of almost any argument. The debate over the Second Amendment powerfully illustrates this, as sides make strong arguments based on the original understanding of the provision.

These critiques of originalism, of course, are familiar. Yet, their significance cannot be overstated in formulating an approach to constitutional law for the 21st century. No theory of constitutional interpretation can provide formalism or significantly reduce judicial discretion. Inevitably, judges in interpreting the Constitution must make choices as to the meaning of open-textured constitutional language and in balancing competing interests.

Antonin Scalia purports to have a more objective approach to constitutional law and repeatedly asserts a moral high ground compared to his colleagues. He finds in the Constitution no protection for reproductive choice, a prohibition of affirmative action, permission for prayer in public schools and government aid to religious schools, and no exclusionary rule. His views seem far more similar to the 2004 Republican platform than to anything in the original meaning of the Constitution.

Third, progressives must defend their alternative vision of constitutional law. Originalists try to put progressives on the defensive by asserting that originalists have a theory of constitutional law, but that others don't. But this is based on their claim of a theory which reduces judicial discretion and offers a seemingly objective method of decision-making. Once this is exposed as false it becomes clear that all judges are engaged in the same enterprise and that none have an objective methodology that permits decisions removed from their own values.

Progressives must offer a more complex and realistic description of judging in constitutional cases. Supporters of originalism present the debate as if there are only two choices: discretion-free judging or judging by whim and caprice. Of course, the reality is neither. Judges always have discretion, but the exercise of that discretion is not about what the judge ate for breakfast. Rather, discretion is about how judges look at multiple sources and decide the meaning of the Constitution. An accurate description of judicial review's reality is needed to compete with the value-neutral models and the rhetoric supporting them.

What, then, is the role for fidelity in constitutional interpretation for the 21st century? It all depends on "fidelity" to what. Constitutional interpretation always must show fidelity to the document's text. But all Justices throughout history have done this and have based their decisions on giving meaning to the text of the Constitution. Surely, too, fidelity must be to the goals of the constitutional provision. But the goals are inevitably abstract, not the specific intent of the framers. In deciding what is "cruel and unusual punishment," judges must be guided by the goal of ending degrading and inhumane punishments, not the specific views of the framers as to which punishments are unacceptable. In deciding that segregation violates equal protection, the Court rightly followed the general goal of equal protection, not the specific views of the Congress that both ratified the Fourteenth Amendment and segregated the District of Columbia public schools. Courts also need to consider all that has occurred since the ratification of a constitutional provision, including judicial precedents. Contemporary needs should be taken into account as well; there is no other way to balance.

This, of course, means that judges will have discretion in interpreting the Constitution. But that is how it always has been. *Marbury v. Madison* [1803], establishing the institution of judicial review, was an exercise of judicial discretion because the Constitution is silent about the authority of courts to invalidate statutes or executive actions.

As progressives articulate a vision of constitutional law for the 21st century, it must be one based on the Constitution's commitments to freedom and equality. It must be based on the Constitution's respect for the dignity of each individual. It must be based on the Constitution's mandate for separation of powers and checks and balances.

Progressives must explain in judicial decisions, law review articles, and op-ed pieces why the Constitution includes protection for reproductive choice, why it allows affirmative action to achieve racial equality, why it requires a separation of church and state, why it does not permit indefinite detentions of human beings without judicial review. This is the challenge of a Constitution for the new century.

THE CONTINUING DEBATE:
Deciding on the Constitution's Meaning

What Is New

The battle over originalism continues to play a key role in many Supreme Court decisions. In *District of Columbia v. Heller* (2008), the court for the first time ruled directly that Americans have at least a limited right to "bear arms." In the majority opinion voiding the District of Colombia's strict gun control law, Justice Antonin Scalia focused on original intent—what was said at the time the amendment was written and adopted—and dismissed everything said afterwards as irrelevant "post-ratification commentary." Scalia noted, "Undoubtedly some think that the Second Amendment is outmoded in [modern] society," but rejected that view as sufficient reason "to pronounce the Second Amendment extinct." By contrast, John Paul Stevens writing for the dissenting justices argued that both original intent and the "post-ratification history of the Amendment...makes [it] abundantly clear that [it] should not be interpreted as limiting the authority...to regulate the use or possession of firearms for purely civilian purposes." According to a 2010 poll, 49% of Americans favored interpreting the Constitution according to "original intent only" and thus agreed with Justice Scalia; 42% favored also considering "changing times," as did Stevens; and 9% were unsure.

Where to Find More

For historical background on the debate, read Johnathan George O'Neill, *Originalism in American Law and Politics: A Constitutional History* (Johns Hopkins University Press, 2005) and Lackland H. Bloom, *Methods of Interpretation: How the Supreme Court Reads the Constitution* (Oxford University Press, 2009). A look at what the authors of the Constitution were or were not thinking is Cass R. Sunstein, *A Constitution of Many Minds: Why the Founding Document Doesn't Mean What It Meant Before* (Princeton University Press, 2009). A good source for a range of recent thinking on interpreting the Constitution, the source from which the two articles here were drawn, is *Advance: The Journal of the American Constitution Society Issues Groups* (Fall 2007), which can be found on the Web site of the American Constitution Society for Law and Policy at www.acslaw.org/advance/. The majority and dissenting opinions in *District of Colombia v. Heller* (2008) provide an excellent look at how justices on both sides of a question use history to buttress their views. One of many sources is OYEZ at www.oyez.org/. Keyboard the case name into the search window.

What More to Do

Have a class debate over what standards to use when interpreting the Constitution. If you adopt the "living constitution" view and use contemporary standards, is there really a "bedrock constitution," or are judges really policymakers interpreting constitutional language according to their own views? But originalism has been compared to "ancestor worship," leaving modern society bound by centuries-old norms. Moreover, how does originalism deal with modern technology and contemporary standards that the founders could not foresee? Perhaps most importantly, are you comfortable with the idea that we all live under a Constitution, but that constitution means what nine, unelected justices with life tenure say it does? How does that square with democracy?

Arizona's Law Encouraging Citizen Identity Checks by Police: State Intrusion into National Policy

ATTORNEYS REPRESENTING THE U.S. GOVERNMENT

In this action, the United States seeks to declare invalid and preliminarily and permanently enjoin the enforcement of S.B. 1070, as amended and enacted by the State of Arizona, because S.B. 1070 is preempted by federal law and therefore violates the Supremacy Clause of the U.S. Constitution. In our constitutional system, the federal government has preeminent authority to regulate immigration matters. This authority derives from the U.S. Constitution and numerous acts of Congress. The nation's immigration laws reflect a careful and considered balance of national law enforcement, foreign relations, and humanitarian interests. Congress has assigned to the U.S. Department of Homeland Security [DHS], Department of Justice [DOJ], and Department of State [DOS], along with other federal agencies, the task of enforcing and administering these immigration-related laws. In administering these laws, the federal agencies balance the complex—and often competing—objectives that animate federal immigration law and policy. Although states may exercise their police power in a manner that has an incidental or indirect effect on aliens, a state may *not* establish its own immigration policy or enforce state laws in a manner that interferes with the federal immigration laws. The Constitution and the federal immigration laws do not permit the development of a patchwork of state and local immigration policies throughout the country.

Despite the preeminent federal authority and responsibility over immigration, the State of Arizona recently enacted S.B. 1070, a sweeping set of provisions that are designed to "work together to discourage and deter the unlawful entry and presence of aliens" by making "attrition through enforcement the public policy of all state and local government agencies in Arizona."

S.B. 1070 pursues only one goal—"attrition"—and ignores the many other objectives that Congress has established for the federal immigration system. And even in pursuing attrition, S.B. 1070 disrupts federal enforcement priorities and resources that focus on aliens who pose a threat to national security or public safety. If allowed to go into effect, S.B. 1070's mandatory enforcement scheme will conflict with and undermine the federal government's careful balance of immigration enforcement priorities and objectives.

The United States understands Arizona's legitimate concerns about illegal immigration and has undertaken significant efforts to secure our nation's borders. The federal government, moreover, welcomes cooperative efforts by states and localities to aid in the enforcement of the nation's immigration laws. But the U.S. Constitution forbids Arizona from supplanting the federal government's immigration regime with its own state-specific immigration policy—a policy that, in purpose and effect, interferes with the numerous interests the federal government must balance when enforcing and administering the immigration laws and disrupts the balance actually established by the federal government. Accordingly, S.B. 1070 is invalid under the Supremacy Clause of the U.S. Constitution and must be struck down.

FEDERAL AUTHORITY AND LAW GOVERNING IMMIGRATION AND STATUS OF ALIENS

The Supremacy Clause of the Constitution mandates that "[t]his Constitution, and the Laws of the United States which shall be made in Pursuance thereof...shall be the supreme Law of the Land." The Constitution [also] affords the federal government the power to "establish an uniform Rule of Naturalization," and to "regulate Commerce with foreign Nations." Further, the federal government has broad authority to establish the terms and conditions for entry and continued presence in the United States, and to regulate the status of aliens within the boundaries of the United States. The Constitution [additionally] affords the President of the United States the authority to "take Care that the Laws be faithfully executed." Further, the President has broad authority over foreign affairs. Immigration law, policy, and enforcement priorities are affected by and have impacts on U.S. foreign policy, and are themselves the subject of diplomatic arrangements.

Congress has exercised its authority to make laws governing immigration and the status of aliens within the United States by enacting the various provisions of the INA [Immigration and Nationalization Act of 1952] and other laws regulating immigration. Through the INA, Congress set forth the framework by which the federal government determines which aliens may be eligible to enter and reside in the United States, which aliens may be removed from the United States, the consequences for unlawful presence, the penalties on persons who violate the procedures established for entry, conditions of residence, and employment of aliens, as well as the process by which certain aliens may ultimately become naturalized citizens of the United States. The INA also vests the executive branch with considerable discretion in enforcing the provisions of the federal immigration laws, generally allowing federal agencies to ultimately decide whether particular immigration remedies are appropriate in individual cases.

In exercising its significant enforcement discretion, the federal government prioritizes for arrest, detention, prosecution, and removal those aliens who pose a danger to national security or a risk to public safety. Consistent with these enforcement priorities, the federal government principally targets aliens engaged in or suspected of terrorism or espionage; aliens convicted of crimes, with a particular emphasis on violent criminals, felons, and repeat offenders; certain gang members; aliens subject to outstanding criminal warrants; and fugitive aliens, especially those with criminal records.

In crafting federal immigration law and policy, Congress has necessarily taken into account multiple and often competing national interests. Assuring effective enforcement of the provisions against illegal migration and unlawful presence is a highly important interest, but it is not the singular goal of the federal immigration laws. The laws also take into account other uniquely national interests, including facilitating trade and commerce; welcoming those foreign nationals who visit or immigrate lawfully and ensuring their fair and equitable treatment wherever they may reside; responding to humanitarian concerns at the global and individual levels; and otherwise ensuring that the treatment of aliens present in our nation does not harm our foreign relations with the countries from which they come or jeopardize the treatment of U.S. citizens abroad. Because immigration control and management is [according to the Supreme Court] "a field where flexibility and the adaptation of the congressional policy to infinitely variable conditions constitute the essence of the program," Congress vested substantial dis-

Immigration and Customs Enforcement ("ICE"), U.S. Customs and Border Protection ("CBP"), and U.S. Citizenship and Immigration Services ("USCIS"). DHS also receives state and local cooperation in its enforcement efforts. In addition, Congress prescribed by statute a number of ways in which states may assist the federal government in its enforcement of the immigration laws.

Through a variety of programs, DHS works cooperatively with states and localities to accomplish its mission to enforce the federal immigration laws. Among these efforts is the Law Enforcement Agency Response program ("LEAR"), an Arizona-specific program for responding to calls from state and local law enforcement officers seeking assistance from ICE regarding suspected unlawfully present aliens. But the opportunity that federal law provides for participation by state and local officials does not mean that states can enact their own immigration policies to rival the national immigration policy; the formulation of immigration policy and balancing of immigration enforcement priorities is a matter reserved for the federal government. Such regulations do not fall within the state's traditional police powers and remain the exclusive province of the federal government.

ARIZONA'S S.B. 1070

On April 23, 2010, [Arizona's] Governor [Janet] Brewer signed into law S.B. 1070, which [among other things] includes a provision that requires, in the context of a lawful stop, detention, or arrest, the verification of an individual's immigration status when practicable where there is "reasonable suspicion" that the individual is unlawfully present in the United States.

On the same day that she signed S.B. 1070 into law, Governor Brewer issued an executive order requiring law enforcement training to "provide clear guidance to law enforcement officials regarding what constitutes reasonable suspicion," and to "make clear that an individual's race, color or national origin alone cannot be grounds for reasonable suspicion to believe any law has been violated." One week after S.B. 1070 was signed into law, the Arizona Legislature passed, and Governor Brewer signed, H.B. 2162, which amended S.B. 1070 for the purpose of responding to those who [according to Governor Brewer] "expressed fears that the original law would somehow allow or lead to racial profiling."

S.B. 1070 (as amended) attempts to second guess federal policies and re-order federal priorities in the area of immigration enforcement and to directly regulate immigration and the conditions of an alien's entry and presence in the United States despite the fact that those subjects are federal domains and do not involve any legitimate state interest. Arizona's adoption of a maximal "attrition through enforcement" policy disrupts the national enforcement regime set forth in the INA and reflected in federal immigration enforcement policy and practice, including the federal government's prioritization of enforcement against dangerous aliens.

S.B. 1070 implements Arizona's stated immigration policy through a novel and comprehensive immigration regime that, among other things, creates a series of state immigration crimes relating to the presence, employment, and transportation of aliens, expands the opportunities for Arizona police to push aliens toward incarceration for those crimes by enforcing a mandatory immigration status verification system, and allows for arrests based on crimes with no nexus to Arizona. [As such], S.B. 1070 conflicts with and otherwise stands as an obstacle to Congress's demand that federal immigration policy accommodate the competing interests of immigration control, national security and public safety, humanitarian concerns, and foreign relations—a balance implemented through the policies of the President and various executive officers with the discretion to enforce the federal immigration laws. Enforcement of S.B. 1070 would also effectively create state crimes and sanctions for unlawful presence despite Congress's considered judgment to not criminalize such status. S.B. 1070 would thus interfere with federal policy and prerogatives in the enforcement of the U.S. immigration laws.

Because S.B. 1070, in both its singularly stated purpose and necessary operation, conflicts with the federal government's balance of competing objectives in the enforcement of the federal immigration laws, its passage already has had foreign policy implications for U.S. diplomatic relations with other countries, including Mexico and many others. S.B. 1070 has also had foreign policy implications concerning specific national interests regarding national security, drug enforcement, tourism, trade, and a variety of other issues. S.B. 1070 has subjected the United States to direct criticism by other countries and international organizations and has resulted in a breakdown in certain planned bilateral and multilateral arrangements on issues such as border security and disaster management. S.B. 1070 has in these ways undermined several aspects of U.S. foreign policy related to immigration issues and other national concerns that are unrelated to immigration.

Numerous other states are contemplating passing legislation similar to S.B. 1070. The development of various conflicting state immigration enforcement policies would result in further and significant damage to (1) U.S. foreign relations, (2) the United States' ability to fairly and consistently enforce the federal immigration laws and provide immigration-related humanitarian relief, and (3) the United States' ability to exercise the discretion vested in the executive branch under the INA, and would result in the non-uniform treatment of aliens across the United States.

Section 2 of S.B. 1070

Section 2 of S.B. 1070 mandates that for any lawful "stop, detention or arrest made by a law enforcement official" (or agency) in the enforcement of any state or local law, including civil ordinances, where reasonable suspicion exists that an individual is an alien and is "unlawfully present" in the United States, the officer must make a reasonable attempt to determine the individual's immigration status when practicable, and to verify it with the federal government. Section 2 also requires that "[a]ny person who is arrested shall have the person's immigration status determined before the person is released."

Section 2 provides that any legal resident of Arizona may bring a civil action in an Arizona court to challenge any official or agency that "adopts or implements a policy that limits or restricts the enforcement of federal immigration laws...to less than the full extent permitted by federal law." Whereas Arizona police (like federal officers and police in other states) formerly had the discretion to decide whether to verify immigration status during the course of a lawful stop, the combination of the verification requirement and the threat of private lawsuits now removes such discretion and mandates verification. This provision also mandates the enforcement of the remaining provisions of S.B. 1070.

The mandatory nature of Section 2, in tandem with S.B. 1070's new or amended state immigration crimes, directs officers to seek maximum scrutiny of a person's immigration status, and mandates the imposition of state criminal penalties for what

tives of Congress in creating a comprehensive system of penalties for aliens who are unlawfully present in the United States.

Section 5 of S.B. 1070

Section 5 of S.B. 1070 makes it a new state crime for any person who is "unauthorized" and "unlawfully present" in the United States to solicit, apply for, or perform work. Arizona's new prohibition on unauthorized aliens seeking or performing work is preempted by the comprehensive federal scheme of sanctions related to the employment of unauthorized aliens. The text, structure, history, and purpose of this scheme reflect an affirmative decision by Congress to regulate the employment of unlawful aliens by imposing sanctions on the employer without imposing sanctions on the unlawful alien employee. Arizona's criminal sanction on unauthorized aliens stands as an obstacle to the full purposes and objectives of Congress's considered approach to regulating employment practices concerning unauthorized aliens, and it conflicts with Congress's decision not to criminalize such conduct for humanitarian and other reasons. Enforcement of this new state crime additionally interferes with the comprehensive system of civil consequences for aliens unlawfully present in the United States by attaching criminal sanctions on the conditions of unlawful presence, despite an affirmative choice by Congress not to criminalize unlawful presence.

Section 5 of S.B. 1070 also makes it a new state crime for a person committing any criminal offense to (1) "transport...an alien..., in furtherance of the illegal presence of the alien in the United States,...if the person knows or recklessly disregards" that the alien is here illegally; (2) "conceal, harbor or shield...an alien from detection...if the person knows or recklessly disregards the fact that the alien" is unlawfully present; or (3) "encourage or induce an alien to come to or reside in this state if the person knows or recklessly disregards the fact that such...entering or residing in this state is or will be in violation of law." This provision exempts child protective service workers, first responders, and emergency medical technicians. This provision contains no further exceptions, including for organizations exempted by federal law from criminal liability, such as religious organizations which "encourage, invite, call, allow, or enable" an alien to volunteer as a minister or missionary.

Arizona's new state law prohibition of certain transporting, concealing, and encouraging of unlawfully present aliens is preempted by federal law. This new provision is an attempt to regulate unlawful entry into the United States (through the Arizona border). The regulation of unlawful entry is an area from which states are definitively barred by the U.S. Constitution. Additionally, because the purpose of this law is to deter and prevent the movement of certain aliens into Arizona, the law restricts interstate commerce. Enforcement and operation of this state law provision would therefore conflict and interfere with the federal government's management of interstate commerce, and would thereby violate Article I, Section 8 of the U.S. Constitution.

Section 6 of S.B. 1070

Section 6 of S.B. 1070 amends a preexisting Arizona criminal statute governing the circumstances under which law enforcement officers can make a warrantless arrest. Section 6 allows the arrest of anyone whom the officer has probable cause to believe "has committed any public offense that makes the person removable from the United States," and does not require coordination with DHS to confirm removability. The warrantless arrest authority provided by Section 6 applies to persons who have committed an offense in another state when an Arizona law enforcement official believes that offense makes the person removable. Arizona law previously allowed for the warrantless arrest of anyone who was suspected of having committed a misdemeanor or felony in Arizona. Although Section 6 authorizes warrantless arrests based on crimes committed out of state, it does so only if the officer believes the crime makes the individual removable. Thus, Section 6 is not intended to serve any new law enforcement interest. Rather, the purpose of Section 6, especially when read in light of S.B. 1070's overall purpose, is plain: Section 6 provides additional means to arrest aliens in the state on the basis of immigration status.

Section 6 makes no exception for aliens whose removability has already been resolved by federal authorities, despite the fact that only the federal government can actually issue removal decisions. Section 6 will therefore necessarily result in the arrest of aliens based on out-of-state crimes, even if the criminal and immigration consequences of the out-of- state crime have already been definitively resolved. For that reason, as with Section 2, Section 6 of S.B. 1070 interferes with the federal government's enforcement prerogatives and will necessarily impose burdens on lawful aliens in a manner that conflicts with the purposes and practices of the federal immigration laws. Additionally, Section 6 will result in the arrest of aliens whose out-of-state crimes would not give rise to removal proceedings at all.

Wherefore, the United States respectfully requests the following relief [be granted by the district court]:

1. A declaratory judgment stating that Sections 1-6 of S.B. 1070 are invalid, null, and void; [and]

2. A preliminary and a permanent injunction against the State of Arizona, and its officers, agents, and employees, prohibiting the enforcement of Sections 1-6 of S.B. 1070;

numerous incidents of serious violence against Arizonans, including the homicide of eight Phoenix police officers since 1999. Almost 50% of illegal aliens enter the United States through Arizona. The Arizona Department of Corrections has estimated that criminal aliens make up more than 17% of Arizona's prison population and 21.8% of felony defendants in Maricopa County [the Phoenix area] Superior Court.

Faced with the ever-escalating social, economic, and environmental costs caused by illegal immigration, the Arizona Legislature determined that it had to take action. After considering these issues and receiving input from numerous and diverse organizations, the Arizona Legislature enacted S.B. 1070 to eliminate sanctuary city policies, to encourage—and, in some instances, mandate—assistance with the enforcement of federal immigration law, and, pursuant to the State's broad police powers, to adopt state crimes that mirror existing federal laws.

The Pertinent Provisions of S.B. 1070

Section 2 has twelve subsections. Plaintiff purports to challenge all of Section 2, but addresses only subsections B and H in its motion. Subsection B states, in pertinent part:

> For any lawful stop, detention *or arrest* made by a law enforcement official or a law enforcement agency of this state…where *reasonable suspicion* exists that the person is an alien *and* is unlawfully present in the United States, a reasonable attempt shall be made, when practicable, to determine the immigration status of the person, except if the determination may hinder or obstruct an investigation. Any person who is arrested shall have the person's immigration status determined before the person is released. The person's immigration status shall be verified with the federal government. A law enforcement official or agency may not consider race, color or national origin in implementing the requirements of this subsection except to the extent permitted by the United States or Arizona Constitution.

Plaintiff argues that S.B. 1070 will require Arizona's law enforcement officers "to verify the immigration status of every person who is arrested in the state," even if no reasonable suspicion of unlawful presence exists. However, this interpretation is inconsistent with the State's interpretation. Moreover, the plaintiff's interpretation ignores recognized principles of statutory construction and defies common sense. The State interprets S.B. 1070 to read that *only* where a reasonable suspicion exists that a person arrested is an alien and is unlawfully present in the United States *must* the person's immigration status be determined before the person is released. [It makes common sense that] the Arizona Legislature could not have intended to compel Arizona's law enforcement officers to determine and verify the immigration status of *every single person* arrested—even for U.S. citizens and when there is absolutely no reason to believe that the person is unlawfully present in the country.

Plaintiff's interpretation suggests the word "person" in the second sentence should be understood to mean both U.S. citizens and aliens. However, a U.S. citizen does not have an immigration status and nowhere in the INA does federal law ascribe an immigration status to any category of U.S. citizen. Accordingly, the only interpretation of the second sentence that is plausible is that "person" means "such person"—namely, aliens referred to in the first sentence where reasonable suspicion exists that the alien is unlawfully present in the United States.

S.B. 1070 does not authorize indefinite detention. S.B. 1070 does not expressly limit the time during which a law enforcement officer may detain an arrested person pending an investigation into his or her immigration status. [However, the law must] be construed in a manner that preserves its constitutionality and is consistent with the Arizona Legislature's intent. The statutory history [of S.B. 1070] confirms that the Arizona Legislature did *not* intend to authorize indefinite detention. Thus, S.B. 1070 must be construed to limit the detention of any person pending an investigation into the person's immigration status to a reasonable time.

Section 3 reinforces and mirrors federal law by imposing the *same* misdemeanor penalties as federal law imposes for violations the INA. The only difference between this provision and the federal statutes is that S.B. 1070 "does not apply to a person who maintains authorization from the federal government to remain in the United States."

Section 4 modifies [existing Arizona law only insofar as it clarifies] law enforcement officers' existing authority to "stop any person who is operating a motor vehicle if the officer has reasonable suspicion to believe the person is in violation of any civil traffic law."

Section 5 will add two provisions to the Arizona Criminal Code. First, [it will be] a Class 1 misdemeanor [1] for an occupant of a motor vehicle…to attempt to hire or pick up passengers for work…if the motor vehicle…impedes the normal movement of traffic; [2] to enter a motor vehicle [in these circumstances]; and [3] or for a person who is who is an unauthorized alien to knowingly [seek or perform] work in a public place. Second, [section 5] will make it unlawful for a person *who is in violation of a criminal offense* to transport, move, conceal, harbor, or shield unlawful aliens, or to encourage an alien to come to this state if the person knows or recklessly disregards that the person would be violating immigration laws to do so. S.B. 1070 is designed to deter persons from inducing persons to enter or remain in the state unlawfully for the purpose of assisting with their criminal enterprise.

Section 6 adds to the authority Arizona peace officers have under [existing law] to arrest a person without a warrant by authorizing such arrests when "the officer has probable cause to believe…[t]he person to be arrested has committed any public offense that makes the person removable from the United States." This provision is based upon a memorandum the DOJ's Office of Legal Counsel prepared in which it concluded that federal law does not "preclude state police from arresting aliens on the basis of civil deportability." Neither Section 6 nor any other federal, state, or local law authorizes Arizona's law enforcement officers to determine whether a person is removable. If, however, a law enforcement officer receives confirmation from the federal government or its authorized agent that a person is removable, this provision permits the officer to handle the initial arrest and processing. S.B. 1070 further reduces the federal government's burden by permitting the officer to transport the person to a federal facility.

S.B. 10 AND THE U.S. CONSTITUTION

None of the Challenged Sections of S.B. 1070 Are Preempted

To establish its claim that federal law preempts S.B. 1070 [under the Supremacy clause], plaintiff must demonstrate that: (1) S.B. 1070 purports to regulate immigration, an exclusively federal power; that (2) federal law occupies the field [that is, Congress intends federal law to be exclusive in that area]; or (3) S.B. 1070 conflicts with and residing in the United States...." And, plaintiff cannot cite to any *congressional* policy that S.B. 1070 supposedly contravenes.

Plaintiff's argument also neglects to demonstrate how the policies underlying S.B. 1070 will (on their face) interfere with any DHS or DOJ enforcement priorities. Arizona cannot require the federal government to take any action with respect to any illegal alien within Arizona's borders—nor does S.B. 1070 attempt to do so. S.B. 1070 merely requires, in limited circumstances, that Arizona's law enforcement officers exercise their existing authority to communicate with the federal government regarding possible immigration violations. This requirement cannot, as plaintiff argues, "force a diversion of federal resources away from federal priorities" because *Congress* determines federal priorities and Congress has not only invited such inquiries but has *required* ICE to respond to them. Further, because S.B. 1070 does not (and could not) provide Arizona's law enforcement officers any authority to determine who should or should not remain in the country, S.B. 1070 does not interfere with the federal government's interest in providing humanitarian relief. In fact, S.B. 1070 expressly requires that the section "be implemented in a manner consistent with federal laws regulating immigration."

S.B. 1070 Does Not Violate the Commerce Clause

The only provision of S.B. 1070 that plaintiff claims violates the Commerce Clause is Section 5. Statutes that do not discriminate and impose no burdens on interstate commerce do not violate the Commerce Clause. Further, even statutes that impose incidental burdens on interstate commerce do not violate the Commerce Clause if they regulate even-handedly to effectuate a legitimate local public interest, and the burden imposed is outweighed by the benefits to the state. Plaintiff generally alleges that S.B. 1070 "restricts the interstate movement of aliens in a manner that is prohibited by [the Commerce Clause]." Plaintiff's argument is misguided as S.B. 1070 does not restrict the interstate movement of aliens nor discriminate against or burden interstate commerce.

In fact, S.B. 1070 does not even address whether aliens can or cannot come to the State, nor does it regulate entry in any way. S.B. 1070 simply provides that individuals, *who are in violation of a criminal offense,* cannot also transport, move, conceal, harbor or shield *illegal* aliens within the state *in furtherance of their unlawful presence,* nor can they encourage an *illegal* alien to *illegally* enter or reside in the state. Plaintiff's misunderstanding about the application of S.B. 1070 and its speculation about the Act's alleged potential impact on interstate commerce is not sufficient to establish a violation of the Commerce Clause. S.B. 1070 does not discriminate against out-of-state interests, burden commerce, or create a preference for in-state commerce.

Plaintiff's Argument That S.B. 1070 Interferes with Foreign Policy [Ignores] the *De Canas* Test

Plaintiff's argument that S.B. 1070 "is independently preempted because it impermissibly conflicts with U.S. foreign policy" is unsupported by the controlling Supreme Court precedent. The premise of plaintiff's argument is that, because S.B. 1070 applies to illegal aliens, it is *per se* preempted under the federal government's foreign affairs power. But plaintiff fails to recognize that the Supreme Court [in *De Canas v. BICA*, 1976] has already rejected the position plaintiff advances and explicitly held that "the fact that aliens are the subject of a state statute" does not mandate a finding of preemption.

De Canas addressed the same type of regulation that is at issue here—regulation designed to address harm specific to Arizona and that touches upon aliens that the federal government has determined are *not lawfully present* in the country. None of the cases plaintiff cites involve the preemption of state regulation touching upon illegal aliens. *De Canas* controls the preemption inquiry and, for the reasons set forth above, plaintiff has not demonstrated preemption under the *De Canas* test.

Plaintiff also seeks to establish that it will suffer irreparable harm if S.B. 1070 is enacted by arguing that S.B. 1070 will interfere with plaintiff's "ability to manage foreign policy." This argument fails to establish irreparable harm because the criticism Arizona has received following S.B. 1070's passage has had little (if anything) to do with any provision in the Act. Arizona and Mexico continue to work together on areas of mutual concern. And, federal officials have, at the very least, been a substantial factor in coloring foreign officials' negative perceptions.

For example, before Governor Brewer even signed S.B. 1070, President Obama criticized the Act by stating that it was "misguided" and instructed the DOJ to evaluate whether the law would violate civil rights. President Obama further stated that a federal solution was necessary to avoid "open[ing] the door to irresponsibility by others," and referred to "the recent efforts in Arizona" as "threaten[ing] to undermine basic notions of fairness that we cherish as Americans." Secretary Janet Napolitano also appeared on television to assert that S.B. 1070 was "bad law enforcement law," after which she admitted that she had not read the Act. [U.S. Attorney General] Eric Holder expressed a concern about the bill as it relates to racial profiling even though he later acknowledged having only "glanced at the bill." And Secretary of State Hillary Clinton announced [that she] expected "a significant negative response from the international community."

Instead of educating the international community about existing U.S. immigration laws, President Obama, Secretary Napolitano, Attorney General Holder, and Secretary Clinton have allowed S.B. 1070 to be distorted in Latin America and around the world. Based on all these statements and misrepresentations, it is impossible to determine to what extent, if any, the foreign policy impact of S.B. 1070 arises out any actual provision of the Act.

THE BALANCE OF EQUITIES TIPS SHARPLY IN ARIZONA'S FAVOR

Plaintiff will not suffer any harm (let alone irreparable harm) if S.B. 1070 goes into effect. Arizona, by contrast, is suffering serious consequences under the status quo. There can be no dispute that Arizona has a serious illegal immigration problem. In 2009, there were approximately 500,000 people in Arizona who were not lawfully present in this country. Arizona has repeatedly asked for federal assistance in dealing with the influx of illegal aliens in Arizona. On June 23, 2010, Governor Brewer wrote to President Obama and explained that "the need for action to secure Arizona's border could not be clearer" and proposed a four-point strategy for addressing Arizona's border-control issues. And, as recently as July 2010, Arizona Attorney General Terry Goddard wrote to President Obama to address the "rampant trafficking of drugs, humans, guns and money across our border" caused by the Mexican drug cartels, which Goddard believes to be "responsible for the murders of more than 22,700 people south of our border since 2007."

Arizona's interest in having S.B. 1070 enforced substantially exceeds plaintiff's supposed interest in having S.B. 1070 enjoined. Enjoining the enforcement of S.B. 1070 would inflict significant and tangible, irreparable harm upon the State and its citizens. Among the documented harms demonstrated by the State herein are: (i) Citizens, including police officers and their families, are exposed to injury and death; (ii) Individuals are subjected to the presence of drug cartels and criminal activity; and (iii) Citizens are denied the use of public lands deemed unsafe and dangerous. These are not speculative, hypothetical harms. These are real-life experiences which have substantially affected the quality of life in Arizona and will continue to do so at an increasing rate if S.B. 1070 is enjoined.

For the foregoing reasons, Governor Brewer and the State of Arizona respectfully request that the Court deny plaintiff's requested injunction.

THE CONTINUING DEBATE
Arizona's Law Encouraging Citizen Identity Checks by Police

What Is New

Passage of S.B. 1070 set off widespread protest. President Barack Obama repeatedly condemned the act. So did numerous other prominent figures including Roman Catholic Cardinal Roger M. Mahony of Los Angeles, who compared the ability of Arizona authorities to demand documents with "Nazism," and Mexico's President Felipe Calderón, who decried S.B. 1070 for "using racial profiling as a basis for law enforcement." Most Americans disagreed, however. Typifying survey results, a *Washington Post* poll in June 2010 found 58% of Americans supporting the law. With regard to legal case that the readings in this debate are part of, U.S. district court judge Susan Bolton soon ruled that Arizona could not put most of S.B. 1070 into effect. Her ruling will hardly be the last. Arizona immediately asked the Ninth Circuit of the U.S. Court of Appeals to end Bolton's injunction. Additionally, several other suits have been filed against S.B. 1070 based on other allegations including racism. Regardless of whoever wins or loses at the district and Circuit Court of Appeals levels, the ultimate decision will almost surely be made by the Supreme Court. Moreover, other states are considering their own approaches to unauthorized immigrants. In August 2010, for example, Florida's attorney general proposed legislation that would include not only having police check immigration papers, but longer detention of suspects during the investigation process and separate state penalties for being an unauthorized alien.

Where to Find More

Background material on federalism as a constitutional issue is available in Louis Fisher and Katy Harriger, *American Constitutional Law: Vol. I, Constitutional Structures: Separated Powers and Federalism* (Carolina Academic Press, 2009). On federalism and immigration, see Daniel Booth, "Federalism on Ice: State and Local Enforcement of Federal Immigration Law," *Harvard Journal of Law & Public Policy* (June 2006). One place to keep up on developments regarding the *United States v. Arizona* is on the Web site of LawBrain at http://lawbrain.com/wiki/Arizona_Senate_Bill_1070. To get background on a suit against S.B. 1070 on civil right grounds, *Friendly House v. Whiting,* read the briefs supporting and opposing the law on the Web site of American Immigration Council at www.legalactioncenter.org/FriendlyHouse-v-Whiting-AmicusBriefs.

What More to Do

As you consider this debate, focus on the federalism issue and try to not let you views on other related issues such as civil rights influence your views here. It is possible, for example, to find the civil rights impact of S.B. 1070 abhorrent, yet to also believe that Arizona was within its authority as a state to pass the law as far as the issues of the supremacy clause, the commerce clause, and foreign policy. The authority of the state on this dimension does not mean the courts in another case could not strike down the law as a civil rights violation. Federalism is an important aspect of the constitutional structure, and an ongoing issue how the powers of the federal government and those of the states interact.

3 | CIVIL LIBERTIES

THE PHRASE "UNDER GOD" IN THE PLEDGE OF ALLEGIANCE:
Violation of the First Amendment *or* Acceptable Traditional Expression?

VIOLATION OF THE FIRST AMENDMENT

Advocate: Douglas Laycock, Professor, School of Law, University of Texas; and Counsel of Record for 32 Christian and Jewish clergy filing an amicus curiae brief with the Supreme Court in *Elk Grove School District v. Newdow*

Source: A discussion of the topic "Under God? Pledge of Allegiance Constitutionality," sponsored by the Pew Forum on Religion and Public Life and held before the National Press Club, Washington, D.C., March 19, 2004

ACCEPTABLE TRADITIONAL EXPRESSION

Advocate: Jay Alan Sekulow, Chief Counsel, American Center for Law and Justice; and Counsel of Record for 76 members of Congress and the Committee to Protect the Pledge filing an amicus curiae brief with the Supreme Court in *Elk Grove School District v. Newdow*

Source: A discussion of the topic "Under God? Pledge of Allegiance Constitutionality," sponsored by the Pew Forum on Religion and Public Life and held before the National Press Club, Washington, D.C., March 19, 2004

This debate focuses on the establishment clause of the Constitution's First Amendment, which requires that "Congress shall make no law respecting an establishment of religion." It is clear that the authors of the First Amendment were reacting against the British practice of establishing and supporting an "official" church, in that case the Church of England. Also certain is that Congress meant the amendment to prohibit any attempt to bar any religion or religious belief. There the certainties end. For example, freedom of religion does not mean that the government cannot proscribe certain religious practices. Polygamy, animal sacrifice, and taking illegal drugs are just a few of the practices exercised in the name religion that have been legally prohibited with subsequent court approval.

Nevertheless, religion has always had a presence in government in the United States. The Great Seal of the United States, adopted in 1782 (and found on the back left of one dollar bills) contains an "all seeing eye of Providence," which probably means God, especially given that it is framed in a triangle, thought to represent the Christian trinity. The Great Seal also contains the Latin phrase "annuit coeptis," which translates as "It/He (Providence/God) has favored our undertakings." Also, first adopted in 1964 and currently on all U.S. paper currency is the motto "In God We Trust." That phrase is also found in the fourth stanza of the Star Spangled Banner (written 1813; officially adopted 1931), which concludes, "And this be our motto: 'In God is our trust.'" Finally, in 1957 Congress added "under God" after "one nation" to the Pledge of Allegiance. This last reference to God is the specific issue in this debate.

Government also has and continues to support religion and to choose among religions in other ways. For example, the military employs chaplains for all the major religious faiths, but does not employ atheist counselors. There is also a level of choosing among religions in having chaplains for the major religions, but not for the lesser-known ones. Each year the president lights an immense Christmas tree, although these days in a bow to restrictions on religious displays on public property the giant fir is called the "national tree" and is lighted as part of the "Pageant of Peace," which, of course, corresponds with the Christmas season. Historically, it has been common to find the Ten Commandments carved in the walls of public buildings or otherwise displayed in them.

Traditionally, displays of the Ten Commandments or similar religious symbols on public property, prayers in public schools, references to God on the country's currency, or affirmations of patriotism were not high-profile issues. This began to change because of the increasing stress on civil rights and liberties and because in *Everson v. Board of Education* (1947) the Supreme Court ruled that the due process cause of the Fourteenth Amendment made the establishment clause of the First Amendment applicable to the states, as well as federal government. During the ensuing years, a significant number of cases involving practices at the state and local levels were brought before the Supreme Court. With regard to the establishment clause, the Court struck down prayers and religious invocations in public schools, most religious displays on public property, and other explicit and implicit supports of religion by public officials. However, the Supreme Court has also allowed religious groups to meet in public buildings as long as there is no discrimination, and has supported prayers opening legislative sessions and having student groups fees go to student religious groups.

In this setting, Michael Newdow filed suit arguing that a California rule requiring students to recite the Pledge of Allegiance with its affirmative reference to God violated the establishment clause of the First Amendment. A U.S. District Court ruled for the school district, but the Ninth Circuit of the U.S. Court of Appeals found for Newdow, and the Elk Grove school district appealed to the U.S. Supreme Court. Shortly before the High Court heard oral arguments, two opposing attorneys who had filed amicus curiae ("friend of the court") briefs with the Court debated the issue and responded to questions from the audience in the readings that follow.

POINTS TO PONDER

➤ Expressing an absolutist position when writing the majority opinion in the *Everson* case, Justice Hugo Black argued that the wall between church and state "must be kept high and impregnable. We [should] not approve any breach." What would be the implications of adopting that no-compromise standard?

➤ Compare the argument of Douglas Laycock that the Pledge, as government-sanctioned religious expression, is "coercive" and Jay Sekulow's contention that the phrase "under God" is merely a "historical statement" reflecting the belief in God by most Americans throughout history.

➤ Does it make any difference that students are not required to say the Pledge, only that schools must lead its recitation?

The Phrase "Under God" in the Pledge of Allegiance: Violation of the First Amendment

DOUGLAS LAYCOCK

Jay [Sekulow, the author of the second article in this debate] and I were on the same side in a case [*Locke v. Davey*, 2004] that the [Supreme] Court decided earlier this year, involving the student from Washington [State] who wanted to take his state scholarship to go to seminary with it. With this case, we're on opposite sides. How does that happen? What's up with me? Explaining that is relevant to what I think about the Pledge of Allegiance.

I come to these cases with a fairly simple theory, which is that people of every religion, including the majority and the minority, and people of no religion at all, are entitled to believe their own beliefs, speak their own beliefs, and act on their own beliefs as long as they're not hurting anybody else, and to be left alone by government and have government not take sides. And a corollary of that is that none of these groups can use the government to try to force the other side to join in or participate in their own religious observances. So when government tries to stop a student prayer club from meeting on its own after school, I think government is wrong. And when that student prayer club—or the supporters of that student prayer club—moves into the classroom and tries to induce everyone else who didn't want to come to participate anyway, I think they're wrong. And I think the Pledge of Allegiance falls on that side of the line.

The country has been fighting about this issue in various forms since the 1820s, when Catholics objected to Protestant religious observances in public schools. We've gotten better about it. In the 1840s and '50s, we had mobs in the street; we had people dead. We don't do that to each other any more, and that's progress. And "one nation under God" may seem like a pretty minimal violation of whatever principle is at stake here. The Supreme Court for 40 years has said consistently, without an exception, that government may not sponsor religious observances in the public schools, and they've said it with respect to things that were pretty short. The first school prayer case, *Engel v. Vitale* in 1962, was a pretty generic, monotheistic prayer composed not by clergymen but by the New York Board of Regents, and it was 22 words long, and the Court said you can't ask children to recite that prayer.

Now we're down to only two words, and it's not a prayer, and it's mixed up in the Pledge of Allegiance, and the question is, Does that change the answer? And the Supreme Court has repeatedly suggested, never in a holding, but over and over in what lawyers call dictums—side comments explaining what this opinion doesn't decide—there is some kind of threshold. It's got to be big enough to matter before it's an Establishment Clause violation [of the First Amendment to the Constitution]. There are little, ceremonial, rote, repetition things that the Court is not going to get involved in striking down. "In God We Trust" on the coins is a classic example; various state mottos around the country; certainly religious references in historical documents and in politicians' speeches, the Supreme Court is not going to strike down. And they have said—without a holding—two or three times that the Pledge of Allegiance is like "In God We Trust" on the coins. It's very short, and it's repeated by rote, and nobody really thinks about it much. Well, most people don't really think about it much.

The Court may say the Pledge of Allegiance—the religious part of the Pledge of Allegiance—is just too short to worry about. It's what lawyers call *de minimis*. That may happen.

I think the Pledge of Allegiance is different from all these other examples of things that might be de minimis. It's different from "In God We Trust" on the coins. It's different from politicians making speeches and so forth. The reason it's different is really unique in the culture. Government doesn't do this to adults; it doesn't do this to children in any other context. In the Pledge of Allegiance, we ask every child in the public schools in America every morning for a personal profession of faith. You don't have to take out your coin and read and meditate on "In God We Trust." You don't have to pay any attention when the politician is talking, and lots of us don't.

But this asks for a personal affirmation: I pledge allegiance to one nation under God. Now if God does not exist, or if I believe that God does not exist, then that isn't one nation under God. We can't have a nation under God unless there is a God. It doesn't say one nation under our god, or some gods, or one of the gods. It pretty clearly implies there is only one God, and if there is only one God, then the God of the Pledge is the one true God, and other alleged gods around the world are false gods.

It says one other thing about this God—it doesn't say much, can't say much in two words—but the nation is "under God." God is of such a nature that God exercises some sort of broad superintending authority so that it is possible for a whole nation to be under Him. Now that doesn't exclude many folks, but it excludes some, right? This is not God as First Cause who set the universe in motion and doesn't intervene any more; this is not God as a metaphor for all the goodness imminent in the universe or imminent in the population. This is God exercising some kind of authority over at least this nation; maybe over all nations.

It's a pretty generic concept of God, and it's comfortable for a lot of people. But we may overestimate how many people. The largest private opinion polls have about 15 percent of the population not subscribing to any monotheistic conception of God. Who is in that 15 percent? Buddhist and other non-theists, Hindus and other polytheists, those with no religion, atheist, agnostic, humanist, ethical culturalists. That's 15 percent of the population, with 7.2 million children in public schools who are being asked to personally affirm every morning a religious belief that is different from the religious belief that is taught or held in their home and by their parents. And it is the personal affirmation request in the Pledge, it seems to me, that makes the Pledge unique. It is different from all the other kinds of ceremonial deism that go on in the country.

In the attempt to defend the Pledge, government and the various friends of the Court supporting the Pledge have said a remarkable variety of things, but probably the most common thing they've said is variations on what appears in the brief of the United States. It is not religious. We don't mean for them to take it literally. We ask the children to say the nation is under God, but we don't expect them to really believe that the nation is under God. Here is a quote from the government's brief: "What it really means is, I pledge allegiance to one nation, founded by individuals whose belief in God gave rise to the governmental institutions and political order they adopted, indivisible, with liberty and justice for all."

Now if that were what it means, if anybody thought that was what it meant, we would not have had the great political outcry in response to the Ninth Circuit's decision. If people want to get mad about this because it had some recital about what the founders believed, or because of the other point the government makes—that it's in reference to historical and demographic facts that most Americans over time have believed in God—that would be one thing. But people don't get angry at a recital of historical and demographic facts. People get angry because they know what it means; it's plain English. They believe what it means, they want people to say what it means, they want their kids to say what it means. And I'll tell you a dirty little secret: They want to coerce other kids to say what it means and what they believe to be true. They know that "under God" means under God.

And if it doesn't mean under God, if we were to take the government seriously for asking children every morning to say the nation is under God but not to mean the nation is under God, well, Christians and Jews have a teaching about that, too. "Thou shalt not take the name of the Lord Thy God in vain." If we don't mean it, if it's a vain form of words that doesn't mean what it says, then it is indeed a taking of the name of the Lord in vain. That is why the [amicus curiae] brief that I filed [with the Supreme Court in the case of *Elk Grove School District v. Newdow*] is on behalf of 32 Christian and Jewish clergy who do care, not only about not coercing other people to practice their religion, but also care that if we are going to practice religion, we mean it seriously. We don't want a watered down religion that we don't really believe.

Jay Sekulow's version [in an opposing amicus curiae brief] is a little different. He says there's a category—and there's some of this in the government's brief as well—of patriotic observances with religious references. You can't do religion in the school, but you can do patriotism with a religious reference. The consequence of that would be, I suppose, that we could undo all the school prayer cases as long as we wrapped them in a coat of patriotism.

Mingling the patriotic and the religious seems to me to make it worse, not better. Think about what the Pledge does to a child who cannot in good faith affirm that the nation is under God and who actually thinks about it. And let me tell you, kids think about it. You don't think about it if you're comfortable with it, if it doesn't challenge anything you believe, you blur right over it. You can say it pretty fast, and most of us don't stop to reflect on the Pledge anymore. But for kids who don't believe it, and maybe most especially for kids who once went to a church and now don't believe it, whether or not to say "under God" becomes a big issue. I don't claim it becomes a big issue for all 7.2 million whose parents show up in opinion polls, but for a substantial minority of kids, to say "under God" or not becomes an issue.

Some kids drop it out. One of the saving graces here is that it's only two words, so you can get away with dropping it out, and your friends may not notice. But there are people who refuse to say those two words because they don't believe them, and there are a few who refuse to say those two words because it's religious in a governmental context, and it shouldn't be there. It belongs somewhere else.

And for the child who cannot say it, here's what we do by putting the religious reference in the middle of the Pledge of Allegiance to the nation: If you are doubtful about the existence of God, you are of doubtful loyalty to the nation. What kind of a citizen can you be? You can't even say the Pledge of Allegiance in the prescribed form that Congress has written. You can't pledge your loyalty to the nation without pledging your belief in the existence of God.

Now over and over and over the Supreme Court has said the reason it will not allow the government itself to take a position on a religious question, will not allow the government to endorse a religious viewpoint or an anti-religious viewpoint is because government should not make any citizen's political standing in the community depend upon his religious beliefs, not even implicitly, not even by implication. The Court says repeatedly that if the government says this is a Christian nation or this is a religious nation, then non-Christians and non-religious folks will think the government really views them as a second-class citizens. That's pretty indirect and implicit. This is very direct and explicit. Now, children, it is time to pledge your allegiance to the United States of America, and to do that, you have to pledge that the nation is under God. We have linked religion and politics, religion and patriotism, religious faith and patriotic standing inseparably right in the middle of one sentence. And the only way to avoid the religious part is literally to drop out mid-sentence and then come back in.

What would follow from a Supreme Court either striking down or upholding the Pledge? I think because of the fact that the Pledge is unique in asking for a personal affirmation, not much follows about other cases from a decision striking it down. Political volcano is going to follow, but not much is going to follow legally. "In God We Trust" doesn't come off the coins, the other religious references in the school curriculum don't come out. Of course the government can teach historical documents that have religious references in them because that is part of the history curriculum. I think they can teach music with religious references in it because that's music. It's important in the culture. I think schools should be more sensitive than they are about the problems faced by nonbelieving children when they're asked to sing that music. I think we can deal with those problems, but I don't think the Constitution requires that all—indeed, I think it forbids—certainly, it's sound educational policy—forbids stripping all religious references out of history. Religion is part of history.

None of those things ask the child to personally affirm his belief that the nation is under God, so in this sense, the Pledge case is unique. A decision taking "under God" out of the Pledge would not really portend much change on anything else.

A decision upholding the Pledge, well, you've got to see how they write it. If the Court wants to say the Pledge is special, we're going to let this go by, but it doesn't mean we're unraveling all the school prayer cases, it doesn't mean anything else much changes. They can write this very narrowly. There is a whole list of objective factors that are special about the Pledge that cut the other way. They could say it is only two words; it is recited by rote; it is not a prayer; it has been around in exactly the same form for 50 years before we got a hold of it; kids don't have to say it—we settled that in 1943 [in West Virginia v. Barnette]; they don't have to say it. For those reasons, in combination with all those reasons, we're going to uphold this. Nothing else will satisfy all those reasons. Nothing else is only two words, for starters, and that would be an opinion that doesn't change much.

If they write an opinion that's like the government's brief—we're going to declare that this really isn't religious—the problem with that is that it's completely standardless and therefore it's completely boundless. It's a fiat. The plain language is religious, but five of us on the Supreme Court—hey, with five votes, you can do anything—we're going to tell the country this is not religious. The Fifth Circuit recently held the Ten Commandments are not religious. A big monument across the top, giant letters, "I am the Lord, thy God. Thou shalt have no other gods before me." Not religious, the Fifth Circuit [of the U.S. Court of Appeals] says.

If the Supreme Court adopts that kind of approach—we'll just decree things not to be religious—then everything's up for grabs. If you're going to arbitrarily decree religious things to be secular, you can do it in any case, and district judges will be asked to do it in any case. So that would be a much scarier opinion, a much more potentially wide-ranging opinion, and then other possibilities sort of range in between. Any religion is okay if you're wrap it in patriotism. I think that's pretty wide open, too, because political officers can be pretty clever about wrapping things in patriotism.

So we may get an opinion either way—we may get a very narrow opinion either way or a very broad opinion, particularly if they uphold it. Watch not only for the result; watch for how they write it.

Question: Please comment on the "notion…of ceremonial deism," the idea that "references to God become meaningless if recited often enough in public places."

Mr. Laycock: I think you're right. I think the principal religious division in the country used to be Protestant-Catholic. It's not that anymore. It is a continuum from intense anti-religion to intensely religious. Intensely devout Protestants, Catholics, Muslims, Jews find themselves on the same side of a lot of issues, given that divide, and ceremonial deism is very comfortable for the vast range in the middle. The religious center in America is low-intensity theist.

I think these ceremonial references are very problematic for the anti-religious and for the seriously religious, and many of the seriously religious, in good faith, defend that kind of watered-down ceremonial deism in court on the theory that it's better than nothing; that's all they'll let us have, that's all we can get in a government-sponsored forum, and it's not for me to tell them they're making a mistake. But it seems to me it is a mistake, and a lot of folks who are intensely religious aren't comfortable with it, and to some extent, it is a position only for the Court. So the Justice Department, representing the United States, says, This is not religious at all. But the form letter from the White House that goes out to people who write in about this issue says it is profoundly religious. They're telling the Court one thing and the public something completely different. The ceremonial deism is a placeholder.

Question: Just to follow up,…comment on whether there is a path that we go down that essentially declares that the public realm—whatever is supported by government—must necessarily be godless, or is there an alternative to this? Does this case take you there or does it not necessarily take you there?

Mr. Laycock: There's no path that leads to the public sphere being godless. There is a path that leads to any activity sponsored by government being godless. The simple absolutist rule is that if the government's sponsoring it, there's no mention of God. In the public schools, the Court has never found a case where a government could mention God, but they've never said this is an absolutist rule with no exceptions either.

This case does not take us there. It does not present the question whether there can ever be any exceptions because this case has the unique feature of requesting a personal affirmation. So a decision in this case wouldn't say anything about whether the rule about what the teacher can do is absolute or the rule about what the president or the governor or the mayor at a public ceremony can do. That's never going to be absolute.

Question: I was wondering what implications this case would have for currency in the message "In God We Trust" on the U.S. dollar notes and coins?

Mr. Laycock: I'm sure there are people who fear it portends that any governmental reference to God goes, and so the currency all has to be changed. I don't think that follows at all because no one has to agree with the currency or pledge allegiance to the currency or even pay any attention to what it says on the currency, beyond the number.

Question: [You argue] "that the Pledge requires an affirmation of personal faith and consequently has got to go." Mr. Sekulow argues, "no, it doesn't—it's not an affirmation of personal faith, so it's okay. One point of view that's not represented here…is that yes, it requires an affirmation of personal faith and that's fine. And the Court should say that's fine. Is that a possible outcome? Can you play around with that a little bit?

Mr. Laycock: I think that's quite unlikely. It's not impossible, but let me just give you 30 seconds of the background. What the Court has said over the years on political issues the government can try to lead public opinion—which it does all the time, it tries to rally public support for its own agenda—but it cannot coerce people to agree with the government or to say that they agree with the government. And that's why in 1943, when the Pledge was entirely secular, it didn't have "under God" in it, and the Pledge case got to the Supreme Court, they said, You can't make students say it. Any student can opt out, but the teacher can lead it. On religious questions in the school prayer cases, they've said opt out isn't enough, because it's really outside the government's jurisdiction, the government isn't responsible for leading public opinion on religion, so the government can't do it at all. It can't ask the kids, even with an opt-out right, to say anything religious, and that's why I agree with Jay [Selulow].

It would be quite unlikely for them to say this really is religious, it really is an affirmation of faith and the government can ask you to say it as long as it gives you the right to opt out. That would be a striking departure from the structure of doctrine they've set up over the past 60 years.

Question: Much has been made of the fact that there are only two words here, but one of those words is a preposition, which, to at least some ears, implies a particular type of God, one that we are under, one that is transcendent. And I wonder if consideration of that aspect would move this particular phrase beyond ceremonial deism? I guess my concern is that if you reject the historical document argument, it does seem to imply that we're asking people to affirm a particular type of God, which in 2004, many, many people do not affirm.

Mr. Laycock: I think that if you want to talk about history, let's talk about history. "One nation under God" does not talk about history. It talks about theology and the relation of this nation today to God today and it does say we're under, that is a particular kind of God. I don't think that's going to trouble the Court much because it doesn't eliminate many conceptions of God, but it does eliminate some, as I said. But it's hard to talk about God without talking about some conception of God. It's impossible to be truly neutral in God-talk because humans have evolved too many radically diverse understandings of God.

Question: If our nation was not under Christianity at the birth of our Constitution, which I think scholars generally acknowledge Thomas Jefferson, whether he was a deist or a heretical Christian or a Unitarian, whatever he was, he was a religious man, obviously. But whether he was a Christian or not isn't relevant as far as the Constitution goes. But why did our Constitution refer to a Christian Sabbath, not a Jewish or a Muslim or an atheist Sabbath? And why was the document dated in the year of our Lord? Would anyone dare to say that Lord is anyone other than Jesus Christ?

Mr. Laycock: I agree with most of what Jay just said. Let me elaborate a little bit further and add a piece that I think is very important here. The founding generation fought hard about religious liberty, but they fought about the issues that were controversial in their time. And the religious liberty issue that was controversial in their time was how do you fund the church? And it was controversial because Protestants disagreed about it, because Episcopalians and Congregationalists had had tax support and nobody else did, and fixing that, not surprisingly, produced a huge fight.

They did not fight about these sort of religious references in public documents and public events because there was broad diversity of opinion, but the country was overwhelmingly Protestant and there wasn't any disagreement there big enough to get a fight going. The disagreement became big enough to get a fight going in the 1820s, when they started creating public schools and conservative Protestants said you Unitarians—Horace Mann was a Unitarian, and he was the founder of the public school movement—you Unitarians are putting watered down Christianity. It's not much more than Unitarianism in the public schools. We want real religion in the public schools. And then the huge Catholic immigration began and you got much bigger fights between Protestants and Catholics about what to do with the schools. And really, today's battles over prayer in the public schools and funding for private religious schools both of those battles date to those early 19th century disputes and the Protestant-Catholic conflicts that comes all the way down.

Now if the Religion Clauses of First Amendment are a guarantee of principle that government will leave each of us alone, give us as much religious liberty as we can, that principle encountered a whole new set of applications when religious diversity became greater and when the public schools got going. And so to say that in the Declaration of Independence, which is our founding political theory but it's also a political document to rally opinion, that they invoked both the secular rationale, natural law, and the religious rationale, nature's God and our Creator, they did both, that's true. And that was shrewd, but I don't think that tells us anything about how the government should handle religion when it has other people's children in its custody.

The Phrase "Under God" in the Pledge of Allegiance:
Acceptable Traditional Expression

JAY ALAN SEKULOW

First, let me say that I probably agree with Doug [Laycock] on more cases than I disagree. In fact, the very first case I argued at the Supreme Court of the United States [*Airport Commissioners v. Jews for Jesus*]—which seems like a long time ago, because it was—Justice [Sandra Day] O'Connor wrote for the Court, and she relied primarily on an article that was written by Professor Laycock. So I've always appreciated that unanimous opinions are rare and getting rarer every day, especially in the Religion Clause cases.

Let me give you five reasons why the Pledge of Allegiance is constitutional and should be affirmed by the Court as not violating the Establishment Clause [of the First Amendment].

1. The Pledge of Allegiance is not in a form of prayer.
2. The Pledge of Allegiance does not refer to Christianity or any other particular religion.
3. The religious portion of the Pledge of Allegiance is only two words.
4. The Pledge of Allegiance was recited unchanged for 50 years before the Court considered the question.
5. And no one can be required to recite the Pledge of Allegiance.

That's the closing portion of the [amicus curiae] brief Professor Laycock filed [in *Elk Grove School District v. Newdow*], where he argued that if the Court was going to rule in favor the Pledge of Allegiance, here's five ways to do it. And it may well be what the Supreme Court does, because it does give a very specific approach, and I think a fairly persuasive one.

Doug [Laycock] talked about the 40 or 50 years of history when the Supreme Court has dealt with the school prayer issue and not allowing for school prayer in that context. There's another history that's over 200 years now, and it goes something like this: "God save the United States and this Honorable Court"—that's how this Supreme Court oral argument's going to start when Dr. [Michael] Newdow presents his arguments before the Supreme Court [in *Elk Grove School District v. Newdow*] next Wednesday.

So the fact of the matter is that the Supreme Court itself has had this cry as part of its opening ceremony described as an invocation. Students attend oral arguments frequently, including kids in high school and even elementary school. And when those justices stand up or walk in, the students stand up. And while they don't have to repeat it, students also don't have to repeat the Pledge of Allegiance, and correctly so, since the Supreme Court's decision in [*West Virginia State Board of Education v. Barnette* (1943)], which is now dating back almost 60 years, said you can't be compelled to violate your conscience [by being required to recite the Pledge of Allegiance], and in that way, if you are objecting to the form of the Pledge of Allegiance.

I think that the words "God save the United States and this Honorable Court," like the words of the Pledge of Allegiance, echo what our founding fathers thought, and that was that our freedoms, rights and liberties are derived not from government but rather from God granting them to mankind. And in a sense, it's a very Lockean [English political philosopher John Locke, 1632–1704] concept. Thomas Jefferson talks about it. And even, of course, in the Declaration of Independence itself, how often have we learned or were required to learn and recite in school the words, the famous portion of the Declaration of Independence where it's written, "We hold these truths to be self-evident, that all men are created equal, endowed by their Creator with certain unalienable rights. Amongst them are life, liberty and the pursuit of happiness."

If the Pledge of Allegiance were to say something like that, I would suspect that there would be the same objection. Why? Because of its reliance on a Creator, and it is a concept where the Creator endows us with our rights. But in the context of the history of our country, that makes a lot of sense. Our country was founded on the concepts that the rights of man don't derive from a king and they can't be taken away from us by a king. The rights of mankind, the basic rights of mankind—liberty, freedom, the things that we cherish in this country—derive from a Creator. That's what our founding fathers mean.

It's often talked about, Thomas Jefferson's famous letter [in 1801] to the Danbury Baptist Connecticut Association, where he talked about what he called the "high and mighty duty in this wall of separation between church and state." There's something else that Jefferson wrote several years before he wrote that famous letter to the Danbury Baptists, and that was during the debates on the First Amendment and also in discussions with friends about the concept of liberty. He wrote, "Can the liberties of a nation be thought secure when we have removed their only firm basis, a conviction in the minds of the people that the liberties are a gift of God and that they are not violated but with His wrath?"

Now, Thomas Jefferson, in the classic understanding of his religious belief, would not fall within what most people would consider an orthodox Christian position. In my view of history anyway, I would not consider him to be—and I'm not speaking as a theologian—he had various views on religion and faith. I don't think faith was insignificant in his life, I don't mean to suggest that at all, but it wouldn't be what we would typically talk about today as a Protestant form of Christianity or Catholic form of Christianity. He kind of had his view of faith, Christianity, and the deity of Jesus, and that's a whole different topic.

But he recognized something very fundamental in that our rights don't come from a king; they are endowed to us. So if the requirement of the school district in *Elk Grove* was that we begin each school day by reminding ourselves, as students, that we should remember the history of this great nation, that we are endowed by our Creator with these rights, they're inalienable, and that the Creator bestowed them upon us—life, liberty and the pursuit of happiness—I submit that many people, Dr. Newdow included, would object, saying again it's this compelled reliance.

Now, nobody can be compelled, nor should they be, as I said, to recite the Pledge. Let's talk about the more recent history, and that is, what happened in 1954? Now, of course, the issue upon which certiorari is granted—and I am frequently reminded of that both when I'm watching arguments and when I argue them myself—is not the congressional action here, which is interesting. The United States asked for review of the 1954 congressional act amending the Pledge of Allegiance. The Supreme Court denied review there. They granted the school district's policy for review, which is a policy that said the school day will start with a patriotic expression. The Pledge of Allegiance would meet that patriotic expression.

In 1954, though, when the Pledge was modified to include the phrase "under God," what was motivating Congress? There were a lot of things motivating Congress. We were in the midst of the Cold War. There was this desire to treat and to establish the difference between how we viewed our rights and liberties, and how communism viewed these things, which is any rights that you have, whatever they might be, are derived from the state; the state is supreme. Congress, reflecting, again, on what the founding fathers thought, said, No, it doesn't work that way. We believe the foundation of our country is different, and this shows the difference. We believe that our rights come from God to mankind.

And I don't know if this is a true fact or not, but it's in one of the briefs, that Dr. Newdow is actually an ordained minister with the Universal Life Church, and I'm not sure if that's correct. What the Universal Life Church has as one of their—and I know they have a pretty broad view of what constitutes God—mission statements, it says that— and they use the phrase "gods" in terms of recognizing that individuals, us, are given what he calls "God-given rights"—freedoms, liberties. Again, this is part of the American experience.

Now, no one's required to believe that, and I don't think that that's the intent of saying the Pledge. Students who don't want to participate don't have to participate, and I think acknowledging the historical significance of how our rights are derived in the foundation of America is correct. The idea that you would be able to tell a student, You cannot be compelled to memorize the Declaration of Independence—which many of us remember having to do—and recite it because of its reference to a Creator, I would think would be wrong. Now, could you argue that there should be a religious exemption? Probably you could argue that under the Free Exercise Clause. These days, though, I don't know if any of us would be too persuasive on how that would go. But I will tell you this much: that is the historical fact. Our founding fathers did recognize—This was part of the Lockean concept of the rights of mankind, and you don't have to be a historian to check this out....

But I don't think it's correct contextually, with due respect, and that is "one nation"— the Pledge of Allegiance, "I pledge allegiance..." one nation under God," and of course ellipses in between. But that's not what the Pledge of Allegiance says. It doesn't say "one nation under God," and context matters in Establishment Clause cases. And I think the context of the Pledge and the history of how this country came into existence is going to point to what I would expect to be a Supreme Court decision affirming the constitutionality of the Pledge.

Let me close with this, and then I know there's going to be some questions. I think it would be revisionist history if we're going to start saying that students cannot say the Pledge of Allegiance, and revisionist in this context: the history, granted, of the Pledge itself is only 50 years old—it's not that old. But I'll tell you something: the religious heritage of the country goes back to its founding, and whether you take the very strict view of church-state separation or a more accommodationist view, or somewhere in between, denying the history is denying the fact. And I think that mandating a change in the Pledge or finding that those statements, those two words, as Professor Laycock pointed out so well in his brief, those two words create a constitutional crisis, I would hope the Court does not go there.

Question: [Please comment on the] notion...of ceremonial deism...the idea that "references to God become meaningless if recited often enough in public places."

Mr. Sekulow: I'll go quickly, because I addressed the issue and covered it, but I'll give you two quick thoughts.

I don't for those who are anti-religious—and I know there are people who are anti-religious—I mean, the fact of the matter is you could be anti-something or pro-something;

it's a free country, and neither the anti-religious nor the majority religion have a veto right over everybody else. And I think that's one thing.

Number two, a lot of people on my side of these issues normally, Doug [Laycock], get nervous about the phrase ceremonial deism. I've never had a problem with it. I think what Justice O'Connor said is right. It's one of these phrases that does tend to solemnize an occasion. It expresses hope for the future and reflects our past, but again, you're not compelling anybody to say this. You're not compelling anybody to believe this, but I suspect there'll be a lot of questions—I mean, I'm guessing again—on the issue of ceremonial deism. I've had that happen on a couple of the cases that I argued on those issues where prayer came up, and even in some of the earlier cases, in the early '90s. That's an issue that's going to come up. The ceremonial deism question is going to, I think, play in this probably significantly.

Question: Just to follow up,…comment on whether there is a path that we go down that essentially declares that the public realm—whatever is supported by government—must necessarily be godless, or is there an alternative to this? Does this case take you there or does it not necessarily take you there?

Mr. Sekulow: I think this case says you don't have to be godless. You can accurately reflect the historical precedent of the country's founding. That's how I would pitch this case. If I were arguing this case to the Court, I would be talking about the historic fact of patriotic expression. Sure, it's got religious overtones, but so does the "Star Spangled Banner" and a host of other religious music and songs and documents of our country. It's part of who we are.

So, yes, I think it can reflect—If you don't want to be in a situation where the next thing—and maybe some do—that we're fighting over is whether you really can have those students memorize the Declaration of Independence and be required to recite it as my teacher required me to recite it flawlessly, and if you didn't do it flawlessly you did it again, and it could go on, for many of us, for weeks.

Question: "I was wondering what implications this case would have for currency in the message "In God We Trust" on the U.S. dollar notes and coins?

Mr. Sekulow: I do think the lawsuit will follow, though. If the Pledge of Allegiance is declared unconstitutional—There have already been a series of cases on the national motto. Most recently, I handled one in Kansas. The district court ruled in our favor, and there was no appeal taken in that case. But I would expect that whether it applies or not, you will see those kind of lawsuits being filed if they declare the Pledge unconstitutional.

Whether they'll succeed or not, that's going to depend on how this opinion's written and what the Court says. But to say that it's not going to have far reaching consequences if the Pledge is struck down as unconstitutional—even if it is a four-four decision, which, as Professor Laycock said, is just an affirmance of the judgment—I will tell you that there will be school districts all over the United States that are going to say, Well, look, we're going to not read the tea leaves here. We don't want to get sued and lose again, so we're just going to stop saying the Pledge. I think that will be a ripple effect of this, too.

Question: Mr. Laycock argues "that the Pledge requires an affirmation of personal faith and consequently has got to go." Mr. Sekulow argues, "no, it doesn't—it's not an affirmation of personal faith, so it's okay." One point of view that's not represented here…is that yes, it requires an affirmation of personal faith and that's fine. And the Court should say that's fine. Is that a possible outcome? Can you play around with that a little bit?

Mr. Sekulow: I can't imagine the Court saying that—if they hold the Pledge constitutional, I think—actually, if they hold the Pledge constitutional, I think, it's going to be for the five reasons that Professor Laycock laid out in his brief. I think that is a pretty straightforward way for the Court to go if they decide it's constitutional. I can't imagine them saying the Pledge is constitutional, and you must believe it when you say it.

Question: Much has been made of the fact that there are only two words here, but one of those words is a preposition, which, to at least some ears, implies a particular type of God, one that we are under, one that is transcendent. And I wonder if consideration of that aspect would move this particular phrase beyond ceremonial deism? I guess my concern is that if you reject the historical document argument, it does seem to imply that we're asking people to affirm a particular type of God, which in 2004, many, many people do not affirm.

Mr. Sekulow: But it's an historical fact that the phrase under God—Most people think it originated in the Gettysburg Address, when President Lincoln said "This nation under God shall have a new birth of freedom." But actually it predates that by almost a hundred years, because General Washington—I think he was Colonel Washington then actually—in his order to the Continental Army said, "Millions of lives are in jeopardy, both born and unborn"—talking about posterity—"and this army under God"—now, does that mean that this army's under God? That's how they viewed the interplay of Divine Providence. That's what they meant by that.

And, again, the Pledge is an historic statement. You can't change the history; you can debate what the history means, but the words they used are—Fortunately for all of us, we have them, and that's what they meant and that's what they said....

Let's say you don't agree with the historical document, say the Declaration of Independence. Again, Mrs. Sopher requiring us to memorize it when I was in junior high. There's no dispute that that's what the document says. It says we're endowed by our Creator with these rights. It was a Lockean concept that rights derived not from the King of England, because then the king could take them away, but derived from God to mankind. That's what they thought, whether they were deists or whatever their views were theologically, that is what their overall and overarching propositions were, and that's their thought process. So you could say you don't agree with the historical documents or you don't assume they're historic, you could argue anything, but I think they're pretty clear.

Question: If our nation was not under Christianity at the birth of our Constitution, which I think scholars generally acknowledge Thomas Jefferson, whether he was a deist or a heretical Christian or a Unitarian, whatever he was, he was a religious man, obviously. But whether he was a Christian or not isn't relevant as far as the Constitution goes. But why did our Constitution refer to a Christian Sabbath, not a Jewish or a Muslim or an atheist Sabbath? And why was the document dated in the year of our Lord? Would anyone dare to say that that Lord is anyone other than Jesus Christ?

Mr. Sekulow: I've just completed a dissertation on a lot of the historical backgrounds, mostly focusing on the Supreme Court justices, not on the founding fathers. But what becomes very clear is that a lot of terminology was used by the founding fathers and by Supreme Court justices that we take in one context and, culturally, at the time, meant something very different. It's not to say that they were not people of faith, but there is no doubt about it, I mean, if you study history in America, it was a pretty broad—even within the founding fathers, a pretty broad swath of faith.

And statements like "In the year of our Lord" were the customary ways in which these documents were signed. It does not mean that they were anti-religious. Obviously they

included them in there. The Declaration of Independence, I think, as a foundational document established how Americans viewed the relationship between rights, liberty, mankind
and God, and I think they did it in one document and actually in one portion of that
document.

A lot of the justices, for instance, had said this is a Christian nation, in 1892, 1864.
We're Unitarians. Now, I'm not saying that they weren't Unitarians, weren't Christians, it's
just that it wasn't what you would typically think of as Protestantism as we know it. So
you've got to look at the cultural context to understand.

Now, having said all of that, to remove that history, I think, would be very dangerous.
The fact that there was this general belief in the way rights derived to mankind, to remove
that, I think, would be wrong....

THE CONTINUING DEBATE:
The Phrase "Under God" in the Pledge of Allegiance

What Is New

The Supreme Court in essence ducked when it ruled in *Elk Grove Unified School District v. Newdow*. Instead of deciding the question, the Court dismissed the case on the grounds that since Michael Newdow's ex-wife had custody of their daughter, he did not have "standing" (enough legal interest) to sue on the girl's behalf. That probably only put off the day when the Supreme Court will have to rule. New lawsuits have been filed, and U.S. district court judges in California and Florida have ruled the Pledge unconstitutional. However, in the latest legal ruling, the California-based Ninth Circuit of the U.S. Court of Appeals upheld the Pledge by a vote of 2 to 1, including describing its religious references as "ceremonial and patriotic [in] nature." The decision is available at Rutgers University's *Jurist* dated March 11, 2010, online using the drop-down menu at www.jurist.law.pitt.edu/gazette.

Where to Find More

One site of a group that believes in a wall between church and state is the "nontheist" Freedom From Religion Foundation at www.ffrf.org/. Taking the opposite view is the Rutheford Institute at www.rutherford.org/issues/religiousfreedom.asp/. A comprehensive view of the Supreme Court's role in the church-state issue is Kent Greenawalt's two-volume set, *Religion and the Constitution*; Volume I: *Free Exercise and Fairness* and Volume 2: *Establishment and Fairness* (Princeton University Press, 2006, 2008). The history of and controversies about the Pledge itself can be found in Richard J. Ellis, *To the Flag: The Unlikely History of the Pledge of Allegiance* (University of Kansas Press, 2005).

What to More to Do

The Supreme Court has sometimes drawn a line between what religious expressions are not permissible and which merely reflect tradition and are permissible. To ponder this distinction, draw up a list of a few expressions of religion ranging from "In God We Trust" on U.S. currency to forced prayers in school and indicate which (if any) are permissible and which are not. Explain the distinction, and also discuss the "OK" and "Not OK" lists of others in your class. Once your views are clear, try jotting down some notes for a hypothetical essay, "How High Should the Wall Between Church and State Be?"

CIVIL RIGHTS

CALIFORNIA'S PROPOSITION 8 BARRING GAY MARRIAGES:
Equal Rights Violation of the U.S. Constitution *or* Valid State Law?

EQUAL RIGHTS VIOLATION OF THE U.S. CONSTITUTION

ADVOCATE: Attorneys representing plaintiffs Kristen M. Perry, et al. and the City of San Francisco seeking to have California's constitutional clause barring gay marriage declared a violation of the U.S. Constitution

SOURCE: *Kristin M. Perry, et al., Plaintiffs, and the City and County of San Francisco, Plaintiff-Intervenor, v. Arnold Schwarzenegger, et al., Defendants, and Proposition 8 Official Proponents Dennis Hollingsworth, et al., Defendant-Intervenors*; Case 3:09-cv-02292-VRW; U.S. District Court for the Northern District of California; Responses to Court's Questions for Closing Arguments, June 15, 2010

VALID STATE LAW

ADVOCATE: Attorneys representing Proposition 8 official proponents Dennis Hollingsworth, et al., seeking to have California's constitutional clause barring gay marriage upheld

SOURCE: *Kristin M. Perry, et al., Plaintiffs, and the City and County of San Francisco, Plaintiff-Intervenor, v. Arnold Schwarzenegger, et al., Defendants, and Proposition 8 Official Proponents Dennis Hollingsworth, et al., Defendant-Intervenors*; Case 3:09-cv-02292-VRW; U.S. District Court for the Northern District of California; Responses to Court's Questions for Closing Arguments, June 15, 2010

The origins of the gay rights issue in the United States began in 1610 when colonial Virginia made sexual contact between same-sex individuals a criminal offense. Thereafter, federal and state policy mostly worked against gays throughout most of U.S. history. This began to change in the 1960s as part of the general civil right movement. Led by Illinois, which decriminalized sexual acts between same-sex adults, laws relating to intimate homosexual relations began to change slowly. Ultimately, the Supreme Court in *Lawrence v. Texas* (2003) declared all such laws unconstitutional. Other laws and policy related to behavior traditionally associated with opposite-sex individuals also changed. In an early instance, a male student in Providence, Rhode Island, successfully sued his school in 1980 to force it to allow him to bring a male date to the senior prom. Social attitudes against homosexuals also moderated, and in 1967, Massachusetts elected the first country's openly gay state legislator. There are now several openly gay members of Congress.

Inevitably, the issue of whether to legalize gay marriages came to the fore. The first major event occurred in 1996 when a judge in Hawaii ruled that barriers to same-sex marriages violated the state constitution. Even though Hawaii soon amended its constitution to reinstitute the ban, an alarmed Congress passed, and President Bill Clinton signed, the Defense of Marriage Act (DOMA, 1996) barring U.S. recognition of same-sex marriages and allowing states not to recognize same-sex marriages licensed by other states. Then in 1999, Vermont's Supreme Court ruled that the state constitution entitled same-sex couples to the same benefits and protections as married heterosexual couples. The following year, Vermont's legislature enacted a civil union bill granting legal status to gay couples. In response, many state legislatures and, in numerous other instances, their citizens through referendums passed laws and even state constitutional amendments barring gay marriages. But some courts and legislatures moved in the opposite direction by allowing civil union and even gay marriages.

The genesis of the events immediately leading to the readings in this debate began in May 2008 when the California Supreme Court ruled the state's ban on same-sex marriage violated the state's constitution. Six months later, California's voters negated that decision by passing a referendum, Proposition 8, with a 52% majority that amended California's constitution to bar same-sex marriage. Gay-rights supporters filed suit challenging the validity of Proposition 8 court on technical grounds, but in May 2009 the state's supreme rejected the appeal.

That set the stage for a female couple and a male couple to file *Perry, et al. v. Schwarzenegger* to be filed in the U.S. District Court in San Francisco. The suit argues that Proposition 8 violates the equal protection clause of the Fourteenth Amendment and other part of the U.S. Constitution. To avoid one bit of possible confusion, note that Arnold Schwarzenegger is technically the defendant as the state's governor, but he opposed Proposition 8 and refused to defend it in court. As a result, anti–gay marriage groups intervened and defending the law in lieu of the governor.

The trial phase of the case began in January 2009 and included not just legal arguments about the Constitution but also testimony about such issues as whether sexual orientation is innate or a matter of choice and the impact of such matters as gay child rearing and other family-related activities. At the end of the trial, Judge Vaughn R. Walker posed a series of questions to the plaintiffs, those seeking to overturn Proposition 8, and to the defendants, proponents of upholding it. The two readings that follow are respectively the replies of the plaintiffs and the defendants [defendant-intervenors] to those questions.

POINTS TO PONDER

➤ The only time clergy can perform a legal act is by marrying people. This arguably conflicts with the First Amendment. Some people advocate having marriages a purely a religious or personal pledge with no legal consequences and having all couples who want a legal connection to do so through a civil union.

➤ Part of the argument is whether the courts should give sexual-orientation, as a classification of people, the same special protections against discrimination given to groups based on race, religion, age, and some other demographic traits. What in principle should determine whether any group is afforded such special protections?

➤ In a democracy, should the courts care that Proposition 8 was passed by California's voters rather than by its legislature?

California's Proposition 8 Barring Gay Marriages: Equal Rights Violation of the U.S. Constitution

ATTORNEYS REPRESENTING PLAINTIFFS KRISTEN M. PERRY, ET AL.

RESPONSES TO QUESTIONS DIRECTED TO PLAINTIFFS

QUESTION: Assume the evidence shows Proposition 8 is not in fact rationally related to a legitimate state interest. Assume further the evidence shows voters genuinely but without evidence believed Proposition 8 was rationally related to a legitimate interest. Do the voters' honest beliefs in the absence of supporting evidence have any bearing on the constitutionality of Proposition 8?

ANSWER: To survive rational basis review, a classification must "bear a rational relationship to an independent and legitimate legislative end." A "law will be sustained" under the rational basis standard *only* "if it can be said to *advance* a legitimate government interest" (emphasis added). [Quotations herein are, unless otherwise attributed, taken from court decisions, usually those of the Supreme Court. Because of space limitations, the citations could not be included, but are available in the original document.] Accordingly, if this Court finds that "the evidence shows Proposition 8 is not in fact rationally related to a legitimate state interest"—as Plaintiffs proved at trial—then Prop. 8 could not survive even rational basis review (let alone, the more stringent requirements of intermediate and strict scrutiny). The voters' allegedly "genuine"—but erroneous—views to the contrary would be insufficient to sustain Prop. 8 because the genuinely held beliefs of voters who enact an arbitrary, irrational, and discriminatory law cannot shield the measure from constitutional scrutiny. Voters' unfounded and discriminatory stereotypes are not a substitute for *proof* that a law actually furthers a legitimate state interest. Indeed, those who disfavor a particular group often genuinely believe and accept negative stereotypes about the disfavored group, even where such stereotypes are wholly unsubstantiated. The constitutionally relevant question for rational basis purposes is whether Prop. 8 in fact "advance[s] a legitimate government interest"—not whether the voters *believed* that it did. In that case, the court found that there was an "absence of" proof that New York's prohibition on marriage by individuals of the same sex failed to further a legitimate state interest. Here, in contrast, Plaintiffs conclusively proved at trial that Prop. 8 does not advance any legitimate state interest, and that it is therefore irrational and unconstitutional under any standard of scrutiny.

QUESTION: What evidence supports a finding that maintaining marriage as an opposite-sex relationship does not afford a rational basis for Proposition 8?

ANSWER: Merely "maintaining marriage as an opposite-sex relationship" is not by itself a rational basis for Prop. 8. As an initial matter, neither tradition nor moral disapproval is a sufficient basis for a State to impair a person's constitutionally protected right to marry. Moreover, the evidence demonstrates that maintaining marriage as an opposite-sex relationship to the exclusion of loving and committed gay and lesbian couples does not promote any legitimate government interest. To the contrary, doing so causes irreparable harm to gay men and lesbians and their families, and is fundamentally stigmatizing and discriminatory.

QUESTION: Until very recently, same-sex relationships did not enjoy legal protection anywhere in the United States. How does this fact square with plaintiffs' claim that marriage between persons of the same sex enjoys the status of a fundamental right entitled to constitutional protection?

ANSWER: The Supreme Court "has long recognized that freedom of personal choice in matters of marriage and family life is one of the liberties protected by the Due Process Clause of the Fourteenth Amendment." Plaintiffs are seeking invalidation of the discriminatory restrictions that Prop. 8 imposes on the existing constitutional right to marry—which is "fundamental[ly] importan[t] for all individuals." Those existing "constitutional protection[s]" for "personal decisions relating to marriage" extend to individuals in a loving, committed relationship with a person of the opposite sex or the same sex because, no matter the sex of the individuals involved in the relationship, marriage is an "expression of emotional support and public commitment" essential to personal fulfillment. Thus, just as the plaintiffs in *Loving v. Virginia*, (1967), were not asking the Supreme Court to recognize a new right to interracial marriage, Plaintiffs here are not asking this Court to recognize a new fundamental right to same-sex marriage. They are instead seeking access to an existing constitutional right that has long been denied to gay men and lesbians. The mere longevity of those discriminatory and irrational restrictions on the right to marry is a constitutionally inadequate ground for continuing to exclude gay men and lesbians from this "vital personal right." [In *Loving v. Virginia*, the Supreme Court struck down a Virginia law that barred marriages between people of different races.]

QUESTION: What is the import of evidence showing that marriage has historically been limited to a man and a woman? What evidence shows that that limitation no longer enjoys constitutional recognition?

ANSWER: Evidence that marriage historically has been limited to a man and a woman does not insulate Prop. 8 from constitutional attack. The historical exclusion of gay men and lesbians from marriage is consistent with the uncontroverted [unchallenged] evidence in this case that gay men and lesbians have suffered a history of discrimination and unequal treatment in virtually all aspects of their lives. Moreover, although there have historically been discriminatory restrictions imposed on marriage, eliminating those restrictions has not deprived marriage of its vitality and importance, but has, in fact, strengthened marriage as a social institution. For example, slaves historically were not allowed to marry but gained that right after emancipation. Similarly, although bans on interracial marriage had their origins in the colonial period, were eventually enacted by 41 States, and remained on the books in more than a dozen States as late as 1967, such restrictions are unthinkable—and flatly unconstitutional—today. Although longstanding, none of these discriminatory restrictions on marriage ever "enjoy[ed] constitutional recognition"—and nor do discriminatory measures that restrict marriage to individuals of the opposite sex.

QUESTION: What empirical data, if any, supports a finding that legal recognition of same-sex marriage reduces discrimination against gays and lesbians?

ANSWER: Uncontroverted evidence demonstrates that invalidating Prop. 8 would immediately and significantly reduce discrimination against gay men and lesbians by removing discriminatory restrictions that prohibit individuals of the same sex from marrying in California.

Affording gay men and lesbians the right to marry would also reduce discrimination by providing them with access to certain tangible benefits, such as health insurance, that flow directly from marriage. Moreover, empirical studies from jurisdictions where marriage between individuals of the same sex is permitted demonstrate the salutary benefits that flow from permitting gay men and lesbians to marry. Empirical evidence also demonstrates that marriage correlates with a variety of measurable health benefits that extend to the married individuals and their children. Indeed, empirical studies have established that gay men and lesbians living in States that do not provide them with antidiscrimination protections are at a significantly higher risk of suffering from psychiatric disorders.

Finally, substantial evidence demonstrates that gay and lesbian couples are stigmatized because they cannot marry. Prop. 8 necessarily relegates the relationships of gay and lesbian individuals to second-class status by communicating the official view that their committed relationships are less worthy of recognition than comparable heterosexual relationships. The resulting harm from that stigmatization is profound and far-reaching.

QUESTION: Even if enforcement of Proposition 8 were enjoined, plaintiffs' marriages would not be recognized under federal law. Can the court find Proposition 8 to be unconstitutional without also considering the constitutionality of the federal Defense of Marriage Act?

ANSWER: Yes. Plaintiffs have challenged only Prop. 8 in this litigation. The Court need not—and in the absence of a federal defendant, should not—address the federal Defense of Marriage Act in this litigation. It may be that the Court's ruling will have implications for the Defense of Marriage Act and other similar laws that discriminate against gay men and lesbians. But such implications, if any, will depend on the parameters of this Court's decision

QUESTION: What evidence supports a finding that the choice of a person of the same sex as a marriage partner partakes of traditionally revered liberties of intimate association and individual autonomy?

ANSWER: Testimony of multiple experts and of Plaintiffs themselves confirms that these liberties are precisely what is at stake in the choice of a same-sex marriage partner. Describing why she is a plaintiff in this case, Sandy Stier explained that "I would like to get married, and I would like to marry the person that I choose and that is Kris Perry." Ms. Stier went on to explain that she feels it is important for the next generation "to at least feel like the option to be true to yourself is an option that they can have, too." Similarly, an American Psychoanalytic Association Position Statement on marriage by same-sex couples has explained that "the milestone of marriage moves a couple and its children into full citizenship in American society."

Of course, the importance that attaches to the "choice" of a person of the same sex as a marriage partner does not mean that gay men and lesbians choose their sexual orientation or could choose to marry a person of the opposite sex. Gay men and lesbians, like all other citizens, have the right to choose the individual with whom they wish to spend their life in marriage. The evidence in this case clearly demonstrates, however, that the vast majority of individuals experience little or no choice in their sexual orientation, and that marrying someone of the opposite sex is not a realistic, viable option for gay men and lesbians.

RESPONSES TO QUESTIONS DIRECTED TO PROPONENTS

QUESTION: Assuming a higher level of scrutiny applies to either plaintiffs' due process or equal protection claim, what evidence in the record shows that Proposition 8 is substantially related to an important government interest? Narrowly tailored to a compelling government interest?

ANSWER: There is no evidence in the record to suggest that Prop. 8 is even rationally related to a legitimate government interest—let alone, substantially related to an important government interest or narrowly tailored to further a compelling government interest. To the contrary, Prop. 8 causes irreparable harm to gay men and lesbians and their families, and is fundamentally discriminatory. Indeed, Proponents cannot conceivably satisfy the requirements of either intermediate or strict scrutiny because they rely exclusively on hoc rationalizations and do not defend any of the arguments advanced in support of Prop. 8 during the campaign itself—such as the purported risk that, in the absence of Prop. 8, children would be taught in school about marriage between individuals of the same sex. The Supreme Court has made clear, however, that, to survive heightened scrutiny, the "justification[s]" offered to defend a discriminatory measure "must be genuine, not hypothesized or invented post hoc in response to litigation."

QUESTION: What evidence in the record supports a finding that same-sex marriage has or could have negative social consequences?

ANSWER: There [is no] evidence in the record that could support a finding that marriage by individuals of the same sex would in fact have negative implications. While Proponents subjected each of the credible and well-qualified experts called by Plaintiffs to lengthy cross-examination, none offered any testimony that would lend support to the premise that allowing gay men and lesbians to marry has or could have negative consequences.

QUESTION: If the motion is granted, is there any evidence to support a finding that Proposition 8 advances a legitimate governmental interest?

ANSWER: There is no evidence in the record to support a finding that Prop. 8 advances legitimate government interests. As Plaintiffs have explained in detail, the record in this case clearly demonstrates that Prop. 8 in fact serves no legitimate government interest.

QUESTION: Why should the court assume that the deinstitutionalization of marriage is a negative consequence?

ANSWER: To the extent that "deinstitutionalization" includes the removal of unfounded and discriminatory restrictions on one or both of the participants in a marriage, this Court should not assume that outcome to be a negative one, and the evidence proves otherwise. For example, as explained by Dr. Nancy Cott, the removal of historically accepted restrictions on the freedom and individuality of women in a marriage, and the lifting of restrictions that have existed over time concerning marriage across different races, are positive developments that have fulfilled the meaning of marriage and helped it to remain a vibrant and important social institution. But even to the extent one assumes that the "deinstitutionalization" of marriage is a harmful or negative thing, the record is devoid of credible, reliable evidence sufficient to show that affording gay men and lesbians the right to marry would lead to such deinstitutionalization. To the contrary, the evidence shows that removing a remaining, unfounded and discriminatory restriction from the meaning of marriage would strengthen, rather than weaken, the institution.

QUESTION: What evidence in the record shows that same-sex marriage is a drastic or far-reaching change to the institution of marriage?

ANSWER: Simply put, there is no evidence that permitting same-sex couples to marry would effect a drastic or far-reaching change to the institution of marriage. First, as Professor Cott testified, civil marriage has never been a static institution. Historically, it has changed, sometimes dramatically, to reflect the evolving needs, values, and understanding of society. Indeed, the institution of marriage has changed repeatedly over its history, from the elimination of the doctrine of coverture [the possession of all of a wife's rights by her husband], to permitting interracial couples to marry, to permitting "no fault" divorces. The institution has easily weathered those changes, and is still seen as a significant institution resonating with social meaning. And allowing same-sex couples to marry is no more drastic than any of those changes.

QUESTION: What evidence in the record shows that same-sex couples are differently situated from opposite-sex couples where at least one partner is infertile?

ANSWER: No evidence in the record shows that same-sex couples are differently situated from opposite-sex couples where at least one partner is infertile. In fact, Plaintiffs presented testimony from Dr. Anne Peplau establishing, based on years of research, that same-sex couples and opposite-sex couples are fundamentally the same in terms of their relationships, what they are looking for in a relationship, and what makes the relationship successful or unsuccessful.

QUESTION: Assume the evidence shows that children do best when raised by their married, biological mother and father. Assume further the court concludes it is in the state's interest to encourage children to be raised by their married biological mother and father where possible. What evidence if any shows that Proposition 8 furthers this state interest?

ANSWER: There is no evidence that Prop. 8 furthers any state interest that may exist in encouraging children to be raised by their married, biological mother and father. Prop. 8 does not change California's laws and policies that permit gay and lesbian individuals to have, adopt, or raise children. Nor does prohibiting marriage by individuals of the same sex have any effect on whether biological parents will choose to raise their biological children or whether biological parents will choose to marry or remain married to raise those children. To the contrary, to the extent the State has an interest in what is "best" for children, the evidence shows that Prop. 8 affirmatively harms the interests of children and does not promote the achievement of good child-adjustment outcomes. By denying same-sex couples with children the right to marry, Prop. 8 deprives the children of those couples the legitimacy that marriage confers on children and the sense of security, stability, and increased well-being that accompany that legitimacy. Indeed, the evidence shows that Prop. 8 stigmatizes the children of same-sex couples by relegating their parents to the separate and unequal institution of domestic partnership. Moreover, because certain tangible and intangible benefits flow to a married couple's children by virtue of the State's (and society's) recognition of that bond, Prop. 8 denies children of same-sex couples access to those benefits.

QUESTION: Why is legislating based on moral disapproval of homosexuality not tantamount to discrimination? What evidence in the record shows that a belief based in morality cannot also be discriminatory? If that moral point of view is not held and is disputed by a small but significant minority of the community, should not an effort to enact that moral point of view into a state constitution be deemed a violation of equal protection?

ANSWER: Legislative action based on moral disapproval of gay men and lesbians as a group is discrimination, and mere moral disapproval is not a legitimate government interest. Accordingly, whether that "moral point of view" is held unanimously—or whether it is disputed by a significant minority of the population—it is not a sufficient basis for sustaining legislation.

QUESTION: What harm do proponents face if an injunction against the enforcement of Proposition 8 is issued?

ANSWER: Excluding individuals of the same sex from the institution of marriage harms Plaintiffs, their children, and hundreds of thousands of other gay men and lesbians (and their families) throughout California. Allowing gay men and lesbians to marry harms no one. Indeed, Proponents' counsel admitted that Proponents "don't know" what effect, if any, marriage by individuals of the same sex would have on opposite-sex marriage. Tellingly, Proponents presented no evidence whatsoever that the 18,000 same-sex marriages that took place between the California Supreme Court's decision in the Marriage Cases and the passage of Prop. 8 have harmed Proponents or anyone else.

RESPONSES TO QUESTIONS DIRECTED TO PLAINTIFFS AND PROPONENTS

QUESTION: What does the evidence show the difference to be between gays and lesbians, on the one hand, and heterosexuals on the other? Is that difference one which the government "may legitimately take into account" when making legislative classifications?

ANSWER: The evidence demonstrates that gay and lesbian individuals and heterosexuals are similarly situated with respect to marriage. The only difference is that gay and lesbian individuals desire to marry a person of the same sex and heterosexual individuals desire to marry a person of the opposite sex. But this difference is not one that the government "may legitimately take into account" when making legislative classifications because it "bears no relation to ability to perform or contribute to society."

Moreover, any difference with respect to procreation is not a basis for barring gay men and lesbians from marrying because marriage has never been limited to procreative unions. And, to the extent that Proponents claim that gay and lesbian couples are less stable and monogamous in their relationships than heterosexual couples, there is no empirical support for this negative stereotype.

QUESTION: What does the evidence show the definition (or definitions) of marriage to be?

ANSWER: Marriage is fundamentally an intimate commitment between two people who choose to build a life and home together—with or without children. This definition of marriage recognizes that, for many, marriage may include childrearing or the legitimization of children, but at its core, procreation is not required for a relationship to constitute a "marriage" as understood through the history of our Nation.

QUESTION: What does it mean to have a "choice" in one's sexual orientation?

ANSWER: Having a "choice" necessarily entails being able to voluntarily decide between two (or more) viable options. Having "choice" in one's sexual orientation would amount to choosing the sex of the person to whom one is attracted. Not surprisingly, no party argued or put on any evidence that heterosexuals feel as though they have a "choice" regarding the sex to which they are attracted. And the overwhelming evidence demonstrates that the same is true for gay men and lesbians.

Notably, despite Proponents' repeated attempts to conflate the two concepts, "choice" is not the same thing as "change." Some percentage of individuals may experience a change in their sexual orientation at some point during their lifetime, but that does not mean that the individual could at any point voluntarily choose to change his or her sexual orientation. There are many reasons why a change may occur—for example, a man may be married to a woman before he realizes that he is gay. But, by definition, "choice" requires a voluntary decision, and there is no testimony or evidence to support the notion that one consciously decides on his or her sexual orientation. As the "Report of the American Psychological Association Task Force on Appropriate Therapeutic Responses to Sexual Orientation" explained:

> [E]nduring change to an individual's sexual orientation is uncommon...[T]he results of scientifically valid research indicate that it is unlikely that individuals will be able to [voluntarily] reduce same-sex attractions or increase other-sex sexual attractions.

QUESTION: If spouses are obligated to one another for mutual support and support of dependents, and if legal spousal obligations have no basis in the gender of the spouse, what purpose does a law requiring that a marital partnership consist of one man and one woman serve?

ANSWER: Plaintiffs agree that spouses are obligated to one another for mutual support and the support of dependants. Plaintiffs further agree that the sex of the spouse is irrelevant to legal spousal obligations. Indeed, changes in society have led spousal roles to become more gender-neutral over time, and changes in the law have ended gender-determined roles for spouses. Accordingly, there is no purpose in limiting marriage to opposite-sex couples. Individuals in marriages of two men or two women are equally capable—and equally obligated—to provide mutual support and support for their dependents as individuals in opposite-sex marriages.

QUESTION: The California Family Code requires that registered domestic partners be treated as spouses. Businesses that extend benefits to married spouses in California must extend equal benefits to registered domestic partners. If, under California law, registered domestic partners are to be treated just like married spouses, what purpose is served by differentiating—in name only—between same-sex and opposite-sex unions?

ANSWER: The fact that California grants gay and lesbian individuals virtually all the tangible rights associated with marriage but denies them the label of "marriage" serves no purpose but to stigmatize and discriminate against gay and lesbian individuals.

The word "marriage" has a unique meaning, and there is a significant symbolic disparity between domestic partnership and marriage. The unique cultural value and social meaning of "marriage" cannot compare to the legal benefits of domestic partnerships. Domestic partnerships—even if they confer virtually all the material benefits of marriage—stigmatize gay and lesbian individuals and relegate them to the status of second-class citizens.

Prop. 8 reflects and propagates the stigma that gay and lesbian individuals do not have intimate relations similar to those of heterosexual couples and conveys the State's judgment that same-sex couples are inherently less deserving of society's full recognition through the status of civil marriage than heterosexual couples. This distinction is stigmatizing—and thus unconstitutional.

QUESTION: What evidence, if any, shows whether infertility has ever been a legal basis for annulment or divorce?

ANSWER: The ability or willingness of married couples to produce children has never been a prerequisite to the validity of a marriage under American law. There is no evidence in the record that an opposite-sex couple not capable of procreating together has ever been barred from marrying simply because their union would not be naturally procreative. Accordingly, Proponents' assertion that "the institution of marriage is, and always has been, uniquely concerned with promoting and regulating naturally procreative relationships between men and women" is factually incorrect and has no support in the trial record.

QUESTION: What are the constitutional consequences if the evidence shows that sexual orientation is immutable for men but not for women? Must gay men and lesbians be treated identically under the Equal Protection Clause?

ANSWER: As a threshold matter, the evidence conclusively demonstrates that sexual orientation is not a choice—it is not consciously changeable for the vast majority of men or women, whether they are heterosexual, gay, or lesbian. Moreover, even if sexual orientation were changeable, gay men, lesbians, and heterosexuals should all be treated equally under the Equal Protection Clause. Because sexual orientation is properly considered a suspect or quasi-suspect classification, discrimination based on sexual orientation is inherently suspect whether it targets a gay man, a lesbian, or a heterosexual.

QUESTION: If the court finds Proposition 8 to be unconstitutional, what remedy would "yield to the constitutional expression of the people of California's will [as expressed in the Prop. 8 referendum]"?

ANSWER: No remedy short of an order permanently enjoining Prop. 8's enforcement in its entirety would be sufficient. If a state constitutional provision is inconsistent with the Fourteenth Amendment of the U.S. Constitution, it can no longer be given effect—regardless of its level of public support.

California's Proposition 8 Barring Gay Marriages: Valid State Law

ATTORNEYS REPRESENTING PROPOSITION 8 OFFICIAL PROPONENTS DENNIS HOLLINGSWORTH, ET AL.

RESPONSES TO QUESTIONS DIRECTED TO PROPONENTS

QUESTION: Assuming a higher level of scrutiny applies to either plaintiffs' due process or equal protection claim, what evidence in the record shows that Proposition 8 is substantially related to an important government interest? Narrowly tailored to a compelling government interest?

ANSWER: Because Proposition 8 neither infringes a fundamental right nor discriminates on the basis of sex, and because gays and lesbians are not entitled to heightened protection under the Equal Protection Clause, Proposition 8 is subject only to rational basis review. Even if heightened scrutiny applied, however, Proposition 8 would readily satisfy such scrutiny.

California's interest in increasing the likelihood that children will be born to and raised by their biological mothers and fathers in stable and enduring family units is a government interest of the highest order. Not only is this core procreative purpose of marriage "fundamental to our very existence and survival," indeed, "It is hard to conceive an interest more legitimate and more paramount for the state than promoting an optimal social structure for educating, socializing, and preparing its future citizens to become productive participants in civil society." [Quotations herein are, unless otherwise attributed, taken from court decisions, usually those of the Supreme Court. Because of space limitations, the citations could not be included, but are available in the original document.] For all of these reasons, the Supreme Court has recognized that marriage is "the foundation of the family and of society, without which there would be neither civilization nor progress."

Thus, "it seems beyond dispute that the state has a compelling interest in encouraging and fostering procreation of the race and providing status and stability to the environment in which children are raised. This has always been one of society's paramount goals." For the same reasons, California has a compelling interest in proceeding with caution when considering changes to the vital institution of marriage that could well weaken that institution and the critically important interests it has traditionally served.

As explained more fully in our responses to [other] questions, Proposition 8 furthers these interests by preserving the traditional definition and form of marriage and by providing special encouragement and recognition to those relationships that uniquely further California's interests in increasing the likelihood that children will be born to and raised by their natural parents in stable and enduring family units.

Proposition 8 is substantially related to at least the two important interests identified above. It does not matter that California could have done more to further these interests, for example by refusing to accommodate either the vested interests of a limited number of same-sex couples who acted in reliance on the California Supreme Court's decision prior to the enactment of Proposition 8 or the interests of gay and lesbian families that are served by domestic partnerships that offer essentially the same rights and obligations of marriage. To the contrary, it is well settled that the Constitution "does not require that a regulatory regime single-mindedly pursue one objective to the exclusion of all others to survive...intermediate scrutiny." Simply put, the fact that California has "struck its own idiosyncratic balance between various important but competing state interests" does not render "its asserted interest" in responsible procreation and parenting "any less substantial than in the states" that have taken a different approach.

Nor does the fact that California permits opposite-sex couples who cannot, or do not intend to, have children to marry render Proposition 8 unconstitutionally over-inclusive. For one thing, allowing such couples to marry does further the State's interest in increasing the likelihood that children will be born to and raised by their natural parents in enduring family units because it reinforces social norms that seek to channel intimate heterosexual relationships into marriage.

The fact that California permits gays and lesbians—as well as single individuals and cohabiting heterosexual couples—to adopt does not in anyway undermine the States' interest in increasing the likelihood that children will be born and raised by their natural parents in stable, enduring family units. Rather, it simply reflects an attempt to provide for the practical reality that this ideal is not always possible. It is simply implausible that by recognizing and making provisions for the reality that an ideal will not be achieved in all cases, the State somehow abandons its interests in promoting and increasing the likelihood of that ideal. Likewise, the fact that California has opted to encourage, rather than require, that opposite-sex couples procreate only within marriage and stay together to raise their children, does not render Proposition 8 unconstitutional.

Allowing [heterosexual] couples to marry furthers the State's interest in other ways as well. Most obviously, couples who do not plan to have children may experience accidents or change their plans, and some couples who do not believe they can have children may discover otherwise. And even in cases of obvious infertility, it is usually the case that only one spouse is infertile. In such cases marriage furthers the State's interest in responsible procreation by decreasing the likelihood that the fertile spouse will engage in sexual activity with a third party, for the State's interest is served not only by increasing the likelihood that procreation occurs within stable family units, but also by decreasing the likelihood that it occurs outside of such units.

Moreover, attempting to determine on a case-by-case basis whether each heterosexual couple seeking to marry will have children would be intolerably burdensome, intrusive, and impractical. As another district court has recognized, because such an approach is simply not a "real alternative" for achieving the state's "compelling interest in encouraging and fostering procreation...and providing status and stability to the environment in which children are raised," allowing "legal marriage as between all couples of opposite sex" is "the least intrusive alternative available to protect the procreative relationship."

Thus, even if intermediate scrutiny applied, no principle of constitutional law bars California from foregoing an implausible and Orwellian attempt to police fertility and childbearing intentions and relying instead on the common-sense presumption that opposite-sex couples are, in general, capable of procreation. Indeed, applying intermediate scrutiny in a closely analogous context, the Supreme Court rejected as "ludicrous" an argument that a law criminalizing statutory rape for the purpose of preventing teenage pregnancies was "impermissibly overbroad because it makes unlawful sexual intercourse with prepubescent females, who are, by definition, incapable of becoming pregnant."

Finally, because there is a clear biological difference between opposite-sex couples who, at least as a general matter, are capable of natural procreation (both intentionally and unintentionally) and same-sex couples who are categorically incapable of natural procreation, California's separate treatment of these two types of couples is neither surprising nor troublesome from a constitutional perspective. Given that same-sex couples and opposite-sex couples are not similarly situated with respect to the state's interest in channeling potentially procreative relationships into stable and enduring family units, intermediate scrutiny does not require the State to prove that limiting marriage to opposite-sex couples is "necessary" to further this interest. In all events, there are very good reasons to believe that redefining marriage to include same-sex couples could weaken that institution and the interests it has always served. In light of these risks, the traditional opposite-sex definition of marriage as reflected in Proposition 8 is substantially related to the State's important interests in increasing the likelihood that children will be born to and raised by their biological mothers and fathers in stable and enduring family units and proceeding with caution when considering changes to the vital institution of marriage that could well weaken that institution and the critically important interests it has traditionally served. For essentially the same reasons, the traditional definition of marriage reflected in Proposition 8 is narrowly tailored to at least the compelling interests identified above.

QUESTION: What evidence in the record supports a finding that same-sex marriage has or could have negative social consequences? What does the evidence show the magnitude of these consequences to be?

ANSWER: There is substantial common ground among the parties relating to the fact that there will be significant consequences flowing from the adoption of same-sex marriage. Professor [Nancy] Cott has acknowledged that the adoption of same-sex marriage will change the public meaning of marriage, that a change in the social meaning of marriage will unquestionably have real world consequences, and that whatever these consequences are, they will be momentous. As Professor Cott told National Public Radio when Massachusetts legalized same-sex marriage: "One could point to earlier watersheds, but perhaps none quite so explicit as this particular turning point," and she added at trial that same-sex marriage is "arguably a highly distinctive turning point." There is ample evidence supporting Professor Cott's view that same-sex marriage would represent a watershed turning point in the history of this venerable institution. For example:

- According to Joseph Raz, professor at both Oxford University and Columbia Law School, "there can be no doubt that the recognition of gay marriages will affect as great a transformation in the nature of marriage as that from polygamous to monogamous or from arranged to unarranged marriage."
- Yale Law School professor and prominent gay rights advocate William Eskridge believes that "enlarging the concept [of marriage] to embrace same-sex couples would necessarily transform it into something new."

Professor Cott also admits that it is not possible to predict with precision the consequences that will flow from same-sex marriage. But there is a wealth of evidence in the record as to the likely negative consequences. Taken together, the evidence supporting these findings strongly suggests that redefining marriage to include same-sex unions will change the public meaning of marriage in ways that will weaken the social norms that seek to discourage procreative sexual relationships and childrearing outside of marital bonds. Redefining marriage in this way would also change its focus from the needs of children to the desires of the adult partners, suggesting that the latter are paramount, as well as weaken the social understanding that, all else being equal, what is best for a child is to be raised by its married, biological parents and to have a mother and father. All of these changes are likely to reduce the willingness of biological parents, especially fathers, to make the commitments and sacrifices necessary to marry, stay married, and play an active role in raising their children. The evidence suggests that as a result, there will be lower marriage rates, higher rates of divorce and cohabitation, more out of wedlock children, and fewer children raised by both of their biological parents.

First, extending marriage to same-sex couples would eliminate the state's ability to specially promote those relationships that uniquely further the vital societal purpose of channeling potentially and naturally procreative conduct into stable and enduring family units. This would have particularly negative consequences for the involvement of fathers in raising their children. The link marriage provides between sex and procreation helps to increase the likelihood that fathers will care for their children.

Second, and relatedly, extending marriage to same-sex couples would likely accelerate and perhaps even complete the "deinstitutionalization of marriage." We discuss deinstitutionalization in more detail in response to the fourth question posed to us, which specifically addresses the concept. In short, a range of social science scholars agree that there is a connection between same-sex marriage and the deinstitutionalization of marriage.

Third, leaving aside the obvious fact that it is far too soon to draw any firm empirical conclusions based on the scant experience with same-sex marriage in those few jurisdictions that have adopted it, the evidence shows that concerns about the potential harms from same-sex marriage have not been negated by experience in those few places where it has been adopted. For example, since becoming the first nation in the world to institute same-sex marriage in 2001, there have been a number of worrisome trends in the Netherlands, including:

- Fewer marriages. There was an average yearly decrease of .07 in the marriage rate from 2001 through 2008, following an average yearly increase of .02 from 1994 through 2000.

- More single-parent families. Single-parent families (as a percentage of all families) increased by an average of .08% annually from 2001 to 2008, after increasing by an average of only .032% annually from 1994 to 2000.

- More unmarried parents raising children. From 2001 to 2008, non-married cohabiting couples with children (as a percentage of all cohabiting couples) increased at a 30% greater average annual rate than it had from 1994 to 2000.

- More opposite-sex couples choosing an alternative status over marriage. In 2001, 2.05% of all opposite-sex couples entering marriage or a new registered partnership chose a partnership. By 2008, that figure climbed to 9.14%.

The evidence also shows that even some same-sex marriage advocates recognize the common-sense wisdom in taking a cautious approach to making such a significant change to the institution of marriage. Indeed, in 2008 leading same-sex marriage advocate Jonathan Rauch recommended that "the way to do this is let different states do different things. Let's find out how gay marriage works in a few states. Let's find out how civil unions work. In the meantime, let the other states hold back."

Refining marriage to include same-sex unions would have other consequences as well. For one thing, it would indisputably eliminate the State's ability to provide special encouragement and recognition to those relationships most likely to further core interests that marriage has traditionally served, namely increasing the likelihood that children will be born to and raised by their natural parents in stable and enduring family units. In addition, such a redefinition will likely infringe, or at least threaten, the First Amendment and other fundamental liberty interests of institutions, parents, and other individuals who support the traditional opposite-sex definition of marriage on religious or moral grounds.

QUESTION: If the motion is granted, is there any other evidence to support a finding that Proposition 8 advances a legitimate governmental interest?

ANSWER: There is a large volume of evidence demonstrating that Proposition 8 advances legitimate government interests. First, by restoring the traditional definition of marriage, Proposition 8 advances the government interests in marriage, especially increasing the likelihood that children will be born to and raised by both their natural parents in stable and enduring family units. Authorities from a wide range of disciplines recognize these as primary interests advanced by marriage.

Second, restoring the traditional definition of marriage also enables California to proceed with caution when considering changes to the fundamental and critical social institution of marriage. In particular, it allows California to observe the results of same-sex marriage in other jurisdictions that have adopted it. As leading same-sex marriage advocate Jonathan Rauch has said: "Let's find out how gay marriage works in a few states. Let's find out how civil unions work. In the meantime, let the other states hold back."

Third, the evidence also demonstrates that Proposition 8 advances a series of other legitimate interests including ensuring democratic control over important social policy, treating different things differently, both in language and in law, and accommodating the First Amendment and other fundamental liberty interests of institutions, parents, and other individuals who support the traditional opposite-sex definition of marriage on religious or moral grounds. In addition, Proposition 8 forestalls the harms that would flow from same-sex marriage.

QUESTION: Why should the court assume that the deinstitutionalization of marriage is a negative consequence?

ANSWER: The court need not assume that the deinstitutionalization of marriage is a negative consequence. The evidence shows that deinstitutionalization weakens marriage, and hence weakens its ability to fulfill its vital societal purposes. Andrew Cherlin, a sociologist at Johns Hopkins University, defines deinstitutionalization as "the weakening of the social norms that define people's behavior in a social institution such as marriage." This weakening of social norms with respect to marriage entails shifting the focus of marriage from serving vital societal needs to facilitating the personal fulfillment of individuals. In other words, people become less likely "to focus on the rewards to be found in fulfilling socially valued roles such as the good parent or the loyal and supportive spouse"; instead "personal choice and self-development loom large in people's construction of their marital careers."

A principal societal purpose of marriage is channeling naturally procreative relationships into stable, long-lasting unions. Deinstitutionalization weakens marriage's ability to perform this function, and thus would likely result in high levels of nonmarital childbearing, cohabitation, and divorce. These consequences directly and negatively impact children. As a leading survey of social science research explains: "Children in single-parent families, children born to unmarried mothers, and children in stepfamilies or cohabiting relationships face higher risks of poor outcomes than do children in intact families headed by two biological parents. Parental divorce is also linked to a range of poorer academic and behavioral outcomes among children. There is thus value for children in promoting stable, strong marriages between biological parents.

QUESTION: What evidence in the record shows that same-sex marriage is a drastic or far-reaching change to the institution of marriage?

ANSWER: The limitation of marriage to opposite-sex unions has been a fundamental, definitional feature of that institution throughout history at common law, in this Country and, almost without exception, in every civilized society that has ever existed. And, with only a handful of exceptions, the same is true today. Redefining marriage to include same-sex unions would constitute a drastic and far-reaching change to that institution.

QUESTION: What evidence in the record shows that same-sex couples are differently situated from opposite-sex couples where at least one partner is infertile?

ANSWER: Same-sex couples are differently situated from opposite-sex couples where at least one partner is infertile in at least three ways. First, determining infertility in opposite-sex couples is extremely burdensome and intrusive, and is not always 100 percent reliable. Second, the fertile partner in an opposite-sex couple is capable of procreative sexual activity with a third party, and allowing all opposite-sex couples to marry discourages the fertile partner of a sterile spouse from engaging in such potentially procreative activity with other individuals. Third, the marriage of opposite-sex couples reinforces social norms that discourage heterosexual intercourse—which generally is potentially procreative—outside the framework of marriage.

QUESTION: Assume the evidence shows that children do best when raised by their married, biological mother and father. Assume further the court concludes it is in the state's interest to encourage children to be raised by their married biological mother and father where possible. What evidence if any shows that Proposition 8 furthers this state interest?

ANSWER: The traditional institutional of marriage has always been understood to further society's interest in increasing the likelihood that children will be raised by their biological mother and father in a stable and enduring family unit. Because Proposition 8 simply restores the opposite-sex definition and form of marriage that has prevailed all but universally throughout history and that continues to prevail in all but a handful of jurisdictions today, the evidence that Proposition furthers society's interest in increasing the likelihood that children will be raised by their biological mother and father in a stable and enduring family unit is the same evidence that establishes that marriage furthers this interest.

The traditional opposite-sex definition of marriage reflected in Proposition 8 is closely aligned with this central concern of that institution. Because sexual relationships between members of the opposite sex can in most cases produce children, either intentionally or not, such relationships have the potential to further—or harm—this vital interest in a way, and to an extent, that other types of relationships do not. By providing special recognition and encouragement to committed opposite-sex relationships, Proposition 8 seeks to channel potentially procreative conduct into relationships where that conduct is likely to further, rather than harm, these interests. Further, by maintaining the traditional definition of marriage, Proposition 8 avoids those harms to the institution of marriage and the purposes it has traditionally served that would very likely flow from the "watershed" redefinition of that institution urged by Plaintiffs.

QUESTION: Why is legislating based on moral disapproval of homosexuality not tantamount to discrimination? What evidence in the record shows that a belief based in morality cannot also be discriminatory? If that moral point of view is not held and is disputed by a small but significant minority of the community, should not an effort to enact that moral point of view into a state constitution be deemed a violation of equal protection?

ANSWER: As an initial matter, Proposition 8 does not legislate based on moral disapproval of homosexuality. Proposition 8 furthers important government interests that have nothing to do with such disapproval. Indeed, it does not matter that voters may have supported Proposition 8 for a variety of reasons, including arguably illegitimate ones. This court must uphold Proposition 8 so long as furthering a legitimate interest is at least one of the purposes of the statute, and may not reject the asserted reasons for the enactment of Proposition 8 unless it determines they could not have been a goal of the legislation. As the Supreme Court has repeatedly explained, even when heightened scrutiny applies, "it is a familiar practice of constitutional law that this court will not strike down an otherwise constitutional statute on the basis of an alleged illicit legislative motive."

Further, religious support for the traditional definition of marriage has a doctrinal and historical basis in the sacred nature of matrimony, which is wholly distinct from religious teachings regarding homosexuality and cannot reasonably be equated with moral disapproval of homosexuality. Religious teachings regarding the sacred nature of marriage developed without regard to issues of sexual orientation, predating by millennia the movement for same-sex marriage. Indeed, it is only that very recent movement that has introduced discussion of sexual orientation into religious discourse regarding marriage.

Furthermore, even if Proposition 8 were based on moral disapproval of homosexual conduct, it would not be unconstitutional. While Proponents have not argued that a belief based in morality can never be discriminatory, it is plain that moral disapproval of homosexual conduct is not tantamount to animus, bigotry, or discrimination. On the contrary, religions that condemn homosexual conduct also teach love of gays and lesbians. To be sure, moral disapproval of homosexual conduct cannot be enforced "through operation of the criminal law," and thus cannot support a law seeking to criminalize "the most private human conduct, sexual behavior, and in the most private of places, the home." But it does not follow that moral considerations cannot influence the formation of public policy. On the contrary, it is well settled that a State need not promote or facilitate what it cannot prohibit. Thus, for example, although with few exceptions a State cannot prohibit abortions, the Supreme Court has "unequivocally" held "that a state has no constitutional obligation to fund or promote abortion" and "is not required to show a compelling interest for its policy choice to favor normal childbirth."

As the Supreme Court has explained, there is a basic difference between direct state interference with a protected activity and state encouragement of an alternative activity consonant with legislative policy. Constitutional concerns are greatest when the State attempts to impose its will by force of law; the State's power to encourage actions deemed to be in the public interest is necessarily far broader." Under these precedents, the fact that a State may not criminalize intimate same-sex relationships in no way suggests that it cannot draw a distinction between such relationships and traditional opposite-sex marriages by preserving the traditional understanding of marriage.

Finally, marriage is inextricably intertwined with religious and moral concerns. As with other issues that are inextricably intertwined with moral values, such as the death penalty, gambling, obscenity, prostitution, and assisted suicide, legislation regarding marriage must inevitably choose between, or attempt to balance, competing moral views. It is not only inevitable, but entirely proper, that voters' decisions be informed by their most deeply held values and beliefs as such debates are resolved, as they should be, through the democratic process.

QUESTION: What harm do proponents face if an injunction against the enforcement of Proposition 8 is issued?

ANSWER: This Court has already held that Proponents have a "significant protectable interest in defending Proposition 8" that is not adequately represented by any other party. That interest would obviously be harmed by an injunction against enforcement of Proposition 8. Additionally, Proponents would be harmed by the issuance of an injunction against the enforcement of Proposition 8 in their capacities as agents for the People and Government of the State of California, recognized as such under state law to defend, in lieu of the defendant public officials, the constitutionality of Proposition 8.

QUESTIONS TO PLAINTIFFS AND PROPONENTS

QUESTION: What does the evidence show the difference to be between gays and lesbians, on the one hand, and heterosexuals on the other? Is that difference one which the government "may legitimately take into account" when making legislative classifications?

ANSWER: First, it is undeniable that only the sexual union of a man and a woman is capable of producing offspring. This unique property of opposite-sex relationships is why marriage is "fundamental to our very existence and survival." The government may legitimately take into account this indisputable biological difference between opposite-sex and same-sex couples.

Second, it is undeniable that only the union of a man and a woman can provide a child with both of its biological parents. The government may legitimately take this into account when making legislative classifications. Social science research indicates that, on average, the ideal family structure for a child is a family headed by two biological parents in a low-conflict marriage. Furthermore, for most children the alternative to being raised by their married, biological parents is being raised by a single parent or in a step-family. As the eminent sociologist Kingsley Davis explained, "the creation, nurture, and socialization of the next generation" are "vital and extremely demanding tasks" for which "society normally holds the biological parents responsible."

Third, it is undeniable that only the union of a man and a woman can provide a child with both a father and a mother. This is another unique property of opposite-sex unions that may form a legitimate basis for legislative classifications. Indeed, "the accumulated wisdom of several millennia of human experience" has not discovered a child-rearing model superior to that centered on the child's married mother and father.

Finally, the evidence demonstrates—and Plaintiffs' experts acknowledge—that there are other meaningful differences between gay and lesbian relationships and heterosexual relationships.

QUESTION: What does the evidence show the definition (or definitions) of marriage to be?

ANSWER: The evidence shows that marriage is, as Justice [John Paul] Stevens has put it, "a license to cohabit and produce legitimate offspring." Marriage confers societal approval to engage in procreative sexual intercourse and the birth of children. This definition of marriage is supported by the historical and anthropological record.

QUESTION: What does it mean to have a "choice" in one's sexual orientation?

ANSWER: Professor [Gregory] Herek's study, referenced by the court, found that 13 percent of self-identified gay men, 30 percent of self-identified lesbians, 41 percent of self-identified bisexual men, and 55 percent of self-identified bisexual women reported that they experienced some, a fair amount, or a lot of choice with respect to their sexual orientation, with the balance reporting that they experienced little choice, or no choice. These statistics, at face value, are wholly inconsistent with any finding that gays and lesbians are a class defined by an immutable characteristic. Indeed, statistics such as these would be unthinkable with respect to other classes, such as race or sex, which the Supreme Court has held to be entitled to heightened protection under the Equal Protection Clause.

Nor does the fact that any given individual reported that he or she experiences little or no choice with respect to his or her sexual orientation mean that his or her sexual orientation has not changed in the past, or that it might not change in the future. This sort of fluidity would be unthinkable with respect to other classes, such as race or sex, which the Supreme Court has held to be entitled to heightened protection under the Equal Protection Clause.

Finally, the fact that substantial numbers of gays, lesbians, and bisexuals reported that they experienced at least some choice with respect to their sexual orientation establishes that that orientation is not determined solely by accident of birth. Not only have plaintiffs presented no evidence that sexual orientation is determined in this manner, but a substantial body of evidence indicates that sexual orientation is not so determined. The American Psychiatric Association [has said], "There are no replicated scientific studies supporting any specific biological etiology for homosexuality."

QUESTION: If spouses are obligated to one another for mutual support and support of dependents, and if legal spousal obligations have no basis in the gender of the spouse, what purpose does a law requiring that a marital partnership consist of one man and one woman serve?

ANSWER: The equal treatment under law of each spouse without respect to gender is an analytically separate issue from the State's interest in preserving the traditional definition of marriage. As explained above, the traditional definition of marriage serves a myriad of governmental interests.

QUESTION: The California Family Code requires that registered domestic partners be treated as spouses. Businesses that extend benefits to married spouses in California must extend equal benefits to registered domestic partners. If, under California law, registered domestic partners are to be treated just like married spouses, what purpose is served by differentiating—in name only—between same-sex and opposite-sex unions?

ANSWER: The California Court of Appeals answered this question when it upheld the California Legislature's decision to differentiate, in name only, between registered domestic partners and married spouses. By retaining the traditional opposite-sex definition of marriage, California preserves the abiding link between that institution and the vital social interests that are implicated by the uniquely procreative capacity of male-female unions and provides special recognition and encouragement to those unions that uniquely serve its interest in increasing the likelihood that children will be born to and raised by both of their natural parents in stable and enduring family units. At the same time, the parallel institution of domestic partnerships recognizes and honors the committed loving relationships of gays and lesbians. These parallel institutions seek to respect and accommodate differing types of relationships that have differing natural capacities and thus serve differing societal interests. It is not irrational that they be called by different names.

Relatedly, redefining marriage to include same-sex couples would work a profound transformation in the meaning and nature of the institution. We cannot escape the reality that the shared societal meaning of marriage—passed down through the common law into our statutory law—has always been the union of a man and a woman. To alter that meaning would render a profound change in the public consciousness of a social institution of ancient origin. It is not unreasonable for the State to proceed incrementally and with caution in balancing the competing interests in this novel and controversial area.

In sum, by retaining the traditional definition of marriage while extending the rights and benefits of marriage to same-sex couples through domestic partnerships, California seeks both to preserve the institution of marriage and its traditional purposes and to recognize and honor gay and lesbian relationships. Nothing in the Constitution requires the state categorically to favor one of these values over the other.

QUESTION: What evidence, if any, shows whether infertility has ever been a legal basis for annulment or divorce?

ANSWER: California courts have allowed annulment on the basis of fraud only "if the fraud relates to a matter which the state deems vital to the marriage relationship." As recently as 2005, the California Court of Appeals has held that procreation is such a vital matter. In fact, "annulments on the basis of fraud are generally granted only in cases where the fraud related in some way to the sexual or procreative aspects of marriage." Thus, the California Court of Appeals has held that an annulment should be granted where one spouse fraudulently concealed known sterility from the other. The justification for the rule is the central place of procreation in marriage.

The historic basis for these legal rules is the centrality of procreation to the institution of marriage. As one commentator explained, "since marriage is a sexual relation, having in view the propagation of the species, a man or woman so imperfect in the sexual organism as to be perpetually and incurably incapable of the connection which precedes parentage cannot enter into indissoluble matrimony with another having no notice of the incapacity."

QUESTION: What are the constitutional consequences if the evidence shows that sexual orientation is immutable for men but not for women? Must gay men and lesbians be treated identically under the Equal Protection Clause?

ANSWER: As an initial matter, the evidence makes clear that sexual orientation is not immutable, either for gay men or for lesbians. Proponents acknowledge, however, that the evidence indicates that there are differences between how gay men and lesbians experience sexual orientation and that for many women, in particular, sexual orientation is a very fluid construct. If this Court were to find, however, that sexual orientation is immutable for gay men but not for lesbians, Proponents are aware of no constitutional precedent for treating gay men and lesbians differently for purposes of a sexual orientation classification under the Equal Protection Clause.

Even if it were appropriate to distinguish between gays and lesbians for purposes of the Equal Protection Clause, a finding that sexual orientation is immutable for gay men would satisfy only one of the requirements for heightened protection; they would still need to satisfy the other requirements for heightened scrutiny, including a lack of political power.

QUESTION: If the court finds Proposition 8 to be unconstitutional, what remedy would "yield to the constitutional expression of the people of California's will [as expressed in the passage of the Prop. 8 referendum]"?

ANSWER: If, as Plaintiffs maintain, Proposition 8 cannot be reconciled with its own non-retrospective application, as interpreted by the California Supreme Court, or with any other feature of California law, the remedy that would "yield to the constitutional expression of the people of California's will" is sustaining Proposition 8 by giving it retrospective effect or invalidating the conflicting feature of California law. Several factors support this conclusion. Proposition 8 is a provision of the California Constitution, and thus "constitutes the ultimate expression of the people's will." The people of California have consistently expressed their commitment to maintaining the institution of marriage in its traditional form as the union of a man and a woman. A contrary result would entail the conclusion that the California judiciary and legislature—the very bodies the people's initiative process is designed to control—have the power to secure the invalidation of a state constitutional provision under the federal constitution by issuing judicial decisions or passing laws that rationally cannot be squared with the expressed will of the people.

[N.B. Unlike the plaintiffs that answered questions to the other side (the proponents/defendants), the proponents did not choose to answer the questions to the plaintiffs. That commentary, had it existed, would have been included here.]

THE CONTINUING DEBATE:
California's Proposition 8 Barring Gay Marriages

What Is New

In August 2010 Judge Vaughn Walker of the U.S. District Court in San Francisco handed down his decision in *Perry v. Schwarzenegger*. He found Proposition 8 to be unconstitutional. After briefly suspending his order not to enforce Proposition 8, he made it permanent. However, before any gay marriages could take place, the Ninth Circuit of the U.S. Court of Appeals ordered that the ban on gay marriages in California remain in place while the opponents of Judge Walker's ruling appealed it. It seems almost certain that whatever the Ninth Circuit decides on the appeal that the case will be finally decided by the Supreme Court. As of mid-2010, 53% of Americans remained opposed to gay marriage, but the level of opposition was down from 68% in 1996.

Where to Find More

For the gay and lesbian perspective, access the Web sites of the Human Rights Campaign at www.hrc.org/ and the National Gay and Lesbian Taskforce at www.thetaskforce.org/. Among those organizations opposing gay marriages are the American Family Association at www.afa.net/ and the Alliance Defense Fund at www.alliancedefensefund.org/. The legality of gay marriages and other forms of union in the 50 states is available at usmarriagelaws.com/. For the international impacts of gay marriages, read M. V. Lee Badgett, *When Gay People Get Married: What Happens When Societies Legalize Same-Sex Marriage* (New York University Press, 2009).

What More to Do

The original documents that served as a base for the two readings were both much longer than the edited versions here, with each side offering an extended legal and substantive justification of their position. One approach to organizing a discussion in class would be to divide the class into groups, assign each one or more of the issues identified in the judge's questions, then have the groups do an in-depth analysis and bring their findings to class.

AMERICAN PEOPLE/ POLITICAL CULTURE

THE CULTURAL ASSIMILATION OF IMMIGRANTS:
The Melting Pot Is Broken *or* Blending Satisfactorily?

THE MELTING POT IS BROKEN

ADVOCATE: John Fonte, Director, Center for American Common Culture, Hudson Institute

SOURCE: Testimony during hearings on "Comprehensive Immigration Reform: Becoming Americans—U.S. Immigrant Integration" before the U.S. House of Representatives, Committee on the Judiciary, Subcommittee on Immigration Citizenship, Refugees, Border Security, and International Law, May 16, 2007

BLENDING SATISFACTORILY

ADVOCATE: Gary Gerstle, James Stahlman Professor, Department of History, Vanderbilt University

SOURCE: Testimony during hearings on "Comprehensive Immigration Reform: Becoming Americans—U.S. Immigrant Integration" before the U.S. House of Representatives, Committee on the Judiciary, Subcommittee on Immigration Citizenship, Refugees, Border Security, and International Law, May 16, 2007

The face of America is changing. A nation that was once overwhelmingly composed of European heritage whites is becoming more diverse ethnically and racially. In 1960 the U.S. population was approximately 82% white, 11% black, and 6% Hispanic, 0.5% Asian American, and 0.5% Native American. By 2000 the U.S. population had become 69% white, 12% African American, 13% Latino, 4% Asian American, and 1% Native American. This diversification is expected to continue, with the U.S. Census Bureau estimating that in 2050, the U.S. population will be 52% white, 24% Latino, 15% African American, 9% Asian American, and 1% Native American. One reason for the change is varying fertility rates, which is the average number of children a woman in her child-bearing years will have. In 2000 the fertility rate was 2.0 for whites, 2.1 for African Americans, 2.3 for Asian Americans, 2.5 for Native Americans, and 2.9 for Hispanics.

Immigration changes are a second factor accounting for growing diversity. As late as the 1950s, more than 70% of immigrants were coming from Europe or from Canada and other European-heritage countries. Then Congress amended the immigration laws in 1965 to eliminate the quota system that favored immigration from Europe. Now, only about 16% of newcomers are from Europe, compared to 48% from Latin America and the Caribbean, 32% from Asia, and 4% from Africa. Adding to this influx are those who come to the United States without going through established immigration procedures. There are an estimated 10 million such immigrants in the United States, and between 400,000 and 500,00 new ones were arriving each year. About 80% of these illegal immigrants are from Central America, especially Mexico.

Not only the racial and ethnic composition of those coming to the United States changed dramatically since the 1960s. There has also been a dramatic increase in the number of immigrants. Legal immigration has nearly tripled from an annual average of 330,000 in the 1960s to annual averages of 978,000 in the 1990s and 1,016,000 between 2000 and 2006. These numbers seems huge, but relative to the U.S. population they are not as high as earlier periods in history. For example, the immigrants who arrived during the decade 1900–1909 equaled 10.4% of the population. Those arriving legally in the ten years between 1997 and 2006 came to 2.9% of the population, with the net inflow of about 4 million illegal immigrants during those years increasing that figure to about 4.3%.

The classic image Americans have of what has occurred with immigrants is in the melting pot analogy, with new immigrants being "Americanized," that is learning English and adopting existing American values and customs. In reality, of course, new immigrants also changed the nature of the American "stew" in the pot by introducing new words, ideas, foods, and other things that existing Americans adopted. Be that as it may, the increased rate of immigration and its increasingly non-European complexion have raised concerns in some quarters that the melting pot is not working adequately and even that some immigrants have no wish to blend in. This view came into particular focus with the book, *Who We Are: The Challenges to America's National Identity* (Simon & Schuster, 2004) written by Harvard University political scientist Samuel P. Huntington. As the *Washington Post* noted, Huntington posed "some of the most critical questions facing our nation" including, "How can a people already preoccupied with ethnic identity absorb and acculturate the millions of immigrants being driven to our shores by global economics?" and "How in the long run will America cohere if everyone feels they belong to a minority?" Huntington was concerned about the melting pot, and his view is furthered in the first reading by John Fonte of the conservative think tank, the Hudson Institute. That is followed by a much more optimistic view of the assimilation process given by historian Gary Gerstle of Vanderbilt University.

POINTS TO PONDER

➤ The traditional goal has been a cultural melting pot in which immigrants merged into existing American culture. Some people now advocate multiculturalism, the coexistence of more than one culture. What are the benefits and drawbacks of the melting pot and multicultural images?

➤ There are people who argue that at least some of those who raise concerns about assimilation are closet racists who are concerned about the "de-Europanization" of the United States, both in culture and the color of its citizen's skins. What is your view?

➤ Think about what changes to immigration policy and naturalization (becoming a U.S. citizen) policy you might make.

The Cultural Assimilation of Immigrants:
The Melting Pot Is Broken

JOHN FONTE

WHAT DO WE MEAN BY INTEGRATION?

Let us start by using the more serious and vigorous term "assimilation." There are different types of assimilation: linguistic, economic, cultural, civic, and patriotic. Linguistic assimilation means the immigrant learns English. Economic assimilation means the immigrant does well materially and, perhaps, joins the middle class. Cultural assimilation means that the immigrant acculturates to the nation's popular cultural norms (for both good and ill). Civic assimilation or civic integration means that the immigrant is integrated into our political system, votes, pays taxes, obeys the law, and participates in public life in some fashion.

These forms of assimilation are necessary, but not sufficient. We were reminded again last week, in the Fort Dix conspiracy that there are naturalized citizens, legal permanent residents, and illegal immigrants living in our country who speak English, are gainfully employed (even entrepreneurs) who would like to kill as many Americans as possible [Fort Dix conspiracy: Six foreign-born Muslim men were arrested in May 2007 and charged with plotting to detonate a terrorist bomb at the U.S. Army installation. Three of the men were illegal immigrants, one was a naturalized citizen, one was a legal immigrant, and the status of the six man was unknown]. The type of assimilation that ultimately matters most of all is patriotic assimilation: political loyalty and emotional attachment to the United States. What do we mean by patriotic assimilation? First of all, patriotic assimilation does not mean giving up all ethnic traditions, customs, cuisine, and birth languages. It has nothing to do with the food one eats, the religion one practices, the affection that one feels for the land of one's birth, and the second languages that one speaks. Multiethnicity and ethnic subcultures have enriched America and have always been part of our past since colonial days.

Historically, the immigration saga has involved some "give and take" between immigrants and the native-born. That is to say, immigrants have helped shape America even as this nation has Americanized them. On the other hand, this "two way street" is 2 not a fifty-fifty arrangement. Thus, on the issue of "who accommodates to whom"; obviously, most of the accommodating should come from the newcomers, not from the hosts.

So what is patriotic assimilation? (or as well shall soon discuss "Americanization"). Well, one could say that patriotic assimilation occurs when a newcomer essentially adopts American civic values, the American heritage, and the story of America (what academics call the "narrative") as his or her own. It occurs, for example, when newcomers and their children begin to think of American history as "our" history not "their" history. To give a hypothetical example, imagine an eighth-grade Korean-American female student studying the Constitutional Convention of 1787.

Does she think of those events in terms of "they" or "we"? Does she envision the creation of the Constitution in Philadelphia as something that "they" (white males of European descent) were involved in 200 years before her ancestors came to America, or does she imagine the Constitutional Convention as something that "we" Americans did as part of "our" history? Does she think in terms of "we" or "they"? "We" implies patriotic assimilation. If she thinks in terms of "we" she has done what millions of immigrants and immigrant children have done in the past. She has adopted America's story as her story, and she has adopted America's Founders—[James] Madison, [Alexander] Hamilton, [Benjamin] Franklin, [George] Washington—as her ancestors. (This does not mean that she, like other Americans, will not continue to argue about our history and our heritage, nor ignore the times that America has acted ignobly).

OUR HISTORIC SUCCESS WITH AMERICANIZATION

Historically America has done assimilation well. As *Washington Post* columnist Charles Krauthammer put it, "America's genius has always been assimilation, taking immigrants and turning them into Americans."

This was done in the days of Ellis Island because America's leaders including Democrat [President] Woodrow Wilson and Republican [President] Theodore Roosevelt believed that immigrants should be "Americanized."

They were self-confident leaders. They were not embarrassed by the need to assimilate immigrants into our way of life and by explicitly telling newcomers that "this is what we expect you to do to become Americanized." Indeed, they didn't use weasel words like "integration," that suggests a lack of self-confidence. They believed in "Americanization." For example, on July 4, 1915 President Woodrow Wilson declared National Americanization Day. The President and his cabinet addressed naturalization ceremonies around the nation on the subject of Americanization. The most powerful speech was delivered by future Supreme Court Justice, Louis Brandeis at Faneuil Hall in Boston in which Brandeis declared that Americanization meant that the newcomer will "possess the national consciousness of an American."

In a sense the views of Theodore Roosevelt, Woodrow Wilson and Louis Brandeis on the need to foster assimilation go back to the Founders of our nation. Indeed, President George Washington explicitly stated the need to assimilate immigrants in a letter to Vice President John Adams. [Washington wrote:]

> The policy or advantage of [immigration] taking place in a body (I mean the settling of them in a body) may be much questioned; for, by so doing, they retain the language, habits, and principles (good or bad) which they bring with them. Whereas by an intermixture with our people, they, or 4 their descendants, get assimilated to our customs, measures, laws: in a word soon become one people.

The Present Day: Americanization and Anti-Americanization

During the 1990s, one of the great members of the House of Representatives, the late Congresswoman Barbara Jordan (D-TX) called for a revival of the concept of Americanization and for a New Americanization movement. Jordan wrote an article in the *New York Times* on September 11, 1995 entitled the "The Americanization Ideal," in which she explicitly called for the Americanization of immigrants. We should heed her words today. Unfortunately, for decades we have implemented what could truly be called anti-Americanization, anti-assimilation, and anti-integration policies—Multilingual ballots, bi-lingual education, [presidential] executive order 13166 that insists on official multilingualism, immigrant dual allegiance including voting and running for office in foreign countries, and the promotion of multiculturalism over American unity in our public schools. [Executive Order 13166, Improving Access to Services for

Persons With Limited English Proficiency, issued August 11, 2000.] The anti-assimilation policies listed above did not place in a vacuum. They are all connected and related to the larger picture. All of these policies and attitudes have hurt assimilation.

Let us examine how assimilation has become more problematic in recent years.
Traditionally the greatest indicator of assimilation is intermarriage among ethnic groups and between immigrants and native-born. Unfortunately a new major study published in the *American Sociological Review* by Ohio State Professor Zhenchao Qian found a big decline in inter-ethnic marriage. Professor Qian declared, "These declines...are significant a departure from past trends" and "reflect the growth in the immigrant population" with Latinos marrying Latinos and Asians marrying Asians.

The survey found that even as recently as the 1970s and 1980s there was an increase in intermarriage between immigrants and native born citizens. In the 1990s however, this situation was reversed with intermarriage between immigrants and native-born declining. Mass low-skilled immigration was an implicit factor cited in the *Ohio State University Research Bulletin*. The researchers pointed out the immigrants with higher education levels were more likely to marry outside their immediate ethnic group and the reverse was true for immigrants with less education. In recent years our immigration policy favors the less education and lower skilled.

My fellow witness, Professor Rumbaut has done some excellent work examining assimilation among the children of immigrants. With Professor Alejandro Portes he produced the "The Children of Immigrants Longitudinal Study," of over 5,000 students from 49 schools in the Miami, Florida and San Diego, California areas. Portes carried out the research in Miami. Their joint findings were published by the University of California Press in 2001 as *Legacies: The Story of the Immigrant Second Generation*. The parents of the students came from 77 different countries, although in the Miami area they were 5 primarily from Cuba, Haiti, Nicaragua, and Columbia. In San Diego there were large numbers from Mexico, the Philippines, and Viet Nam.

Portes and Rumbaut pointed out that it is significant that although the youths' knowledge of English increased during their three or four years of school between the longitudinal interviews, their American identity decreased:

> Moreover, the direction of the shift is noteworthy. If the rapid shift to English...was to have been accompanied by a similar acculturative shift in ethnic identity, then we should have seen an increase over time in the proportion of youths identifying themselves as American, with or without a hyphen, and a decrease in the proportion retaining an attachment to a foreign national identity. But...results of the 1995 survey point in exactly the opposite direction.

In other words, linguistic assimilation has increased, but patriotic assimilation has decreased. After four years of American high school the children of immigrants are less likely to consider themselves Americans. Moreover, the heightened salience (or importance) of the foreign identity was very strong. Portes and Rumbaut declare that:
Once again, foreign national identities command the strongest level of allegiance and attachment: over 71% of the youths so identifying considered that identity to be very important to them, followed by 57.2% hyphenates [as in, for example, Irish-American], 52.8% of the pan-ethnics [such as Latino, a regional, rather than specific country reference], and only 42% of those identifying as plain American. The later

[plain American] emerges as the "thinnest" identity. Significantly, in the 1995 survey, almost all immigrants groups posted losses in plain American identities....Even private-school Cubans, over a third of whom had identified as American in 1992, abandoned that identity almost entirely by 1995–1996.

In 2002 the Pew Hispanic Survey revealed that around seven months after 9/11 only 34% of American citizens of Hispanic origin consider their primary identification American. On the other hand, 42% identified first with their parent's country of origin (Mexico, El Salvador, etc.) and 24% put ethnic (Latino, Hispanic) identity first.

An empirical survey of Muslims in Los Angeles was conducted in the 1990s by religious scholar Kambiz Ghanea Bassiri (a professor at Reed College). The study found that only one of ten Muslim immigrants surveyed felt more allegiance to the United States than to a foreign Muslim nation. Specifically, 45% of the Muslims surveyed had more loyalty to an Islamic nation-state than the United States; 32% said their loyalties "were about the same" between the U.S. and a Muslim nation-state; 13% were "not sure" which loyalty was stronger; and 10% were more loyal to the United States than any Muslim nation. All of this data suggests problems with assimilation.

In a Chicago *Tribune* article on April 7, the head of the Office of New Americans in Illinois, the person in charge of assimilation in the state, made the following statement. "The nation-state concept is changing. You don't have to say, 'I am Mexican,' or, 'I am American.' You can be a good Mexican citizen and a good American citizen and not have that be a conflict of interest. Sovereignty is flexible."

He is a dual citizen who is actively involved in Mexican politics. He votes in both the U.S. and Mexico and is active in political campaigns in both nations. His political allegiance is clearly divided. He will not choose one nation over the other. One hundred years ago the President of the United States in 1907, Theodore Roosevelt, expressed a different point of view:

> If the immigrant who comes here in good faith becomes an American and assimilates himself to us, he shall be treated on an exact equality with everyone else, for it is an outrage to discriminate against any such man because of creed, or birthplace, or origin. But this is predicated upon the man's becoming in very fact an American, and nothing but an American...There can be no divided allegiance here. we have room for but one sole loyalty and that is a loyalty to the American people.

Those are two very different views of the meaning of the oath of allegiance in which the new citizens promises to "absolutely and entirely" renounce all allegiance to any foreign state.

What is to be done?

What do we do then, in a practical sense? For one thing, it makes no sense to enact so-called comprehensive immigration reform, which means both a slow motion amnesty and a massive increase in low skilled immigration further exacerbating our assimilation problems. What we do need is comprehensive assimilation reform for those immigrants who are here legally.

First, we have to dismantle the anti-assimilation regime of foreign language ballots, dual allegiance voting by American citizens in foreign countries, bi-lingual education, and executive order 13166.

Second, we should follow Barbara Jordan's lead and explicitly call for the Americanization of immigrants, not integration.

Third, we should enforce the oath of allegiance. The Oath should mean what it says:

> I hereby declare, on oath, that I absolutely and entirely renounce and abjure all allegiance and fidelity to any foreign prince, potentate, state, or 7 sovereignty, of whom or which I have heretofore been a subject or a citizen; that I will support and defend the Constitution and laws of the United States of America against all enemies foreign and domestic; that I will bear true faith and allegiance to the same; that I will bear arms on behalf of the United States when required by law; that I will perform noncombatant service in the Armed Forces of the United States when required by law; that I will perform work of national importance under civilian direction when required by law; and that I take this obligation freely, without any mental reservation or purpose of evasion; so help me God.

Clearly, if we are a serous people, naturalized citizens should not be voting and running for office in their birth nations.

Fourth, Senator Lamar Alexander of Tennessee has introduced bi-partisan legislation "to promote the patriotic integration of prospective citizens into the American way of life by providing civics, history and English as a second language courses." There is a "specific emphasis" on "attachment to the principles of the Constitution" and to the "heroes of American history (including military heroes)." This initiative will be administered by the Office of Citizenship in the United States Citizenship and Immigration Services (USCIS). Also, this legislation incorporates "a knowledge and understanding of the Oath of Allegiance into the history and government test given to applicants for citizenship." This amendment passed the Senate last year by 91–1. Its enactment should be implemented with or without any "comprehensive" measure.

Fifth the mandate of the Office of Citizenship should be to assist our new fellow citizens in understanding the serious moral commitment that they are making in taking the Oath, and "bearing true faith and allegiance" to American liberal democracy.

Because we are a multiethnic, multiracial, multireligious country, our nationhood is not based on ethnicity, race, or religion, but, instead, on a shared loyalty to our constitutional republic and its liberal democratic principles. If immigration to America is going to continue to be the great success story that it has been in the past, it is essential that newcomers have an understanding of and attachment to our democratic republic, our heritage, and our civic principles.

To this end, the Office of Citizenship should strengthen the current educational materials used by applicants for American citizenship. Since the Oath of Allegiance is the culmination of the naturalization process, an examination of the Oath and what it means, "to bear true faith and allegiance" to the United States Constitution should be part of those educational materials, and should be included on any citizenship test. Further, the Office could (1) examine ways to make citizenship training and the swearing-in ceremony more meaningful; (2) cooperate with other government agencies that work with immigrants such as the U.S. Department of Education's English Literacy-Civics 8 program; and (3) continue to reexamine the citizenship test to see how it can be improved (as it is currently doing, so kudos to the Office of Citizenship on this point). Sixth English Literacy Civics (formerly English as a Second Language-Civics or ESLCivics) is a federal program that provides grants to teach English with a civics education emphasis to non-native speakers. The program is administered by the U.S. Department of Education through the states. The money goes to adult education schools, community colleges, and non-governmental organizations to integrate civic instruction into English language learning.

Logically, EL-Civics is a program that should promote the Americanization of immigrants. As noted, in becoming American citizens, immigrants pledge, "True faith and allegiance" to American liberal democracy. This requires some knowledge of our history and our values. If the money expended annually on EL-Civics assisted our future fellow citizens in understanding America's heritage and civic values, the money would be well spent. This appears to have been the intent of Congress in creating the program in the first place.

Unfortunately, there are problems with EL-Civics programs. In many federally funded EL-Civics classes "civics" is defined narrowly as pertaining almost exclusively to mundane day to day tasks such as how to take public transportation or make a doctor's appointment. Obviously, these "life-coping skills" (as they are called in the jargon) could be part of EL-Civics classes, but the classes should focus primarily on American values, or what veteran civic educator Robert Pickus calls "Idea Civics."

The problem is that many state guidelines for EL-Civics are rigid and inflexible. These state guidelines have been influenced heavily by language professionals; who define "civics" in a very narrow way, and resist the idea of teaching American values through English language training.

It is time to put American civic principles at the head of the taxpayer supported English Literacy Civics program. Federal guidelines to the states should be revised, insisting on the use of solid content materials that emphasize our American heritage, and our civic and patriotic values. In our post-9-11 world, "Idea Civics," that will assist newcomers in understanding the meaning of "bearing true faith and allegiance" to our democratic republic must be emphasized.

In sum, it is time to promote the patriotic assimilation of immigrants into the mainstream of American life. Today as in the past, patriotic assimilation is a necessary component of any successful immigration policy. This does not mean that we should blindly replicate all the past Americanization policies of Theodore Roosevelt and Woodrow Wilson. But it does mean that we have much to learn from our great historical success. In the final analysis it means that we should draw on a usable past, exercise common sense, and develop an Americanization policy that will be consist with our principles and effective in today's world.

What about "Comprehensive Immigration Reform"?

The irony is that so-called "comprehensive" immigration reform is not "comprehensive." There are no serious assimilation components to the legislation. Moreover the eventual promised amnesty and the massive increase in low-skilled immigration promoted formula would weaken assimilation. Assimilation policy cannot be separated from immigration policy. We need comprehensive assimilation reform (for legal immigrants), before we need comprehensive immigration.

Unfortunately, comprehensive immigration reform is primarily about the special needs of particular businesses, not the interests of the American people as a whole, ignores assimilation and puts the market over the nation, but Americans must always remember that we are a nation of citizens before we are a market of consumers.

The Cultural Assimilation of Immigrants: Blending Satisfactorily

GARY GERSTLE

Since its founding, the United States has arguably integrated more immigrants, both in absolute and relative terms, than any other nation. In the years between the 1820s and 1920s, an estimated 35 million immigrants came to the United States. Approximately 40 to 50 million more came between the 1920s and 2010s, with most of those coming after 1965. The successful integration of immigrants and their descendants has been one of the defining features of American society, and, in my view, one of this country's greatest accomplishments. Can we find descendants of the immigrants who came in such large numbers one hundred years ago who today do not regard themselves as Americans? We can probably identify a few, but not many. Even those groups once known for their resistance to Americanization—Italians, for example—today count themselves and are considered by others as being among the America's most ardent patriots. Throughout the nation's history, moreover, newer Americans and their descendants have contributed a dynamic quality to our society through their Americanization. As President Woodrow Wilson proudly told a group of immigrants in 1915, America was "the only country in the world that experiences a constant and repeated rebirth," and the credit went entirely to the "great bodies of strong men and forward-looking women out of other lands" who decided to cast their lot with America.

In my testimony today, I have four aims: first, to acquaint you with the so-called "new immigrants" who came by the millions to the United States one hundred years ago and who were widely regarded as lacking the desire and ability to integrate themselves into American society; second, to discuss with you how these immigrants and their children confounded their critics by becoming deeply and proudly American; third, to lay out for you what I think a successful process of immigrant integration requires; and fourth, to suggest to you ways this earlier experience of successful integration can guide an exploration of the prospects of integrating immigrants who are living in America today.

My most important point is twofold. First, that the United States has been enormously successful in making Americans out of immigrants, even among immigrant populations who were thought to have cultures and values radically different from America's own. Second, immigrant integration does not happen overnight. Typically it takes two generations and requires both engagement on the part of immigrants with American democracy and an opportunity for them to achieve economic security for themselves and their families. If we approach questions of immigration today with a realistic and robust sense for what a successful process of immigrant incorporation requires, we have reason to be optimistic that America will once again demonstrate its remarkable ability to absorb and integrate foreign-born millions.

THE "NEW IMMIGRANTS" OF ONE HUNDRED YEARS AGO

An estimated 24 million immigrants came to the United States between the 1880s and the 1920s. They entered a society that numbered only 76 million people in 1900. A large majority of these new immigrants came from Europe, and they came mostly from impoverished and rural areas of eastern and southern Europe: from Italy, Russia, Poland, Lithuania, Hungary, Slovakia, Serbia, Greece, and other proximate nations or parts of the Austro-Hungarian Empire. Few of these immigrants were Protestant, then the dominant religion of the United States; most were Catholic, Christian Orthodox, or Jewish. The integration process of these turn-of-the century immigrants, however, was not quick and it was not easy. Indeed, the label applied to these immigrants—"the new immigrants"—was meant to compare them unfavorably to the "old immigrants" who had come prior to 1880 from the British Isles, Germany, and Scandinavia and who were then thought to have been the model immigrants: industrious, freedom-loving, English-speaking, and ardently patriotic. If I could parachute you, the members of this Subcommittee into American society in a year when the "new immigration" was at its height—in 1910, for example, or 1920—you would encounter a pessimism about the possibilities of integrating these immigrants more intense than what exists in American society today. That the outcome was so positive and so at variance with the pessimistic expectations of 1910 or 1920 should caution us against giving ourselves over to pessimism today.

In the early years of the twentieth century, a majority of Americans were Protestants who cared deeply about the Protestant character of their society. Protestantism, in their eyes, had given America its mission, its democracy, its high regard for individual rights, and its moral character. These Americans worried that the largely Catholic, Orthodox, and Jewish immigrants who dominated the ranks of the "new immigrants" would subvert cherished American ideals, and that the great American republic would decline or even come to an end.

America, at the time, was also a deeply racist society. Black-white segregation was at its height. Chinese immigrants had been largely barred from coming to the United States in 1882 and Japanese immigrants were largely barred in 1907. A naturalization law stipulated that only those immigrants who were free and white were eligible for citizenship, a law that effectively prohibited almost all East and South Asians immigrants from becoming citizens between 1870 and 1952. For a twenty year period in the early twentieth century, the U.S. government attempted to rule that several peoples from the Middle East and West Asia, including Arabs and Armenians, were nonwhite and thus also ineligible for U.S. citizenship. In 1924, Congress stopped most eastern and southern Europeans from coming to the United States because these peoples were also now thought to be racially inferior and thus incapable of assimilating American civilization and democracy. This is how a member of Congress (Fred S. Purnell of Indiana, R) described eastern and southern European immigrants in 1924, [saying,] "There is little or no similarity between the clear-thinking, self-governing stocks that sired the American people and this stream of irresponsible and broken wreckage that is pouring into the lifeblood of America the social and political diseases of the Old World."

Purnell quoted approvingly the words of a Dr. Ward, who claimed that Americans had deceived themselves into believing that "we could change inferior beings into superior ones." Americans could not escape the laws of heredity, Ward argued. "We cannot make a heavy horse into a trotter by keeping him in racing stable. We can not make a well bred dog out of mongrel by teaching him tricks." The acts that Ward dismissed as "tricks" including the learning by immigrants of the Gettysburg Address and the Declaration of Independence.

Given these attitudes, it is not surprising that many immigrants felt unwelcome in the United States. Nevertheless, America was then what it is today: a society for the enterprising, for those who wanted to raise themselves up in the world. Many immigrants perceived America as a land in which they could improve their economic circumstances. They worked endless hours to make that happen. But would America become for them more than a place to work? Would it become their home, a place where they would feel comfortable, where they would raise their families, where they could come to consider themselves—and be considered by others as—Americans? Many immigrants doubted that this would ever be the case. Many intended to make some money in the United States and return home. In the early years of the 20th century, it is estimated that the repatriation rates (those who chose to return home) among Italian immigrants ran as high as 40 to 50 percent. Among immigrants from the Balkans in the years prior to the First World War, it is estimated that as many 80 percent returned home. Those who did not or could not return to their original lands often sent remittances to their families in Europe. For many of these immigrants, becoming U.S. citizens and learning English were goals that were secondary to the primary challenge of earning a living and raising the standard of one's family, either in the United States or one's home country. Yet these immigrants and their children did become integrated into America and deeply committed to America. How and when did this integration happen?

INTEGRATING THE "NEW IMMIGRANTS"

Three factors are particularly important for understanding the integration of the "new immigrants": learning to practice American democracy; the transition in immigrant communities from the first to second generation; and the achievement of economic security.

Practicing American Democracy: As anti-immigrant sentiment grew in America across the early decades of the 20th century, immigrants who had been reluctant to enter American politics now believed that they had no alternative but to become so involved, if only to protect their most basic interests. In the 1920s, they began to naturalize and then to vote in large numbers. Immigrants wanted to elect representatives who supported their freedom to enter the United States, to pursue a trade or occupation of their choice, to school their children and raise their families in ways that corresponded to their cultural traditions and religious beliefs. They also wanted the government to end discrimination against immigrants in employment, housing, and education. Immigrants lost some major elections, as in 1928, when Herbert Hoover (R) defeated the pro-immigrant candidate, Al Smith (D) [for the presidency], but they also scored some major victories, as when Franklin D. Roosevelt (D) won a landslide re-election in 1936 with the help of millions of new voters, many of them immigrant, casting their ballots for the first time. These immigrant voters believed that FDR was opening up American politics to immigrant participation in ways that few previous presidents had done. In response to this opening, these new immigrants and their children became an important part of the Democratic Party voting majority that would keep Democrats in the White House and in control of Congress for a majority of years between the mid-1930s and late 1960s.

Political parties were important in brokering the entrance of immigrants into American politics. The Democratic Party in particular played a pivotal role not just in registering immigrants to vote but in teaching them the practical arts of American politics—running for office, building constituencies, raising money for campaigns, getting out the vote, writing legislation and building coalitions. The "political boss" and "political machines" were central institutions in many American cities of the time, and both played important roles in bringing immigrants into politics. Although the national Republican Party was not as important as the Democratic Party in assisting immigrants, particular state and local Republican parties often were important players in this brokerage process.

The ability of immigrants to participate in politics and to feel as though their votes made a difference was crucial to their engagement with and integration into America. In the 1920s and 1930s, immigrants began to assert their Americanness and their right to participate in debates about America's best interests. In the short term, this generated more political conflict than political consensus, as immigrant Americans often disagreed sharply with the native-born about what course to chart for America's future, and whether (and how) to open up American workplaces, occupations, universities, and neighborhoods to the full participation of immigrants. But there can be no doubt that immigrant engagement in American politics, with all the conflict it entailed, worked to bind the native-born and foreign born together, and make both groups feel part of one American nation. And that engagement worked, too, to change America in ways that allowed Catholics and Jews to assert their claims on America and to assert that they had as much right to live in America, to speak on its behalf, and to access its opportunities as did long-settled populations of American Protestants.

Generational Transition: Equally important to the integration of the new immigrants was a shift in the balance of power within immigrant families from the first to second generation. This shift occurred sometime between the 1920s and the 1940s, as the immigrant generation aged and the second generation came into maturity. The children of immigrants (or those who had come to America as very small children) were comfortable with their Americanness in ways that their parents frequently had not been. Some of this second-generation Americanization occurred invisibly, through the daily experiences of these children with American society—walking down the streets of their cities, scouring the ads in newspapers and magazines for alluring consumer goods, listening to the radio, going to the movies, playing sports, and discovering the latest innovation in American popular music. Popular culture in America has always been a great assimilator. Some of the second generation's Americanization occurred more formally, through institutions, most notably high schools (which significantly expanded their enrollments in the 1930s and 1940s) and the World War II military, which took more than sixteen million young Americans out of their homes and neighborhoods between 1941 and 1945, mixed them up with other young Americans from every region of the country, and then asked every one of them to give their life for their country.

Even prior to their entry into these powerful institutions, mother-tongue monolingualism had fallen dramatically among these young men and women. For the second generation, bilingualism or English monolingualism became the norm; the third generation, meanwhile, was almost entirely English monolingual. Most members of the third generation could not speak and not even understand the language of their grandparents. By this time, too, many private institutions in "new immigrant" ethnic communities— churches, synagogues, fraternal and charitable organizations, ethnic newspapers— had begun to see themselves as agents of Americanization, in part to keep the younger generation engaged with issues of concern to the ethnic community.

Economic Security: We should not underestimate the importance of economic security in persuading immigrants to cast their lot with America. The welfare of one's family was almost always a key consideration for the "new immigrants" of the early 20th century. While some immigrants found opportunities in America and prospered, many were stuck in low paying, unskilled jobs in American manufacturing and construction, with little promise of advancement and no security that they would be able to keep even these jobs. Many had to make do with wages that were chronically insufficient. Many lived with the fear that they would fail as breadwinners, that the American dream would never be theirs, and that their employers would toss them aside for yet younger and cheaper workers. When the Great Depression plunged the

U.S. economy into crisis for twelve long years, this fear spread to the second generation who were trying to find their first jobs at a time when neither the private nor public sector was able to bring the nation's unemployment rate below 15 percent. In these dire circumstances, many immigrants and their children began to turn to collective institutions of economic self help, the most important of which was the labor movement. Labor unions were Americanizing institutions during these years, convincing ethnic workers both that they had rights as American workers and that their ability to improve their circumstances would contribute to the overall well-being of American society. Labor movement advocates argued that wages must be raised to a decent level, that hours of work should not exceed human endurance, that the government must make some provision for those who lost their jobs through no fault of their own, and that those who had spent a life time at work should be rewarded by the government with an old age pension. The labor movement provided critical support for two of the most important government policies of the 1930s and 1940s, the Social Security Act and the GI Bill of Rights, both of which meant a great deal to the new immigrants and their children. One can make the case that the labor movement played a major role in helping to lift immigrant workers and their children out of poverty and thereby in giving them a stake in the American dream.

To identify the labor movement as an important institution of immigrant incorporation is to venture onto controversial political terrain. But whatever one thinks of the proper role of labor unions, it remains the case that questions of economic security and opportunity must be part of our discussion of immigrant integration. An immigrant population that finds itself unable to move out of poverty or to gain the confidence that it can provide a decent life for their children is far more likely to descend into alienation than to embrace America.

By 1950s, the integration of the "new immigrants" and their children had been successfully accomplished. Most of the children and grandchildren of these immigrants were enthusiastic Americans. But the success of the process had taken forty to fifty years and had required immersion in the practice of American democracy, a transition in generational power from the first o the second generation, and the achievement of economic security.

TODAY'S IMMIGRANTS: QUESTIONS AND ANSWERS

Today's immigrants are sometimes depicted by their critics as are far more different from "us" than were past waves of immigrants and as far less interested in integrating themselves into American society. The charge is also leveled that there are simply too many of immigrants residing in America today for this country to absorb and integrate.

Below I examine each of these beliefs in light of the background I have provided on the "new immigrants" who came between the 1880s and 1920s.

1. *Are today's immigrants too different from "us?"* Immigrants today are different from earlier waves of immigrants in the diversity of their origins, in the diversity of their economic backgrounds, and in the fact that a majority are nonwhite. At earlier periods of U.S. history, most immigrants came from Europe. Today they come from every continent, with South America (and Latin America more generally), Asia, and Africa being the largest sources. Today's immigrants are also more diverse in economic backgrounds than any previous wave of immigrants. In earlier waves, the immigrants were overwhelmingly poor and generally lacking in education. Such individuals are amply represented in the ranks of immigrants today, but so too are those who are highly trained professionals, managers, and small retailers who have decided that their skills will be more fully used and rewarded in the United States than at home, and that the opportunities for their children will be greater here as well. Thus the proportions of professionals and managers in the immigrant streams coming from the Philippines, India, Taiwan, and Korea regularly reach or exceed fifty percent. These immigrants are generally thought not to be "problem immigrants" and so they don't form a significant part of our discussion about immigration today. But these kinds of immigrants are well represented in today's immigrant population, especially among those groups who have come from East and South Asia. They are generally thought to be important contributors to America, and so they should be included in any overall assessment of current immigration.

Discussion of today's immigrants generally focuses on those who are at the poor end of the immigrant spectrum. Poverty alone, of course, is hardly a distinguishing feature of today's immigrants, since past groups of immigrants were overwhelmingly poor. What does distinguish today's immigrant poor is that they are nonEuropean. Coming from nonEuropean cultures, they are sometimes thought by their critics to lack the cultural attributes—what we commonly refer to as the values of "western civilization"—that allowed earlier waves of poor immigrants to climb out of their poverty, to embrace America's creed of freedom and individualism as their own, and to become active contributors to American enterprise and American democracy.

The irony of this critique is that the "Europeans" held up as model immigrants of yesteryear were, at the time of their immigration, depicted much as poor nonwhite immigrants are today: as so racially and culturally different from Americans, as so different from the earlier waves of immigrants who had come from western and northern Europe, that they could never close the gap between who they were and what "we," America, wanted them to be. Because they were allegedly unassimilable, the United States made a fateful decision in the 1920s to all but close its immigrant gates to eastern and southern Europeans. America was successful in barring them from entry, but it was wrong to believe that they lacked the ability to integrate themselves into American society. As I have argued in earlier sections of this testimony, the millions of eastern and southern Europeans already here did Americanize, and today we celebrate them as exemplary Americans. Why repeat that earlier mistake today and designate large sections of the world's population as inappropriate material for inclusion in America? To do so is not only to discriminate on the grounds of race but also to confess our own lack of faith in the promise and transformative power of American freedom.

2. *Are today's immigrants too little interested in integrating themselves into American society?* It is true that many immigrants today retain strong ties to their homeland and

that many return home or aspire to do so. Technological innovations have made travel back and forth relatively easy, and the communications revolution has made it possible to stay in constant and instantaneous touch with one's family and friends back home. Many immigrants are not eager to relinquish the cultures they brought with them. Among adult immigrants who work in unskilled occupations where literacy is not important (construction, agriculture, landscaping, and personal services), some are slow to learn English. But these patterns are hardly novel. To the contrary, they are similar to patterns evident among the European immigrants who came at the beginning of the twentieth century. They are patterns that tend to be characteristic of immigrant groups in which recent arrivals form a large part of the immigrant population.

If we want to develop an accurate picture of the progress of integration (or lack thereof), we should not be content to take snapshots of a group at a particular point in time. We should want to supplement those snapshots with an examination of immigrants across time and across generations. Studies done by social scientists are beginning to supply us with this kind of data, and they are revealing patterns of integration that are similar to those associated with European immigrants a hundred years ago. For example, among the children of Latino immigrants, the rates of Spanish monolingualism (those who speak only Spanish) are very low and the rates of English-Spanish bilingualism are very high. Moreover, English monolingualism has made surprising inroads among the children of Latino immigrants, so much that some Latino parents worry that their children are losing touch with their cultural roots. These patterns become even more pronounced among third generation immigrants. The patterns of language loss and acquisition among today's immigrant generations, in other words, seem to be similar to those that shaped the lives of the European immigrants who came one hundred years ago.

Successful integration depends not simply on language and generational transition but on immigrant engagement with American democracy and on the experience of economic opportunity, advancement, and security. Some social scientists have argued that institutions that were once so important in involving past generations of immigrants in American politics (political parties) and for helping them to achieve economic security (the labor movement) have either so changed in nature or have become so weak that they can no longer perform a similar function with today's immigrants. There is some truth to this argument, although the events of the past two years have demonstrated both that political parties still retain the capacity to mobilize immigrants and that labor unions, in cities such as Los Angeles where they remain strong, can still play an important role in promoting immigrant economic interests. Nevertheless, it seems clear that the successful integration of today's immigrants requires either that these older institutions find ways to broaden their involvement with immigrants or that other institutions step forward to engage immigrants in the practice of American democracy and to assist the poor among them with the pursuit of economic opportunity and security. Among Latino immigrants, the Catholic Church has demonstrated that it can become an important mechanism for immigrant integration. Ideally, institutions that assist immigrants in the pursuit of economic opportunity will bring them into alliance rather than conflict with the native-born poor.

3. *Has the number of immigrants coming to America reached such a numerical level that integration has become impossible?* In absolute terms, the number of immigrants is at all time high: approximately 35 million. A few years ago, the number arriving in a single

year passed one million and topped the previous one year record that had been record-ed in the early years of the twentieth century. In proportional terms, however, we have not yet reached the immigrant density that prevailed in America in the early twentieth century. The million who were arriving annually in those years were entering a society that possessed between one-fourth and one-third the population of America today. To reach that earlier level of immigrant density, America would have to admit three to four million immigrants a year and sustain that rate for a decade or more.

It is possible, of course, for a society to reach levels of saturation whereby the num-bers coming overwhelm mechanisms of integration. Saturation can be a national phe-nomenon or one that affects a particular region or city. Current immigrant density in the United States, however, is not at an all time high. Moreover, it is wrong to assume that demography is destiny, and that, for the sake of integration, we must close the immigrant gates once a pre-selected immigration density index is reached. If we can put in place mechanisms or institutions that broaden immigrant immersion in the practice of American democracy and broaden the access of poor immigrants to economic oppor-tunity and security, then we can have every reason to believe that the integration of this wave of immigrants will be as successful as the last one was. The process will take time and we should expect it to be complex and contentious. But it can yield success, prov-ing yet again the remarkable ability of America to take in people from very different parts of the world, to make them into Americans, and to allow them an important role in defining what it means to be an American.

THE CONTINUING DEBATE:
The Cultural Assimilation of Immigrants

What Is New

Perhaps because of the stumbling economy, American attitudes toward undocument-ed immigrants was less open in 2010 than a few years earlier. When asked whether immigration reform should focus on allowing (1) "illegal immigrants who have jobs to become legal U.S. residents," or (2) "developing a plan for stopping the flow of illegal immigrants into the U.S. and for deporting those already here" only 42% favored emphasizing legalization, while 57% wanted to stress interdiction and depor-tation. Yet this opinion about undocumented immigrants has not led to a strong move to cut legal immigration. According to a 2010 poll, a plurality of Americans (47%) wanted current immigration levels to remain the same, 35% wanted them decreased, and 17% wanted them increased. This is actually more open than attitudes in 1995, when a majority (51%) wanted a decrease, only 42% favored the status quo, and a scant 3% supported an increase. As for the melting pot idea, 2010 found 60% favoring that approach over 34% who thought immigrants should strive to maintain their culture.

Where to Find More

A review of immigration policy is Jeb Bush and Thomas F. McLarty, chairs, Report of the Independent Task Force on U.S. Immigration Policy (Council on Foreign Relations, 2009). Current immigration statistics are available from the Department of Homeland Security at www.dhs.gov/files/statistics/. Also see the Congressional Budget Office's *Immigration Policy of the United States* (February 2006) at the agency's Web site, www.cbo.gov/. A group favoring tough immigration laws is NumbersUSA at www.numbersusa.com/. An opposing viewpoint is held by the National Immigration Forum at www.immigrationforum.org/.

What More to Do

One thing to do is to be careful of the history of immigration. It is common to think that things once went smoothly and now have somehow gone off the tracks. Is that true? Talk to people who are, say, third and fourth generation Americans and see what they can recall about how fast their parents, grandparents, and great grandparents "melted in the pot." Then talk to first or second generation Americans, especially from the newer immigrant groups, such as Latinos. Also explore the data on the acculturation of immigrants from these groups and the generations that follow them at the Pew and Kaiser sites noted above and others that are available. Has accultura-tion really slowed?

6 | PARTICIPATION

ALLOWING NONCITIZENS TO VOTE:
Expanding Democracy *or* Undermining Citizenship?

EXPANDING DEMOCRACY

ADVOCATE: Ron Hayduk, Associate Professor of Political Science, Borough of Manhattan Community College, CUNY

SOURCE: "The Case for Immigrant Voting Rights," an original essay, 2009

UNDERMINING CITIZENSHIP

ADVOCATE: Stanley Renshon, Professor of Political Science, City University of New York Graduate Center

SOURCE: "The Debate Over Non-Citizen Voting: A Primer," on the Web site of the Center for Immigration Studies, April 2008

At the very root of Democracy is the idea that the legitimacy of the government rests on the consent of the people. Under the doctrine of popular sovereignty, all political power rests with the people, who are thus sovereign. They can exercise that power directly through such methods as initiatives and referendums. Or the people can chose to exercise their power indirectly by establishing a republic and electing representatives to pass laws and otherwise govern on their behalf. Representing this belief and its role in justifying the American Revolution, virtually all American school children learn that "no taxation without representation" was the rallying call of their country's early patriots as they defied British taxes and other burdens by such acts of civil disobedience as dumping imported tea into the harbor during the Boston Tea Party of 1773.

No student of democracy would disagree that it requires the voice of the people. However, there is wide disagreement about who exactly are "We the people of the United States," as the preamble to the Constitution put it, and what part of those people must be included in the decision-making process in order for it to be democratically legitimate.

Three points are immediately clear about who "We the people" are. First, voter eligibility was initially very limited. Few people, usually only white men and often only those with property, were eligible to vote in the countries that had democratic governments in the early 1800s.

Second, voter eligibility gradually expanded. The first country to guarantee women the right to vote was New Zealand in 1893. The United States did so in 1920 with the Nineteenth Amendment to the Constitution. The age of adulthood and the vote was universally 21 until Czechoslovakia dropped it to 18 in 1946. With the Twenty-sixth Amendment in 1971, the United States joined the ranks of those allowing 18-year-olds to vote. American history has also been the story of other extensions of the vote. The Fifteenth Amendment (1970) barred denying the vote to anyone because of race. After nearly a century, the federal government actually enforced that law through various steps such as the Voting Rights Act (1965). Indeed, the right to vote in the United States and elsewhere has become so inclusive that it is arguable that democracy demands that the burden of proof for excluding anyone should rest on those who favor the exclusion rather than on those who favor inclusion.

The third obvious thing about democratic practice is that despite the expansion of the franchise, all countries exclude some people. Children, for example, are universally excluded. Few countries permit noncitizens to vote at any level.

Fourth, the expansion of democracy continues. The age of adulthood provides an example. Austria lowered its voting age to 16 in 2007, and about a dozen countries now have national voting ages of 16 or 17. There are moves in several U.S. states to follow suit, and about a third of U.S. states already allow 17-year-olds to vote in primaries if they will be 18 by the time of the election.

There are about 300 million people in the United States. The largest block of people without the vote are the 75 million or so people under age 18, or about 25% of the population.

That leaves a voting age population (VAP) of about 225 million. Of these, 19.5 million people, or 8.6% of all adults are barred from voting because they are not citizens. The only other sizeable group of adults barred from voting are about 3.4 million convicted felons.

This debate takes up the nearly 20 million residents in the United States that cannot vote because they are not citizens. Professor Ron Hayduk takes up their cause in the first reading. He argues enabling noncitizens to vote is a logical extension of the evolution of democracy toward increasingly expanding the franchise. Professor Stanley Renshon disagrees in the second reading and predicts that Americans will likely to do damage to their country by giving in to demands for erasing the distinction between immigrants and citizens.

POINTS TO PONDER

➤ Does it make sense to give noncitizens the vote at local levels of government but not at state and national levels?

➤ Professor Renshon rhetorically asks, but does not answer, "What would happen if…non-citizens nationwide were given the right to vote? What do you think would happen?

➤ Professor Hayduk argues, "Democracy means rule by the people—all the people—not merely some of the people." If that is true for resident noncitizens, then is it not true for those under age 18 and those barred because they have committed felonies?

Allowing Noncitizens to Vote: Expanding Democracy

RON HAYDUK

To many, the idea of allowing noncitizens to vote may sound odd or outlandish. For most Americans, voting is the essence of citizenship. But it was not always so; nor need it be. In considering the case for (or against) immigrant voting rights, there are three things to keep in mind:

1 *It's legal.* The Constitution does not preclude it and the courts—including the Supreme Court—have upheld voting by noncitizens. Noncitizens have enjoyed voting rights for most of U.S. history and continue to do so today.

2. *It's rational.* There are moral and practical reasons to restore immigrant voting—including notions of equal rights and treatment—as well as mutual benefits that accrue to all community members, citizen and noncitizen alike.

3. *It's feasible.* Noncitizen voting is making a comeback in U.S. and globally.

Americans are usually surprised to learn that immigrants enjoyed voting rights for most of our history and throughout the vast majority of the country. In fact, from 1776 to 1926, forty states and federal territories permitted noncitizens to vote in local, state and even federal elections. Noncitizens also held public office, such as alderman, coroner and school board member. Moreover, these practices promoted civic education and citizenship. Immigrants learned civics by practice and voting facilitated political incorporation. In other words, the notion that noncitizens should have the vote is older, was practiced longer, and is more consistent with democratic ideals than the idea that they should not. Curiously, this 150-year history has been eviscerated from national memory.

Nor is immigrant voting merely a relic of the past. Noncitizens currently vote in local elections in over a half dozen cities and towns in the U.S., most notably in Chicago's school elections and in all local elections in six towns in Maryland. In addition, campaigns to expand the franchise to noncitizens—primarily in local elections—have been launched in more than a dozen other jurisdictions from coast to coast during the past decade, including in New York, Massachusetts, Washington D.C., California, Maine, Colorado, Minnesota, Wisconsin, Connecticut, Vermont, New Jersey, and Texas.

Moreover, the effort to expand the franchise to immigrants is not particular to the U.S.; it is a global phenomenon. More than forty five countries on nearly every continent allow resident noncitizens to vote at various levels in the host countries' elections, with most countries adopting such legislation during the past three decades.

Before proceeding with this discussion, note that the terms "immigrants," "foreign born," "aliens," "émigrés," "refugees," "asylees," "green card-holders," "newcomers," and "noncitizens" refer to the same persons—persons who are not citizens by birth right or naturalization—and the terms are used interchangeably. Similarly, "noncitizen voting," "alien suffrage," "immigrant voting," "resident voting" and "local citizenship" refer to the same practice—voting by individuals who are not U.S. citizens. There is some variation, however, in which categories of noncitizens are permitted to vote. Some cities and towns allow both so-called undocumented or "illegal" immigrants to vote, while other places grant suffrage only to documented or "legal" immigrants.

Differences also exist regarding which elections noncitizens can vote, such as in school board elections, in municipal elections, or in state races, depending on the city or state.

ARGUMENTS FOR IMMIGRANT VOTING

Contemporary campaigns for immigrant voting rights are part of the broader movement for immigrant and human rights. The effort to create a truly universal suffrage is but one policy option to insure that government is representative, responsive and accountable to all. Toward these ends, immigrant rights advocates utilize moral and political claims to achieve voting rights for noncitizens. Indeed, advocates often employ many of the same moral and political arguments used in past struggles to expand the franchise to previously excluded groups, including blacks, women, and youth. There are three basic arguments:

1. the social contract, which posits a just government can exist only if it rests on the consent of the governed;

2. discrimination and bias, which are the inevitable consequences of being politically excluded; and

3. the mutual benefits that accrue to all community members who share common interests in a political democracy.

One of the basic tenets of democratic theory is the social contract: the legitimacy of government rests on the consent of the governed. Members of democratic communities are rightfully obliged to obey the laws they are subject to if they possess a means to participate in governance, such as by voting. Citizens consent to be governed in exchange for the power to select their representatives, a mechanism that can hold elected officials accountable to the people. The Founding Fathers enshrined this notion in the phrase "No taxation without representation," which provided a rallying cry for the American Revolution.

Voting rights were not and are not intrinsically tied to citizenship. Recall that voting was originally restricted to white, male property owners. Women and post-emancipation blacks—who were citizens at the time—could be denied voting rights (until 1920 and 1965 respectively). Voting rights were tied to gender and race rather than citizenship per se. Similarly, age also determined who could vote (the 26th Amendment lowered the voting age from 21 to 18). In short, voting rights have always been linked to questions about who would be included and excluded in the polity, and who would wield political power, whether one was a citizen or not.

Democracy means rule by the people—all the people—not merely some of the people. Otherwise, as Thomas Paine and others argued—and as the experience of African Americans and women demonstrated—those excluded from participation could be subject to discrimination and oppression. Although voting is a relatively crude democratic instrument, it is an important power that the people can wield to keep elected officials responsive and accountable. Joaquin Avila, a professor at Seattle University School of Law, summed it up this way:

> ...noncitizens have the same obligations as citizens and should therefore enjoy some of the same privileges....A society's interests are not furthered when a substantial number of its inhabitants are excluded from the body politic and have no meaningful way to petition for a redress of grievances through the electoral

process. Such a continued exclusion from political participation is detrimental to achieving a more cohesive society. The ultimate product of such exclusion is a political apartheid.

Federal, state, and local governments already treat noncitizens—both legal residents and undocumented individuals—like other community members. The most obvious example is that all residents must pay income taxes regardless of their immigration status. In fact, contrary to popular belief, most immigrants pay more in taxes than they receive in benefits (except refugees) and more than the average American, while contributing positively to the nation's economy on the whole. Immigrant households paid an estimated $133 billion in taxes to federal, state, and local governments—from property, sales, and income taxes—and the typical immigrant pays an estimated $80,000 more in taxes than they receive in federal, state, and local benefits over their lifetimes.

Noncitizen immigrants, or resident aliens, work in every sector of the economy, own homes and businesses, attend colleges and send children to schools, pay billions of dollars in taxes each year, make countless social and cultural contributions, are subject to all the laws, participate in every aspect of daily society including serve in the military and even die defending the U.S., but they are without formal political voice. You see them in every walk of life and neighborhood: teachers, students, firefighters, police officers, nurses, doctors, small business owners, entertainers, construction workers, gardeners, and domestic workers. In a country where "no taxation without representation" was once a rallying cry for revolution, such a proposition may not, after all, be so outlandish.

But, one might wonder, if immigrant voting was so prevalent, why was it eliminated? The short answer is fear. Fear about what newcomers—who spoke different languages, practiced different religions, and had different cultural habits—might mean for America. Immigrant voting rights were rolled back during periodic influxes of different kinds and increasing numbers of immigrants. For example, the War of 1812 slowed and even reversed the spread of alien suffrage, by raising the specter of foreign "enemies." Leading up to the Civil War, the South opposed immigrant voting because many of the new immigrants (especially the Irish) opposed slavery. In fact, one of the first planks in the Confederate Constitution was to exclude voting to anyone who was not a U.S. citizen. After the Civil War and during Reconstruction, alien suffrage spread in the South and West with the growing need for new labor. Many new states and territories used voting rights as an incentive to attract new immigrant settlers and as a pathway to citizenship, though not as a substitute. Immigrants who declared their intent to become citizens could gain voting rights.

As the twentieth century approached and large numbers of Southern and Eastern European immigrants came to the U.S.—who were not universally seen as "white" at the time and who often held politically "suspect" views—immigrant voting was increasingly challenged. These newer immigrants—coupled with the rise of mass social movements and third political parties (e.g., Populist, Labor, and Socialist)—posed a potential threat to the dominant political and social order, and noncitizen voting was gradually eliminated state by state. The anti-immigrant backlash culminating after World War I led to the elimination of this long-standing practice.

Importantly, noncitizen voting rights were abolished at the same time that other restrictive measures were enacted by political elites in both major parties, including literacy tests, poll taxes, felony disenfranchisement laws, and restrictive residency and voter registration requirements—all of which combined to disenfranchise millions of voters. Voter participation dropped precipitously from highs of nearly 80 percent of the voting-age population in the mid- to late nineteenth century down to 49 percent in 1924. Additional legislation drastically reduced the flow of immigrants into the U.S. and limited the proportion of non–Western European immigrants. These changes had profound effects on American political development. It is revealing—but not coincidental—that immigrant voting has been buried in the annals of American history.

As we know, the Civil Rights Movement swept away many of these obstacles to voting and also established crucial anti-discrimination laws. But the American Dream is still out of reach for far too many. Immigrants are the new outsiders who suffer discrimination and exploitation.

Today, about one in five people in the U.S. are immigrants or the close relative to one. More than twenty five million adults are barred from voting because they lack U.S. citizenship. In many places immigrant political exclusion approximates the level of disenfranchisement associated with African-Americans and youth before the Voting Rights Act of 1965. Noncitizen adults comprise over 10 percent of the adult voting age population in seven states and the District of Columbia, and more than 20 percent of all Californians. If these noncitizens were enfranchised, they could wield decisive power in state races. At the local level, noncitizens are even more highly concentrated. Adult noncitizens in Los Angeles make up more than one third of the voting-age population; in New York City, they are 22 percent of adults. In some cities and towns, noncitizens make up 40 to 50 percent—or more—of all voting-age residents. Their taxation without representation challenges basic democratic notions that "government rests on the consent of the governed" and "one person, one vote."

Rising numbers of noncitizens challenges democratic ideals not only because immigrants are excluded from formal political participation, but also because they are all too often relegated to the lower social order. Noncitizens are more likely to score poorer on nearly every social indicator, including working and living conditions, health, education, and safety. According to the Urban Institute, one in four low-wage workers are foreign-born, and one in four low-income children is the child of an immigrant. Despite the fact that immigrants work more than most other Americans—more hours and often at two or more jobs—large numbers of immigrants and their families have low incomes, lack health insurance, and are "food insecure" (a euphemism for going hungry).

Noncitizens suffer such inequities, in part, because policy makers can ignore their interests. Discriminatory public policy and private practices—in employment, housing, education, healthcare, welfare, and criminal justice—are the inevitable by-products of immigrant political exclusion, not to mention racial profiling, xenophobic hate crimes, and arbitrary detention and deportation. Denying immigrants local voting rights makes government officials less accountable, undermines the health of our democracy, and the legitimacy of our public policies.

Thankfully, noncitizen voting is making a comeback. Today, immigrants vote in local elections in six towns in Maryland and also in school elections in Chicago. Not long ago New York City also allowed noncitizens that had children in the public schools to vote in community school board elections from 1969 until the school boards were dismantled in 2003 (for unrelated reasons). Cambridge and Amherst, Massachusetts, extended voting rights to noncitizens for local offices, but they await state action to implement these home rule laws. As aforementioned, advocates in more than a dozen cities and towns from coast to coast are currently waging—or have recently waged—campaigns to extend voting rights to noncitizens in local and state elections (not federal).

Noncitizen voting would extend the visibility and voices of immigrants, which in turn, could make government more representative, responsive and accountable. Winning voting rights could help advance other struggles important to immigrants—and to working people and people of color more generally—from speeding up the naturalization process and enacting comprehensive immigration reform to improving healthcare and education.

One thing is for sure: immigrants are here to stay. Population projections indicate the foreign born will grow in number and disperse further throughout the United States, given current family reunification policies, birth rates, and domestic economic arrangements. Their large and growing numbers make them increasingly important political players, especially at the state and local levels. Although questions remain about the direction U.S. immigration policy will take, there is little doubt that how immigrants will be incorporated—socially, politically, culturally, economically—will remain a burning issue for years to come. In other words, it is not a question about whether the millions of immigrants in the United States will be incorporated, but *how* they will be incorporated.

"Resident" voting rights offers a way to facilitate immigrant civic education and political incorporation. Inclusion and equality, which were core goals of the civil rights movement, now appear in the form of a growing immigrant rights movement. The main point—and one that runs through all these arguments—is fairness. In sum, noncitizen voting is legal, it's rational, and it's the right thing to do.

ANSWERS TO OBJECTIONS

Citizens understandably question why immigrants should be able to vote before they become U.S. citizens. The most common objection is that noncitizens already have access to the vote—by becoming citizens. New York City Mayor Michael Bloomberg argued: "the essence of citizenship is the right to vote, and you should go about becoming a citizen before you get the right to vote." Similarly, Representative Tom Tancredo (R-CO) asked, "Is it really too much to ask that American citizenship be a prerequisite for voting in American elections?"

Most immigrants want to become U.S. citizens but the average time it takes to naturalize is eight to ten years, or longer. That's the cycle for a two-term mayor, city council members, governors, and state representatives. Mario Cristaldo, born in Paraguay and a resident of the District of Columbia since 1994, said, "I invite anyone who says we don't want to become citizens to navigate the [immigration] system. It is not easy." In addition, not all immigrants are eligible to become U.S. citizens, unlike earlier times when almost everyone that came to the U.S. was able to naturalize. It used to be a much easier and faster process. Today, millions are currently barred from the pathway to citizenship. And they are not merely the undocumented—foreign students, people with work visas, and so on—are not currently eligible to naturalize.

While advocates of resident voting support efforts to speed up the naturalization process and to increase pathways to citizenship, they view these goals as complimentary rather than mutually exclusive. Noncitizen voting can be a pathway to citizenship, and can also promote civic education and political engagement at the same time.

Others object by arguing that immigrants are ill prepared for voting, possessing limited knowledge of U.S. laws, customs, and values. But specific knowledge is not a prerequisite for political participation. If it were many native-born citizens would fail tests of even basic political knowledge, as survey research has consistently shown. Such objections are eerily reminiscent of rationales previously used to bar women, African-Americans and youth from the vote.

Some object that granting noncitizens voting rights would reduce incentives for immigrants to naturalize and cheapen the meaning of citizenship. Daniel Stein, executive director of the Federation of American Immigrant Reform, a Washington D.C.–based organization that supports stricter immigration controls, argues: "No one should be given the franchise without taking the Pledge of Allegiance. If you divorce citizenship and voting, citizenship stops having any meaning at all." Like a relationship, some opponents argue, there are different "degrees of commitment," and it is not unreasonable to ask and expect immigrants to wait and develop a deeper relationship to and knowledge of U.S. culture and politics.

Proponents of noncitizen voting counter by noting that immigrants are legitimate stakeholders who can rightly claim the vote. For example, Catherine Jones a noncitizen who has resided in New York City since 1993 testified at a 2005 hearing at the New York City Council:

> New York has become my home. I have made friends, fallen in love, had my heart broken, and gotten promoted at work. I was asked to be present and assist at the birth of a friend's baby and have watched that baby grow up. I have become integrated. I have watched my community change over the years…I take the buses, pay taxes, eat at restaurants and buy my groceries. I say this to illustrate that I am already here, already immersed in this city.

There are many such New Yorkers, Floridians, Texans, Californians, and so on across the country.

Moreover, there are at least ten rights and privileges that immigrants gain when they naturalize; voting is only one. Pending and proposed legislation would permit residents to vote in municipal and/or state elections—not federal elections—leaving plenty of incentives to naturalize. Distinctions between citizens and noncitizens would remain. What would change is the silencing of noncitizens.

Equally important, resident voting rights would benefit all community members. We all have the same interests in safe streets, good schools, affordable housing, health care, and good jobs, whether newcomers arrive to neighborhoods from Delaware or the Dominican Republic. Noncitizens are legitimate stakeholders in communities and have vested interests in local and state elections. We're a stronger society when everyone participates because we all benefit when decisions are made democratically. Noncitizen voting would help insure that government will be more representative, responsive, and accountable to all its members. We would all benefit from immigrants' political inclusion.

Although there are effective representatives at every level of government, good fortune should not play a role in elections and governance. Voting is a crucial mechanism to insure democratic government is truly of the people, by the people, and for the people.

Immigrant rights are the civil rights of the day and noncitizen voting is the suffrage movement of our time. The burgeoning movement to create a truly universal suffrage calls forth America's past and future as an immigrant nation. Democracy is an evolving concept and resident voting is a logical step forward. Restoring immigrant voting rights would update our democracy for these global times. By doing so, we would make history, again.

Allowing Noncitizens to Vote: Undermining Citizenship

STANLEY RENSHON

There is no more iconic feature of American democracy and citizenship than the right to vote. Men and women have marched for it, fought for it, and died for it. Historically, those without property, women, and African-Americans have all legitimately counted their progress toward full citizenship by their ability to vote. And they have correctly judged America's progress toward living up to its ideals by the extension of the vote to all of the country's citizens.

Given these facts, it is understandable that the average American might well ask: What debate?

A DEBATE GAINING MOMENTUM

The answer to that question is that this debate has been slowly gathering momentum out of the public view for some time. While most Americans have been understandably preoccupied with terrorism, Iraq, the economy, illegal immigration, and other issues, a steady drumbeat of advocacy has been gathering force trying to legitimize and implement the idea that the United States should allow new immigrants to vote without becoming citizens.

Advocates of this position use many arguments—about fairness, representation, teaching democracy, increasing participation, expanding democracy, being welcoming to immigrants, the large number of Hispanics who are not yet citizens, and so on. They buttress their claims with the fact that several foreign counties now allow immigrants to vote in local elections, that some American states and territories once allowed it, and that some localities allow it now.

This last fact, that there are several municipalities in the United States that currently allow non-citizens to vote in local elections, may come as somewhat of a surprise. The best known of these is Takoma Park, Md., which introduced the practice in 1992, although its legality has never been tested in the courts. In addition, legislation has been formally introduced in a number of cities, including New York City and Washington, D.C., and in at least two states—New York and Minnesota—to allow non-citizens to vote in local elections. In Massachusetts, the cities of Amherst, Cambridge, and Newton have approved measures to allow non-citizens to vote in local elections, but the ordinances require approval by the state legislature, which has not yet acted favorably on these proposals. A number of other cities are in the initial stages of considering such schemes.

Chicago allows non-citizens to vote in school board elections, and New York did until elected school boards were abolished in 2003. Boulder, Colo., recently introduced a measure to allow non-citizens to serve on city boards and commissions. And in City Heights, Calif., all residents, regardless of citizenship, are able to vote for members of the Planning Committee.

ICONIC WORDS, PROSAIC MOTIVATIONS

Anyone who delves into the arguments put forward in favor of giving non-citizens the right to vote soon encounters iconic terms like "justice," "fairness," and "democracy." A great deal of the advocacy for non-citizen voting makes extensive use of what Mary

Ann Glendon [Learned Hand Professor of Law at Harvard Law School] refers to as "rights talk," the tendency to turn every policy debate into a clash of rights. From the advocate's perspective this is a winning strategy. One of the chief advocates of the non-citizen voting movement, Ron Hayduk [author of the first reading in this debate], is quite direct about this strategy: "The use of democratic and moral claims on the polity has often been an effective tool used by social justice advocates in struggles for equality." In their view, advocates are simply pressing for what they believe many would agree in theory would be a good thing—more democracy, higher morality, more social justice, and more equality, to name all four iconic terms used in that single sentence.

The problem with these iconic words is that they have many meanings. Their incantation is not necessarily synonymous with persuasive argument. Advocates use expansive definitions of these terms to further their goals, and rarely address the political, cultural, and policy implications of their proposals. Moreover, while advocacy rhetoric emphasizes lofty theoretical sentiments, there often are much more prosaic motives at work. Many supporters of non-citizen voting are seeking what they feel will be a large and reliable source of votes for their progressive political agenda. Hayduk, for instance, writes that for allies it is important to drive "home the potential benefits of non-citizens to forge progressive political majorities."

Others are more interested in furthering the political fortunes of the ethnic groups they favor. Louis DeSipio [associate professor of political science, University of California–Irvine] and Rodolfo de la Garza [Eaton Professor of Administrative Law and Municipal Science, Columbia University] argue that non-citizens should be given the right to vote, although their focus is on the Spanish-speaking community. Mr. DeSipio details in a separate book "the low level of citizenship among Latino immigrants," but argues that "Latino permanent residents offer a new pool of citizens and new voters. Sufficient numbers could naturalize to have influence in the next election." And some proponents are simply interested, as one would expect from incumbents who wish to remain in office, in having what they envision as a large pool of reliable voters for their reelection.

It would be tempting to dismiss calls for non-citizen voting as an idea that is not likely to get very far. That however, would be a mistake. There is now a concerted campaign by a vocal group of liberal (or progressive, if you prefer) academics, law professors, elected public officials, and community activists, working in tandem, to decouple voting from American citizenship. Their odds are long, but the stakes are high.

These activists are trying to erase the distinction between citizen and alien, or between national and foreigner…[speaking] directly to the nature of state sovereignty itself." This sounds like a somewhat abstract argument, but it is a debate with the most immediate, direct and profound consequences.

SOME NON-CITIZEN VOTING PROPOSALS

Advocates for non-citizen voting have put forward a variety of proposals. Some focus on gaining non-citizens the vote in local school board elections. Others see granting voting rights at the local level, in less-threatening venues like school board elections, as a bridge to a wider expansion of voting rights for non-citizens. Others focus on gaining voting rights for non-citizens at the local level, even though as one advocate has written, "it is admittedly hard to think of any principled way to justify the inclusion of aliens in local elections, but exclude them from state elections. The problem is that the

U.S. constitution categorically makes all persons enfranchised in state legislative elections into federal electors, and alien participation in national elections presents a far more troubling proposition."

Some want non-citizens to have voting rights at the state as well as the local level. They advocate this despite, or perhaps because of, the fact is that, as noted, given the structure of constitutional law this would inevitably involve granting voting rights at the national level as well. Some want the Supreme Court to declare non-citizen voting a federal right, thereby nullifying the overwhelming number of state constitutions that specifically state that voting is a right reserved for citizens. And some see no reason why non-citizens should not be allowed to run and serve in public office, as well as vote.

The New York City Proposal. In the spring of 2005, William Perkins, then the New York City Council's Deputy Majority Leader, introduced a bill that defines a municipal voter as, "a person who is not a United States citizen, but is lawfully present in the United States, and has been a resident of New York City, as defined herein, for six months or longer by the date of the next election, and who meets all qualifications for registering to vote under the New York State election law, except U.S. citizenship, and has registered to vote with the New York City Board of Elections under this provision." This proposed bill would allow non-citizens to vote for "any municipal officer, including, but not limited to, the mayor, the comptroller, the public advocate, members of the council, borough presidents, and any other future elected municipal official." These new voters may vote in, "without limitations, primary elections, and on municipal ballot questions."

This proposal effectively bypasses all the requirements for learning about the immigrant's new country that are built into the nationalization process. It does not require a demonstrated familiarity with the English language. It does not require a demonstration of any knowledge of American civics and history. And it does not require any knowledge of the issues on which the person would be voting, since the person need only have been in the country for six months.

The most immediate (but not the only) drawbacks to such a proposal are obvious. The new non-citizen voters would be unfamiliar with the United States, its politics, its history, its culture, its language, and the issues on which they are being allowed to vote. Further, having been granted a green card simply acknowledges that a person has applied for and been granted permanent residence. Allowing non-citizens to vote before they have gone through the naturalization process is likely to diminish immigrants' interest in undertaking that process. And this in turn is likely to marginalize a process through which many immigrants increase their emotional and psychological attachment to their new American community. Proposals to allow non-citizens to vote fail to recognize that attachment is an important part of integrating immigrants into the American national community, and that the naturalization process has an important role to play in this regard.

The DeSipio/de la Garza Hispanic Non-citizen Voting Proposal. As noted, some proposals for non-citizen voting have come from ethnic advocates interested in furthering the political clout of their favored ethnic groups. Louis DeSipio…and Rodolfo de la Garza…first put forward such a proposal in 1993. Their proposal "is a modified form of the current effort to make non-citizens eligible to vote." They, however, "add two twists;"

> "First, we would allow noncitizens to vote for the five-year period during which they are statutorily ineligible to naturalize. Under this system, recently immigrated permanent residents would be able to obtain a five-year voter registration card (transferable across jurisdictions, but not extendible). After five years, they would no longer be eligible for permanent resident voting privileges, but would be able to naturalize. Recognizing that the INS suffers from frequent backlogs, we would allow some provision for extending the temporary privileges while the application is on file."

The proposal's authors disagree on the range of elections to which their proposal would apply. "Because of their ability to shape national policy, de la Garza would extend this limited non-citizen voting only for state and local elections." His co-author, DeSipio, however "fears the administrative burdens to local election officials of having to create two sets of voting lists and two ballots would allow permanent residents to vote in all elections during the first five years of residence."

This proposal, like that of New York Councilman William Perkins noted above, raises the same set of voting readiness issues. Here too, new non-citizen voters would not have to be familiar with or knowledgeable of any aspect of the country's history, language, politics, or culture. Yet what is truly unique about this proposal is the authors' highly unusual reassurance as to why it should be adopted: Hispanics won't make use of it.

In surely one of the oddest underlying arguments put forward in favor of non-citizen voting, the authors note, "We think that regardless of one's philosophical attitudes toward noncitizen voting in the contemporary political environment it has one serious flaw: Few noncitizens would use the right." A few pages later, they remind their readers thusly: "Again, it is important to make note that neither one of us thinks that many noncitizens would vote in large numbers under this proposal."

The question immediately arises then: Why bother? Well, it seems that the authors are really of two minds about their proposal. On one hand, their view is that most of those for whom it is intended won't use it. On the other hand, they think it might have a "great impact" on cities where there is a sizable non-citizen population. One reviewer of a book authored by Mr. DeSipio notes that he calls for "a massive, national citizenship campaign targeting these noncitizens [because it] would foster a sense of Latino unity and purpose, and translate into a serious political movement. The momentum created by hundreds of thousands of immigrants joining the polity would spur all Latinos toward greater political participation, culminating in a Latino electorate taking its place among the major new electorates of this century." Allowing non-citizens to vote for a five-year period that could be renewable for some further period would be very consistent with that aim.

The professors also point out that there could be national implications to such a policy. They write that "it must be noted that the only national race—the campaign for the presidency—is in fact just fifty state races in which the winner takes all of the states' electoral votes. Thus in a very close race that is determined by the votes of the larger states (most of which are immigrant receiving states), an empowered noncitizen electorate could swing the election." These advocates try to be reassuring by noting that,

"The scenarios vary from the possible—influence in local elections—to the highly unlikely, that is, national or state level influence."

So, their point seems to be that non-citizens are unlikely to use the vote if it is given to them. On the other hand, if they do use it, they may be able to tip elections. This raises a very basic and direct question: Why should the United States have to take any chance that persons who have literally just arrived in the country and are very unlikely to know anything about its politics—much less the complex issues that citizens are called upon to address—have the opportunity to hold the fate of public decisions in their hands?

IN LIEU OF NATURALIZATION?

The DeSipio/de la Garza proposal, like others that would allow an immigrant to vote within a short time of arrival, would substantially downgrade the importance of naturalization. That is because the second of their "two twists" involves allowing noncitizen voters to substitute evidence that they have voted for having to take the naturalization test. In their words, "naturalization applicants who can show that they voted in most primary and general elections would be exempt from the naturalization examination. The examination is designed to test good citizenship through indirect measures such as knowledge of American history and civics. We propose that voting is an equally good measure of commitment to and understanding of the American system."

The authors make a number of basic mistakes in this statement. They err in equating the knowledge of American history and citizenship with "commitment." Such knowledge can be part of the basis for forming an emotional attachment, and that attachment in turn can grow into a commitment over time, but it is a mistake to equate abstract knowledge with the emotional attachments that go into developing a commitment.

The authors also err in failing to see that knowledge of American history and citizenship, as well as knowledge of English (that the authors belatedly added to their list of items tested by the citizenship test) are not so much measures of good citizenship, indirect or otherwise, as they are a foundation for it. Knowledge of the English language and American history and civics does not automatically make you a good citizen, but it does provide a starting point for becoming one.

It is hard to see how immigrants who know little of American history or American politics and its debates and who do not speak the language will develop that foundation by just pressing a lever three or four times over a five-year period. In practice this would mean that they have voted in "most" of the five elections that take place in any five-year period. In a later publication, they change the requirement of voting in "most" elections to a requirement that such immigrants vote "regularly." It is unclear what this term means. Perhaps this would require new immigrants to vote in a minimum of three or maybe four elections. In return for this, the authors would "grant citizenship automatically upon application." No civics test. No American history test. No test of minimum English language facility. And no further mechanism for encouraging new immigrants to get that important basic knowledge. On all these matters, the proposal is very ill advised. Proposals that would grant non-citizens the right to vote will severely curtail the importance of the naturalization process, and that process plays an important role in the integration of new citizens into the American national community.

POTENTIAL IMPACT

Whether or not non-citizens would make use of the vote is one question. How many would be eligible to do so is another question. Those numbers give us some indication of the potential impact of such proposals. It is useful to begin framing the issues that underlie the debate by first asking a deceptively easy question: What is the number of non-citizens in this country that would potentially be affected by allowing non-citizens to vote? That is not an easy number to ascertain. Some studies include persons residing in the country illegally. Some count those "recently naturalized," while others count all naturalized citizens, whenever they were naturalized. And finally, different studies rely on different data sets that add variations to the figures. With those caveats in mind, we can at least attempt to narrow the range of estimates of the numbers of legal non-citizen residents who would be affected by the proposals to allow non-citizens to vote.

The Eligible Pool of Non-citizen Voters. The March 2007 Current Population Survey, conducted by the Census Bureau, reported that there were about 20.2 million adult non-citizens in the country, about half of whom are believed (based on other research) to be illegal immigrants. Adding to this figure are two important factors. The first is the number of legal immigrants admitted to the country every year. These constitute the pool of potential non-citizen voters for any given five-year period before they begin the naturalization process and become citizens (if they do so). Let us stipulate that the whole process from entry to oath takes six years to complete. So, to take the previous six-year period the numbers would be 1,058,902 for 2001; 1,059,356 for 2002; 703,542 for 2003; 957,883 for 2004; 1,122,373 for 2005; and 1,226,264 for 2006. Thus, in 2006, the pool of non-citizen voters would be the number of new immigrants for the preceding five years, which totals 4,902,056 minus the number that were below voting age (18) in any single year. So, in 2006, the country admitted 1,226,264 immigrants of whom 78 percent were over 18 and thus immediately eligible to vote under most of the non-citizen voting proposals. This figure would need to be added to the number of immigrants from previous years over 18 who had not naturalized.

A number of new immigrants will become naturalized citizens, thus reducing the pool of potential non-citizen voters, but how many? Here again, numbers and the means by which they are calculated vary. A 2007 study by the Pew Hispanic Center estimated that naturalization rates among those eligible were 52 percent for the year 2005. These rates, however, have varied over time depending on levels of immigration and political circumstances. In 1970, the naturalization rate was 64 percent but it dropped over time until in 1996 it stood at 39 percent.

Assuming a continuing robust naturalization of 50 percent, we can then estimate that the pool of non-citizen voters will increase somewhere between 400,000 and 500,000 each year. So a prudent working assumption would be that there are today about 10.5 million legally resident non-citizens, with that number growing at the rate of 400,000 to 500,000 each year.

State and Local Impact. The numbers above are figures for the United States as a whole, but given immigrant settlement patterns it is clear that some localities and elections would be affected more than others. One way to look at this impact is to begin to look at the state distributions of new immigrant settlement. The Passel study of naturalization lists six states as major destinations. They are (with the number of persons eligible but not yet naturalized): California (2.6 million), New York (1.1 million), Texas (766,000,) Florida (607,000), New Jersey (373,000), and Illinois (340,000). In addition, each of the major destination states has a pool of soon-to-be eligible immigrants ranging from a high of 717,000 (California) to 142,000 (Illinois).

Seen from a slightly different perspective, a U.S. Census report from 2003 found that non-citizens accounted for about 10 percent or more of the populations of six major states plus the District of Columbia: California (15.5 percent), D.C. (10.4 percent), Florida (9.5 percent), Nevada (11.3 percent), New Jersey (10.3 percent), New York (10.2 percent), and Texas (10.2 percent).

Within states, some cities and metropolitan areas are magnets for new immigrants. Within New York City's foreign-born population of 2.87 million foreign-born residents in 2000, 65.5 percent or 1.59 million were non-citizens. When introducing his noncitizen voting bill into the New York City Council, Mr. Perkins used a figure of 1,361,007 non-citizens of voting age living in New York as of 2005.

Hayduk provides us with some further information on the number of non-citizens in various kinds of local geographical areas. Twenty-nine states contain cities with a non-citizen voting population of more than 10 percent. In immigrant-rich states, the figures can be dramatic. In California, 19 percent of the state population is made up of non-citizens. In at least 85 cities, 25 percent of the population consists of non-citizens. Eighteen percent of municipalities have non-citizen populations of between 40 and 49 percent. In 12 other municipalities, non-citizens comprise a majority of the adult population—between 50 and 63 percent.

However, the potential political impact of allowing non-citizens to vote is unlikely to be felt only in California. Across the United States, 874 cities have an adult non-citizen population of more than 10 percent; 193 cities have a non-citizen population of more than 25 percent. And 21 cities have an adult non-citizen population of 50 percent or more.

The 10 most populous cities in the United States have a large percentage of adult non-citizens. These range from a high of 32.2 percent (Los Angles) to a low of 13.8 percent (Austin). Other major cities with substantial adult non-citizen populations include New York City (22.9 percent), Chicago (16.4 percent), Houston (22.9 percent), Phoenix (17.5 percent), San Diego (16.6 percent), Dallas (22.27 percent), San Francisco (16.7 percent), and San Jose (24.9 percent).

The Consequences of Non-citizen Voting on American Political Culture. For many advocates, non-citizen voting represents the so-far unachieved holy grail of liberal politics, the creation of a major and sustainable progressive voting majority. Commenting on the possibilities of non-citizen voting, Hayduk writes that the "Creation of a truly universal suffrage would create conditions conducive to forming progressive coalitions." He then immediately goes on to exalt: "Imagine the progressive political possibilities in jurisdictions of high numbers of immigrants such as New York City; Los Angles; Washington, D.C.; and Chicago—as well as in such states—if non-citizens were re-enfranchised."

Hayduk and many of his allies nurture high hopes for the impact of these initiatives. He writes, "noncitizen adults already comprise over 10 percent of the voting-age population in seven states and the District of Columbia, and 19 percent of all California voters. If these noncitizens were enfranchised, they could yield decisive power in state races." And one might add here, a number of cities, towns, and municipalities.

There is, however, one question that advocates of non-citizen voting do not address: What would happen to America's politics and political culture were advocates to get their wish? What would happen if they were able to successfully accomplish their goals and non-citizens nationwide were given the right to vote? How would American citizens in any state, city, or county feel about having an election decided by people who had not yet joined the community of citizenship and might never do so?

What if the political center of gravity in those places shifted decisively to the left because of the influx of these new voters as advocates hope? How would most Americans who, on repeated national surveys, see themselves as moderate, react to having their city, town, and state policies determined by a surging influx of progressive voters who have not become citizens?

These thought experiments lead easily to the conclusion that such occurrences would be profoundly upsetting to many, if not most, Americans. And it is easy to develop scenarios based on the overwhelming rejection of illegal immigration in this country by Americans in general that the responses to these circumstances would be emotionally vivid and strong.

One legitimate question, as yet unanswered by advocates, is whether such political trauma is really necessary. The United States is not a country that keeps immigration to a minimum. It takes in for permanent settlement more people from more countries every year than any other country on earth. It does not base its citizenship on blood or lineage as other countries do, keeping its immigrants in a perpetual state of limbo. Instead, it offers citizenship to almost every legal immigrant after a modest waiting period and after the satisfaction of several other relatively simple requirements. And it offers immigrants, before they become citizens, many ways to take part in politics other than voting.

Non-citizen voting is a potentially politically traumatic and clearly unnecessary answer to a problem that is not very pressing.

ARGUMENTS FOR NON-CITIZEN VOTING

Advocates of non-citizen voting make many arguments for what would be a radical historic change. In just one article, one author claimed 30 separate benefits. It is only fair, advocates say, since non-citizens already pay taxes and can serve in the military. It provides an ideal way for new immigrants to learn about citizenship, they assert. It helps new immigrants feel more welcomed and included, they argue. It ensures that those who are not yet citizens will be represented, they suggest. And, it will help to increase declining rates of political participation, they promise.

These arguments seem reasonable. To advocates they are compelling. Yet, a closer look at each suggests they are neither.

Voting has always been a critical element of full citizenship; courts have called it the essential element. It is true that over 80 years ago, some states allowed resident non-citizens to vote. However, this was always an exception to a more general rule that preserved voting for citizens. By the 1920s, non-citizen voting had been ended by legislation, duly debated and passed by the people's representatives and signed into law by their governors, and with good reason.

Voting is one of the few, and doubtlessly the major, difference between citizens and non-citizens. Citizenship itself, and open access to it, is one of the major unifying mechanisms of E Pluribus Unum. When citizenship loses its value—and it would if voting were not an earned privilege—a critical tie that helps bind this diverse country together will be lost. Given the challenges that face us, this should not be done lightly.

What of fairness? Don't non-citizens pay taxes, and therefore isn't it unfair to not allow them to vote? That argument assumes that non-citizens get nothing for their taxes, and need the vote to compensate for that. However, the truth is that immigrants from most countries enjoy an immediate rise in their standard of living because of this country's advanced infrastructure—for example, hospitals, electricity, communications. They also get many services for their taxes—like public transportation, police, trash collection, and so on. Most importantly and immediately they get what they came for: freedom and opportunity.

What of serving in the armed forces? If they can serve, why can't they vote? The difference here is between can and must. Non-citizens can serve if they volunteer, but they are not required to serve as part of the citizenship process. When they do volunteer, they earn this country's gratitude and, by presidential order, a shortening of the time period before they can become citizens.

Doesn't voting help immigrants learn about their new country? Yes, but the fallacy of that argument is the assumption that there are not other, less damaging ways, to do so. No law bars non-citizens from learning democracy in civic organizations or political parties. No law keeps them from joining unions or speaking out in public forums. Indeed, no law bars them from holding responsible positions within all these groups. In all of these many ways, legal residents can learn about their new country and its civic traditions. Voting is not the only means to do so, and may not even be the best since it can be done from start to finish with the pull of a lever.

What of representation? Isn't it bad for democracy and against democratic principles to have so many people unrepresented? The first problem with this argument is that the condition is temporary and easily remedied by time and patience. Second, the very fact that advocates push non-citizenship voting undercuts the argument that this group's interests are not represented. This country is a republic, not a democracy. We depend on our representatives to consider diverse views. The views of legal non-citizen residents are no exception. The more such persons take advantage of the many opportunities to participate in our civic and political life, the more likely it is that their voices will be heard.

Well, what about participation? Won't giving non-citizens the vote increase participation, and isn't that good for democracy? The answers to those two questions are no and maybe. The record of non-citizen voters should lead all of us to pause and reflect. When New York City allowed non-citizens to vote in local school-board elections, presumably something in which they had a direct, personal, and immediate stake, less that 5 percent of that group did so. Takoma Park, Md., often cited as a model by advocates, refuses to ascertain whether non-citizen voters are in the country legally. Even so, their participation went from a high point of 25 percent in 1997, to 12 percent in the next election, and 9 percent in the election thereafter. In November 2007, only 10 non-citizens voted. In a special election held that year, "officials took extra steps to get the word out. They mailed a notice, in Spanish and English, to every home. They sent a second notice to every registered voter," yet not a single non-citizen voted. In the end, the touted benefits of non-citizen voting participation turn out to be very small and in some cases non-existent—very small gain upon which to sacrifice such a core element of American citizenship.

There are many things this country could and should do to make new immigrants feel welcomed. We could, and should, provide free English classes to all those who want them—and that want is great. We could set up classes to help immigrants learn about the nuts and bolts of our country's life—how do you get insurance, why do you raise your hand in class. We take these things for granted, but new immigrants cannot. If elected officials really want to help new immigrants, these initiatives would be of direct and immediate benefit and won't have the downside of destroying citizenship.

Every effort should be made to integrate legal immigrants into our national community. Yet, isn't it fair to ask that they know something about that community before they fully take up the responsibilities, and not just the advantages, of what has been the core of citizenship? Some non-citizen voting proposals would require three years as a legal resident—saving a mere two years before naturalization and the vote. Others suggest a period of only one year or less, allowing people practically just off the plane to help make complex public decisions.

Advocates of non-citizen voting do not discuss whether these new voters would need to demonstrate language proficiency or knowledge of this country, as they must now do for naturalization. Would that requirement be waived? Nor have they said what they would do if many decided there was no longer a need to become a citizen—since they already can vote.

In the end, we do immigrants, and this country, no favor—indeed, we likely do damage—by giving in to demands for erasing the distinction between immigrants and citizens.

THE CONTINUING DEBATE:
Allowing Noncitizens to Vote

What Is New

Because determining voting eligibility still largely remains with the states, any effort to give national voting rights to noncitizens would require a constitutional amendment. That is extremely unlikely, and so the campaign to extend the vote to noncitizens continues at the state and local levels. Perhaps the most initiative is the current efforts of several city commissioners in Portland, Oregon to extend the franchise. As for public opinion, one survey that asked about who was entitled to vote in federal elections found that only 49% of the respondents thought franchise was limited to citizens. Another 45% thought that voting eligibility extended to everyone in several categories that include both citizens and noncitizens. These categories included "legal residents" (27%), taxpayers (11%), and residents (7%). The remaining 6% were unsure who could vote. However when asked in another survey if "persons in this country who are not citizens" should be permitted to vote in any elections, should be permitted only in local elections, or should be permitted to vote in all elections, an overwhelming 84% opposed any noncitizen voting. Voting in local elections only was supported by 6% and voting in all elections by 8%, with 2% unsure.

Where to Find More

A claim that noncitizens are already voting—illegally—is made by Hans A. von Spakovsky in "Illegal Voting: The Non-citizen Electorate," in *National Review* online, July 10, 2008 at www.nationalreview.com/. An extended version of Professor Hayduk's view can be found in his *Democracy for All: Restoring Immigrant Voting Rights in the United States* (Routledge, 2006).

More on international practice is available in David C. Earnest, 2006, "Neither Citizen Nor Stranger: Why States Enfranchise Resident Aliens," *World Politics* (2006) and Daniel Munro, "Integration Through Participation: Non-Citizen Resident Voting Rights in an Era of Globalization," *Journal of International Migration and Integration* (2008).

What More to Do

It is probable that most of the members of your class, like most Americans, will react negatively to the idea of anyone but citizens voting. Whichever is the right answer, it is important to square it with the basic democratic notion that those who are governed should have a say in their governance. If some of the objections to noncitizen voting, like unfamiliarity with the U.S. political system, are valid, then would they not be valid for everyone? Debate whether a fair approach would be a basic test of knowledge about the political system as a gateway to voting for U.S. residents whatever their status with regard to citizenship, age, or any other characteristic.

7

MEDIA

THE FUTURE OF QUALITY JOURNALISM:
Imperiled *or* Secure?

IMPERILED

Advocate: David Simon, creator and executive producer of the HBO television series *The Wire*

Source: Testimony during hearings on Senate Subcommittee on "The Future of Journalism" before the U.S. Senate, Committee on Commerce, Science, and Transportation; Subcommittee on Communications, Technology, and the Internet, May 6, 2009

SECURE

Advocate: Arianna Huffington, founder of the *Huffington Post*

Source: Testimony during hearings on Senate Subcommittee on "The Future of Journalism" before the U.S. Senate, Committee on Commerce, Science, and Transportation; Subcommittee on Communications, Technology, and the Internet, May 6, 2009

Journalism is undergoing profound change. Until about 40 years ago, the daily sources of news easily available to most Americans were limited to one newspaper, perhaps two in the larger cities, and to the three major broadcast television networks, ABC, CBS, and NBC. Then, like now, radio was ubiquitous, but its role in news delivery was marginal.

Then technology began to rapidly and dramatically reconfigure the news media. In 1980 CNN began broadcasting on the technological upstart, cable television. Then Fox network with its news programming was launched, in the 1990s Microsoft and NBC joined to begin MSNBC, cable companies added foreign sources of news like the BBC, and specialty new channels like the Weather channel and CNBC (business) emerged, as did Univision and other foreign language networks with newscasts. The advent of the Internet further accelerated change. Now almost all U.S. daily newspapers and scores of foreign dailies, often in English, are available online. All the broadcast and cable news networks and many of their foreign counterparts are also available online. Beyond these, there is a wide range of relatively new ways to transmit news widely and quickly. Some are organized operations such as the liberal *Huffington Post*, edited by the author of the second article in this debate, the conservative *Drudge Report*, and the less ideological *Politico.com*. At the other end of the organizational range are the billions of email and text messages that people use daily to exchange their views individually. For collective interchanges, there are at least 112 million blog sites. Almost all of this wide array of Internet sites are free, and many include streaming video and other innovative techniques to enhance their product.

Because such ways of transmitting news are so new and because getting good data is exceptionally difficult, it is unclear what their overall impact is or will be. For now, though, consider the following indications of the rise of non-traditional sources of news:

- 37% of Americans go online daily to get news, and another 8% do so 3 to 5 days a week.

- 29% reported recently getting online news from a source other than a newspaper Web site.
- 27% report getting a news story from a friend by email within the last week.
- 14% report sending a news story to a friend by email within the last week.
- 36% have news feeds on their homepage.
- 15% regularly and 21% sometimes read blogs about politics or current events.
- 3% regularly and 9% sometimes read online magazines such as *Salon* or *Slate.*
- 10% regularly and 20% sometimes get news through social networking pages such as MySpace and Facebook.
- 6% regularly and 18% sometimes share information about local, national, or international news through a social networking page.

Among the traditional sources of news, newspapers have suffered most from this competition. Most Americans (61%) still cite television as their primary news source, but in 2007 the Internet (17%) replaced newspapers (16%) as the second most used primary source. Concomitantly, daily newspaper circulation between 1985 and 2008 sagged 62 to 48 million copies. Drops in circulation, led to declines in ad revenues. These forced major cutbacks, with newspapers losing 17% of their staff between 2001 and 2008. The increases that print newspapers have gained in online readership and ad revenue have fallen far short of losses from their print side. As a result, some papers like the *Baltimore Examiner, Tucson Citizen,* and *Cincinnati Post* have closed. The *Seattle Post-Intelligencer, Detroit Free Press, Christian Science Monitor,* and others have either gone entirely online or only publish printed editions a few times a week.

The debate here is about the "so what" of this shift in the sources of news. David Simon sees dire results from the decline of newspapers. He partly blames the newspaper industry, but whatever the cause, he believes that in-depth professional journalism is in danger, thereby endangering the ability of the people to keep track of their government. He views news sources like the *Huffington Post,* as "parasites" that contribute little more than "repetition" and "froth." Anne Huffington disagrees, and sees the new era of journalism as a "golden age" of increased opportunities for people to get news through a range of quality sources.

While the debate here focuses on newspapers, television news is also struggling. The number of people watching the evening news on one of the major broadcast or cable networks fell 35% to 26.3 million between 1993 and 2008. Adding to the worries that many have about the traditional press is the criticism that it has tried to boost its audience and revenues by "dumbing down" its coverage to the point where it is ever harder to distinguish, for example, between the *CBS Evening News* and *Entertainment Tonight,* which follows on many CBS stations.

POINTS TO PONDER

➤ Simon implicitly equates professional journalists with high quality news. Do you agree that newspaper offer high quality journalism?
➤ Think about what sources you go to for news, and ask yourself why you use these sources.
➤ Consider Huffington's praise of "citizen journalism," and ask yourself whether you agree.

The Future of Quality Journalism: Imperiled

DAVID SIMON

Thank you all for the invitation and opportunity to speak on this issue today, but I start by confessing reluctance.

My name is David Simon, and I used to be a newspaperman in Baltimore. Head and heart, I was a newspaperman from the day I signed up at my high school paper until the day, eighteen years later, when I took a buyout from the *Baltimore Sun* and left for the fleshpots of Hollywood [Simon became involved in popular entertainment, most notably creating the HBO police series set in Baltimore, *The Wire*].

To those colleagues who remain at newspapers, I am therefore an apostate, and my direct connection to "newspapering"—having ended in 1995—means that as a witness today, my experiences are attenuated.

Ideally, rather than listening to me, you should be hearing from any number of voices of those still laboring in American journalism. I am concerned that the collective voice of the newsroom itself—the wisdom of veteran desk editors, rewrite men and veteran reporters is poorly represented in this process. But of course newspapers are obliged to cover Congress and its works, and therefore the participation of most working journalists in today's hearing would compromise some careful ethics. I know your staff tried to invite working journalists but were rebuffed on these grounds. And so, tellingly, today's witness list is heavy with newspaper executives on the one hand, and representatives of the new, internet-based media on the other.

And so, I've accepted the invitation, though to be honest, I'm tired of hearing myself on this subject; I've had my say in essays that accompany this testimony, and in the episodes of a recent television drama, and I would be more inclined to hear from former colleagues if they were in a position to speak bluntly....

What I say will likely conflict with what representatives of the newspaper industry will claim for themselves. And I can imagine little agreement with those who speak for new media. From the captains of the newspaper industry, you will hear a certain "martyrology"—a claim that they were heroically serving democracy to their utmost only to be undone by a cataclysmic shift in technology and the arrival of all things web-based. From those speaking on behalf of new media, weblogs and that which goes twitter, you will be treated to assurances that American journalism has a perfectly fine future online, and that a great democratization in newsgathering is taking place.

In my city, there is a technical term we often administer when claims are plainly contradicted by facts on the ground. We note that the claimant is, for lack of a better term, full of it. Though in Baltimore, of course, we are explicit with our nouns.

High-end journalism is dying in America and unless a new economic model is achieved, it will not be reborn on the web or anywhere else. The internet is a marvelous tool and clearly it is the informational delivery system of our future, but thus far it does not deliver much first-generation reporting. Instead, it leeches that reporting from mainstream news publications, whereupon aggregating web sites and bloggers contribute little more than repetition, commentary and froth. Meanwhile, readers acquire news from the aggregators and abandon its point of origin—namely the newspapers themselves.

—In short, the parasite is slowly killing the host.

It is nice to get stuff for free, of course. And it is nice that more people can have their say in new media. And while some of our internet commentary is—as with any unchallenged and unedited intellectual effort—rampantly ideological, ridiculously inaccurate and occasionally juvenile, some of it is also quite good, even original.

Understand here that I am not making a Luddite argument against the internet and all that it offers. But democratized and independent though they may be, you do not— in my city—run into bloggers or so-called citizen journalists at City Hall, or in the courthouse hallways or at the bars and union halls where police officers gather. You do not see them consistently nurturing and then pressing sources. You do not see them holding institutions accountable on a daily basis.

Why? Because high-end journalism—that which acquires essential information about our government and society in the first place—is a profession; it requires daily, full-time commitment by trained men and women who return to the same beats day in and day out until the best of them know everything with which a given institution is contending. For a relatively brief period in American history—no more than the last fifty years or so—a lot of smart and talented people were paid a living wage and benefits to challenge the unrestrained authority of our institutions and to hold those institutions to task. Modern newspaper reporting was the hardest and in some ways the most gratifying job I ever had. I am offended to think that anyone, anywhere believes American institutions as insulated, self-preserving and self-justifying as police departments, school systems, legislatures and chief executives can be held to gathered facts by amateurs pursuing the task without compensation, training, or for that matter, sufficient standing to make public officials even care to whom it is they are lying or from whom they are withholding information.

The idea of this is absurd, yet to read the claims that some new media voices are already making, you would think they need only bulldoze the carcasses of moribund newspapers aside and begin typing. They don't know what they don't know—which is a dangerous state for any class of folk—and to those of us who do understand how subtle and complex good reporting can be, their ignorance is as embarrassing as it is seemingly sincere. Indeed, the very phrase citizen journalist strikes my ear as nearly Orwellian. A neighbor who is a good listener and cares about people is a good neighbor; he is not in any sense a citizen social worker. Just as a neighbor with a garden hose and good intentions is not a citizen firefighter. To say so is a heedless insult to trained social workers and firefighters.

—So much for new media. But what about old media?

When you hear a newspaper executive claiming that his industry is an essential bulwark of society and that it stands threatened by a new technology that is, as of yet, unready to shoulder the same responsibility, you may be inclined to empathize. And indeed, that much is true enough as it goes.

But when that same newspaper executive then goes on to claim that this predicament has occurred through no fault on the industry's part, that they have merely been undone by new technologies, feel free to kick out his teeth. At that point, he's as fraudulent as the most self-aggrandized blogger.

Anyone listening carefully may have noted that I was bought out of my reporting position in 1995. That's fourteen years ago. That's well before the internet ever began to seriously threaten any aspect of the industry. That's well before Craigslist and department-store consolidation gutted the ad base. Well before any of the current economic conditions applied.

In fact, when newspaper chains began cutting personnel and content, their industry was one of the most profitable yet discovered by Wall Street money. We know now—because bankruptcy has opened the books—that the *Baltimore Sun* was eliminating its afternoon edition and trimming nearly 100 editors and reporters in an era when the paper was achieving 37 percent profits. In the years before the internet deluge, the men and women who might have made *The Sun* a more essential vehicle for news and commentary—something so strong that it might have charged for its product online—they were being ushered out the door so that Wall Street could command short-term profits in the extreme.

Such short-sighted arrogance rivals that of Detroit in the 1970s, when automakers—confident that American consumers were mere captives—offered up Chevy Vegas, and Pacers and Gremlins without the slightest worry that mediocrity would be challenged by better-made cars from Germany or Japan.

In short, my industry butchered itself and we did so at the behest of Wall Street and the same unfettered, free-market logic that has proved so disastrous for so many American industries. And the original sin of American newspapering lies, indeed, in going to Wall Street in the first place.

When locally-based, family-owned newspapers like *The Sun* were consolidated into publicly-owned newspaper chains, an essential dynamic, an essential trust between journalism and the communities served by that journalism was betrayed.

Economically, the disconnect is now obvious. What do newspaper executives in Los Angeles or Chicago care whether or not readers in Baltimore have a better newspaper, especially when you can make more putting out a mediocre paper than a worthy one? The profit margin was all. And so, where family ownership might have been content with 10 or 15 percent profit, the chains demanded double that and more, and the cutting began—long before the threat of new technology was ever sensed.

But editorially? The newspaper chains brought an ugly disconnect to the newsroom, and by extension, to the community as well. A few years after the A.S. Abell Family sold *The Sun* to the Times-Mirror newspaper chain, fresh editors arrived from out of town to take over the reins of the paper.

They looked upon Baltimore not as essential terrain to be covered with consistency, to be explained in all its complexity year in and year out for readers who had and would live their lives in Baltimore. Why would they? They had arrived from somewhere else, and if they could win a prize or two, they would be moving on to bigger and better opportunities within the chain.

So, well before the arrival of the internet, as veteran reporters and homegrown editors took buyouts, newsbeats were dropped and less and less of Baltimore and central Maryland were covered with rigor or complexity.

In a city in which half the adult black males are without consistent work, the poverty and social services beat was abandoned. In a town where the unions were imploding and the working class eviscerated, where the bankruptcy of a huge steel manufacturer meant thousands were losing medical benefits and pensions, there was no longer a labor reporter. And though it is one of the most violent cities in America, the Baltimore courthouse went uncovered for more than a year and the declining quality of criminal casework in the state's attorney's office went largely ignored.

Meanwhile, the editors used their manpower to pursue a handful of special projects, Pulitzer-sniffing as one does. The self-gratification of my profession does not come, you see, from covering a city and covering it well, from explaining an increasingly complex and interconnected world to citizens, from holding basic institutions accountable on a daily basis. It comes from someone handing you a plaque and taking your picture.

The prizes meant little, of course, to actual readers. What might have mattered to them, what might have made the *Baltimore Sun* substantial enough to charge online for content would have been to comprehensively cover its region and the issues of that region, to do so with real insight and sophistication and consistency.

But the reporters required to achieve such were cleanly dispatched, buyout after buy-out, from the first staff reduction in 1992 to the latest round last week, in which near-ly a third of the remaining newsroom was fired. Where 500 men and women once covered central Maryland, there are now 140. And the money required to make a great newspaper—including, say, the R&D funding that might have anticipated and planned for the internet revolution—all of that went back to Wall Street, to CEO salaries and to big-money investors. The executives and board chairman held up their profit mar-gins and got promoted; they're all on some golf course in Florida right now, comfort-ably retired and thinking about things other than journalism. The editors took their prizes and got promoted; they're probably on what passes for a journalism lecture cir-cuit these days, offering heroic tales of past glory and jeremiads about the world they, in fact, helped to bring about.

—But the newspapers themselves?

When I was in journalism school in the 1970s, the threat was television and its immediacy. My professors claimed that in order to survive, newspapers were going to have to cede the ambulance chasing and reactive coverage to TV and instead become more like great magazines. Specialization and detailed beat reporting were the future. We were going to have to explain an increasingly complex world in ways that made us essential to an increasingly educated readership. The scope of coverage would have to go deeper, address more of the world not less. Those were our ambitions. Those were my ambitions.

In Baltimore at least, and I imagine in every other American city served by newspa-per-chain journalism, those ambitions were not betrayed by the internet. We had trashed them on our own, years before. Incredibly, we did it for naked, short-term prof-its and a handful of trinkets to hang on the office wall. And now, having made ourselves less essential, less comprehensive and less able to offer a product that people might pur-chase online, we pretend to an undeserved martyrdom at the hands of new technology.

I don't know if it isn't too late already for American newspapering. So much talent has been torn from newsrooms over the last two decades and the ambitions of the craft are now so crude, small-time and stunted that it's hard to imagine a turnaround. But if there is to be a renewal of the industry a few things are certain and obvious:

First, cutting down trees and printing a daily accounting of the world on paper and delivering it to individual doorsteps is anachronistic. And if that is so, then the indus-try is going to have to find a way to charge for online content. Yes, I have heard the post-modern rallying cry that information wants to be free. But information isn't. It costs money to send reporters to London, Fallujah and Capitol Hill, and to send pho-tographers with them, and to keep them there day after day. It costs money to hire the best investigators and writers and then to back them up with the best editors. It costs money to do the finest kind of journalism. And how anyone can believe that the industry can fund that kind of expense by giving its product away online to aggregators and bloggers is a source of endless fascination to me. A freshman marketing major at any community college can tell you that if you don't have a product for which you can charge people, you don't actually have a product.

Second, Wall Street and free-market logic, having been a destructive force in journalism over the last few decades, are not now suddenly the answer. Raw, unencumbered capitalism is never the answer when a public trust or public mission is at issue. If the last quarter century has taught us anything—and admittedly, with too many of us, I doubt it has—it's that free-market capitalism, absent social imperatives and responsible regulatory oversight, can produce durable goods and services, glorious profits, and little of lasting social value. Airlines, manufacturing, banking, real estate—is there a sector of the American economy where laissez-faire theories have not burned the poor, the middle class and the consumer, while bloating the rich and mortgaging the very future of the industry, if not the country itself? I'm pressed to think of one.

Similarly, there can be no serious consideration of public funding for newspapers. High-end journalism can and should bite any hand that tries to feed it, and it should bite a government hand most viciously. Moreover, it is the right of every American to despise his local newspaper—for being too liberal or too conservative, for covering X and not covering Y, for spelling your name wrong when you do something notable and spelling it correctly when you are seen as dishonorable. And it is the birthright of every healthy newspaper to hold itself indifferent to such constant disdain and be nonetheless read by all. Because in the end, despite all flaws, there is no better model for a comprehensive and independent review of society than a modern newspaper. As love-hate relationships go, this is a pretty intricate one. An exchange of public money would pull both sides from their comfort zone and prove unacceptable to all.

But a non-profit model intrigues, especially if that model allows for locally-based ownership and control of news organizations. Anything that government can do in the way of creating non-profit status for newspapers should be seriously pursued. And further, anything that can be done to create financial or tax-based incentives for bankrupt and near-bankrupt newspaper chains to transfer or even donate unprofitable publications to locally-based non-profits should also be considered.

Lastly, I would urge Congress to consider relaxing certain anti-trust prohibitions with regard to the newspaper industry, so that the *Washington Post*, the *New York Times* and various other newspapers can sit down and openly discuss protecting their copyright from aggregators and plan an industrywide transition to a paid, online subscriber base. Whatever money comes will prove essential to the task of hiring back some of the talent, commitment, and institutional memory that has been squandered.

Absent this basic and belated acknowledgment that content has value—if indeed it still does after so many destructive buyouts and layoffs—and that content is what ultimately matters, I don't think anything else can save high-end, professional journalism.

The Future of Quality Journalism: Secure

ARIANNA HUFFINGTON

Thank you for inviting me to be a part of today's discussion on the future of journalism. Like any good news story, let me start with the headline: Journalism Will Not Only Survive, It Will Thrive.

Despite all the current hand wringing about the dire state of the newspaper industry—well-warranted hand wringing, I might add—we are actually in the midst of a Golden Age for news consumers. Can anyone seriously argue that this isn't a magnificent time for readers who can surf the net, use search engines, and go to news aggregators to access the best stories from countless sources around the world—stories that are up-to-the-minute, not rolled out once a day? Online news also allows users to immediately comment on stories, as well as interact and form communities with other commenters.

Since good journalism plays an indispensable role in our democracy, we all have a vested interest in making sure that our journalistic institutions continue producing quality reporting and analysis. But it's important to remember that the future of quality journalism is not dependent on the future of newspapers.

Consumer habits have changed dramatically. People have gotten used to getting the news they want, when they want it, how they want it, and where they want it. And this change is here to stay.

As my compatriot Heraclitus put it nearly 2,500 years ago: "You cannot step into the same river twice." [Huffington's maiden name is Stassinopoulos]

The great upheaval the news industry is going through is the result of a perfect storm of transformative technology, the advent of Craigslist, generational shifts in the way people find and consume news, and the dire impact the economic crisis has had on advertising. And there is no question that, as the industry moves forward and we figure out the new rules of the road, there will be—and needs to be—a great deal of experimentation with new revenue models. But what won't work—what can't work—is to act like the last 15 years never happened, that we are still operating in the old content economy as opposed to the new link economy, and that the survival of the industry will be found by "protecting" content behind walled gardens. We've seen that movie (and its many sequels, including TimesSelect). News consumers didn't like them, and they closed in a hurry.

And the answer can't be content creators attacking Google and other news aggregators. No, the future is to be found elsewhere. It is a linked economy. It is search engines. It is online advertising. It is citizen journalism and foundation-supported investigative funds. That's where the future is. And if you can't find your way to that, then you can't find your way.

Online video offers a useful example of the importance of being able to adapt. Not that long ago, content providers were committed to the idea of requiring viewers to come to their site to view their content—and railed against anyone who dared show even a short clip.

But content hoarding—the walled garden—didn't work. And instead of sticking their finger in the dike, trying to hold back the flow of innovation, smart companies began providing embeddable players that allowed their best stuff to be posted all over the web, accompanied by links and ads that helped generate additional traffic and revenue.

When I hear the heads of media companies talking about "restricting" content or describing news aggregators as "parasites," I can't help feeling the same way I did in 2001, when I was one of the cofounders of The Detroit Project, and watched as the heads of the auto industry decided that instead of embracing the future they would rather spend considerable energy and money lobbying the government for tax loopholes for gas-guzzling behemoths, fighting back fuel efficiency standards, and trying to convince consumers through billions in advertising that SUVs were the cars that would lead America into the 21st century.

Instead of trying to hold back the future, I suggest that media executives read *The Innovator's Dilemma* by Clayton Christensen, and see what he has to say about "disruptive innovation" and how, instead of resisting it, you can seize the opportunities it provides.

And that's why it's imperative that Congress and the FCC [Federal Communications Commission] make sure they have in place smart policies that bridge the digital divide, ensure competition among Internet service providers, and protect innovators and consumers from attempts to undermine net neutrality or impose unjustified charges—like metering—on Internet users.

Digital news is a classic case of "disruptive innovation"—a development that newspapers ignored for far too long.

Even so, I think all the obituaries for newspapers we're hearing are premature. Many papers are belatedly but successfully adapting to the new news environment. Plus, it's my feeling that until those of us who came of age before the Internet all die off, there will be a market for print versions of newspapers. There is something in our collective DNA that makes us want to sip our coffee, turn a page, look up from a story, say, "Can you believe this?" and pass the paper to the person across the table. Sure, you could hand them your Blackberry or laptop…but the instinct is different (and, really, who wants to get butter or marmalade on your new MacBook Pro?).

I firmly believe in a hybrid future where old media players embrace the ways of new media (including transparency, interactivity, and immediacy) and new media companies adopt the best practices of old media (including fairness, accuracy, and high-impact investigative journalism).

This hybrid future will include nonprofit/for profit hybrids, like the Investigative Fund the *Huffington Post* recently launched.

As the newspaper industry continues to contract, one of the most commonly voiced fears is that serious investigative journalism will be among the victims of the scaleback. And, indeed, many newspapers are drastically reducing their investigative teams. Yet, given the multiple crises we are living through, investigative journalism is all the more important. For too long, whether it's coverage of the war in Iraq or the economic meltdown, we've had too many autopsies and not enough biopsies.

The Investigative Fund is our attempt to change this—backed by nonprofit foundations interested in giving freelance reporters, many of whom have lost their jobs, the ability to pursue important stories. Others, like ProPublica, The Center for Public Integrity, Spot.US, and The Center for Investigative Reporting are pursuing different not-for-profit investigative models. More will follow.

We will also see more citizen journalism—not as a replacement for traditional journalists, but as a way of augmenting their coverage.

"Citizen Journalism" is shorthand for a collection of methods for producing content by harnessing the power of a site's community of readers, and making it a key element of the site's editorial output. These engaged readers can, among other things, recommend stories, produce raw data for original reported stories, write original stories themselves, record exclusive in-the-field video, search through large amounts of data or documents for hidden gems and trends, and much more. By tapping this resource, online news sites can extend their reach and help redefine newsgathering in the digital age.

In the process, they will also expand their online community—which, in turn, will attract more users and help build a more viable business model.

For too long, traditional media have been afflicted with Attention Deficit Disorder—they are far too quick to drop a story—even a good one, in their eagerness to move on to the Next Big Thing. Online journalists, meanwhile, tend to have Obsessive Compulsive Disorder…they chomp down on a story and stay with it, refusing to move off it until they've gotten down to the marrow.

In the future, these two traits will come together and create a much healthier kind of journalism. The discussion needs to move from "How do we save newspapers?" to "How do we strengthen journalism—via whatever platform it is delivered?"

We must never forget that our current media culture led to the widespread failure (with a few honorable exceptions) to serve the public interest by accurately covering two of the biggest stories of our time: the run-up to the war in Iraq and the financial meltdown.

That's why, as journalism transitions to a new and different place, the emphasis should not be on subsidizing what exists now but on how to rededicate ourselves to the highest calling of journalists—which is to ferret out the truth, wherever it leads. Even if it means losing our all-access-pass to the halls of power.

Unfortunately, this is a concept that has fallen out of favor with too many journalists who, like Pontius Pilot, wash their hands of finding the truth and instead are obsessed with a false view of "balance" and the misguided notion that every story has two sides. And that the truth can be found somewhere in the middle. But not every story has two sides and the truth is often found lurking in the shadows. The earth is not flat. Evolution is a fact. Global warming is real.

The most exciting thing for both journalists and news consumers, is the fact that technology will continue to give readers more and more control over what kind of information they get, and how that information will be presented. The days of publishing pooh-bahs dictating what is important and what is not are over. And thank goodness. As the legendary journalist I.F. Stone once said of a leading newspaper of his time: it's a particularly exciting paper to read because "you never know on what page you will find a page-one story."

We stand on the threshold of a very challenging but very exciting future. Indeed, I am convinced that journalism's best days lie ahead—just so long as we embrace and support innovation and don't try to pretend that we can somehow hop into a journalistic Way Back Machine and return to a past that no longer exists and can't be resurrected.

THE CONTINUING DEBATE:
The Future of Quality Journalism

What Is New

The decline in circulation of newspapers continues and has even accelerated, dropping by more than 10% during the period March–September 2009 alone. Reflecting this ongoing trend, 166 newspapers closed or ceased publishing printed edition between 2008 and late 2010. Because of the financial pressures, the surviving papers reduced their staffs by about 35,000 during the period, thus cutting down on news coverage. Americans are divided about what it portends. A 2009 poll found that 61% believe that they would "still be able to get the information they need as citizens," if the newspaper in their community shut down. Also worrisome for newspapers, in 2009 only 25% of Americans expressed significant confidence in newspapers, while 43% had only "some" confidence, and 31% had little or no confidence in them, with 1% unsure.

Where to Find More

A first-rate source for more information on newspapers and all the other news media is the annual port, *State of the News Media*, by the Pew Research Center's Project for Excellence in Journalism at www.stateofthemedia.org. More on newspapers specifically can be found on the Web site of the American Society of Newspaper Editors at www.asne.org/. To follow the media more generally, go to National Public Radio's *On The Media* program found at www.onthemedia.org/. The hearings in Congress at which Simon and Huffington testified sparked considerable interest in the media. One commentary is John Nichols, "David Simon, Arianna Huffington and the Future of Journalism," *The Nation*, May 11, 2009 www.thenation.com/. From a political science perspective, the future of journalism is heavily connected to the issue about the role the press plays in democracy and governance. A good look at that is Doris Graver, "The Media and Democracy: Beyond Myths and Stereotypes," *Annual Review of Political Science* (2003).

What More to Do

First, discuss how important newspapers are to society, particularly democracy. Thomas Jefferson once said that, if it was "left to me to decide whether we should have government without newspapers, or newspapers without a government, I should not hesitate a moment to prefer the latter." Do you agree? If you are worried about the decline of newspapers, and also what many see as the "infortainmentization" of television news, what would you do to fix that? Expanding public funding of public television news, giving commercial stations tax breaks for news operations, designating newspapers as tax exempt organizations, or making newspaper subscriptions tax deductible are a few ideas. Brainstorm to find others and debate them.

PERMITTING CORPORATIONS TO PARTICIPATE IN ELECTION CAMPAIGNS:
A Blow to Democracy *or* Constitutionally Appropriate?

A BLOW TO DEMOCRACY

Advocate: Monica Youn, Counsel at the Brennan Center for Justice at the New York University School of Law

Source: Testimony during hearings on the "First Amendment and Campaign Finance Reform After *Citizens United*," before the Committee on the Judiciary, U.S. House of Representatives, February 3, 2010

CONSTITUTIONALLY APPROPRIATE

Advocate: M. Todd Henderson, Assistant Professor of Law, University of Chicago Law School

Source: "*Citizens United*: A Defense," Faculty Blog, University of Chicago Law School, March 12, 2010

Elections are big business. During the 2008 election cycle (2007–2008) alone, candidates, parties, interest groups, and individuals spent approximately $5.5 billion on the campaigns for the nominations and election for federal, state, and local offices. Of this total, almost two-thirds went to federal elections, including $2 billion to the presidential campaign and another $1.5 billion or so to the campaigns for Congress.

Although some wealthy candidates spend millions of their own dollars trying to get elected, more than 95% of the overall money that goes to influencing who gets nominated for and elected to Congress comes from sources other than the candidates themselves. In an ideal democracy, most of this money would come from small donations by a sizeable proportion of the electorate supporting one or another candidate. Reality is different. The vast majority of money comes from "big money" sources. Only about 15% of the money donated to congressional candidates for the 2008 campaigns came from small donors (those giving less than $1,000), while about 45% came from large donors. Political action committees (PACs) representing interest groups accounted for about another 25% of congressional campaign funds. Tax-exempt advocacy groups (TAGs) are also major players in the campaign finance picture. Also called 501(c) groups and 527 groups in reference to the sections of the Internal Revenue Code designating them as tax exempt, TAGs are not supposed to support or oppose the election of candidates for federal office. Nevertheless, a significant percentage of the more than $400 million that TAGs spent promoting their causes during the 2008 election cycle went to de facto partisan electoral activity.

Concern about the impact of big money on elections led Congress to enact the Federal Election Campaign Act (FECA) in 1971 to limit individual and PAC "hard money" contributions to political parties and candidates. The FECA did not cover "soft money" that various groups use to oppose or support federal candidates without donating to any candidate directly. In part to address soft money, Congress in 2002 enacted the Bipartisan Campaign Reform Act (BCRA). Among other things, the act prohibits federal candidates from raising or spending soft money and also limits its flow into federal elections via state and local party funds. The act also expanded the definition of campaign advertisements (versus issue ads) by specifying that messages depicting a candidate prior to an election and targeting that candidate's constituency are campaign communications subject to federal regulations. These two laws have helped restrain the flow of big money into politics, but their impact has been limited by Supreme Court decisions voiding some of their provisions as violations of the First Amendment. Most importantly for this debate, the Court ruled in *Citizens United v. FEC* (2010) that the BCRA's provision prohibiting corporations from sponsoring independent "electioneering communications" close to elections was an unconstitutional restraint on free speech. Corporations, it should be noted, are considered legal "persons" with at least some constitutional rights under Supreme Court decisions dating as far as *Dartmouth College v. Woodward* (1819) and *Santa Clara County v. Southern Pacific Railroad* (1886). Also worth noting is that the Court's decision in *Citizens United* probably means that the BCRA's limits on labor union electioneering are also unconstitutional.

What *Citizens United* did not do, despite much erroneous reporting, was to strike down long-standing laws that bar corporations (since 1907) and unions (since 1947) from giving money directly to federal candidates and political parties. The justices did, however, invalidate state laws barring corporate independent election activity, thereby reversing the Court's decision in *Austin v. Michigan Chamber of Commerce* (1990) upholding a Michigan law barring corporations from using their funds to support or opposed a candidate independently.

Fueled at least in part by the worry that *Citizens United* will result in increased spending by corporations to help Republicans, the decision drew an angry condemnation by President Obama and congressional Democrats. In the first reading, Marcia Youn of the Brennan Center at NYU's School of Law, tells a congressional hearing that the Court's *Citizens United* decision was misguided and will harm the democratic process by increasing the influence of big money in politics. University of Chicago Law School Professor M. Todd Henderson disagrees in the second reading. He contends that the Supreme Court made the appropriate decision in *Citizens United* and that the decision enhances democracy by increasing the number of views be expressed.

POINTS TO PONDER

➤ If corporations, which are organizations, can have their "free speech" limited, can unions, advocacy groups, and other organizations also be restricted from using their money to independently support candidates?

➤ Youn and Henderson have very different view of what the *United Citizens* decision will mean in terms of corporate political spending. Whose view seems more likely to be right?

➤ If restraining corporate political spending both restrains free speech and serves to keep the political playing field more even between wealthy interests and others, which is more important?

Permitting Corporations to Participate in Election Campaigns: A Blow to Democracy

MARCIA YOUN

Since its creation in 1995, the Brennan Center has focused on fundamental issues of democracy and justice, including research and advocacy to enhance the rights of voters and to reduce the role of money in our elections. That work takes on even more urgency after the United States Supreme Court's decision in *Citizens United v. Federal Election Commission* on January 21, 2010. *Citizens United* rivals *Bush v. Gore* [2000] for the most aggressive intervention into politics by the Supreme Court in the modern era. Indeed, *Bush v. Gore* affected only one election; *Citizens United* will affect every election for years to come. [In *Bush v. Gore*, the Supreme Court rejected a challenge to Florida's awarding of its electoral votes to George W. Bush, thereby, in effect, giving him a majority of the Electoral College votes and the presidency.]

[There is a] five-vote majority on the Supreme Court [that] has imposed a radical concept of the First Amendment, and used it to upend vital protections for a workable democracy. We must push back against this distorted version of the Constitution. We must insist on a true understanding of the First Amendment as a charter for a vital and participatory democracy. And there are other values in the Constitution, too, that justify strong campaign laws—values such as the central purpose of assuring effective self-governance.

The Court blithely asserts that unlimited corporate spending poses no threat of corruption. That is simply not the case. We urge, above all, that this committee build a record to expose the actual workings of the campaign finance system. Such a record is vital for the public's understanding, and even more to make clear to Justices in future litigation that a strong record undergirds strong laws.

THE POLITICAL STAKES OF *CITIZENS UNITED*

Last week, the Supreme Court's decision in *Citizens United v. FEC* undermined 100 years of law that restrained the role of special interests in elections. By holding—for the first time—that corporations have the same First Amendment rights to engage in political spending as people, the Supreme Court re-ordered the priorities in our democracy—placing special interest dollars at the center of our democracy, and displacing the voices of the voters. There is reason to believe that future elections will see a flood of corporate spending, with the real potential to drown out the voices of every-day Americans. As Justice [John Paul] Stevens warned in his sweeping dissent, American citizens "may lose faith in their capacity, as citizens, to influence public policy" as a result.

After news of the *Citizens United* ruling sent shock waves through political, legal, and news media circles throughout the nation, some commentators took a jaundiced view, arguing, in essence, that since the political system is already awash in special-interest dollars, this particular decision will have little impact. It is undoubtedly true that heretofore, corporations have engaged in large-scale spending in federal politics—primarily through political action committees ("PACs") and through more indirect means such as lobbying and nonprofit advocacy groups. However, the sums spent by corporations in previous elections are miniscule in comparison to the trillions of dollars in corporate profits that the Supreme Court has now authorized corporations to spend to influence the outcome of federal elections. The difference, in short, changes the rules of federal politics.

Prior to *Citizens United*, a corporation that wished to support or oppose a federal candidate had to do so using PAC funds—funds amassed through voluntary contributions from individual employees and shareholders who wished to support the corporation's political agenda. Such funds were subject to federal contribution limits and other regulations. Now however, the *Citizens United* decision will allow corporations that wish to directly influence the outcome of federal elections to draw from their general treasury funds, rather than PAC funds, to support or oppose a particular candidate. This difference is significant enough to amount to a difference in kind rather merely a difference in degree, as demonstrated by the following:

- In the 2008 election cycle, the nation's largest corporation, Exxon-Mobil, formed a PAC that collected approximately $700,000 in individual contributions. Thus, Exxon-Mobil was limited to spending this amount on advertisements directly supporting or opposing a federal candidate. During the same 2008 election, Exxon-Mobil's corporate profits totaled more than $80 billion. Thus, *Citizens United* frees this one corporation to increase its direct spending in support or opposition to federal candidates by more than 100,000 fold.

- During the 2008 election cycle, all winning congressional candidates spent a total of $861 million on their campaigns—less than one percent of Exxon-Mobil's corporate profits over the same period.

Furthermore, corporations have demonstrated that they are willing to spend vast sums of money to influence federal politics. Since corporations have been banned from contributing to candidates and restricted in their campaign spending, their political spending has generally taken the form of lobbying.

- In the same year that it was able to raise only $700,000 for its federal PAC, Exxon Mobil spent $29 million on lobbying.

- In 2008, the average expenditures in a winning Senate race totaled $7.5 million and $1.4 million for the House.

- The health care industry in 2009 spent approximately $1 million per day to lobby Congress on health care reform.

- During the 2008 election, all congressional candidates spent a total of $1.4 billion on their campaigns. This is only 26 percent of the $5.2 billion corporations spent on lobbying during the same two-year period.

Thus, merely by diverting a fraction of their political spending budgets from lobbying to direct campaign advocacy, corporations could easily outspend the candidates themselves by a factor of many multiples. The same is true even if one factors in party spending:

- The single largest lobbying organization—the U.S. Chamber of Commerce—spent more than $144 million in lobbying, grassroots efforts, and advertising in 2009, compared to $97.9 million spent by the RNC and $71.6 million spent by the DNC. Thus, this single corporate-backed trade association is able to outspend the national committees of both political parties *combined*.

- According to *The Atlantic*'s Marc Ambinder, the Chamber's 2009 spending included electioneering in the Virginia and Massachusetts off-year elections, as well as "sizeable spending on advertising campaigns in key states and districts aimed at defeating health care, climate change, and financial reform legislation."

Even corporations that are reluctant to throw their hat into the ring of political spending may find themselves drawn into the fray just to stay competitive in the influence-bidding arms race this decision creates.

Indeed, despite the campaign finance regulations that—until *Citizens United*—attempted to protect our democracy against overt influence-peddling, there are numerous examples to demonstrate that absent such safeguards, special interests will attempt to use all means at their disposal to insure favorable legislative treatment.

- In 2006, the FEC levied a $3.8 million fine—the agency's largest in history—against mortgage giant Freddie Mac for illegally using corporate treasury funds to raise over $3 million for members of the House subcommittee that had regulatory authority over that corporation. Approximately 90% of those funds directly benefited the chair of the subcommittee.

Moreover, corporate campaign ads may be a much more effective route than lobbying for corporations to pressure elected officials to comply with their agendas. Even the most aggressive lobbying effort cannot exert the same direct political pressure on an elected official that a campaign expenditure can. Such corporate campaigning impacts the political survival of elected officials in a way that mere lobbying cannot. An elected official might hesitate to oppose a corporation on a particular piece of legislation if she knows that the corporation could unleash a multimillion attack ad blitz in her next reelection campaign.

Such an example came before the Court just last year in *Caperton v. Massey Coal Co.* In that case, the Supreme Court recognized that large independent expenditures can create actual and apparent bias in the context of judicial elections. In *Caperton,* the CEO of a coal company with $50 million at stake in a case before the West Virginia Supreme Court spent almost $3 million dollars in independent expenditures in support of that candidate's campaign. Writing for the majority, Justice Kennedy, wrote that such large expenditures—expenditures which exceeded the combined expenditures of both candidate committees by $1 million—had "a significant and disproportionate influence on the electoral outcome" and created a "serious, objective risk of actual bias."

In *Citizens United,* the Supreme Court has handed corporate special interests a loaded weapon—whether they ever fire the weapon is, arguably, beside the point. There is every reason to believe that the threat of corporate funded campaign attack ads is likely to distort policy priorities and to allow special interests to dominate federal politics. Perhaps even more profoundly, the Court in *Citizens United* has given the stamp of constitutional approval to corporate electioneering. The Court has invited corporations into elections, telling them that they have a First Amendment right to spend their vast resources to try to influence the outcome of an election. If even a few major corporations with stakes in current policy battles take the Court up on its invitation, the resulting wave of special interest money could undermine the foundations of our democracy.

THE ROBERTS COURT'S "DEREGULATORY TURN"

The limits on corporate campaign spending at issue in *Citizens United* represent the fourth time challenges to campaign finance laws have been argued before the Roberts Court, and the fourth time the Roberts Court majority has struck down such provisions as unconstitutional. As Professor Richard Hasen has explained, this "deregulatory turn" represents an about-face—by contrast, the Rehnquist Court had generally taken a deferential approach to campaign finance reform regulations enacted by federal and state lawmakers. However, now that Chief Justice [John] Roberts and Justice [Samuel] Alito have replaced Chief Justice [William] Rehnquist and Justice [Sandra Day] O'Connor on the Supreme Court, the newly constituted majority has moved with stunning haste to dismantle decades-old safeguards intended to limit the effect of special interest money in politics. Indeed, as Justice Stevens wryly noted, "The only relevant thing that has changed since *Austin* and *McConnell* is the composition of this Court."

With *Citizens United,* the current Supreme Court's majority's hostility to campaign finance law has become apparent to even the most casual observer. At oral argument in *Citizens United,* Justice Antonin Scalia exemplified the majority's unwarranted suspicion of long-standing campaign finance reform safeguards, assuming in his questions that such safeguards represented nothing more than incumbent self-dealing:

> Congress has a self-interest. I mean, we—we are suspicious of congressional action in the First Amendment area precisely because we—at least I am—I doubt that one can expect a body of incumbents to draw election restrictions that do not favor incumbents. Now is that excessively cynical of me? I don't think so.

Justice [Anthony] Kennedy also speculated during oral argument that "the Government [could] silence a corporate objector" who wished to protest a particular policy during an election cycle. Similarly, in the *Citizens United* opinion, Justice Kennedy simply assumed, without any factual basis, that Congress' motives were invidious, stating of the law at issue, "[i]ts purpose and effect are to silence entities whose voices the Government deems to be suspect." And Chief Justice Roberts famously expressed his impatience with campaign finance safeguards, striking down regulations on corporate electioneering in the *Federal Election Commission v. Wisconsin Right to Life* decision, saying "Enough is enough." The Court has used its skepticism of congressional motives—based not on facts or a record below but on the instincts of a majority of justices—to justify its utter lack of deference to legislative determinations in this arena. Such a cavalier dismissal of Congress' carefully considered legislation ignores the years of hearings, record, debate and deliberation involved in creating these reforms.

Unfortunately, *Citizens United* will not be the Roberts Court's last word on the issue. Seeking to take advantage of the majority's deregulatory agenda, the same coalition of corporate-backed groups that filed the *Citizens United* lawsuit have launched an armada of constitutional challenges to state and federal reforms, now advancing rapidly toward the Supreme Court.

These challenges include attacks on public financing systems, campaign finance disclosure requirements, "pay-to-play" restrictions on government contractors and lobbyists, and "soft money" restrictions on political parties and political action committees. Challengers seek to use the First Amendment as a constitutional "trump card" to strike down any reform that attempts to mitigate special interest domination of politics. Several of these challenges will be ripe for decision by the Supreme Court within the year.

This committee has an important role to play in helping to create a factual record that would correct unfounded assumptions about money and politics embedded in the Court's decisions, and could be useful in defending both new and existing reforms against judicial overreaching. In addition, we urge the committee to endorse several reforms to counter the impact of *Citizens United*—supporting public financing of congressional and presidential elections; enacting federal voter registration modernization legislation; and enacting federal legislation that requires shareholder approval for corporate political spending, as well as effective disclosure of such spending.

CONCLUSION—ADVANCING A VOTER-CENTRIC VIEW OF THE FIRST AMENDMENT

Perhaps the most troubling aspect of *Citizens United*—worse than its political implications, worse than its aggressive deregulatory stance—is that the Court embraces a First Amendment where voters are conspicuously on the sidelines. At the start of the *Citizens United* opinion, Justice Kennedy correctly noted that "The right of citizens to inquire, to hear, to speak, and to use information to reach consensus is a precondition to enlightened self-government and a necessary means to protect it." As the opinion proceeded, however, it became evident that the majority was in fact taking a myopic view of campaign finance jurisprudence, one that focuses exclusively on campaigns—candidates, parties and corporate interests—at the expense of the voting citizenry. The Court's ultimate judgment held, in effect, that whatever interest is willing to spend the most money has a constitutional right to monopolize political discourse, no matter what the catastrophic result to democracy.

This aspect of *Citizens United*—like many others—constitutes a break with prior constitutional law. The Court has long recognized that "constitutionally protected interests lie on both sides of the legal equation." Accordingly, our constitutional system has traditionally sought to maintain a balance between the rights of candidates, parties, and special interests to advance their own views, and the rights of the electorate to participate in public discourse and to receive information from a variety of sources. It is crucial that this committee and Congress recognize the Roberts Court's one-sided view of the First Amendment as a distortion—one which threatens to erode First Amendment values under the guise of protecting them. In truth, our constitutional jurisprudence incorporates a strong First Amendment tradition of deliberative democracy—an understanding that the overriding purpose of the First Amendment is to promote an informed, empowered, and participatory electorate. This is why our electoral process must be structured in a way that "build(s) public confidence in that process," thereby "encouraging the public participation and open discussion that the First Amendment itself presupposes." In this post-*Citizens United* era, a robust legislative response will be critical. It is similarly imperative, however, that we reframe our constitutional understanding of the First Amendment value of deliberative democracy. In the longer term, reclaiming the First Amendment for the voters will be the best weapon against those who seek to use the "First Amendment" for the good of the few, rather than for the many.

Permitting Corporations to Participate in Election Campaigns: Constitutionally Appropriate

M. TODD HENDERSON

Let me say at the outset, some of my prior beliefs. First, I believe in the marketplace of ideas and think that more speech is generally better than less speech. I believe the Founders shared this belief and enshrined it in the "no law" component of the First Amendment. I believe this is especially true for speech about politics. Why else would we allow the Nazis to march in Skokie? [This is a reference to a 1978 decision by an Illinois court that under the First Amendment a neo-Nazi group could march and pro-claim its views in Skokie, Illinois, a suburb of Chicago with a large Jewish population.] Other countries don't let Nazi's march because they (rightfully) view their ideas as repugnant. But we let them march. We do so because we are more confident in our cit-izens' ability to know right from wrong, to look beyond rhetoric for substance, and to be able to weigh competing claims of truth. If we didn't trust the people to make deci-sions based on all available information, if we didn't trust the people to be able to filter speech according to its source and content, if we didn't trust the people to know what is good for them, we wouldn't let the Nazi's march. But we let them march.

Second, I believe that we should view extensions of government activity under a pre-sumption of error, especially where there is no evidence of a market failure or where the case for government regulation is suspect, say because of the potential for an incum-bency bias or the possibility of abuse by the forces of totalitarianism. The control we have over our government, which, after all, has a monopoly on legal physical violence, is tenuous and something that requires constant vigilance. Giving incumbent politi-cians the ability to write rules that will make it more likely they will be reelected is something that should be done only, if at all, in the face of overwhelming evidence of the inability of citizens to make sensible political decisions in the absence of these rules.

Third, I believe that people generally want to restrict "corporations" in the abstract from influencing politics, a belief that is born out by recent polling data showing about 70% of people disagree with the result in *Citizens United.* In other words, if we voted on *Citizens United,* I think we would have voted the other way. As I describe below, I do not think this should matter. Based on the first two priors, I think the Court got the case right, and that its countermajoritarian instincts here are a sign of strength in the decision, not weakness.

Here are some thoughts about the case and its aftermath.

First, I think it is amusing how the case is perceived on both sides of the political aisle. Political commentators on the Left have said the case has "more dire implications than Dred Scott" and that "within 10 years every politician in this country will be a prostitute." [In *Dred Scott v. Sandford* (1857) the Supreme Court ruled that escaped slave Dred Scott could not sue for his freedom in federal court because he was proper-ty, not a citizen.] Or take this zinger from Justice [John Paul] Stevens's opinion: "The Court's ruling threatens to undermine the integrity of elected institutions across the Nation" and "do damage to this institution" as well.

The law that was struck down was passed in 2002: The Bipartisan Campaign Reform Act. It was upheld against a facial challenge in a 2003 case called McConnell, which was based on a precedent from 1990, called *Austin [v. Michigan Chamber of*

Commerce]. So pick your time period, pre 2002, pre 1990, whichever. Were all politicians prostitutes of corporate interests, whatever that is, in 1989?

Or, looking at the issue another way, does the fact that the conduct permitted by *Citizens United* was legal in 26 states prior to *Citizens United*, suggest that politicians are hopelessly corrupt in over half our states? What about the fact that prior to the case, companies, unions, and advocacy groups and other agglomerations of individual interests that chose the corporate form could do exactly what *Citizens United* allows them to do if the speech was funneled through "separate segregated funds," commonly known as Political Action Committees? The belief in disaster must be based on a claim that when corporations or unions can fund political speech directly, from so-called treasury funds, instead of indirectly, the flood gates will open and companies will spend much, much more on politics. This is a claim about how corporations act that is highly suspect, a point I will return to in a moment.

Moreover, what about all the money the so-called special interests spend on lobbying members of our legislatures? The campaign finance laws say nothing about this, and which is more likely to influence public policy creation, a drug company running an ad in New Jersey 30 days before the election telling citizens that Senator Henderson is a Marxist who wants to nationalize drug development or that same company spending millions on lobbyists to jawbone existing legislators about the virtues of our current system?

A final point about the hysteria: Do critics of more political speech have such little faith in the people to make decisions that the inevitable consequence of more information about politics will be to bias it in a socially negative direction? Was it really the case that 2 U.S.C. section 441(b), the law at issue in the case, is all that was preserving our democracy? I for one have more faith in the strength of our Union and the wisdom of the people than to think that the byzantine structure of federal election law is all that distinguishes American politics from that of the Ukraine or Nigeria. Even if you believe, as many do, that the average corporation is analogous to the National Socialist party, this does not mean we must necessarily regulate their speech. Remember, we let the Nazis speak.

On the Right the fans are just as simple minded. An op-ed in the Wall Street Journal after the decision argued (lamely) that *Citizens United* is a key victory for business in the battle to reduce the influence of trial lawyers. The unstated suggestion is that companies will give more money and this is a good thing. This is highly suspect, and I suspect that businesses are not in favor of the decision. Every penny spent to influence law is a penny not spent to pay managers, hire workers, innovate, or make shareholders wealthy.

Campaign finance laws can be thought of as a solution to a simple collective action problem: every firm would prefer not to pay politicians not to treat them badly, but none individually have an incentive to refrain from doing so absent collective agreement of the same. An obvious solution to the collective action problem is an agreement among firms to refrain from spending on politics. But this agreement would be illegal under our antitrust laws. Campaign finance laws may be a rough substitute. (Note the irony that laws restricting speech are necessary because of other laws prohibiting firms from acting rationally in their self-interest.)

The zero-sum game aspect of corporate giving can be seen by looking at the donations by businesses in the 2008–2009 election cycle. Business corporations gave $1.96 billion to political campaigns, 50.6% to Republicans, 49.4% to Democrats. They play both sides, making claims of *Citizens United* meaning more corporate influence or better for Republicans somewhat fanciful.

While we are on the subject of partisanship, it is interesting to compare business giving with that by the other major corporate contributors—labor unions, specifically public-employee unions. Unions donated $674 million in 2008–2009 (about one third of what businesses gave), but they gave overwhelmingly to Democrats (92% to 8%). The net contributions from "corporations" were $1.6 billion for Democrats and $1.0 billion for Republicans. The conservative majority of the Court hardly gave Republicans a gift, assuming these ratios continue when the rules are liberalized across the board, and we have no reason to believe they won't be. (For reference, one candidate, our president, raised nearly $1 billion in donations from individuals in that year.)

So it is not at all clear that this case will make things worse or that it favors one political party or the other. It is not even clear that it favors things corporate or business over things uncorporate. After all, there are corporations on the side of almost all issues, especially when we remember that the ACLU, NRA, Sierra Club, AARP, Citizens United, and others are corporations too. Are those anti-corporate readers out there afraid of all of them or just some of them? If you like the ACLU and the Sierra Club, but not the NRA and the AARP, and as a consequence want to ban the speech of the former and not the latter, this is the road to totalitarianism. The Supreme Court is adamant that restrictions on speech cannot be based on content. Tolerating the speech of those we disagree with is one of our most sacred core values.

This case is about just this kind of toleration and the threat of unchecked political power. To see this, consider this passage from the Court in *Citizens United*:

> The law before us is an outright ban, backed by criminal sanctions. Section 441b makes it a felony for all corporations—including nonprofit advocacy corporations—either to expressly advocate the election or defeat of candidates or to broadcast electioneering communications within 30 days of a primary election and 60 days of a general election. Thus, the following acts would all be felonies under §441b: The Sierra Club runs an ad, within the crucial phase of 60 days before the general election, that exhorts the public to disapprove of a Congressman who favors logging in national forests; the National Rifle Association publishes a book urging the public to vote for the challenger because the incumbent U.S. senator supports a handgun ban; and the American Civil Liberties Union creates a Web site telling the public to vote for a presidential candidate in light of that candidate's defense of free speech. These prohibitions are classic examples of censorship.

Let me reframe the Court's holding: the government may not ban political documentaries in the 60 days before an election. This is the end of democracy? The government tried to ban speech about government! Imagine a [Sarah] Palin Administration banning the Michael Moore movie "Dumb as the Average Moose," before the 2016 presidential election? How would those on the Left react to that decision?

The [U.S.] Solicitor General [Elena Kagan] admitted during oral argument that the logical extreme of the law would allow the government to ban book publishers, who happen to have chosen to organize their economic affairs as corporations, from publishing political books before elections. Yes, you read that right. Book banning. This goes to the heart of the First Amendment. Imagine James Madison and Thomas Jefferson traveled to our era and asked about the Bill of Rights. If *Citizens United* came out the other way, we would have to tell them that virtual child pornography and pole dancing are protected by the First Amendment, but books or documentaries about politicians are not. I'm not suggesting that we limit our constitutional interpretation to a what-would-the-Founders-think analysis or even to the plain text (which, by the way, says Congress shall pass no law restricting the freedom of speech), but if the First Amendment means anything, it means protecting speech about politics.

Of course, one could argue that books or documentaries about politicians are OK, so long as the speaker was you or me or all of us acting together, so long as we didn't organize as a corporation. But why should the value of political speech be determined by whether the entity doing the speaking or enabling the speaking is a corporation or person, partnership, or sole proprietorship? Or whether the corporation speaking was a "media corporation," a class of corporations that were exempted from the regulation. So our First Amendment, as previously interpreted, said that the *New York Times* or Fox News could say whatever they want about politics whenever they wanted, but that the ACLU and Apple could not. I see no basis for this in the text of the Amendment or in common sense. What is the difference between a non-media company and a media company? What if Apple started a newspaper? Could it then speak? How about a blog? Is that media? Why should Rupert Murdoch [head of a huge multimedia empire including Fox Network] get to spend and say what he wants on politics, but not News Corp. [the corporation Murdoch controls]? And what is the reason for encouraging businesses that want to speak to choose to organize as partnerships or individuals instead or corporations? Imagine a corporation with one owner—should the corporation not be allowed to speak the same as its sole owner?

One possibility is a concern that when News Corp. spends money on politics, it is spending shareholders' money, or, depending on your point of view, employees' money or other stakeholders' money. This is as true as it is irrelevant. For one, investing is voluntary, and there is no demand for any individual firm's stock. If you own shares in Exxon Mobil, and it decides to spend $1 million to fund ads supporting Sarah Palin for president, you can convert your shares to cash and buy shares of Apple Computer, which is running ads supporting President Obama's reelection. The only time this voting with your feet argument doesn't work is if the conduct causing you to sell also is the cause of a loss of firm value, thus making your shares worth less than they would have been. Given the trivial amounts firms spend or could possibly spend on politics, this is in the world of law-school hypotheticals. (ExxonMobil had political expenditures of about $500,000 in 2008, on profits of nearly $50 billion, or less than 0.001%. We will, of course, have to wait and see how much they spend next year, but, for the reasons I describe below, I'd be shocked if it was orders of magnitude more. Even if they spent 1,000 times more, the expenditures would be only 1 percent of profits, something unlikely to move the stock price needle significantly.)

Business corporations exist to make money, and donations to candidates will be aimed in that direction. Insofar as they are, shareholders should be happy, and if they aren't, they can exert influence by selling their shares. If instead, the claim is just corporate influence, as opposed to this agency costs story, then we are back to puzzles about individual contributions, donations by PACs, lobbyists, and so on. Corporations spend handsomely to lobby politicians, and shareholders don't complain. Why? Because presumably the lobbying is about increasing firm value—that is, making money for shareholders. Why do we think other forms of political spending would be different?

Moreover, firms are very jealous and protective of their reputations. Do you think Nike is going to risk its brand by spending billions to elect politicians that may offend 49% of the population? And if they do, don't we have faith in other constraints on such attempts at manipulation? Consumer boycotts, news reports, publicity by non-profits, and so on are likely to cause firms to be quite cautious in their attempts to buy politicians outright.

Finally there is the claim that business are creatures of the state and therefore the state should be able to tell them what to do. This certainly used to be the case, when state legislatures gave businesses permission to do only certain things in return for, well, political contributions and favors. But thankfully we've moved past this so-called concession theory. The concession theory is plainly inconsistent with the contractarian model of the firm, which treats corporate law as nothing more than a set of standard form contract terms provided by the state to facilitate private ordering. Limited liability can be created by contract as easily as it can by state diktat, and no matter what, if we have this view of government power, it has no end. Everything exists in some way because of government action or inaction, but that is not the basis of our government. We believe our rights exist not because of the government, but rather the other way around—the government exists to protect our preexisting rights.

Let me close with three final observations.

First, I think the case is interesting in how it reveals the schism on the Court (and in all of politics) between those with faith in experts and those with faith in markets. The campaign finance laws, and the dissenters' views of elections law, are premised on a belief that we can design rules, no matter how layered and complex, that can be implemented by well-meaning bureaucrats with the result that we can take the money/corporate influence/corruption out of politics and finally create Democracy. These people are uncomfortable with uncertainty and unknown outcomes, and believe we should plan our way to some sort of utopia. The *Citizens United* majority, on the other hand, seems to have a distrust in experts and regulating natural things out of existence, preferring instead to rely on markets to work toward the optimal state of affairs. Of course, there is a tradeoff between a belief in centralized versus diffuse knowledge, and the question is how much of each. In short, I think the *Citizens United* majority looked at the elaborate regulatory regime, the relative ineptness of the Federal Election Commission bureaucrats charged with implementing it, and decided to err on the side of the marketplace of ideas.

Second, we should not forget the history of our regulation of corporate speech, which, by the way, survives *Citizens United*. The first law banning corporate contributions in federal political elections was based in part about the content of corporate speech. The Tillman Act, passed in 1907 is named for Senator Benjamin Ryan "Pitchfork Ben" Tillman from South Carolina, one of the most reprehensible public servants in our history. Tillman argued that, "The negro must remain subordinated or be exterminated," and openly called for the murder of blacks in order to, "keep the white race at the top of the heap." Tillman wanted to restrict corporate speech to reduce the influence of Northern corporations, which were opposed to segregation. We should not condemn restrictions of corporate speech for this reason, but we should remember that the motives behind allegedly idealistic legislation are not always what they seem. Sometimes corporations have good things to say; sometimes they have bad things to say. Telling them they cannot speak prevents us from hearing both during a crucial period before our elections.

Finally, some critics deride the case as "activist" and inconsistent with claims about the proper judicial role made by some of the justices in the majority. Of course the claim of activism is as silly as the claim of courts as simply calling balls and strikes, as the Chief Justice [John Roberts] has argued. Some of the Court's job is calling balls and strikes, but most is about policy. And, some of the best court decisions are countermajoritarian. Consider *Meyer v. Nebraska* (1923), which dealt with a state law banning foreign language instruction for young children, passed during the anti-German hysteria of World War I. The Nebraska Supreme Court had upheld the ban, writing, "The legislature had seen the baneful effects of permitting foreigners, who had taken residence in this country, to rear and educate their children in the language of their native land." [Justice] Oliver Wendell Holmes followed his views about judicial restraint and dissented. But the Court got it right. Activism was essential to preserve our liberty.

In *Citizens United*, the Court decided that we cannot trust the government to tell us what we should be hearing about our political system. In the view of this corporate law professor, this is a victory for our democracy.

THE CONTINUING DEBATE:
Permitting Corporations to Participate in Election Campaigns

What Is New

Congress did nothing in the aftermath of the *Citizens United* decision to try to mitigate the impact of the decision. At least one reason is that incumbents in Congress are much more likely to get large donations from interests groups and other corporations than are challengers. Therefore it is to the disadvantage of the incumbents, whether Republican or Democrat, to limit the flow of money. As for this writing, it is too early to tell what, if any, impact the decision will have on the 2010 election cycle.

Where to Find More

Details of campaign fund raising and spending, including by your members of Congress, are on the site of The Center for Responsive Politics at www.opensecrets.org/. Also good is the Hoover Institution's site on campaign finance at www.campaignfinancesite.org/. More officially, you can find information from the Federal Elections Commission at www.fec.gov/. Good information on reform legislation and regulations should also be on the site of the Campaign Legal Center at www.campaignlegalcenter.org/.

What More to Do

This is one of those cases where the details are very important. Even if you support reform, it is important to see that at some point limiting what individuals and groups can spend to influence elections begins to unduly restrict their free speech and their right to try to influence policy—abilities that are at the core of democracy. It is also worth considering how appropriate it is to distinguish between organizations based on their professed purpose: business, union, civic organizations, ideological groups, and so on. Also, should wealth be a barrier to fully airing one's views, even if they are corporate? Yet democracy also entails some degree of equality among people's ability to have influence, and the money factor clearly skews that. What would you advise Congress to do, if anything?

9 POLITICAL PARTIES

THE FORESEEABLE FUTURE OF PARTY POLITICS:
Dominant Democrats *or* Resurgent Republicans?

DOMINANT DEMOCRATS

ADVOCATES: David W. Brady, Professor of Political Science; Douglas Rivers, Professor of Political Science; and Laurel Harbridge, graduate student in Political Science, all at Stanford University

SOURCE: "The 2008 Democratic Shift," *Policy Review* (December, 2008)

RESURGENT REPUBLICANS

ADVOCATE: Jay Cost, political analyst and blogger, Real Clear Politics

SOURCE: "The 'Enduring Majority'—Again: No, the Democrats Will Not Be in Power Forever," *National Review* (June 8, 2009)

This debate brings to mind the classic tune, "The Party's Over," originally made famous by Judy Holliday in the 1956 Broadway musical *Bells Are Ringing* and also recorded by Frank Sinatra and others. The theme of the lyrics is captured in two lines:

> The party's over, it's time to call it a day,
> They've burst your pretty balloon and taken the moon away.

Judy Holliday was singing about lost love. In the first reading of this debate David W. Brady, Douglas Rivers, and Laurel Harbridge might use the words to back up their theme that the Republican Party has faded from the affections of a majority of American voters, who have found increased and enduring new warmth for the other major party, the Democrats. In the second reading, Jay Cost recognizes the electoral pounding Republicans took in 2006 and 2008, but concludes that the idea of an "enduring Democratic majority" is a false image.

There can be little doubt that the immediate picture was bright for Democrats when Brady, Rivers, and Harbridge published their article in late 2008. The Democrats had regained control of Congress in 2006. Then a Democratic landslide in 2008 brought a Democrat to the presidency and further decimated the Republicans in Congress. Overall between 2000 and 2009, Republican membership plummeted from 55 to 40 in the Senate and from 228 to 178 in the House.

Recent history clearly shows, however, that current success does not necessarily translate into positive long-term prospects. Just three decades ago, the Watergate scandal that forced President Richard M. Nixon to resign in August 1974 also tainted his Republican Party, which lost 48 House seats in that November's elections. When the new Congress convened in 1975, the Democrats held 291 seats in the House, more than two-thirds of the total, against only 144 Republicans. The GOP also lost five Senate seats, leaving it almost nearly as lop-sided, with 60 Democrats, 38 Republicans, and 2 independents. The Democrats made even further gains in both houses in 1976 when their presidential nominee, Jimmy Carter, captured the

White House, and the opinion columns and talk-show airwaves around the country were full of predictions about the imminent demise of the Republican Party.

That did not occur. Republicans Ronald Reagan and George H.W. Bush won the presidency in 1980 and 1984 and in 1988 respectively. The GOP also gained in Congress and was the majority party in the Senate for six years under Reagan. Then Democrat Bill Clinton won the 1992 presidential election, but the uncertain start of his presidency helped cost Democrats 54 House seats in 1994. When the 104th Congress convened in January 1995, the GOP controlled both houses of Congress for the first time since 1954. The pundits touted the so-called "Republican revolution." Then George W. Bush completed the Republican trifecta by edging Al Gore for the presidency in 2000. To make matters even better for the Republicans, they gained seats in Congress in 2002, thereby overcoming the tradition of the president's party losing seats in the off-year elections.

Do these shifts in recent decades mean that one or the other party cannot dominate for a significant period? The answer is no. The Republicans controlled both houses of Congress for all but six years (1913–1919) between 1901 and 1933. During this time, Woodrow Wilson (1913–1921) was the sole Democratic president. Then the Democrats took control with the election of President Franklin D. Roosevelt. Except for four years (1947–1949, 1953–1955), they then were a majority in the Senate until 1981 and in the House of Representatives until 1995. Furthermore, Democrats served as president for 8 of the 12 presidential terms between 1933 and 1981.

The difference between short-term reverses for the parties and long-term shifts in their relative power relates to whether defeats are based on immediate questions such as specific candidates or issues, or if defeats reflect a major shift in voter attitudes. The later can occur in three ways. One is when party strength in an important group of voters shifts. Women, for example, have become considerably more Democratic in recent decades. A second shift is when members of a group vote in increasing numbers. African Americans, who are solidly Democratic voters, have increased their participation rate considerably. Third, a group can grow in size. Latinos are a rapidly growing demographic group, and their party leaning, pro-Democrat so far, is beginning to have a marked impact on elections.

POINTS TO PONDER

➤ Why is it that many more Americans say they are Democrats than Republicans if 41% say they are conservative, compared to just 17% saying they are liberal (with 39% moderate, and 3% unsure)?

➤ Republicans are debating whether the best change to regain their strength is by being even truer to their conservative principles or being more flexible to attract middle-of-the-road voters. Which strategy would you recommend?

➤ Think about how Cost analyzes Latino partisan preferences. Would you be as optimistic as he is that Latinos are slowing becoming more Republican?

The Foreseeable Future of Party Politics:
Dominant Democrats

DAVID W. BRADY, DOUGLAS RIVERS, AND LAUREL HARBRIDGE

After the 2004 presidential election, Republicans appeared to be in good shape. They had won the presidency, had a 30-seat margin in the House of Representatives and 55 U.S. Senators. Four years later, the situation is very different. Republicans lost 31 House seats, six Senate seats, and control of both chambers of Congress in the 2006 midterms. In addition to losing the presidency, Republicans lost approximately 20 more House seats and at least six more Senate seats in the 2008 elections. Not since the Hoover administration have Republican fortunes been reversed so clearly and precipitously.

These shifts are, we think, indicative of a more fundamental change in partisan loyalties that could reshape American politics for a generation. Starting in the late 1960s and continuing through 2004, Republicans posted consistent, steady gains in standard measures of partisan support. Democrats held almost a 20-point advantage over Republicans in the period from 1952, when the American National Election Studies (ANES) started measuring party identification, through the mid–1960s. Starting in the 1970s and accelerating during the Reagan years, Republicans narrowed this gap to less than five percent, with near partisan parity in the 2000 and 2004 presidential elections. At the same time, the geographic bases of the parties shifted, with Democrats winning the Northeast and West Coast and Republicans holding almost everything in between.

In four short years, Democrats have reclaimed most of the ground they lost during the Reagan era…[The] percentage of Democrats and Republicans in six different media polls between 2005 and 2008…show the trend in Democratic self-identification and the trend in Republican self-identification, with Democrats now having an advantage between 5 and 10 percent. The question wording and procedures used by the different polls vary, but the pattern is unmistakable. Pew, Gallup, *New York Times*/CBS, *Washington Post*/ABC, and *Wall Street Journal*/NBC all show party identification moving away from the Republicans. Only the *Time* polls show gains for Republicans and even here the net shift is toward the Democrats.

In this article, we investigate why voters shifted toward the Democrats following the 2004 election and its short- and long-term implications for party competition. Part of Republicans' difficulties comes from widespread dissatisfaction with the Bush administration and its handling of the economy and the war in Iraq. These are retrospective evaluations whose effects will tend to diminish over time. But another cause of Republican troubles appears to be the ideological positioning of the Republican Party, particularly on social issues. The positions that appeal to the Republican base are repelling moderates the party needs to maintain its long-term competitiveness. These voters are not lost to Republicans—yet. Most consider themselves independents or leaning or weak Republicans, not Democrats. They are not liberals and remain closer, on average, to Republican positions than those espoused by the Democrats, but they are up for grabs.

THE NATURE OF PARTISAN CHANGE

While the polls generally agree about the magnitude of the Democratic shift, these surveys do not tell us why such a shift has occurred. To understand why Republican support has fallen off so dramatically, we utilize a unique data source. Starting in 2004, YouGov/Polimetrix has interviewed samples of American voters using Web surveys.

The sample used here consists of 12,881 respondents who participated in at least one interview during the 2004 election campaign and were re-interviewed in 2008 as part of a series of surveys for the *Economist*. This allows us to trace individual voters over this time-span. We can identify actual voters who said they were Republicans in 2004, but who had become independents or even Democrats by 2008.

In both 2004 and 2008, our respondents were asked to place themselves on the traditional seven-point party-identification scale. This is a two-part question that first asks:

> Generally speaking, do you think of yourself as a Republican, a Democrat, an independent, or what?

Democrats and Republicans were then asked whether they are a "strong" or "not-so-strong" Democrat or Republican, while independents and others were asked if they "lean toward" one party or the other. This yields a seven category scale: strong Democrat, weak Democrat, leaning Democrat, independent, leaning Republican, weak Republican, and strong Republican.

Very few Republicans actually become Democrats. Only 1.2 percent of the strong Republicans and 8.0 percent of the weak Republicans from 2004 say they are Democrats or lean Democratic in 2008. Instead, the decline of Republican strength occurs when strong Republicans become weak Republicans, weak Republicans become independents, and independents lean more Democratic or even becoming Democrats. These voters are not necessarily permanently lost to the Republican Party, but this has the look of an emerging party-realignment, with the Republican base shrunken substantially.

Some more detail on the nature and size of the Democratic shift is shown in Table 1, which shows how respondents in each of the seven party-identification categories moved between 2004 and 2008. For example, among pure independents (i.e., independents who did not lean toward either party), 34.6 percent were stable and gave the same answer in 2008 as 2004. Of the remainder, 37.5 percent moved in the Democratic direction (either identifying as weak or strong Democrats or as leaning toward the Democrats) while 27.9 percent moved in the Republican direction, for a net gain of 9.6 percent for the Democrats. Overall we see a shift of 6.0 percent toward the Democrats, consistent with the shifts seen in media polling.

TABLE 1

Shifts in Party Identification 2004–2008

2004 Party Identification	Change from 2004 to 2008		
	More Democratic	Stable	More Republican
Strong Democrat	—	85.1%	14.9%
Weak Democrat	39.5%	0.8%	19.7%
Lean Democrat	41.9%	48.9%	9.2%
Independent	37.5%	34.6%	27.9%
Lean Republican	16.1%	49.6%	34.3%
Weak Republican	26.3%	38.6%	35.2%
Strong Republican	21.1%	78.9%	—
Total	21.1%	63.7%	15.1%

Respondents in the two extreme categories—strong Democrats and strong Republicans—can move only in one direction. Because there are only seven categories, strong Democrats cannot become "stronger" on this scale. Similarly, strong Republicans can only become more Democratic. However, if we compare strong Democrats with strong Republicans we see that the Democratic losses among strong identifiers are smaller than the corresponding Republican losses among their strong identifiers. The same pattern holds for weak identifiers and leaners. Weak Republicans actually became more Republican by a 35.2 percent to 26.3 percent margin, but weak Democrats became more Democratic by an even larger 39.5 percent to 19.7 percent margin. Across the board, Democrats do better with their identifiers than Republicans do with theirs. The Republican net-losses are smallest among their base of strong identifiers and somewhat larger among weak Republicans and largest among independents leaning Republican.

WHAT CAUSED THE DEMOCRATIC SHIFT?

What caused these voters to switch their party identification between 2004 and 2008? The increase in Democratic support was not limited to independents, who typically exhibit more volatility in their partisan loyalties than voters in each party's base. These are, for the most part, voters who supported George Bush's reelection in 2004 and voted for Republican congressional candidates, but who have subsequently become more Democratic (or, perhaps more accurately, less Republican). One can think of any number of reasons for them to have moved in this direction, but most explanations fall into two broad categories; dissatisfaction with the performance of the Bush administration or estrangement from the Republican Party on ideological grounds. An obvious answer would appear to be President Bush's unpopularity.

Presidents and their parties are usually blamed for bad economic news (and sometimes credited for positive news) that occurs on their watch. The second Bush administration has had a large share of bad economic news with little positive to report. Rapid increases in oil prices and the most severe financial crisis since the onset of the Great

Depression alone would be enough to make a president and his party unpopular. In fact, much of the decline in Republican support is associated with negative assessments of President Bush. Table 2 shows the percentage of Republicans who shifted toward the Democrats between 2004 and 2008 among different groups of voters. For instance, 63.0 percent of persons who were strong Republicans in 2004 and strongly disapproved of President Bush's job performance became more Democratic. There are, of course, not many Republicans (much less strong Republicans) who came to hold such a negative assessment of Bush, but those who did are now much weaker Republicans than they were previously.

TABLE 2

Percentage Becoming More Democratic 2004–2008

2004 Party Identification	Strong Republican	Weak Republican	Leaning Republican
Ideology			
Very Conservative	14.1%	11.0%	14.4%
Conservative	20.9%	21.8%	13.0%
Moderate	39.0%	34.7%	20.3%
Gay Marriage			
Strongly oppose	19.6%	19.4%	8.1%
Somewhat oppose	17.0%	22.2%	14.7%
Somewhat favor	23.3%	27.3%	19.2%
Strongly favor	53.2%	47.7%	27.5%
War in Iraq			
Not a mistake	20.3%	25.8%	13.1%
Not sure	29.4%	28.6%	24.5%
A mistake	60.0%	51.4%	46.4%
Bush approval (2008)			
Strongly approve	7.6%	13.9%	9.7%
Somewhat approve	21.6%	19.2%	11.3%
Somewhat disapprove	37.8%	30.2%	22.8%
Strongly disapprove	63.0%	57.8%	41.9%

However, Bush's steep decline in popularity, as well as Republicans' loss of control of Congress, preceded the economic events of 2007–08. An obvious alternative explanation is the war in Iraq, which 54 percent of the public now thinks was a mistake. Opposition to the war is much stronger among Democrats than Republicans, but even among Republicans enthusiasm for the war has waned considerably over the past five years. A majority of strong and weak Republicans who turned against the war by 2008 moved in the Democratic direction. This is a fairly sizable group, and the proportions becoming more Democratic are large. The public has tired of the war in Iraq and one casualty may be the Republican Party.

Dissatisfaction with the performance of President Bush and the U.S. intervention in Iraq are matters of retrospective evaluation, not fundamental ideology. We also have examined the relationship between voters' ideological preferences and their support for the Republican Party. Among "very conservative" Republicans, between 11.0 percent and 14.4 percent became more Democratic between 2004 and 2008—a fairly modest number, offset (except among strong Republicans) by larger numbers of voters who became more Republican. This is the new Republican base: ideologically committed to conservative positions across a wide range of issues, including not only taxes and the size of government, but also abortion, gay rights, immigration, and gun control. Among those who consider themselves just "conservative" (and not "very conservative") there is more movement in the Democratic direction (between 13.0 percent and 21.8 percent become more Democratic), but the movement is not that big or significant.

In contrast, among self-described "moderates" there have been large losses, with 39.0 percent of the strong Republican moderates becoming more Democratic. These are (or were) marginal Republicans and the last four years have shrunken their numbers substantially. The larger losses among peripheral Republicans mean that the Republican base is not just smaller, but more conservative than it was before 2004.

Nowhere is this trend more apparent than on the issue of gay marriage. In 2004, all eleven states which had a referendum involving gay marriage on the ballot voted to ban the practice. A majority of voters still oppose gay marriage, as evidenced by the passage of Proposition 8 banning gay marriage in California. The Republican Party is clearly associated with opposition to gay marriage, and most Republican voters also oppose it. However, Republicans who do not share the party's enthusiasm for attacking gay marriage have weakened their ties to the party. Approximately half of the Republicans strongly in favor of gay marriage became more Democratic between 2004 and 2008.

Dislike of President Bush and his policies was one driving force behind movement toward independence and becoming Democratic. It is possible that some Republicans moved Democratic because on issues not specifically related to President Bush, they favored Democratic issue positions. In order to test this hypothesis, we selected a set of issues where party differences are apparent: universal health care, worries over global warming, gay marriage, abortion rights, and illegal immigration. The Republican response was coded as follows: Opposed to universal health care, think effects of global warming haven't started, opposed to any legal recognition of same-sex couples, favor no abortions or abortion only in cases of rape and incest and, finally, favor deportation of illegal immigrants. [We then plotted] the percent taking the Republican response for each of the three categories of respondents: stable Republicans, Republicans who moved to independent, and Republicans or independents who moved to Democratic. The results consistently show that those who remain Republican are more likely to favor the Republican position on these issues. However, the opinions of Republicans who moved to independent are quite close to the opinions of stable Republicans. Only those respondents who now identify as Democrats are, on average, between 40 and 60 points different from stable Republicans in their positions. Those who left the Republican Party to become independents or Democrats were more likely to favor universal health care, gay marriage, pro-choice abortion rights and believe that global-warming effects were already present. Only on deporting illegal immigrants is the support from stable Republicans and Republicans who moved to independents equivalent. Thus, a combination of disliking President Bush and his policies and beliefs that the government should do more to guarantee health care, combat global warming, ensure rights for same-sex couples, maintain or strengthen pro-choice abortion rights and not deport illegal immigrants moved a significant number of Republicans toward the Democratic Party.

The shape of the new electoral landscape [shows that]...not surprisingly, strong Republicans are to the right of weak and leaning Republicans, who are to the right of independents. [During their respective elections, voter perceived] Barack Obama and John Kerry...to be about halfway between the "liberal" and "very liberal" labels. (Interestingly, Democrats perceive their candidates as being more moderate than Republicans do, but our focus here is on Republican voters.) President Bush [was] perceived as being almost as far to the right by these voters as Kerry and Obama [were] to the left. John McCain, on the other hand, [was] judged to be fairly close to the center, almost on top of the average location of weak and leaning Republicans.

In electoral competition, the median position will, *ceteris paribus* [all other things being equal], defeat any other position. In 2008, we witnessed the anomaly of a better situated candidate—McCain—doing worse than a more extreme candidate—Bush— did in the preceding election. The problem is that other things are not equal in this case. The combination of a poor economy, an unpopular war, and a party (rather than a candidate) positioned too far to the right is too much for a candidate to overcome. Even quite explicit attempts by McCain to distance himself from the Bush administration did not convince many voters that he represented a real break from Bush.

It is important to note that these voters are still closer to either the Bush or McCain positions in terms of general ideology than they are to either of the Democratic candidates. The Republican Party doesn't have to move too far to recapture these voters. The dilemma Republicans face, however, is that the Republican base prefers to have candidates close to their own views on social issues, even if this means losing elections.

2008 AND BEYOND

The evidence of a significant erosion in Republican support is consistent, but its meaning is unclear. Dissatisfaction with the state of the economy or the war in Iraq or Bush's job performance are matters of retrospective evaluation. The public was, at one point, supportive of the war and of Bush. That they turned sour on these does not necessarily have long-term implications for the viability of Republican candidates. In 1964, Lyndon Johnson won an FDR-like victory over the Republican candidate, Barry Goldwater, capturing over 60 percent of the popular vote and 486 Electoral College votes. On the congressional front, Democrats held 68 Senate seats and 290 seats in the House of Representatives. Articles abounded on the dismal future of the Republican party, yet in 1968, Richard Nixon defeated Hubert Humphrey and Republicans dominated presidential elections for the next 40 years (7 of 10 presidential elections, to be exact). In 1976, however, a poor economy and the residue of Watergate prevented Republican Gerald Ford from being elected (though he came close). Yet the presidency of Jimmy Carter, who beat Ford, was a single term, and Republicans won five of the subsequent seven presidential elections. The Republican comeback from 1964 and 1976 were largely the result of the failed policies of Johnson and Carter and not of any shifts in permanent party-identification toward the Democrats. Such short-term fluctuations in party identification are the norm, whereas relatively permanent party realignments are often forecast, but rarely realized.

We cannot rule out a similar trajectory today, with the trends that we have identified being transitory rather than permanent. But it is also possible, and in our judgment more likely, that we are witnessing an election similar to 1980, in which the election signified a longer-term trend that lasted nearly a quarter century. Today we have two parties with quite distinct ideological positions and electoral bases. The Democratic base is urban and liberal, while the Republican base is suburban or rural and conservative. The problem for Republicans is that their base is slowly shrinking and they cannot win without the support of moderates.

Bush's reelection strategy in 2004 depended upon mobilizing the Republican base. This strategy succeeded brilliantly in securing his reelection, but the perils of playing to one's base are evident in the losses Republicans have incurred among moderates and moderate conservatives. This has been compounded by the unpopularity of the Bush administration and the war in Iraq. The 2004 strategy of mobilizing the Republican base seems, in retrospect, to have been an effective way of winning a battle but losing the war. Despite nominating a candidate in 2008 who is perceived by most Republicans to be less conservative than George W. Bush, moderate Republicans have been fleeing the party in large numbers.

In 2008, the McCain campaign tried to focus on foreign policy and personality, areas in which McCain was perceived to be more experienced and less risky than Obama. McCain called himself a "maverick" and tried to separate himself from President Bush on several issues (such as global warming). But on most issues the actual differences between McCain and Bush were small. On abortion, gay marriage, and universal health care, McCain's positions appeal more to the base than to the switchers. In the end, none of this positioning could have much impact in the face of a financial crisis, regarding which Republicans, rather than Democrats, seemed like the riskier alternative.

The national exit poll showed that McCain won the votes of 90 percent of self-identified Republicans, while Obama won 89 percent of self-identified Democrats. Unfortunately for McCain and Republicans, only 32 percent of voters now call themselves "Republicans" (compared to 39 percent who say they are Democrats) and Obama won the independent vote by a 52–44 margin. Particularly concerning for Republicans is that 18- to 24-year-olds voted overwhelmingly for Obama (by a 66–32 margin).

The Republican Party left in the Senate and the House is more conservative than in any of the Bush Congresses, as Republican losses were predominantly moderates like Chris Shays of Connecticut. The average Republican in the Senate has shifted rightward and the policies he prefers are distinctly to the right of those preferred by the average voter in the electorate. The voters who left the Republican Party over the last four years are like the independents who make up about a third of the electorate—political moderates—and unless the Republican leadership can figure out how to combine fiscal conservatism with moderate views on social and other issues, the trend away from the Republican Party is likely to continue.

After any electoral defeat, there is always a predictable debate between those who attribute the loss to a compromise of principles versus those who think not enough was compromised. The post-election analysis among Republicans will have to deal with the question of declining membership and what issue-position mix will bring back lost members and appeal to independents. The declining Republican base makes it obvious that purity on social issues is an unpromising strategy for a conservative party that needs to widen its appeal. A political party that starts an electoral cycle with 7 percent fewer party identifies than its competitor and a base that prefers policies to the right of independents and moderates is set up for a long, dry run similar to that of the post-FDR era Republicans.

The Foreseeable Future of Party Politics: Resurgent Republicans

JAY COST

After the Democrats' triumphs in two consecutive elections, left-wing pundits have returned to an old meme: The party's majority will be enduring. In a report published by the Center for American Progress, liberal author Ruy Teixeira boldly proclaimed: "A new progressive America has emerged with a new demography, a new geography, and a new agenda....All this adds up to big change that is reshaping our country in a fundamentally progressive direction....These trends will continue." Other liberals—most notably John Judis of *The New Republic* and Alan Abramowitz of Emory University— have similarly argued that Obama's election ushered in a new, enduring Democratic majority.

This essay will rebut some of the claims made by advocates of this idea. It will also offer a broader perspective on how to understand the 2008 election, and what it means for the Republican party and conservatives in the future.

What makes this task difficult is that it's hard to nail down exactly what the phrase "enduring Democratic majority" is supposed to mean. Which "progressive" policies will be passed? How much control over the government will Democrats have? For how long will they have it? Just how enduring will it be? These questions are typically left unanswered. Recently Judis commented to the *Huffington Post*: "The only circumstances that could bring back the Republicans is Obama's failure to stem the recession." This, of course, would make it indistinguishable from just about every majority in the country's history.

If this sounds like an unfalsifiable hypothesis to you, you're not alone. Judis and Teixeira floated a version of the same argument in their book *The Emerging Democratic Majority* in 2002, just a few months before the Republicans regained control of the Senate and increased their majority in the House. After the 2006 midterm election, they resurrected their thesis in an article for *The American Prospect* titled "Back to the Future" and subtitled "The re-emergence of the emerging Democratic majority." To explain away the years of GOP dominance, they invented a new psychological concept—"de-arrangement." What this means, they explained, is that:

> the focus on the war on terror not only distracted erstwhile Democrats and independents but appeared to transform, or de-arrange, their political worldview. They temporarily became more sympathetic to a whole range of conservative assumptions and approaches.

This is a textbook case of special pleading. If creating an ad hoc concept out of whole cloth is the only way to salvage a theory, it's time to find a new theory. The concept is not particularly helpful to them, either. After all, couldn't conservatives explain away 2006 and especially 2008 with "de-arrangement"? Perhaps our cool, ultra-liberal president bewitched true Republicans with his post-partisan campaign gibberish, and these voters will soon see the error of their ways.

Ultimately, engaging with the advocates of the "enduring Democratic majority" hypothesis is like punching sand. The rules of the game are set up so that the majority is considered enduring even if a recession terminates it or it is interrupted by years of Republican governance. In other words: Heads they win, tails you lose.

It is fairly easy to get away with this kind of unrigorous thinking when you are preaching to the liberal choir. However, this argument has found its way into conservative circles, usually among pundits who blame the party's decline on a lack of attention to their favorite issue. That's misguided, because while the party has been in tough spots before, it has bounced back pretty quickly. Every time the party has suffered a setback, like 1992, it was not long before a comeback, like 1994. Even after Franklin Roosevelt swept the Democrats into office in the 1932 elections, and extended Democratic gains in 1934 and 1936, Republicans came bouncing back in 1938, returning to Capitol Hill with enough numbers to block New Deal legislation with the first of many bipartisan conservative coalitions.

Nevertheless, I sense that many conservatives think the current period in the wilderness will actually last 40 years. This feeling of dread is not a huge surprise, given the attention the "enduring Democratic majority" hypothesis has received from the iron triangle of the mainstream media, the Democratic party, and left-wing interest groups. What follows should help conservatives see that there is a lot more sizzle than steak to this idea.

As we go through the details, it's important to keep the big picture in mind. Analysts like to talk about the movement of this or that group in the last election, but the context is of crucial importance. Voters cast their ballots last fall amid an economy that was shrinking at a 6.3 percent annual rate. This was a dramatic contraction, precipitated by a financial calamity that had struck just weeks before. Additionally, President Bush's job approval had fallen to less than 30 percent due to largely non-ideological concerns like his handling of Iraq and Hurricane Katrina. That's an unwinnable environment for any party. When you're losing, you're losing. Nothing in the data looks particularly good, but this does not mean the data are always going to look bad. The course of politics is not a straight line, and liberal analysts are simply wrong to assume that subsequent elections will look like the previous one.

One point often cited by proponents of the enduring-majority hypothesis is the voting preference of young Americans. There is no doubt that President Obama scored a huge victory among young voters, winning 66 percent of those under 30. Proponents think this group of voters will be important to the party's continuing success.

Perhaps—but this is the same argument we might have heard in 1972, when George McGovern lost the popular vote by 23 points but won voters aged 18 to 24 by a point. In 1976, now aged 22 to 28, this cohort voted for Jimmy Carter roughly in line with the whole country. They went slightly for Ronald Reagan in 1980, and in 1984 and 1988 the GOP had a breakthrough, as they voted for Reagan and then for George H. W. Bush at the same rate as the whole country. By 2008, these voters—most of them now in their late 50s—went for Obama by a point. Given that the whole country voted for Obama by 7 points, we'd have to conclude that they now have a Republican tilt. In other words, though this cohort of voters looked quite Democratic when they were young, the GOP won them over later, when the political pendulum swung its way again.

It's like your financial analyst's disclaimer: Past performance is no guarantee of future results. As young voters age, their lives change, and so can their politics. One big source of change is marriage. Typically, committed conservatives vote Republican and committed liberals vote Democratic, regardless of marital status. But for moderates and the non-ideological, marriage makes a big difference. In 2000 and 2004, George W. Bush did better than Al Gore and John Kerry among moderate voters of nearly all ages if they were married. The big question for the future, which advocates of the enduring-majority view cannot yet answer, is: Will young, unmarried voters follow the older cohorts and trend to the GOP after they marry, or will they stay with the Democrats? None of this is meant to minimize the significance of Obama's accomplishment in bringing young voters to his side, or the work that conservatives will have to do to win over the so-called Millennial Generation. The point is that one cannot simply extrapolate from the 2008 results.

Then there are the "professionals." This is the rather tendentious term typically applied to anybody with a graduate degree. The idea here is that these voters—driving hybrids, shopping at co-ops, hyphenating their last names, and so on—are more sympathetic to progressive views, and are solid Democrats.

Indeed they are. But so what? First of all, the fraction of "professionals" has held fairly constant since 1988, making up 16 to 18 percent of the electorate. They have consistently voted 3 to 7 more points Democratic than the rest of the nation. Given their relatively small size, they have not been decisive. They have not stopped the GOP from winning three of the last six presidential elections, or holding the House of Representatives for twelve years in a row.

It's hard to argue that there's been much of a shift along educational lines. Of all college-educated voters who voted for one of the two major parties, Obama won 53 percent. Ditto non-college voters. In 1992, Bill Clinton performed about the same across education groups, after factoring out the Perot vote: He won 53 percent of college grads and 55 percent of non-college grads. So in 16 years, not much has changed.

Those who expect an enduring Democratic majority also make much of the fact that, in a few decades, the United States will be a minority-majority nation, with whites making up less than half the population. Whether or not this is true, I can say that they tend to overstate the consequences of the underlying trend.

Let's start with black voters. There is no doubt Obama performed very well with them. Typically, the GOP wins about 10 percent of the black vote. In 2008, John McCain won just 4 percent. Obama also brought an unprecedented number of black Americans to the polls. Last year, blacks actually constituted a larger share of the electorate than they do of the population as a whole.

The critical question, as yet unanswerable, is whether these numbers can be sustained. Is this a "personal" vote for Obama, or the beginning of a new trend? It is too soon to say. Nevertheless, we can say that the GOP's performance with blacks has been horrible. George W. Bush won only 26 percent of self-identified conservative blacks in 2004. In other words, black Americans who are ideologically sympathetic to the GOP still vote heavily Democratic. The Republicans need to work on this. Minimally, they should strive to make black conservatives comfortable voting for the conservative party.

Hispanics are another matter, though you can't tell that to most advocates of the enduring-majority hypothesis. In a recent article, Abramowitz—arguing that demographic trends will favor the Democrats for decades—allocated white conservatives to the GOP and white liberals to the Democrats, and predicted that white moderates would be swing voters. He then allocated all ethnic and racial minorities to the Democrats. This must have come as a shock to the 3.67 million Hispanics who voted for McCain last year. They are a testament to the fact that Hispanic voters cannot be viewed through the same lens as black voters. In fact, they have recently behaved more like white voters, breaking for the party that is closer to their ideology. George W. Bush won 69 percent of Hispanic conservatives and 41 percent of Hispanic moderates in 2004. He did better than any previous Republican by winning about 40 percent of all Hispanics.

Hispanics swung against McCain in 2008, but the Arizona senator still won the same share as George H. W. Bush did in 1988, even though the latter ran in a much more favorable political climate. Additionally, McCain did better than Gerald Ford in 1976 and Bob Dole in 1996. In other words, Hispanics have slowly become more Republican in recent cycles. To place them in the Democratic column so confidently is to ignore this, as well as Bush's breakthrough in 2004. But maybe these deviations can be chalked up to de-arrangement, too.

Nevertheless, conservatives must make outreach to Hispanics a priority—especially if they want to win states such as Nevada, Colorado, and New Mexico. Even though Bush did better with Hispanic conservatives than with black conservatives, too many still "defected" to Kerry. Obama probably won many more Hispanic conservatives, so there is a lot of work to be done. Abramowitz and other Democrats might be content to overlook Bush's performance among Hispanics, but conservatives should not overlook Obama's.

Finally, any discussion about the burgeoning minority vote favoring the Democrats must acknowledge that the GOP has done better with white voters in recent decades. No Democrat has won a majority of whites since Lyndon Johnson in 1964, although Jimmy Carter came close in 1976. Bill Clinton nearly won a plurality in 1992 and 1996. Yet Al Gore lost the white vote to George W. Bush by twelve points in 2000, and Bush improved among whites in 2004, winning 58 percent despite a tough war in Iraq and weak job growth after the 2001 recession. This was about the same share his father pulled in 1988, though the elder Bush had the benefit of running on years of peace and job-creating prosperity.

John McCain won 55 percent of the white vote, the largest share ever to go to a losing presidential candidate, even though President Bush was hugely unpopular and the country was plummeting into a deep recession. Part of McCain's success with whites was probably due to hesitation among some to vote for a black candidate; just as Obama may have won some votes because of his race, he may have lost others. Still, the 2008 result fits with a trend we have seen for 40 years. Whereas Carter and Clinton won Arkansas, Kentucky, Louisiana, Tennessee, and West Virginia thanks to strong showings among white voters, those voters have since flocked to the Republican party, pushing these states out of reach for the Democrats, even in years that favor their party as heavily as 2008 did.

This migration of whites to the GOP has helped counter the advantage the Democrats might otherwise have enjoyed from demographic changes. The net effect of all this has been imperceptible to date. Compare the election of 2008 with the last time the Democrats took the White House, in 1992. That year, the Democrats nominated a fresh-faced, 40-something governor promising change amid a weak economy and an unpopular incumbent named Bush. He won 53.5 percent of the two-party vote and 370 Electoral College votes. In 2008, they nominated a fresh-faced, 40-something senator promising change amid a weak economy and an unpopular incumbent named Bush. He won 53.7 percent of the two-party vote and 365 Electoral College votes.

Ultimately, the increasing share of non-whites in the population might tip the scales to the Democrats, as proponents of the enduring-majority hypothesis suggest. But that claim rests on the assumption that the GOP will not match their gains with equal improvements among whites and Hispanics. In other words, those partial to the "enduring Democratic majority" hypothesis are arguing for the continuation of some recent trends but against the continuation of others.

The comparison between 1992 and 2008 is instructive. From a certain perspective, they are extremely similar: a weak economy, an unpopular incumbent, and so on. The top-line numbers look identical—but underneath them are dramatically different voting coalitions. What conclusions can we draw from this?

First, voting coalitions are in flux. This is the principal reason to question the "enduring Democratic majority" hypothesis—it rests on the false assumption that the parties' electorates are static. Voting coalitions change because the parties work to change them. In 2000 Governor Bush surveyed President Clinton's voting coalition and realized that it was vulnerable in several spots. He exploited those vulnerabilities in his race against Clinton's vice president, Al Gore. Eight years later, Senator Obama found weaknesses in Bush's coalition that he could exploit in his race against Senator McCain. This process is not unique. Each successful challenger finds marginal voters on the other side who can be persuaded to switch. The fact that Obama did this does not mean that the 200-year process is somehow at an end. It means that it is continuing.

This is precisely what we should expect from two broad-based political parties whose objective is to acquire power in our diverse republic: The losers will adapt to the new environment, and the winners will have trouble keeping their voters in the fold. Governing coalitions are stitched together around limited, common goals, and as politicians achieve those goals the coalitions unravel. How was it, for instance, that high earners voted Democratic in 2008? One reason was the GOP's 1980s cuts in tax rates. Those tax cuts have long since come to be taken for granted, removing an issue for the party and thus making it a victim of its own success.

Defeating the party of an unpopular incumbent is the easy part. The hard part is governing to the satisfaction of a majority coalition—which the Democrats have not yet done. Holding his coalition together could be real trouble for Obama. It remains to be seen whether the people who voted for him can be united around some positive goals, or whether they simply voted against Bush and the recession. Candidate Obama was adept at obfuscation during the campaign, trying hard to be all things to all people, but you can't do that when you're actually running the government; you have to decide who wins and who loses.

Michael Barone [a mildly conservative political commentator] has noted that Obama has a top-bottom voting coalition, which could be unstable. The core of Bush's support came from middle earners, with a tilt toward the upper end. Obama's electorate, on the other hand, samples heavily from the poles. This presents an obvious policy problem. The president is promising large increases in government benefits, which will go mostly to lower-income voters. How to pay for it? Heavy tax increases on high earners will damage him among his upper-income voters. If he raises taxes too many times, the wealthy suburbs around Philadelphia and D.C. will suddenly start trending red again. So what to do? It seems the president's solution is $1 trillion budget deficits from here to eternity. Will the middle tolerate that? Those who earn between $50,000 and $100,000 per year were not terribly partial to Obama last November—and their incomes are such that they are already sacrificing important goals as they balance their family budgets. How will they react when they see Obama abandoning the last pretenses of fiscal discipline?

In the final analysis, I'd suggest that the "enduring Democratic majority" theory consists of a few good ideas surrounded by a lot of wind. The liberals who offer it are honest and well-intentioned, but their enthusiasm has gotten the best of them. Their thesis appears to be impervious to falsifying evidence. Its empirical claims are overstated and offered without appropriate context. It fails to take into account American electoral history, in particular how and why the parties have shared power over time and why we can expect that to continue into the future. Conservatives should focus on finding a way back to the majority, and ignore those who say it can't be done.

THE CONTINUING DEBATE:
The Foreseeable Future of Party Politics

What Is New

The first test of the competing ideas in this debate came in the November 2010 congressional elections. When this book went to press less than three months before those elections, President Obama's public approval rating had plummeted from 68% when he was inaugurated in January 2009 to 45% in late August 2010. While the Democrats had led national voting for the House of Representatives in 2008 by an impressive 53% to 47%, an August 2010 poll of registered voters showed 47% of them saying they would vote Republican in 2010, with only 44% intending to vote Democratic and 9% unsure. Most analysts were projecting a Democratic debacle in November, possibly including the loss of control of the House. What occurred? If the dire predictions of a massive setback for the Democrats were accurate, then the idea of an emerging, long-term dominant Democratic era was dealt a considerable blow. But if the Democrats' losses were moderate or less, then the idea was at least partially validated because the president's party usually loses some seats, especially in the House, during "off-year" elections. During such elections from 1954 through 2006, the president's party lost seats all but twice and lost an average of 16 seats. Given the very difficult economic times, a Democratic loss in 2010 near that average could be interpreted as a sign of Democratic strength. Losses up to the mid-thirties, allowing the Democrats to retain control of the House, could arguably be construed as not undermining the idea of an emerging Democratic dominance.

Where to Find More

There are various theories about cycles, party eras, and other periodic changes in the strengths of political parties. To explore these, see Samuel Merrill, Bernard Grofman, and Thomas L. Brunell, "Cycles in American National Electoral Politics, 1854–2006: Statistical Evidence and an Explanatory Model," *American Political Science Review* (2008) and Norman Schofield, Gary Miller, and Andrew Martin, "Critical Elections and Political Realignments in the USA: 1860–2000," *Political Studies* (2003). An article on how voters deal with the intersection of parties and policies is Thomas M. Carsey and Geoffrey C. Layman, "Changing Sides or Changing Minds? Party Identification and Policy Preferences in the American Electorate," *American Journal of Political Science* (2006). For day-to-day politics, go to the Web sites of the two major parties: the Republican National Committee is at http://www.rnc.org/ and the Democratic National Committee at http://www.democrats.org/. Also good for ongoing politics is the *National Journal* at www.nationaljournal.com/njonline/.

What More to Do

Conduct your own post-election analysis of what happened in November 2010. Also look at polls to see if Americans have shifted their party loyalties. Even if the Democrats suffered sharp losses in 2010, that may have been just a short-term phenomenon if more people have not started to identify as Republicans and fewer people are identifying as Democrats. Two sites to find polls on party identification are the Gallup Poll at www.gallup.com and the Harris Poll at www.harrisinteractive.com/.

10 VOTING/CAMPAIGNS/ELECTIONS

ELECTING THE PRESIDENT
Adopt the National Popular Vote Plan *or* Preserve the Electoral College?

ADOPT THE NATIONAL POPULAR VOTE PLAN

ADVOCATE: National Popular Vote, an advocacy organization

SOURCE: "Agreement Among the States to Elect the President by National Popular Vote," from the Web site of National Popular Vote, April 29, 2009

PRESERVE THE ELECTORAL COLLEGE

ADVOCATE: John Samples, Director, Center for Representative Government, Cato Institute

SOURCE: "A Critique of the National Popular Vote Plan for Electing the President," *Policy Analysis*, October 13, 2008

Most Americans do not understand clearly how they elect their presidents. When one poll asked "What is meant by the Electoral College?" only 20% of those surveyed correctly responded that it elected the president. Another 35% gave various incorrect answers, and 46% admitted they did not know. Another survey asked how the election would be resolved if there was a tie in the Electoral College. "By the House of Representatives," the correct answer, was chosen by 25% of the respondents, while 24% incorrectly chose the Senate. Another 32% thought that whomever had won the popular vote would become president, 2% guessed that a coin toss would decide the election, and 17% said they did not know.

It is worrisome that most people did not know what the Electoral College is, but they can hardly be blamed for not knowing the intricacies of the complex procedure. Basically, the Electoral College is an indirect process for selecting the U.S. president. Each state selects a number of electors equal to its combined representation in the U.S. House and Senate, and the District of Columbia gets three electors, for a total of 538 electors. The exact process for choosing electors varies by state, but as a general rule each party or candidate selects a slate of electors. It is for one of these slates that the people vote in November. In all states except Maine and Nebraska, there is a "winner-take-all" system in which the slate that receives the most votes wins. Then the individual electors cast their separate ballots for president and vice president in December. The ballots are sent to Congress, where they are counted in early January. It takes a majority of all electoral votes (270) to win. If no individual receives a majority, then the House selects a president from among the candidates with the three highest electoral votes. Each state casts one vote in the House, and it requires a majority of the states (26) to win. The Senate, with each member voting individually, chooses a vice president from among the top two electoral vote recipients. This type of election by Congress as happened twice (1800 and 1824).

You will see in the following readings that there are many objections to, and countering defenses of, the Electoral College. The most important is that it is possible for one candidate to win the popular vote and another to win the Electoral College and become president. This has occurred three times (1876, 1888, and 2000). In 2000, Al Gore received 51,003,238 popular votes to only 50,459,624 votes for George W. Bush in the 2000 presidential election. Yet Bush became president when he received 271 electoral votes to Gore's 266. More generally, the winning candidate's share of the popular vote and share of the electoral vote are never the same. In 2008, for example, Barack Obama received 67.8% of the electoral votes, while getting only 52.9% of the popular vote.

Whether such outcomes are acceptable is for you to decide, but they are a product of the way the electoral college was consciously designed. Congress is constructed to balance the equality of the states in a federal system (with each state getting two votes in the Senate) and the idea of majority rule (with each state's population largely determining its number of seats in the House). Thus, there was never any assumption that the president should or would be elected by a majority popular vote when the delegates at the Constitutional Convention in Philadelphia created the Electoral College. Indeed, a second motive for the Electoral College was to insulate the selection of president from the people. As Alexander Hamilton explained in *Federalist* #68 (1788), he and others worried that the "general mass" would not "possess the information and discernment requisite to such complicated investigations," raising the possibility of "tumult and disorder." This is part of the reason why the Constitution left it up to each state to determine how its electors are chosen. At first most states had their legislature choose the electors. During the first presidential election in 1789, the electors were chosen by popular vote in only four states. It was the presidential election in 1804 before a majority of states used the popular vote to pick electors, and the last state legislature did not give up its ability to choose electors until South Carolina did so in 1860.

Over time members of Congress have introduced over 700 proposals to reform or eliminate the Electoral College, and polls dating back to 1944 show a majority of Americans up until the 1960s favoring its dissolution. Yet it survives in part because amending the Constitution is so difficult. Some years ago, those who favor electing the president by popular vote thought of a possible way to get around the need for a constitutional amendment and launched an effort to institute the National Popular Vote (NPV) plan. It is well described in the first reading, which also advocates its adoption and decries the Electoral College. The second reading defends the Electoral College in general and criticizes the NPV plan as an alternative.

POINTS TO PONDER

➢ Remember that it is possible to both (a) favor eliminating or revising the Electoral College and (b) oppose the NPV plan.
➢ Which is more important, the aspect of federalism that is part of the Electoral College vote calculation or the "majority rules" aspect of the NPV plan?
➢ What do you make of the arguments that the NPV plan is/is not constitutional?

159

Electing the President:
Adopt the National Popular Vote Plan

NATIONAL POPULAR VOTE

The National Popular Vote bill would guarantee the Presidency to the candidate who receives the most popular votes in all 50 states (and the District of Columbia).

The National Popular Vote bill has been enacted by states possessing 61 electoral votes—23% of the 270 necessary to activate the law (Hawaii, Washington, Illinois, New Jersey, and Maryland).

The bill has passed 27 legislative chambers in 17 states, including Arkansas, California, Colorado, Hawaii, Illinois, Maine, Maryland, Massachusetts, Michigan, Nevada, New Jersey, New Mexico, North Carolina, Oregon, Rhode Island, Vermont, and Washington.

The bill is currently endorsed by 1,659 state legislators—763 sponsors (in 48 states) and an additional 896 legislators who have cast recorded votes in favor of the bill.

In numerous Gallup polls conducted since 1944, about 70% of Americans have supported a national popular vote for President (with only about 20% opposed and about 10% undecided). The *Washington Post*, Kaiser Family Foundation, and Harvard University poll show 72% support for direct nationwide election of the President.

State-level polls (most taken after the November 2008 election) show strong support for a national popular vote for president in battleground states, small states, Southern states, border states, and numerous other states. Support is strong among Republican voters, Democratic voters, and independent voters, as well as every demographic group surveyed. State polls have been conducted in Arkansas (80%), California (70%), Colorado (68%), Connecticut (73%), Delaware (75%), Kentucky (80%), Maine (77%), Massachusetts (73%), Michigan (73%), Mississippi (77%), Missouri (70%), New Hampshire (69%), Nebraska (74%), Nevada (72%), New Mexico (76%), New York (79%), North Carolina (74%), Ohio (70%), Pennsylvania (78%), Rhode Island (74%), Vermont (75%), Virginia (74%), Washington (77%), and Wisconsin (71%). Details, including cross-tabs, are available at www.NationalPopularVote.com/.

The *New York Times* endorsed National Popular Vote's plan (March 14, 2006) by calling it an "innovative new proposal" and "an ingenious solution" urging that "Legislatures across the country should get behind it." The *Chicago Sun-Times* called National Popular Vote's plan "thinking outside the box" and said "It's time to make the change with this innovative plan" (March 1, 2006). The *Minneapolis Star-Tribune* said "It's a lot to ask the Legislature to do the right thing and endorse the new compact. But it really should. So should other states—both red and blue—join, for the sake of a better democracy" (March 27, 2006). The *Los Angeles Times* endorsed the plan on June 5, 2006. The *Sacramento Bee* endorsed the bill saying "The governor and senators can get this process rolling in other states by acting this session" (June 3, 2006). Common Cause and Fair Vote have also endorsed the plan.

The National Advisory Board of National Popular Vote includes former congressmen John Anderson (R-Illinois and later independent presidential candidate), John Buchanan (R-Alabama—the first Republican elected to represent Birmingham), Tom Campbell (R-California), and Tom Downey (D-New York), and former Senators Birch Bayh (D-Indiana), David Durenberger (R-Minnesota), and Jake Garn (R-Utah).

The National Popular Vote bill is described in the 620-page book, *Every Vote Equal: A State-Based Plan for Electing the President by National Popular Vote*. The book was first released at National Popular Vote's press conference on February 23, 2006 in Washington, DC.

SHORTCOMINGS OF THE CURRENT SYSTEM

The current system of electing the president has several shortcomings—all stemming from the winner-take-all rule (i.e., awarding all of a state's electoral votes to the presidential candidate who receives the most popular votes in each state).

Because of the state-by-state winner-take-all rule, a candidate can win the presidency without winning the most popular votes nationwide. There have been four "wrong winner" elections out of the nation's 56 presidential elections. This is a failure rate of 1 in 14. But because half of American presidential elections are landslides (i.e., a margin of greater than 10% between the first- and second-place candidates), the failure rate is actually 1 in 7 among the non-landslide elections. Given that we are currently in an era of non-landslide presidential elections (1988, 1992, 1996, 2000, 2004, and 2008), it is not surprising that we have already had one election in this recent string of six elections won by the second-place candidate. Moreover, a shift of a handful of votes in one or two states would have elected the second-place candidate in five of the last 12 presidential elections. A shift of 60,000 votes in Ohio in 2004 would have elected Kerry, even though President Bush was ahead by 3,500,000 votes nationwide. A switch of fewer than 22,000 votes in 2004 in New Mexico, Nevada, and Iowa would have wiped out President Bush's majority in the Electoral College. The second-place candidate was elected in 2000, 1888, 1876, and 1824.

Another shortcoming of the current system is that voters in two thirds of the states are effectively disenfranchised in presidential elections because they do not live in closely divided "battleground" states. Under the winner-take-all rule, presidential candidates have no reason to poll, visit, advertise, organize, or campaign in states that they cannot possibly win or lose. In 2008, candidates concentrated over two-thirds of their campaign visits and ad money in just six states and 98% in just 15 states. This means that voters in two thirds of the states are ignored in presidential elections.

Both shortcomings have a single cause—the states' use of the winner-take-all rule. The winner-take-all rule is not mentioned in the U.S. Constitution. It is not a federal law. It was not the choice of the Founding Fathers. It was used by only three states in the nation's first presidential election. The winner-take-all rule exists only in state law. States have the power to change these state laws at any time.

HOW THE NATIONAL POPULAR VOTE BILL WOULD WORK

At the present time, the Electoral College reflects the voters' *state-by-state* choices for president in 48 states. In Maine and Nebraska, the Electoral College reflects the voters' *district-by-district* choices. The United States can have nationwide popular election of the president if the states change the manner of choosing their presidential electors so that the Electoral College reflects the voters' *nationwide* choice. This means changing the state laws that establish the state-level winner-take-all rule (or, in Maine and Nebraska, the district-level winner-take-all rule).

Under the state legislation proposed by National Popular Vote, the popular vote counts from all 50 states and the District of Columbia would be added together to obtain a national grand total for each presidential candidate. Then, state election officials in all states participating in the plan would award their electoral votes to the presidential candidate who receives the largest number of popular votes in all 50 states and the District of Columbia.

Under the proposal, no state would act alone in offering to award its electoral votes to the nationwide winner. Instead, the National Popular Vote plan would take effect only when the plan has been enacted by states collectively possessing a majority of the electoral votes—that is 270 of the 538 electoral votes. This threshold guarantees that the presidential candidate receiving the most popular votes nationwide would win enough electoral votes in the Electoral College to become president. The 270-vote threshold corresponds essentially to states representing a majority of the people of the United States. The result would be that every vote in all 50 states and the District of Columbia is equally important in presidential elections.

The National Popular Vote plan is an interstate compact—a type of state law authorized by the U.S. Constitution that enables states to enter into a legally enforceable contractual obligation to undertake agreed joint actions. There are hundreds of interstate compacts, and each state in the United States belongs to dozens of compacts. Examples of interstate compacts include the Colorado River Compact (allocating water among seven western states), the Port Authority (a two-state compact involving New York and New Jersey), and the Multi-State Tax Compact. Some compacts involve all 50 states and the District of Columbia. Interstate compacts are generally subject to congressional consent.

As an additional benefit, National Popular Vote's plan would eliminate the (unlikely) possibility of faithless presidential electors. The presidential candidate receiving the most popular votes in all 50 states and the District of Columbia would receive a guaranteed majority of at least 270 electoral votes coming from the states enacting the compact, and the nationwide winner candidate would receive additional electoral votes from whatever non-compacting states happened to be carried by the nationwide winner. Thus, in practice, the presidential candidate receiving the most popular votes nationwide would end up with about three-quarters of the electoral votes—more than enough to eliminate the remote possibility that an unfaithful elector could affect the outcome.

Because the presidential candidate receiving the most popular votes nationwide would be guaranteed enough electoral votes in the Electoral College to become president, another benefit of the National Popular Vote plan is that it would eliminate the possibility of a presidential election being decided by the House of Representatives (where each state would have one vote) and the vice-presidential election being decided by the U.S. Senate.

Nationwide election of the president would reduce the possibility of close elections and recounts. The current system regularly manufactures artificial crises even when the nationwide popular vote is not particularly close. Even though President Bush was 3.5 million votes ahead of Kerry in 2004 on election night, the nation had to wait until Wednesday to see if Kerry would dispute Ohio's all-important 20 electoral votes. A shift of 60,000 votes in Ohio in 2004 would have given Kerry a majority of the electoral votes, despite President Bush's 3,500,000-vote lead in the nationwide popular vote. Similarly, the disputed 2000 presidential election was an artificial crisis created by one candidate's 537-vote lead in Florida in an election in which the other candidate had a 537,179-vote lead nationwide (1,000 times greater). In the nation's most controversial presidential election, Tilden's 3.1%-lead in the popular vote in 1876 was greater than Bush's substantial 2.8%-lead in 2004; however, a constitutional crisis was created by very small popular-vote margins in four states (889, 922, 1,050, and 1,075). With a single massive pool of 122,000,000 votes, there is less opportunity for a close outcome or recount (and less incentive for fraud) than with 51 separate smaller pools, where a few hundred popular votes can decide the presidency.

To prevent partisan mischief between the November voting by the people and the mid-December meeting of the Electoral College, the compact contains a six-month blackout period if any state ever wishes to withdraw from the compact. The blackout period starts on July 20 of each presidential election year and runs through the January 20 inauguration. Interstate compacts are contracts. It is settled compact law and settled constitutional law that withdrawal restrictions—very common in interstate compacts—are enforceable because the U.S. Constitution prohibits a state from impairing any obligation of contract.

Under existing law in 48 of the 50 states, the state's electoral votes are cast by a group of presidential electors who were nominated by the political party whose presidential candidate carried their particular state. People nominated for this position are almost invariably long-time party officials or activists. Under the proposed compact, the 270 or more electoral votes possessed by the states belonging to the compact would be cast by a group of presidential electors nominated by the political party whose candidate won the nationwide vote in all 50 states and the District of Columbia. This group of electors—sufficient to guarantee the election of a president—would reflect the will of the voters nationwide. None of these presidential electors would be voting contrary to his or her political inclinations or conscience. Instead, the 270 (or more) presidential electors associated with the candidate who won the nationwide vote would simply vote for their own party's presidential nominee (i.e., the nationwide choice of the voters from all 50 states and the District of Columbia). This approach implements the desire of an overwhelming majority of Americans (over 70% in recent polls), namely that the candidate who gets the most votes nationwide should become president.

Some may argue that voters would be uncomfortable with the electoral votes of their state being cast for a candidate that won the national popular vote—but not necessarily their state's vote. However, the public is not attached to the current system. Indeed, less than 20% of the public supports it. A nationwide popular vote for president inherently means that the winner would no longer be determined on the basis of which candidate carries individual states but, instead, on the basis of which candidate receives the most citizen votes in all 50 states and the District of Columbia. All of the 270 (or more) presidential electors from the states enacting the compact will be from the political party associated with the nationwide winner. When these electors cast their votes for the candidate who received the most votes nationwide, they will be implementing the method of electing the president that has long been supported by an overwhelming majority of Americans; the method that the people's elected representatives have enacted into law; and the method under which the campaign will have been conducted.

THE EXCLUSIVE POWER OF THE STATES TO AWARD THEIR ELECTORAL VOTES

The U.S. Constitution gives the states exclusive and plenary control over the manner of awarding their electoral votes. The manner of conducting presidential elections is covered in Article II, Section 1, Clause 2 of the U.S. Constitution. "Each State shall appoint, in such Manner **as the Legislature thereof may direct**, a Number of Electors...." (emphasis added).

The constitutional wording "as the Legislature thereof may direct" contains no restrictions. It does not encourage, discourage, require, or prohibit the use of any particular method for awarding a state's electoral votes. In particular, the U.S. Constitution does not mention two of the most prominent present-day features of American presidential elections—the winner-take-all rule (awarding all of a state's electoral votes to the candidate winning the state) and citizen voting for president. These features were not part of the original Constitution, nor were they installed by any subsequent federal constitutional amendment. Instead, these features were established by state laws that were enacted, over a period of decades, on a state-by-state basis.

The winner-take-all rule was used by only three states when the Founding Fathers went back to their states to organize the nation's first presidential election in 1789. Today, it is used by 48 of the 50 states. A federal constitutional amendment was not required, nor used, to enact the winner-take-all rule in these 48 states. The 48 states simply used the power that the Founding Fathers gave them to enact this particular method for awarding their electoral votes on a state-by-state basis. The states may change their decisions concerning the winner-take-all rule, at any time, by enacting a different state law.

Only half the states participating in the nation's first presidential election gave voters a voice in presidential elections, whereas no state legislature has chosen the state's presidential electors since 1876. A federal constitutional amendment was not required, nor used, to confer the presidential vote on the people. States simply enacted state laws implementing this concept.

The fact that Maine enacted a congressional-district system in 1969 (and Nebraska did the same in 1992) is a reminder that the manner of awarding electoral votes is entirely a matter of state law. Maine and Nebraska did not need a federal constitutional amendment to modify the winner-take-all rule because the winner-take-all rule was never part of the U.S. Constitution in the first place. The legislatures of Maine and Nebraska simply used the power that the Founding Fathers gave the states to decide how to award their electoral votes.

The U.S. Supreme Court has repeatedly characterized the authority of the states over the manner of awarding their electoral votes as "plenary" and "exclusive."

In short, there is nothing in the U.S. Constitution that needs to be changed in order to implement nationwide popular vote of the president. This change can be accomplished in the same manner as the current system was originally adopted—namely the states using their exclusive and plenary power to decide the manner of awarding their electoral votes.

NATIONWIDE POPULAR ELECTION WILL GIVE A VOICE TO SMALL STATES

It is sometimes asserted that the current system helps the nation's least populous states. It is also sometimes asserted that the small states confer a partisan advantage on one political party. In fact, neither statement is true.

Twelve of the 13 smallest states are almost totally ignored in presidential elections because they are politically non-competitive. Idaho, Montana, Wyoming, North Dakota, South Dakota, and Alaska regularly vote Republican, and Rhode Island, Delaware, Hawaii, Vermont, Maine, and DC regularly vote Democratic. These 12 states together contain 11 million people. Because of the two electoral-vote bonus that each state receives, the 12 non-competitive small states have 40 electoral votes.

However, the two-vote bonus is an entirely illusory advantage to the small states. Ohio has 11 million people and has "only" 20 electoral votes. As we all know, the 11 million people in Ohio are the center of attention in presidential campaigns, while the 11 million people in the 12 non-competitive small states are utterly irrelevant. Nationwide election of the president would make each of the voters in the 12 smallest states as important as an Ohio voter.

The fact that the bonus of two electoral votes is an illusory benefit to the small states has been widely recognized by the small states for some time. In 1966, Delaware led a group of 12 predominantly low-population states (North Dakota, South Dakota, Wyoming, Utah, Arkansas, Kansas, Oklahoma, Iowa, Kentucky, Florida, Pennsylvania) in suing New York in the U.S. Supreme Court. Delaware and the other states argued that New York's use of the winner-take-all rule effectively disenfranchised voters in their states. The Court declined to hear the case (presumably because of the well-established constitutional provision that the manner of awarding electoral votes is exclusively a state decision). Ironically, defendant New York is no longer a closely divided "battleground" state (as it was in the 1950's and 1960's) and today suffers the very same disenfranchisement as the 12 non-competitive small states. A vote in New York is, today, equal to a vote in Wyoming—both are equally worthless and irrelevant in presidential elections.

NATIONWIDE POPULAR ELECTION WILL MEAN A 50-STATE CAMPAIGN

Although no one can accurately predict exactly how a presidential campaign would be run if every vote were equal throughout the United States, it is clear that presidential candidates would have to run 50-state campaigns. It would be politically impossible, under a nationwide vote, for presidential candidates to ignore two-thirds of the states, as they now do.

In round numbers, both major party candidates have time for about 450 campaign visits during a three-month presidential campaign (coincidentally, a number that is roughly equal to the number of congressional districts in the country, namely 435). Presidential candidates now concentrate their 450 visits heavily in battleground states, such as Ohio and Wisconsin, while virtually ignoring the equally-populous near-by states of Illinois and Indiana. In a nationwide vote for president, every vote would be equally important throughout the country. The Republican Party would suddenly care about whether its share of the vote in Indiana was 58% or 62% (as opposed to its 60% share in 2004), and it would therefore campaign in Indiana. Similarly, the Democratic Party would campaign in Indiana because it would care whether its (losing) share was 38%, 40%, or 42%. Therefore, in a nationwide vote for president, both presidential candidates would have to start paying specific attention to issues of concern to Indiana. Failure to campaign in every state, or failure to campaign in the current spectator states, would be punished as surely and severely as a gubernatorial or senatorial candidate is punished if he or she ever seems to be ignoring areas inside a state, presidential candidates could not continue to concentrate over two-thirds of their campaign visits in just six states, and over 80% in just nine states. Thus, in a nationwide vote, each presidential campaign would have to reallocate its limited campaigning resources over all the states. On average, candidates would allocate one visit to each congressional district.

A small state such as Idaho with two congressional districts could reasonably expect two visits from both the Democratic candidate and the Republican candidate.

Currently, of course, Idaho receives no attention from either party because the Republican candidate has nothing to gain in Idaho, and the Democratic candidate has nothing to lose. Although Idaho would undoubtedly continue to deliver a popular-vote majority to the Republican presidential candidate, every vote in Idaho would suddenly matter to both the Democrat and the Republican candidates. It would be folly for John Kerry to write off Idaho because he would care if he lost Idaho by 227,000 versus a somewhat smaller or larger number. Similarly, it would be folly for George Bush to take Idaho for granted because he would care if he won by 227,000 versus some larger or smaller number. As the *Idaho State Journal* editorialized in 2004, "As we enter the home stretch of the quadrennial horse race known as the presidential election, it's time to remember that this is an election for the president of the United States of America—all 50 states, not an election for the president of the Swing States of America."

The expenditure of money for advertising, organizing, and campaigning is allocated in a manner that parallels campaign visits. In round numbers, both major-party candidates (and their closely allied groups) had about a half billion dollars at their disposal in 2004 (that is, an average of roughly $1 million for each of the nation's 435 congressional districts). Under a nationwide vote, each presidential campaign would have to reallocate its campaigning resources over all the nation's 435 congressional districts. Thus, on average, candidates could be expected to allocate one visit to each congressional district and $1,000,000.

Although it is sometimes conjectured that a national popular election would focus only on big cities, it is clear that this would not be the case. Evidence as to how a nationwide presidential campaign would be run can be found by examining the way presidential candidates *currently* campaign *inside* battleground states. Inside Ohio or Florida, the big cities do not receive all the attention. And, the cities of Ohio and Florida certainly do not control the outcome in those states. Because every vote is equal inside Ohio or Florida, presidential candidates avidly seek out voters in small, medium, and large towns. The itineraries of presidential candidates in battleground states (and their allocation of other campaign resources in battleground states) reflect the political reality that every gubernatorial or senatorial candidate in Ohio and Florida already knows—namely that when every vote is equal, the campaign must be run in every part of the state.

Further evidence of the way a nationwide presidential campaign would be run comes from national advertisers who seek out customers in small, medium, and large towns of every small, medium, and large state. A national advertiser does not write off Indiana or Illinois merely because a competitor makes more sales in those particular states. Moreover, a national advertiser enjoying an edge over its competitors in Indiana or Illinois does not stop trying to make additional sales in those states. National advertisers go after every single possible customer, regardless of where the customer is located.

Electing the President: Preserve the Electoral College

JOHN SAMPLES

The U.S. Constitution provides for the election of the president of the United States in Article II, section 1 and in the Twelfth Amendment. Article II states: "Each State shall appoint, in such Manner as the Legislature thereof may direct, a Number of Electors, equal to the whole Number of Senators and Representatives to which the State may be entitled in the Congress." The Twelfth Amendment provides for the casting of electoral ballots, a majority of which suffices for election. For well over a century, almost all states have elected to cast their votes by the unit rule in which the winner in a state receives all of that state's electoral votes. The National Popular Vote (hereinafter NPV) plan proposes an interstate compact to bring about direct election of the president of the United States. States that join the compact would agree to cast their electoral votes for the winner of the national popular vote for president. The compact would become valid once states with a majority of presidential electors sign on. Congress must approve of the compact before states can agree to it. By July 1, 2008, four states—Hawaii, Illinois, New Jersey and Maryland—had passed NPV; the four together control 50 electoral votes. Supporters also say the proposal has been introduced in 42 states. They hope NPV will govern the 2012 presidential election. I begin this analysis by examining the differences between NPV's plan for electing the president and the Constitution's method for doing so. I then turn to NPV's effects on the relative influence of the states in presidential elections. Although the NPV seeks to equalize the power of voters, it is Congress and state legislators that will decide the fate of this proposal. The latter will wish to know if the NPV enhances or depreciates the influences of their constituents on a presidential election. Finally, I will evaluate the costs and benefits of NPV.

NPV AND THE STATUS QUO

NPV sets as its goal implementing a nationwide popular election of the president and vice president, a significant change from the constitutional status quo. Under NPV, presidential electors "would reflect the nationwide will of the voters—not the voters' separate statewide wills." The states that are parties to the compact would award all their electoral votes to "the presidential slate receiving the most popular votes in all 50 States and the District of Columbia." Taken together, those votes would number at least 270 electoral votes, i.e. the necessary majority for election.

NPV does not necessarily impose election by a majority. If a plurality suffices for election, a majority of voters may have chosen someone other than the winner. Under NPV, the nation is the electoral district. In the current way of electing the president, the states are important. States qua states are represented in a presidential election because electors are allocated on the basis of both population and states. State legislatures also decide how to allocate their electors. Each state constitutes an electoral district for purposes of allocating a state's electors. NPV thus proposes to change the way Americans elect a president by eliminating the states as election districts in favor of the nation.

The current system allows states more choices in how to allocate electors. As noted, NPV proposes a winner-take-all system that follows the national popular vote; each state in the compact allocates all its electors to the candidates with the most popular votes nationwide. The Constitution empowers state legislatures to decide how to allocate electors. In practice, almost all states have selected a winner-take-all rule for allocating their electoral votes. A few states have chosen other methods of allocation, now and in the past. All votes would be equally weighted under NPV. As we shall later learn, there are several ways of measuring the influence of individual votes under the Electoral College. Clearly the framers did not intend to create a means to elect presidents that depended on equal weighting of individual votes. The representation given states qua states precluded such equality from the start. This move toward equal weighting of votes also suggests how different NPV would be from the constitutional status quo.

We may summarize the differences between the two ways of electing a president. The Constitution assigns importance to the states in electing the president. NPV recognizes only a national electoral district in which individuals cast equally-weighted votes. The states matter only as contractors to the NPV compact; the agreement itself makes the allocation of state electors a function of a plurality of voters in the national district. The constitutional plan does not restrict how states may allocate their electors although almost all have chosen a winner-take-all system. NPV requires the states to have a winner-take-all system that follows the votes of a national plurality or majority. The actual majority or plurality vote for president in a state has no influence on the election of the president. In general, NPV proposes two changes to the current means of electing the U.S. president. It eliminates states as electoral districts in presidential elections. It creates through a state compact a national electoral district for the presidential election. In that way, the NPV advances a national political identity for the United States.

THE INTERESTS OF THE STATES

The U.S. Constitution allocates electors to the states on the basis of their population (each gets one per House seat) and their equality (because each gets two electors regardless of size) (Article II, section 1). The most populous states would be less influential in electing the president than they would be under a direct election proposal. This difference is not large. The constitutional plan (known as the electoral college) reflects population by allocating electors according to House membership, which is four times greater than the Senate membership. Moreover, a state's influence in an actual presidential election may depend on more than its relative population. A state whose electoral votes are crucial to determining the winner of an election enjoys more influence than a state whose votes do not affect the outcome of the election. State legislatures will likely decide the fate of the NPV. Although many factors will affect these decisions, each legislature is likely to consider whether NPV increases or decreases the influence of their state over the presidential election. There are two ways to look at the question of which states would win and which would lose by moving to direct elections. First, I will examine the question on the basis of state's share of the total electors and its eligible voters (*the relative measure*). Next, I will turn to some estimates of the relative influence of each state in determining the winner of the presidency (*the power measure*).

The Relative Measure

Under the current system, a particular state's influence over a presidential election may be measured by dividing a state's electoral votes by the total electoral votes for the nation. The influence of a state under direct election is measured by dividing the number of eligible voters in a state in 2000 by the total number of eligible voters in the nation in 2000. The absolute gain or loss of a state from moving to direct election equals the difference between this measure of its influence under the electoral college and the same number under direct election. This absolute measure of state influence is difficult to interpret. I have thus constructed a relative measure of how much each state wins or loses from direct election. The relative gain or loss of a state equals its absolute gain or loss divided by the measure of its influence under the electoral college.

NPV would move us from the presidential status quo to direct election. Twenty states may expect to gain from moving to direct election. Most of these gains are quite small. Six states may expect to gain more than 10 percent in influence according to this measure. In contrast, 29 states and the District of Columbia lose influence from the move to direct election. Of those, 20 states and the District of Columbia may be expected to lose more than 10 percent of their influence over the presidential election by the change. A large part of this group would lose about half their current influence over the presidential election.

Power Measures

In practice, the influence of a state in selecting a president depends on how likely it is that the state will cast the pivotal vote that constitutes a majority in the electoral college for a candidate. States that are more likely to cast the deciding vote have more influence over the selection. If the deciding vote were distributed randomly, larger states would tend to be more powerful in presidential elections simply because they have more electoral votes, the Senate bonus not withstanding. Of course, the deciding vote in the electoral college has not been distributed randomly. States that are more competitive are more likely to cast the deciding vote. In other words, battleground states will have the most actual influence over the presidential outcome.

State officials who wish to determine whether their state benefits from the electoral college face the daunting task of determining whether their state is likely to be competitive (i.e. likely to cast a deciding vote for president). We might reasonably assume that the NPV would enact direct election of the president for the foreseeable future. A state legislator thus would like to know whether their state will be competitive in the future. No study has offered that knowledge. A study by George Rabinowitz and Stuart Elaine Macdonald ["The Power of the States in U.S. Presidential Elections," *American Political Science Review* (1986)] has estimated which states have the most influence under the current electoral college plan, taking into account their likely competitiveness. We can also examine in a less systematic way which states have been competitive in recent elections.

Rabinowitz and Macdonald collected data about the partisan and ideological leanings of the states in presidential elections from 1944 to 1980. They then simulated a large number of elections to determine how often a state occupies the pivotal position in a presidential election. The results of that simulation are interesting. Once again, the most powerful state comes first in the list, the least influential at the bottom. The power of a state in the electoral college is highly correlated to its size. California is by far the most influential state followed by Texas, New York, Illinois, and Ohio. States with small populations also tend to have less influence by the Rabinowitz-Macdonald measure. That is not surprising. Large states are less likely to be politically or otherwise homogeneous, which may be related to more competition in presidential elections.

In contrast to the earlier ranking of states, the Rabinowitz-Macdonald measures suggests that large states have the most influence in the selecting of a president. Where the voting measure suggests that large states would benefit by moving to direct election, the Rabinowitz-Macdonald study suggests they dominate the current system.

Another study found that voters in large states have more influence over presidential elections than voters from small states. Lawrence Longley and James Dana ["The Biases of the Electoral College in the 1990s," *Polity* (1992)] examined the relative influence of voters within states in the 1990s.

They did not attempt to estimate how likely it was a state would be competitive as part of their investigation. Instead, they calculated both the likelihood that a state would cast the pivotal vote in the electoral college and that a voter could change the way his state's electoral votes were cast by changing his vote. Longley and Dana found that citizens in all but six of the states have lower than average voting power in presidential elections. Voters in the six most populous states have greater than average influence. The study concluded, "the electoral college in the 1990s contains partially countervailing biases which result in a net advantage to large states as much as 2.663 to one, and a net *disadvantage* to states with from 3 to 21 electoral votes." [emphasis in original]

Two recent studies offer new insights about the power of voters and states under the electoral college and under the direct vote. Jonathan Katz, Andrew Gelman, and Gary King ["Empirically Evaluating the Electoral College," in *Rethinking the Vote: The Politics and Prospects of American Election Reform,* ed. Ann N. Crigler, Marion R. Just, and Edward J. McCaffery (New York: Oxford University Press, 2004)] examined the relative power of a vote under the electoral college and a direct vote system. Looking at presidential elections since 1960, they found minimal difference between the two systems in the estimated average probability of a voter being decisive. The method of voting did not affect the actual power of voters in these presidential elections.

The most recently published study of the electoral college uses a different measure of power: candidate attention to a state as measured by the number of visits. This measure of power fits well with the concerns of the NPV proposers who criticize the current system because only a few states receive attention from candidates under the electoral college. David Strömberg ["How the Electoral College Influences Campaigns and Policy: The Probability of Being Florida," *American Economic Review* (2008)] examines the actual number of visits to all states in the presidential elections from 1948 to 2000. He then constructs a model to predict the number of visits each state would receive under direct election of the president. He calculates which states will gain and lose visits under each voting system. Strömberg also concludes that small states do not benefit from the electoral college on balance.

By Strömberg's calculations, [the] twenty states that control 221 electoral votes would receive more visits under a direct vote for president; [the] twenty states that control 210 electoral votes receive more visits under the electoral college. Ten states and the District of Columbia (107 electoral votes) neither gain nor lose visits by moving to a direct vote. Looked at this way, the states that would benefit from a direct vote are 49 electoral votes short of the majority needed to pass NPV. The states that would gain comprised 41 percent of eligible voters in the 2006 elections; the states that would lose under direct election comprised 38 percent which implies that 21 percent of the nation's eligible voters lives in states that would neither gain nor lose by moving to direct election. In sum, the same number of states would lose from a direct vote as would gain, and the losers control almost as many electoral votes as the gainers. Finally, if we add the states that have reason to be indifferent since they neither gain nor lose from a direct vote to the states that would lose visits, we discover a coalition of states who have no reason to move to a direct vote and control a majority of 317 electoral votes. The number of eligible voters tells a similar story. Fifty-nine percent of eligible voters in 2006 lived in states that would either lose influence under direct election or would be indifferent about moving away from the electoral college.

Implications

It is often said that the electoral college benefits small states that block efforts to amend the Constitution to institute direct election of the president. This assumption implies most states would benefit from moving to direct election but are stymied by the super-majority requirements of amending the basic law and the determination of small states to hold on to their privileges. In fact, these matters are much more complicated than most people assume.

In practice, actual influence under the electoral college depends on the likelihood a state and its voters will have a competitive election and be decisive in determining the outcome of the presidential election. Some studies indicate some more populous states are more likely to decide an election under the electoral college and thus have more power. More recent studies, however, indicate either the power of a vote is about the same under the electoral college and the direct vote or that state size has little relationship to actual influence under either system. It is far from clear that most states would enjoy more influence over the presidential election in a direct vote system.

Moving away from the electoral college involves transaction costs and risks. To justify those costs and risks, a state legislator should have clear evidence that its voters will enjoy more influence under direct election than they do under the electoral college. We have seen that more than a few states will do worse under direct election. Several other states by various measures can expect to wield about as much influence under direct election as under the electoral college. Given the costs of moving away from the status quo, these indifferent states have little reason to support NPV. Adding the indifferent states to those who lose from the change may well form a coalition of states who control a majority of electoral votes. The electoral college, not NPV, may be the preference of a majority of states.

Legislators in most states should find it difficult to determine whether their constituents will gain or lose influence over presidential elections by moving away from the electoral college toward direct election. Given that uncertainty, the costs of trying to change the status quo, and the relative apathy of constituents about the way the nation selects the president, it is not surprising that the electoral college has not been seriously challenged within memory.

NPV poses other problems beyond calculations of political advantage. It raises deep questions of legitimacy and institutional change. In this regard, the benefits of the proposal also seem doubtful.

COSTS OF THE NPV PROPOSAL

Legitimacy

The Oxford English Dictionary defines legitimate as "conformable to law or rule; sanctioned or authorized by law or right; lawful; proper." Similarly, the same dictionary defines the noun legitimacy as "the condition of being in accordance with law or principle." The word itself can be traced to a Latin root that means "to be declared lawful." A legitimate government action should conform to the law and ultimately to the fundamental law, the U.S. Constitution. The idea of legitimacy is particularly important for actions that changed the law and especially the fundamental law. If *any* action changing a law could be considered legitimate, the fundamental law would be irrelevant for practical purposes. A second, related meaning of legitimacy may be found in the social sciences: "to ask whether a political system is legitimate or not is to ask whether the state, or government, is entitled to be obeyed." The idea of legitimacy thus links "being in accordance with law" with being worthy of being obeyed. Article V of the U.S. Constitution provides a procedure for amending the fundamental law. It depends on demanding supermajorities; typically, an amendment requires approval by two-thirds of Congress and three-fourths of the states. The supermajority requirement tends to inhibit amendments but does not preclude them. It favors amendments that have broad support. The amendment process thus protects significant (but not quite small) minorities.

Some supporters of NPV concede that their proposal seeks to circumvent the amendment process. The prominent journalist, E. J. Dionne ["Bypassing the Electoral College," *Washington Post,* April 2, 2007] wrote of the NPV plan: "this is an effort to circumvent the cumbersome process of amending the Constitution. That's the only practical way of moving toward a more democratic system. Because three-quarters of the states have to approve an amendment to the Constitution, only 13 sparsely populated states—overrepresented in the electoral college—could block popular election." Some who believe the constitutional method of electing the president should be changed agree that the NPV plan circumvents the Constitution. The editorial board of *The Milwaukee Journal Sentinel* concluded, "The U.S. Constitution, when it comes to the Electoral College, is flawed. However, rather than take the direct route to fix that, amending the Constitution, this proposal simply subverts it. This method complies with the letter of the Constitution but violates the spirit."

NPV advocates argue that their proposal comports with the Constitution and no amendment is necessary. They argue that the states are empowered by the Constitution to appoint electors "in such Manner as the Legislature may direct" which arguably includes assigning electors with regard to the outcome of the national popular vote. They suggest that the power to appoint electors is unconstrained by the Constitution. It is accurate that the Constitution does not explicitly constrain the power of state legislatures in allocating electors. But a brief consideration of the history of the drafting of this part of the Constitution suggests some implicit constraints on state choices.

The Framers considered several ways of electing a president. The three major ways were the current system, direct election by the people, and selection by Congress. On July 17, 1787, the delegates from nine states voted against direct election of the president; the representatives of one state, Pennsylvania, voted for it. The Framers chose an alternative to direct election which is described in Article II, section 1 of the Constitution. Of course, that decision by the framers need not bind Americans for all time. The Constitution also permits overturning the decisions of the framers through amendments to the Constitution. In contrast, NPV proposes that a group of states with a majority of electoral votes should have the power to overturn the explicit decision of the Framers against direct election. Since that power does not conform to the constitutional means of changing the original decisions of the framers, NPV could not be a legitimate innovation.

The authors of NPV strongly suggest that congressional consent to the proposed interstate compact is not necessary. Robert Bennett [*Taming the Electoral College*

(Stanford University Press, 2006)] argues the Supreme Court might not require a compact be approved by Congress if the agreement did not "enhance the political power of the [agreeing] States at the expense of other States or have an 'impact on the federal structure.'" But NPV does not meet these conditions. It harms those states whose citizens benefit from the current system of election. NPV also eliminates all states as electoral districts. Those states that adopt the NPV may see that elimination as a boon; others outside the compact may find the change to be a cost. The elimination of the states as electoral districts surely has "an impact on the federal structure" of presidential elections. For all practical purposes, NPV eliminates the federal character of presidential elections. For these reasons, Congress should have the chance to consent to NPV or to reject it.

E.J. Dionne's comment suggests that the demands of democracy should take precedence over constitutional constraints on the will of the people. The current means of electing the president may slightly reduce the influence of states that comprise a large majority of the eligible voters in the United States. Democracy in this regard may be taken to mean: the majority shall rule. Here again we have a question of legitimacy. The United States was designed to be a republic, "a government which derives all its power directly or indirectly from the great body of the people." It was not designed to be a government ruled by unconstrained majorities.

Would E.J. Dionne agree that the wishes of a majority should trump the Constitution's guarantee that Congress shall make no law abridging freedom of the press? The number of constraints against majority rule could be extended, but the point has been made. Circumvention of the Constitution in the name of majority rule cannot be legitimate in the United States. In sum, the NPV group poses the question whether we wish to have legitimate presidential elections and a constitutional government. If NPV succeeds, we will have less of both, at the margins.

Nationalization

The U.S. Constitution allocates presidential electors according to the federalist principle. Anti-federalists feared the new Constitution would centralize power and threaten liberty as well as subordinate the smaller states to the larger. The founders sought to fashion institutional compromises that responded to the concerns of the states and yet created a more workable government than had existed under the Articles of Confederation. With regard to presidential elections, they pursued a middle course that rejected both election by state legislatures and election by a national popular vote. The constitutional plan instead offers a compound means of election in which the states are considered as both co-equals in an association and as unequal members.

This same balancing of state and national elements may be found elsewhere in the Constitution. This general preference for federalism signaled that the new Constitution would not be wholly national in character and that the national government would be part of a larger design of checks and balances that would temper and restrain political power, a major concern of both the Founders and their Anti-Federalist critics.

These expectations for federalism have not been realized. In the past fifty years, the national government has increasingly treated the states as administrative units for larger national undertakings. Looked at historically, the role of the states in electing a president would be a likely target for elimination as part of these nationalizing trends. The nationalization of the political parties has also vitiated the selection of electors as state representatives; they now are chosen for their loyalty to national parties rather than as citizens of a state.

The realization of the NPV plan would continue this trend toward nationalization and centralized power. The president is the most important elected official in the nation. Under the NPV proposal, he or she will be elected by the nation acting as an electorate. Inevitably, this change will foster the creation of a national consciousness among Americans, a unified and centralized political identity. The president will thus be empowered as the choice of this national electoral district; he or she will speak for a plurality of that nation. As the renowned constitutional scholar Martin Diamond said, direct election of the president will not "increase the democracy of the election or the directness of the election but the pure nationalness of the election. The sole practical effect of [direct election] will be to eliminate the States from their share in the political process." A president so elected may be more likely to pursue national interests at a cost to state or regional concerns because state identities and considerations will no longer matter at all since the states will no longer exist so far as presidential elections go. Such a president "might also be likely to pursue policies that enhance or enlarge the scope and power of the federal government."

While direct election may not have strong partisan effects, the further empowering of the federal government and a subsequent increase in its ambit would run counter to the founding aspirations for limited government and individual liberty. It would be fully in line with the progressive emphasis on the national community, a purely national electorate, and the empowered executive. In other words, if people create institutions, institutions also create people, and the NPV will lead to a more nationalized and progressive electorate. Skeptics might object that the United States has already developed a centralized, national political identity. Few people are said to think of themselves as citizens of a particular state. The same skeptics might also note that the integration of the states into a unified national Leviathan has been a natural development fostered by the preferences of voters. Yet in our lifetime the hope for limited government has proven politically popular, and the states have enjoyed a renaissance based on policy achievements. The possibility of a renewed decentralization of power remains open.

The NPV plan also mistakenly assumes that the people living in the United States are a unified nation that should act as one in selecting their leader. But the United States today is deeply polarized along partisan, ideological, and other dimensions. These differences relate strongly to territorial and regional differences. Rather than forcing all these differences into a single national electoral district, the nation would do better to foster institutions that allow people who deeply disagree to live at some distance from one another in fact and in politics. Instead of further fostering a national identity, we should hold open the possibility of a more decentralized government in which people who profoundly disagree about things can live separately in peace. The NPV proposal would make that decentralization of identity marginally more difficult.

Disputed Outcomes

As in 2000, it is possible that one state will experience an election dispute that could affect the outcome of the presidential race. The struggles associated with such a dispute will be relatively confined. The same would not be true of the NPV alternative. Rational candidates or party leaders would have reason to dispute results throughout the nation to overturn close outcomes. Indeed, what constitutes a close election would become broader since the necessary votes to overturn the result could be found nation-wide. That would be more difficult and more contentious than the current system. As political scientist David Lublin ["Popular Vote? Not Yet. Problems With a Plan to Kill the Electoral College," *Washington Post*, July 16, 2007] has noted, the parties and the media would have difficulty supervising recounts and litigation around the country. As Lublin argues, "We might not even be able to have a national recount. All existing recount laws were designed to address elections within states. Compact states cannot compel other states to participate." NPV's supporters say it tends toward a clear result. But in a close election, the scope of its electoral district might well preclude a settled outcome in a close presidential contest.

PUTATIVE BENEFITS OF THE NPV PLAN

Ignored States

The authors of NPV note that under the current system candidates write off many uncompetitive states, which means those states are ignored by the campaigns. Several political scientists recently wrote that "Presidential campaigns have a clear tendency to concentrate their resources on a relatively small number of competitive states—states that both candidates have some legitimate prospect of carrying—while ignoring states that appear solidly to favor one camp or the other." This is not a new story. Scholars found that candidates in both the 1960 and 1976 campaign concentrated their resources in this manner. In contrast, the NPV advocates argue, a direct popular election would value all votes equally. Candidates would presumably seek votes in all states since they would all count equally toward victory.

The states, and not the Constitution, create the problem complained of by the NPV authors. Currently 48 states allocate their electors according to the winner-take-all standard; the District of Columbia also employs this method. This has been true for some time. By 1824 only six of twenty-four states selected electors by state legislatures. By 1832, all but one chose by popular election. After 1832, selecting electors by popular vote meant popular vote by general ticket which meant "winner take all." This rule offers the dominant party in the state legislature (and thus probably in the presidential contest) more electors than under say, a division of electors along the lines of the popular vote.

Of course, state legislatures need not choose a "winner take all" rule for selecting electors. They could divide electors according to the popular vote if they believed it would attract attention from presidential candidates thereby benefiting their state. But few states do so. That suggests most legislators believe "winner take all" benefits their state more than the candidate attention that might come from a division according to the popular vote. Since these legislators are elected by the people, we have to reason to think the "winner take all" system reflects the popular will.

This judgment by legislators raises another issue. Why should citizens in a state be concerned about being ignored because of a lack of competition? Voters can easily gather sufficient information from the national media to cast their ballot. Businesses in a neglected state may miss the tax receipts generated by the candidate, her entourage, and the media, but such losses do not seem relevant. After all, the nation does not hold presidential elections to foster local economic development. Neglected states may be concerned that if a candidate can take a state for granted during the campaign, he or she will do less for the state once in office, at least compared to what they might have done if the state had been competitive. NPV thus appeals to the material and thus political interests of voters in neglected states.

As a political tactic, the appeal to neglected states seems likely to fail. Imagine that a presidential candidate has the same sum to spend on votes under NPV as he does under the Electoral College. Imagine also, as predicted, the candidate decides to spend more under NPV on formerly neglected states (for example, by budgeting more public works for them once in office). Where would the president find the money for this spending with a fixed budget? It would have to come from states that were competitive under the Electoral College. With a fixed budget, NPV would impose losses on battleground states to benefit previously neglected states. However, individuals and groups tend to value losses more than identical benefits. All things being equal, the voters who lose by moving to NPV would care more than voters who gain from it which suggests the appeal to the material interests of neglected states would fail as a political tactic.

The "neglected state" argument also raises budgetary and moral questions. If a president under NPV simply spends more public money to reward voters in formerly neglected states, competitive states will not face losses, but the federal deficit will rise and will be financed by public borrowing. Future voters will pay higher taxes because of this increased debt. Such voters, however, will have no say about the decision to incur the debt; many of them are either too young to vote or do not exist. NPV aspires to an equality of votes for the current generation. Its political appeal, however, may rely on exploiting an inequality of voting power between the current generation and future voters.

Even if all votes are weighed equally in an election, the cost of attracting a marginal vote for president would vary. For example, it would be less expensive per voter to attract votes in populous states because of the structure of media markets. As noted earlier, there is a relationship between population size and competitiveness in presidential elections. In that respect, the marginal effect of the NPV plan would be to draw candidates toward large, competitive states. The cost of votes also depends on the efficiency of a campaign and party organization. The least costly votes are thus likely to be found in large, competitive states where the organizations have become efficient through competition and in large, non-competitive states where party organizations may have unique advantages in "running up the score." In that way, the NPV plan might bring some candidate attention to states that are now non-competitive and ignored. But running up the score in party strongholds may also increase the regionalization of presidential politics. In general, because of the relative costs of attracting votes, the NPV proposal seems likely at the margin to attract candidate attention to populous states. Many voters outside low-cost media markets may be as ignored under NPV as they are under the status quo.

Certainty of Election

NPV advocates have argued that their compact will create a clear, nationwide winner of the presidential election. Direct election of the president by a plurality or majority would almost certainly lead to a clear winner. But NPV seeks to attain direct election through an interstate compact. The question of certainty turns on whether the interstate compact will work as NPV advocates hope.

State legislatures might have strong incentives to withdraw from the compact if their commitment elects a president opposed by a majority in the legislature. Indeed, the voters who elected the legislature might demand they withdraw from the compact or face the consequences at the next election. The backers of the NPV plan outline a model compact that prevents a state from withdrawing until a president is qualified for office. NPV supporters argue the U.S. Supreme Court would enforce the agreement against a state wishing to withdraw from it; they rely on the Court's decision in *West Virginia ex rel. Dyer v. Sims,* a 1950 case involving the Ohio River Valley Water Sanitation Compact. They also cite the influence of public opinion and "safe harbor" provisions in federal law that give preference to election returns that are in accord with laws enacted prior to election day.

The Constitution empowers states to select presidential electors within the constraints implicit in the work of the Constitutional Convention. It does not say a legislature cannot change its manner of selection or that its choice must be made prior to election day. The significance of this grant of power should not be underestimated; it is one aspect of how the Founders included the states in the new government. The Constitution includes other clauses, of course, including one forbidding states to impair contracts. The Supreme Court might force a state legislature to hold to the terms of the NPV compact, but the issue would certainly be litigated, perhaps between election day and the day when electoral votes are cast. In any case, the compact has no backup provision if a state withdraws. That state's electoral votes would remain in limbo. If a legislature has withdrawn from the compact, we may presume public opinion approves or perhaps even demands a withdrawal. To be sure, a majority outside of a state may disapprove of the withdrawal, but no legislator in the withdrawing state will face those disapproving voters unless he or she runs for president. The "safe harbor" provision, if effective, will simply mean that a state withdraws prior to election day. Modern polling often enables legislators to guess the outcome of a state's presidential election.

The NPV compact may work as advertised in practice. But in a close election legislators will be under tremendous pressure, and many voters may see their states casting electoral votes for a candidate who finished second in their state. It is not clear that outcomes under the NPV compact will be any more certain than under current arrangements.

INCENTIVES FOR HIGHER TURNOUT

NPV advocates argue that the current system depresses voter turnout because voters in non-battleground states doubt their participation matters. If all votes counted equally, so the argument implies, more people would feel their votes mattered and would turn out on election day. Others have suggested that direct election would increase the incentives for a state to increase turnout. It seems unlikely that switching to direct election would actually increase turnout. Several experts on voting behavior have noted: We would expect voter participation among the most informed segments of the electorate to respond positively to the popular election of the president. This effect is probably small if not trivial. The most informed and attentive voters are already predisposed to vote. Replacing the Electoral College with the popular election of the president is not likely to be perceived by inattentive and less informed voters and will have only a trivial influence on the likelihood of voting among the most informed voters.

Should increasing voter turnout be an important goal of the nation? Current levels of turnout do not seriously bias election results; the sample of voters reasonably well represents the partisan and ideological views of the entire population of voters. Voting turnout is highly correlated to education which in turn is the best predictor of economic literacy. As the economist Bryan Caplan [*The Myth of the Rational Voter: Why Democracies Choose Bad Policies* (Princeton University Press, 2007)] discovered, increasing turnout to 100 percent would mean candidates "have to compete for the affection of noticeably more biased voters than they do today." Even lesser increases would be expected, all things being equal, to increase the number of biased (i.e. ill-informed) voters compared to the status quo. Insofar as candidates follow the wishes of voters, increased turnout would mean worse (i.e. more irrational) economic policies.

Increasing voting turnout should not be a high priority for American policymakers and even if it were, moving to direct election, perhaps especially in such a complicated way as NPV, would not bring out more voters.

CONCLUSION

NPV offers a way to institute a means of electing the president that was rejected by the Framers of the Constitution. It does so while circumventing the Constitution's amendment procedures. Implicitly, NPV advocates believe that direct election of the president by the greater number of voters weighs so heavily on the normative scales that bypassing constitutional propriety should be accepted. Yet the U.S. Constitution establishes a liberal republic not a majoritarian democracy. The NPV plan appears unlikely to deliver its promised benefits and likely to impose other costs, not least by throwing into question the legitimacy of our presidential contests. NPV gives the supporters of a losing presidential candidate little reason to accept the outcome. Legitimacy and political obligation are rooted in law, and the NPV plan circumvents our legal procedure for changing presidential elections. That alone should be enough to convince legislators in the various states that this proposal should not be adopted. The fate of NPV will also depend on the play of political interests. Would states controlling a majority of electoral votes benefit from joining NPV? Many people believe small states benefit from the electoral college. Certainly, many small states would do relatively poorly by moving to the NPV. That result does not mean, however, that large states would benefit from direct election of the president. Populous states tend to hold the most actual power over the election of the president under the current system since they tend to be the most competitive and more likely to decide an election. Medium-size states may expect few gains from NPV and losses from the change if they are competitive. It is often assumed that the electoral college persists because of the difficulty of amending the Constitution. But it appears that both small and large states have reasons to support the status quo in electing a president, and other states have good reason to be indifferent toward a change to direct election. The electoral college, though much maligned, may satisfy the interests of more states and voters than any other alternative means of electing the president including NPV.

THE CONTINUING DEBATE:
Electing the President

What Is New

On August 4, 2010, Massachusetts' governor signed an NPV plan into law. That made Massachusetts the sixth state to adopt the NPV plan, joining Hawaii, Illinois, New Jersey, Maryland, and Washington. These states have a combined 73 electoral votes, or 27% of those needed for the plan to go into effect. In June 2010, New York State's Senate passed an NPV bill by 52 to 7, and almost half the members of state's Assembly have announced their support. Should New York also enact the NPV plan, the state's 31 electoral votes would bring the electoral votes of the state's supporting the plan to 39% of those needed to put it into operation. It has been since 2007 that a national poll has tested public sentiment on using a national popular vote system rather than the Electoral College to elect the president, but that poll showed 72% favoring the popular vote.

Where to Find More

The National Archives at www.archives.gov/federal-register/electoral-college/ has extensive information on the Electoral College. The National Popular Vote organization's Web site is www.nationalpopularvote.com/. Another group opposed to the Electoral College is FairVote, and its Web site has a good discussion of options beyond the NPV. Go to www.fairvote.org/ and choose "Electoral College" in the drop-down issues menu. Additional critiques of the NPV plan and defenses of the Electoral College are available from Daniel P. Rathbun, "Ideological Endowment: The Staying Power of the Electoral College and the Weaknesses of the National Popular Vote Interstate Compact," *Michigan Law Review* (2008); and Bradley A. Smith, "Vanity of Vanities: National Popular Vote and the Electoral College," *Election Law Journal* (2008). Taking the opposite point of view is Alexander S. Belenky, "The Good, the Bad and the Ugly," *Michigan Law Review* (2008). An edited book in which contributors discuss various alternatives to the Electoral College and the implications of each is Paul D. Schumaker and Burdett A. Loomis, *Choosing a President: The Electoral College and Beyond* (Chatham House, 2002).

What More to Do

Calculate three things: your state's percentage of the national population, its percentage of the electoral vote, and given its turnout in 2008, its percentage of the presidential vote. Keep in mind, your state's seats in the U.S. House of Representatives, and therefore the number of its electoral votes, may change on the basis of the 2010 census. These numbers should be available early in 2011. Based on these updated calculations, would your state gain or lose political advantage if the Electoral College were to be abolished? Also expand your consideration past just the NPV plan discussed here. Do some research on alternative plans at the FairVote site noted above, and compare all the possibilities before making your decision.

CONGRESS

SENATE FILIBUSTERS:
Blocking Majority Rule *or* Preventing Majority Tyranny?

BLOCKING MAJORITY RULE

ADVOCATE: Thomas E. Mann, W. Averell Harriman Chair and Senior Fellow, Brookings Institution

SOURCE: Testimony during hearings on "Examining the Filibuster: Legislative Proposals to Change Senate Procedures" before the Committee on Rules and Administration, U.S. Senate, June 23, 2010

PREVENTING MAJORITY TYRANNY

ADVOCATE: Lee Rawls Faculty Member, National War College and Adjunct Professor, College of William and Mary

SOURCE: Testimony during hearings on "Examining the Filibuster: Legislative Proposals to Change Senate Procedures" before the Committee on Rules and Administration, U.S. Senate, June 23, 2010

James Madison and many of the other delegates to the Philadelphia Constitutional Convention of 1787 were wary of democracy, at least too much of it. One thing they worried about was how to protect minority rights from the tyranny of the majority. As Madison put it, there was a need to ensure that "no common interest or passion will be likely to unite a majority of [Americans] in an unjust pursuit." It should be noted that the delegates did not mean the rights of minority racial and ethnic groups. Instead, they were worried about the rights of the propertied class being threatened by the poor majority. One thing that the delegates did to restrain democracy was to design the U.S. Senate to play something of a "cooling" role, to temper the passions of the democracy manifested in public sentiment and the popularly elected House of Representatives. To accomplish this function, the Constitution as written in 1787 took several steps. First, senators were chosen indirectly by their respective state legislatures instead of directly by popular vote like members of the House. Second, any law passed by the House also had to be agreed to by the Senate. James Madison, the "father" of the Constitution depicted the Senate as "the great anchor of the government" and a "temperate and respectable body of citizens" that would resist public passions "until reason, justice, and truth can regain their authority over the public mind." Third, the Senate, unlike the House, was given two key unilateral legislative powers: ratifying treaties and confirming presidential appointments. Fourth, the Constitution gave senators six-year terms of office, three times longer than those of House members. Madison explained that the longer term of senators would make them less likely than members of the House to yield to the public's "sudden and violent passions."

The smaller number of senators and the sense that the chamber was meant to carefully deliberate on issues—especially anything pushed forward by unstable public passions and the House that might threaten and be adamantly opposed by a minority—led the Senate in 1806 to abolish any method of forcing a vote on a measure before all senators were willing to do so. This set the stage for the first filibuster in 1826. Filibusters are a parliamentary tactic whereby one or more senators continue to speak on a measure in order to prevent it from coming to a vote. This tactic can be used to force a compromise or to even have a measure withdrawn from Senate consideration in order to continue with other, more pressing business. Even the threat of a filibuster can have such an impact.

Prior to 1917 there was no way other than making concessions to end a filibuster, but that year the Senate adopted a rule that allowed it to invoke cloture (end debate) by a vote of two-thirds of all senators present and voting. The vote necessary to invoke cloture was changed in 1975, and Senate Rule 22 now requires a vote of three-fifths of the entire Senate membership, or normally 60 senators, to end debate. The Senate also has a number of other procedures that enable one or a few senators to delay or even prevent final action. A "hold" is one of these tactics. Senate Rule 7, which bars the Senate from floor consideration of any matter without the "unanimous consent of the membership" allows individual senators to put a hold on a measure by refusing to give their consent. Like a filibuster, a hold can be overcome, but it is difficult to do so.

Although the use of filibusters and similar delaying tactics is almost as old as the country, there is growing concern about them because of their increased use. Before the mid-1960s, filibusters were rare. They began to increase as Southern senators used the tactic to block civil rights legislation. That factor has waned, but intensifying partisanship in the Senate has escalated the number of filibusters even more steeply. Among other uses, filibusters have become a much more common method by which the minority can delay or defeat presidential judicial nominations. Indeed, filibuster activity has become nearly routine on the most important votes ("key votes") in Congress. Filibusters occurred, or were threatened on, 50% or more of the key votes since 1990, including more than 80% of these votes in 2008. It is now often reported that passing a piece of legislation will require a "supermajority" of 60 votes, the de facto number given the cloture threshold, instead of 51 votes, the normal majority in the Senate.

The frequent need for a supermajority of 60 is questionable as a matter of democracy and also increases the chances for stalemate in the Senate. Given this and the increase in filibuster activity, Thomas E. Mann, a well-know scholar in the area of Congress who is at the Brookings Institution, focuses on the confirmation processes and contends that whatever advantages filibusters may have, their costs outweigh their benefits. Also focusing on the confirmation process, Lee Rawls, who teaches at the National War College, counters that the filibuster should not be abolished because it continues to foster moderation and consensus in the picking the federal judiciary and executive branch officials.

POINTS TO PONDER

➢ What relationship, if any, does the filibuster have to the familiar notion of having "majority rule with respect for minority rights"?

➢ Is the original "cooling" role of the Senate still desirable? Was it ever in a democracy?

➢ Note the suggestions for reform made by Professors Mann and Rawls and think of yet other possibilities.

Senate Filibusters:
Blocking Majority Rule

THOMAS E. MANN

Testimony [already] presented at [these] hearings usefully [has] clarified the origins of unlimited debate in the Senate, circumstances surrounding the adoption of Rule XXII in 1917 and its subsequent amendment, changing norms and practices regarding the use of filibusters, holds, and cloture petitions, and in recent years the extraordinary increase in the frequency of extended-debate-related problems on major measures before the Senate.

I concur with the scholarly consensus that the emergence of an ideologically polarized Senate, with sharp party differences on most important issues, appears to be a major force behind the routinization of the filibuster. The striking unity within each of the party caucuses reflects this ideological separation but also arises from the rough parity between the parties. Control of the Senate is now regularly up for grabs. Both parties have powerful incentives to use the available parliamentary tools to wage a permanent campaign to retain or regain majority status. The resulting procedural arms race has served individual and partisan interests but has diminished the Senate as an institution and weakened the country's capacity to govern.

The focus of my testimony at this hearing is the impact of the increasing use of filibusters and holds on the Senate confirmation of presidential appointees. The Constitution provides that the President "shall nominate, and by and with the Advise and Consent of the Senate, shall appoint Ambassadors, other Public Ministers and Counsels, Judges of the Supreme Court, and all Other Officers of the United States, whose Appointments are not herein otherwise provided for, and which shall be established by Law..." The Framers differed amongst themselves on the proper role of the Senate in the nomination and confirmation process so it is no surprise that this has been a bone of contention between the branches throughout the course of American history. Because it holds the constitutional authority to withhold its approval of presidential appointments, the Senate can wield formidable negative power. How responsibly the Senate exercises that power importantly shapes the performance of the executive and judicial branches.

All presidential appointments subject to Senate confirmation are not equal. Approximately 65,000 military appointments and promotions are routinely confirmed each Congress, with very few (though occasionally prominent) delays or rejections. Many of the roughly 4,000 civilian nominations considered each Congress are handled by the Senate in a similar fashion. These include appointments and promotions in the Foreign Service and Public Health Service as well as many nominations to part-time positions on boards and advisory commissions. In many other cases (U.S. attorneys, U.S. Marshals, and U.S. district judges), a long-standing custom of "senatorial courtesy" gives home-state senators support to object if they are not fully consulted by the White House before nominations are submitted. In addition, a number of fixed-term appointments to commissions, boards, and other multi-member entities are required by their enabling statutes to maintain political balance in some way or to follow an explicit selection procedure. In both cases, these consultations and selection processes go some distance in limiting the potential friction between the branches in resolving their shared responsibility. (Not the entire distance, to be sure. Nominees to the Federal Election Commission have often been subject to prolonged delays, even denying it the ability to have a quorum to conduct business during much of the 2008 election campaign. Similar examples can be found with the Election Assistance Commission and other regulatory bodies and boards.) Consequently, it is no surprise that 99% percent of presidential appointees are confirmed routinely by the Senate. More problematic are appellate judicial nominations (numbering roughly 25 to 50 per Congress) and the 400 or so Senate-confirmed senior positions in cabinet departments and executive agencies (excluding ambassadors) who serve at the pleasure of the president. In the case of the former, the confirmation process over the last three decades has become increasingly prolonged and contentious. The confirmation rate of presidential circuit court appointments has plummeted from above 90% in the late 1970s and early 1980s to below 50% in recent years. A particularly acrimonious confrontation over the delay of several judicial nominations in 2005 led then Majority Leader Bill Frist (R-TN) to threaten to use the so-called "nuclear option"—a ruling from the chair sustained by a simple majority of senators to establish that the Constitution required the Senate to vote up or down on every judicial nomination (effectively cloture by simple majority). Before Frist's deadline for breaking the impasse arrived, a group of 14 senators (seven Democrats and seven Republicans) reached an informal pact to oppose Frist's "reform-by-ruling" and to deny Democrats the ability to filibuster several of the pending nominations. This diffused the immediate situation but did little to alter the long-run trajectory of the judicial confirmation process. Lifetime appointments and high ideological stakes provided ample incentives for senators whenever feasible to use holds and silent filibusters to prevent a majority of their colleagues from acting on judicial nominations.

Theses delays in confirming appellate judges have led to increased vacancy rates, which has produced longer case processing times and rising caseloads per judge on federal dockets. Moreover, the conflict over appellate judges is spilling over to the district court appointments, which are beginning to produce similarly low rates of confirmation.

Even more disconcerting has been the impact of the changing confirmation process on the ability of presidents to staff their administrations. My colleague on this [hearing] panel, Cal Mackenzie, this country's preeminent student of the presidential appointments process, has in his prepared testimony made a powerful case that "we have in Washington today a presidential appointment process that is a less efficient and less effective mechanism for staffing the senior levels of government than its counterparts in any other industrialized democracy." Professor Mackenzie summarizes the longstanding flaws in the present system and documents how it has steadily deteriorated over the last several decades. That deterioration has occurred at both ends of Pennsylvania Avenue.

In fact, delays in filling senior executive positions are substantially larger at the nomination than the confirmation stage. This reflects in substantial part a defensive posture by new administrations seeking to reduce or eliminate any possibility of adverse publicity about any of their nominees surfacing after they are chosen. But the trends over the last four administrations place an increasing responsibility for delays with the Senate. As Professor Mackenzie, drawing on important new work on this subject by Professor Anne Joseph O'Connell of the University of California, Berkeley School of

Law, notes, the average time taken to confirm nominees in the first year of new administrations has steadily increased (from 51.5 days under George H.W. Bush to 60.8 days under Barack Obama) while the percentage of presidential nominations confirmed by the end of the first year declined (from 80.1% under Bush 41 to 64.4% under Obama).

These discouraging statistics actually understate the problem. Cabinet secretaries are usually confirmed within a couple of weeks while top noncabinet agency officials take on average almost three months. Some nominees have been subject to much more extended delays, putting their personal lives on hold for many months and critical positions unfilled for much or all of a president's first year in office. Some Cabinet secretaries have had to manage with only skeleton senior staffs, with few empowered with the formal authority that is contingent on Senate confirmation. Recent administrations have many horror stories associated with the absence of timely confirmation of its top executives.

The Obama administration is no exception. Indeed, its stories are more numerous and telling than those that came before it. Consider just a few examples. In the midst of a financial meltdown and critical decisions to be made on the implementation of TARP [the Troubled Asset Relief Program enacted in 2008], the Treasury Department had no Senate-confirmed officials in many high-ranking policy positions, including: Deputy Secretary, Undersecretary for International Affairs, Undersecretary for Domestic Finance, Assistant Secretary for Tax Policy, Assistant Secretary for Financial Markets, Assistant Secretary for Financial Stability, and Assistant Secretary for Legislative Affairs. One of those nominees, Lael Brainard, a former colleague of mine at Brookings, was nominated for the key position of Undersecretary for International Affairs on March 23, 2009 but did not get confirmed until April 20, 2010, over a year later. Her problem was tax-related, reportedly over a deduction she claimed on a home office. Yet her husband, Kurt Campbell, was nominated for a post at the State Department and confirmed by the Senate in about two months, even though they filed a joint tax return.

Other critical positions with urgent responsibilities for a Senate-confirmed appointee subject to extended vacancies included Commissioner of U.S. Customs and Border Protection, director of the Transportation Security Administration, head of the National Highway Traffic Safety Administration, and director of the Centers for Medicare and Medicaid Services. To be sure, delays associated with filling these and other senior executive positions often arose during the nominating process and sometimes were associated with genuine concerns about the nominee. But the evidence strongly supports the view that many nominees get caught in ideological and partisan battles in the Senate or become hostages to the personal agendas of individual senators, often unrelated to the nominee or the position to be filled.

Currently, there is no foolproof way of discerning how many nominations are subject to holds by individual senators. The effort to limit secret holds initiated by Senators [Ron] Wyden (D-OR) and [Charles] Grassley (R-IA) as part of the 2007 ethics bill has loopholes that have rendered it largely ineffective. One can, however, examine the list of nominations that have been approved by committees and placed on the Senate executive calendar. One presumes that absent a hold or other signal of a filibuster, the Majority Leader would move expeditiously to call up these nominations. Not that long ago it was rare that nominees would linger on the list of pending confirmation for days, weeks, and months. On Memorial Day 2002, during George W. Bush's administration,

13 nominations were pending on the executive calendar. Eight years later, under Obama, the number was 108. Senators have long viewed the confirmation process as an opportunity to express their policy views and to get the administration's attention on a matter of importance to them or their constituents. But the culture of today's Senate provides no restraints on the exercise of this potential power and no protection of the country's interest in having a newly-elected president move quickly and effectively to form a government. One telling indicator of the arbitrary and self-indulgent use of holds on nominees is when a successful cloture vote to overcome a longstanding hold is followed by a near-unanimous vote for confirmation. This happens with increasing frequency in the Senate.

In my view and that of virtually the entire policy and scholarly communities, the costs of the serious flaws on our appointment and confirmation process outweigh the benefits. Government agencies are ill-equipped to operate effectively and to be held accountable by Congress; able individuals willing to serve their country are subject to uncertainty and major disruptions in their personal and professional lives; huge amounts of precious time in the White House and Senate are diverted from much more pressing needs.

I understand that subsequent hearings will deal more directly with remedies to the shortcoming of governance associated with obstruction in the Senate. Let me conclude by urging you to consider two proposals: an effective end to anonymous holds on nominations and, more ambitiously, a fast-track system that sets time limits on committee and floor action for the confirmation of senior executive nominations.

Senate Filibusters: Preventing Majority Tyranny

LEE RAWLS

"These opposed and conflicting interests which you considered as so great a blemish in your old and present constitution interpose a salutary check to all precipitate resolutions. They render deliberation a matter not of choice, but of necessity."

Edmund Burke

"The disposition of people to impose their own opinions can only be restrained by an opposing power."

John Stuart Mill

"Partisan competition has been at the center of our struggle to advance as a people and as a nation. It has been our most important engine for adaptation and change—one that remains in full motion."

John Hilley (Chief of Staff to Majority
Leader Senator Mitchell, and Legislative
Affairs Director for President Clinton)

I am here today because of my previous life as Chief of Staff to Senator Frist (R-TN) when he was Senate Majority Leader and also as an Assistant Attorney General for Legislative Affairs at the Department of Justice in the early 1990s. Among my responsibilities at the Department were nominations for the Federal Judiciary, along with nominees for all the senior positions at the Department itself, including that of Attorney General.

I have opened my prepared remarks with several quotes to telegraph my general view of the value of the filibuster, and to preclude me from having to inflict my full philosophical theories of the filibuster on the members. Moreover, my longer musings can be found in my 2009 book *In Praise of Deadlock*—whose title captures much of my thinking.

Instead, I will open with a quote from the famed journalist Eric Sevareid, who wisely noted that "the chief cause of problems is solutions." I have taken a look at the committee's previous hearings on the filibuster which in the aggregate present a thorough review of the filibuster and during which many former members, scholars and practitioners have offered a wide range of possible solutions. My advice to the committee on these proposals comes down to one word: Don't.

At the War College, we train the senior military commanders who attend to ask one question at the start of any discussion on a problem: So What? What is it about a situation that demands a remedy, and what assurances are there that the proposed solution will not make the problem worse?

The filibuster is a perfect candidate for this line of questioning. The Committee has been told that both partisanship and the use of the filibuster are on the rise. You have been told that the American legislative system is "broken," that the nominations process, particularly for the federal judiciary is in disarray, and that strong medicine is necessary to cure the situation.

Let me make 5 points in response, and leave any nuances to questions the members of the Committee may have.

1. Any legislative system that in the face of a deep financial recession and two wars that can enact in the space of two years TARP legislation, $750 billion dollars in stimulus funding, a major overhaul of the world's largest health care system and is preparing to enact a far-reaching reform of its financial system is by definition not broken. Moreover, any nomination process that has not had a single nominee for the federal judiciary rejected as the result of an unsuccessful cloture vote is by definition not in disarray.

2. If rising partisanship is a concern, the sole source in the entire American legislative system of bipartisanship, moderation, continuity and consensus is found in the United States Senate because of the role of the filibuster. The leverage provided to the minority by the filibuster is a two-sided coin. On one side it is the source of bipartisanship throughout the entire legislative process. On the other, it slows down the legislative process that in turn leads to inaccurate cries of "gridlock" which are loudly echoed by the press. In Burke's words, quoted above, the filibuster renders deliberation a "matter of necessity, not choice." This moderating, consensus forming role of the filibuster has been going on for 170 years. As Sarah Binder told the committee, organized use of the filibuster by the political parties started in the 1840s, and as Senator [Robert] Byrd (D-WV) noted in his remarks, "bitter partisan periods in our history are nothing new." In fact, scholars note that parts of the 19th century were clearly more partisan than today.

3. The United States Senate is the most intricate legislative body in the known universe, unique for its permissive rules. At the core of its genius is its ability to moderate a large number of vital political forces all of which have their dark side For example, the filibuster is an essential element in moderating the extremes of our competitive party system. It also moderates the hubris and moral aggression noted by the Mill quote above in those who actually make the rules. Of particular importance it lessens the risks of united government when one party "hijacks" the Constitution's separation of power system and in the name of all Americans exercises power in all branches of government at the same time.

The First amendment explicitly provides for special interests to engage in the political process. These groups range from economic interests to single-interest advocates, all of whom have a narrow focus, and who usually are not interested in compromise. The filibuster, by providing resistance within the legislative system, often smoothes out the worst abuses of this special interest participation. Thus, although the First Amendment guarantees special interest participation, it is often the filibuster that protects the public interest in the legislative process. Professor Smith in his remarks to the Committee lamented the "obstruct and restrict syndrome" that he believes the filibuster has caused. From my vantage point as a practitioner within the system, I believe that the "continuous resistance" that the filibuster provides on a daily basis to these vital, but occasionally dangerous forces, is the essential component in the genius of the United States Senate.

4. The above points lead to the conclusion that if you change the filibuster rule, you unalterably change the nature of the Senate. Chairman [Charles] Schumer (D-NY) has been quite fair-minded in his quest for answers to the filibuster riddle. In particular, because he has been both in the majority and minority, he has asked the right question as to whether one's views of the filibuster are completely dependent on one's political

status of the moment, or whether there are more fundamental issues at stake. I believe such larger issues are at stake. These relate to what it means to have a full and productive Senate career. Such a career requires continuous involvement; namely a full body of legislative work that gives personal satisfaction and contributes to the public needs of the American people. Moreover, such a career requires the full engagement of one's skills whether one is in the majority or minority. A career where minority status means effective banishment falls short of these criteria. In fact, for those who have had acknowledged successful careers, such as the late Senator [Edward] Kennedy (D-MA) or the recently retired Senator [Peter] Domenici (R-NM), the key to their success has often been the important role they played as leaders of the minority skillfully negotiating with the majority.

For the members of the minority, the value of filibuster in achieving a full career is obvious. I believe it is worth noting that the members of the Majority also run some risks if the filibuster were abolished. The first is that the power of the president would be substantially increased, particularly in united government. Given his visibility and power to influence grass roots forces, members of a Senate devoid of a filibuster would be under increased pressure to toe the line of a president of the same party.

Members of the Senate Majority may not appreciate how much they are in control of the entire legislative machine in the American system. The resistance provided by the Minority makes their political judgments the essential ingredient in establishing and implementing legislative strategy. Without such resistance, they will lose their strategic function and their role becomes one of either supporting or opposing the policies of an executive branch of the same party.

The other risk that a Majority party without a filibuster runs is being overwhelmed by the special interests. Every year thousands of bills that reflect strong special interest input are introduced but are not addressed by the Senate because of the filibuster. Absent such a constraint, it is difficult to conceive of the Majority party in the Senate resisting the whole range of special interest legislation that is introduced on an annual basis. For Majority senators who do not conceive of themselves as handmaidens of special interests, this change would be an unwelcome shock.

5. With these first principles in mind, let me make 2 concluding remarks on the nominations process.

a. The virtues of the filibuster in fostering moderation and consensus are important in picking the federal judiciary. These are lifetime posts vested with immense importance in our system. Trust is perhaps the most important element in the Rule of Law which the federal judiciary oversees. Brilliance and other intellectual virtues are second order virtues, particularly if they come wrapped in strong ideological packaging. Anything that forces matters to the middle is a virtue, and the filibuster certainly does that. Every member here has had discussions as to whether a nominee will face opposition and what a minority armed with a filibuster is likely to do.

In addition, the leverage provided by the filibuster allows for a more thorough examination of candidates for the federal bench. Documents, extensive hearings, additional face-to-face meetings, all these flow form the leverage of a minority armed with the filibuster. As with any tool, or instrument, mistakes and abuses occur. But my view is that in the aggregate, given the importance of the federal judiciary, and their lifetime appointments, the leverage of the filibuster provides for a more thorough vetting process of the federal judiciary than a process without such leverage. As an aside, I also wonder how much of an issue this is at present. During 2003–4 when I was Senator Frist's Chief of Staff, the Senate was split 51–49. We spent a lot of floor time on judicial nominees, winning some and losing some. Today's Majority of 59 votes has a perfect record on judicial cloture votes which leaves me wondering what part of the puzzle I am missing, if any.

b. Some of the same considerations hold for executive branch nominees. Here the problem is numbers. My experience is that the Senate is reasonably prompt in providing the president with his senior Cabinet leadership. With exceptions, usually cases where the nominee has self-inflicted problems, the Senate does a good job on the Cabinet. Where matters get off the rails is the mid-level management of the executive branch on which the Senate insists on providing advice and consent. There are a variety of ways to address this issue, but overall the Senate insists on confirming too many nominees. The problem is not the filibuster; it is the Senate's inability to set priorities. In my own case, I was held up for a period of time with two other nominees after our nominations to the Justice Department. The Senator who held us had a perfectly legitimate beef with the Department, and after some negotiations, the issue was resolved.

Since the post of Assistant Attorney General for Legislative Affairs is really a fancy title for flak-catcher, it seemed to me that the elaborate gyrations surrounding my nomination was wasted effort. In my view, if the nomination is important enough for a Senator to personally meet with the nominee and attend the confirmation hearing then the confirmation process is appropriate. If not, then drop the Senate confirmation requirement. In my case, no courtesy visits were asked for, and one poor junior member of the committee had to be dragooned into chairing the hearing. If following such an effort at establishing priorities to determine which positions actually need confirmation, there is still a substantial problem, then perhaps other measures could be considered.

THE CONTINUING DEBATE:
Senate Filibusters

What Is New

Potential filibusters were a major threat to some key measures in 2010, but most of the important ones moved forward. The Senate leadership used an arcane parliamentary maneuver to avoid a Republican filibuster on the final passage of the reconciled heath care reform legislation early in the year. In April, Republicans filibustered financial reform for several days, but they gave way when they concluded that continuing to block the bill would put them in political peril during the impending congressional elections. Then in August, the nomination of Elena Kagan to the Supreme Court was confirmed without a filibuster when it became clear that there would not be enough votes to block a cloture motion. As far as any reform of the Senate's Rule 22 on filibusters, nothing occurred beyond the hearings. For all the criticism of the filibuster, it is hard to change the rules in part because many senators see the filibuster as a valued Senate tradition. Additionally, whichever party is in the majority—and could perhaps change the rules—knows that it will surely someday be the minority party and will then want to use filibusters to gain leverage in the Senate.

Where to Find More

A good place to begin further study is Gregory Koger, *Filibustering: A Political History of Obstruction in the House and Senate* (University of Chicago Press, 2010). The Senate Committee on Rules and Administration held a series of hearings on the filibuster and related procedures. The third hearing was "Examining the Filibuster: Legislative Proposals to Change Senate Procedures." It is available on the committee's Web site at http://rules.senate.gov. Since filibusters are not declared formally, the easiest way of finding and counting them is through is by counting cloture petitions and votes, which are formal procedures. The best source for researching the parliamentary maneuvers is the Historian of the United States Senate on the Web at www.senate.gov/pagelayout/feference/cloture_motions/.

What More to Do

It can be hard to evaluate filibusters in the abstract. So for some applied analysis, go back in history and identify the top ten or so most important filibuster using Gregory Koger's book *Filibustering* mentioned above or other studies such as Gregory J. Wawro and Eric Schickler, *Filibuster: Obstruction and Lawmaking in the U.S. Senate* (Princeton, NJ: Princeton University Press, 2006) and Sarah A. Binder, Eric D. Lawrence, and Steven S. Smith, "Tracking the Filibuster, 1917 to 1996," *American Politics Research* (2002). See what the outcomes were. Did the filibuster defeat the bill at which it was aimed, result in compromise, or fail? For each, was the result one that you think was good or bad? Ask yourself how the outcomes, and your reactions to them, impact your views on filibusters.

PRESIDENCY

THE WAR POWERS OF THE PRESIDENT:
Curb *or* Leave As Is?

CURB

ADVOCATE: Jules Lobel, Professor of Law, University of Pittsburgh

SOURCE: Testimony during hearings on "War Powers for the 21st Century: The Constitutional Perspective" before the U.S. House of Representatives, Committee on Foreign Affairs, Subcommittee on International Organizations, Human Rights, and Oversight, April 24, 2008

LEAVE AS IS

ADVOCATE: Stephen G. Rademaker, Senior Counsel, BGR Holding and former Associate White House Counsel to President George H.W. Bush

SOURCE: Testimony during hearings on "War Powers for the 21st Century: The Executive Branch Perspective" before the U.S. House of Representatives, Committee on Foreign Affairs, Subcommittee on International Organizations, Human Rights, and Oversight, April 24, 2008

"We're going to find out who did this, and we're going to kick their asses," President George Bush vowed angrily to Vice President Richard Cheney just after the 9/11 terrorist attacks. Bush soon asked Congress for a resolution supporting action against terrorists in Afghanistan. But in doing so he asserted that he already had the right to strike "pursuant to my constitutional authority...as commander in chief." In other words, support by Congress would be nice, but it was not necessary. Bush's assertion of a unilateral power to wage war brings into focus the issue about when presidents may use military force without congressional authorization. The dispute begins with two clauses in the Constitution. Article I empowers Congress "to declare war." Article II designates the president as "commander in chief" of the military. It is clear that the framers of the Constitution believed both that the president should sometimes be able to act unilaterally and that there were limits to the president's war power. The distinction, according to delegate Roger Sherman, was that presidents should "be able to repel and not commence war."

There is a long history of the use of the president's war powers, but the matter became more controversial after World War II. Two things changed. First, the United States became a superpower that deployed its forces around the world and used them often. Second, beginning with the Korean War (1950–1953), presidents began to assert unprecedented powers as commander in chief. In Korea for the first time the United States fought a full-scale war without congressional authorization. President Harry Truman asserted he could act alone because, "the president, as commander in chief of the armed forces,...has full control over [their] use" and because North Korea's attack threatened "interests which the president...can protect by the employment of...[U.S.] forces...without a declaration of war."

This view prevailed unchallenged until the Vietnam War led Congress in 1973 to try to reign in the president's war powers by passing the War Powers Resolution (WPR). Section 2c specifies that the president can only send U.S. forces into action or put them in imminent danger (harm's way) if (1) Congress has declared war, (2) Congress has given the president "specific statutory authorization" to act, or (3) "a national emergency [has been] created by attack upon the United States, its territories or possessions, or its armed forces." Unfortunately a later section, 5b, muddied the WPR's intent by stipulating that within 60 days after ordering troops into combat or harms way, the president has to terminate the action unless Congress has authorized it to continue. Some read section 5b to mean that the president has unilateral authority for 60 days. Others take the language to mean that the 60 days applies only to the three circumstances indicated in section 2c and that, in other cases, the president must get prior authority from Congress to act.

President Richard Nixon vetoed the WPR claiming it put the country in danger by hamstringing the president and also violated his constitutional authority as commander in chief. Congress overrode that veto, and the WPR became law. However, its effect has been marginal. In nearly every case since then when presidents have used military force—with or without congressional authorization—they have claimed the unilateral right to act as commander in chief. When, for example, Congress authorized Bush to take action against Iraq, he was careful to say that "my signing this resolution does not constitute any change in the long-standing positions of the executive branch on either the president's constitutional authority to use force to deter, prevent, or respond to aggression or other threats to U.S. interests or on the [un]constitutionality of the War Powers Resolution."

Such assertions of presidential authority prevail for two reasons. One is that despite several challenges to "presidential wars" in recent years, the Supreme Court has refused to hear such cases, leaving the matter in legal limbo. The second factor is that Congress has been unwilling to challenge the president. It has never refused to pass a resolution supporting action, and when the president has acted without one or seemingly exceeded the limits of Congress' intent, it has been unwilling to assert its authority through a variety of tools at its disposal ranging up to the ability to impeach and remove the president for violating the law. Whatever the cause, University of Pittsburgh Law School Professor Jules Lobel contends that president does need to be retrained, that the WPR has failed, and that it should be replaced by a more effective measure. Former White House Associate Counsel Stephen Rademaker disagrees, arguing that because the president is constitutional commander in chief, there are very serious limits on Congress' ability to tell him when and where he can use the military.

POINTS TO PONDER

➤ It is important to distinguish between your view about whether a particular military action is wise policy or not and the constitutional process by which that decision should be (or have been) made.

➤ Ask yourself, under what circumstances the president may not unilaterally use force or send troops into harm's way?

➤ If a president ignores the War Powers Resolution and claims to be acting under his authority as commander in chief, what do you think Congress should do?

The War Powers of the President: Curb

JULES LOBEL

Thank you for inviting me to testify before this Subcommittee on the critical issue of how to ensure that decisions to go to war be made by Congress. The constitutional principle that those decisions not be made by one person is too important to our nation's well-being and security to be a partisan issue.

My own experience with this issue has been bipartisan. I have not only written extensively on the question of constitutional war powers, but I am Vice President of the Center for Constitutional Rights, on whose behalf I have represented members on both sides of the aisle in lawsuits challenging presidential usurpations of congressional authority over warfare. In 1990, I was lead counsel for Congressman [Ron] Dellums (D-CA) and more than 50 Democratic members of Congress in a case challenging President George H. W. Bush's claim that he could go to war against Iraq without congressional authorization. In 1999, I was lead counsel for Congressman Tom Campbell (R-CA) and more than 20, mostly Republican members of Congress who sought declaratory and injunctive relief against President Clinton's use of force against Yugoslavia after this House had refused, by tie vote, to specifically authorize hostilities. My experience both as a scholar and in my representation of both Republican and Democratic members of this House leads me to conclude that the constitutional framework prohibiting the president from initiating warfare without congressional approval is as important in the 21st century as it was in the 18th, that the War Powers Resolution has failed to serve its purpose and should be replaced by a more effective measure, and that H.J.R. [House Joint Resolution] 53 is an excellent step in that direction.

CONSTITUTIONAL FRAMEWORK

The framers vested the power to decide on warfare in Congress for three main reasons. First, they believed that war was, in [James] Madison's words, "among the greatest of national calamities," and therefore wanted to provide what [Thomas] Jefferson termed an "effectual check on the dogs of war." They sought to slow down or "clog" the process of initiating warfare by providing careful review by independent minds, thus ensuring that the United States would not, as a key framer James Wilson put it, "hurry…into war." Second, they were suspicious of allowing the Executive to make the decision to go to war alone, for many agreed with Madison that war "in fact is the true nurse of executive aggrandizement." Third, they wanted broad democratic participation in the momentous decision to initiate warfare, and therefore required the approval of a broadly representative legislative body. Therefore the Constitution provides that only Congress can initiate warfare—whether it be major military conflicts, small skirmishes or little wars—with the sole exception that the president can use force to respond to a sudden attack against us.

These reasons are as valid today in the 21st century as they were in the 18th century. Madison's claim that, "in no part of the Constitution is more wisdom to be found, than in the clause which confides the questions of war or peace to the legislature and not to the executive department," has been affirmed by the last half century of our history, which demonstrates the need for more independent review by Congress before going to war, not less. While the nature and source of the threats to our national security have dramatically changed since the 18th century, the cost of warfare in lives lost, injuries suffered, and national resources expended is even greater today than it was in 1787. Indeed, one lesson of the current Iraq war is that the need to put a brake on the rush to war and ensure that independent minds evaluate whether war is really necessary is still as compelling today as it was in 1787. Today the rule of law encapsulated in the Constitution and our treaty commitments require the authorization of not only Congress but also the U.N. Security Council before the United States initiates non-defensive warfare.

Modern presidents have distorted our constitutional framework, engaging in dozens of military actions against other nations without first seeking the constitutionally required consent of Congress. Moreover, they have articulated broad theories of presidential power under which the president alone can use force in a broad array of circumstances. As President George H. W. Bush colloquially stated, "I didn't have to get permission from some old goat in the United States Congress to kick Saddam Hussein out of Kuwait."

For example, post–World War II presidents have claimed that smaller uses of military force, such as the [President Bill] Clinton administration's planned invasion of Haiti in 1995 do not rise to the level of war requiring congressional approval. The Justice Department in *Dellums v. Bush* [1990] took the even more extreme position that the term war had no fixed meaning whatsoever and therefore what was a war for purposes of the Declare War Clause [in Article I of the Constitution] could not be determined by a court. This position is in error and was fortunately rejected by [U.S. District Court] Judge Greene in the *Dellums* case. The Article I congressional power to declare war is not limited to the formal power of issuing a declaration, nor to authorizing full-scale wars, but was intended to give Congress the power to decide whether the United States should initiate any offensive military hostilities, however big or little, or for whatever purposes.

Moreover, to the extent there is any doubt as to the meaning of the Declare War Clause, the clause immediately following it gives Congress the power to "grant letters of marque and reprisal." In the 18th century, letters of marque and reprisal had two meanings. The first, now obsolete, referred to authorization given to private merchantmen to fight the enemy. Second, and still relevant today, letters of marque and reprisal referred to imperfect wars, special wars, limited wars, reprisals—all of which constituted hostilities that were something less than full-scale war. For example, both Alexander Hamilton and Secretary of War James McHenry advised President John Adams in 1798 that any use of American naval force beyond repelling attack on the nation's seacoast, armed vessels or commerce within American waters, "comes within the sphere of reprisals and…requires the explicit sanction of that branch of the government which is alone constitutionally authorized to grant letters of marque and reprisal."

Various administrations and their supporters have also argued that the traditional limit of the commander-in-chief's power to repel sudden attack or resist invasion no longer controls in the modern world. The Justice Department argued that the president had the unilateral power to send troops to Vietnam because the interdependence of the 20th century world meant that all warfare anywhere in the world might "impinge directly upon the nation's security." Similarly, the [President George W.] Bush administration acknowledged the Iraq Resolution passed by Congress in 2002 as a "resolution of support" but claimed that the president had independent authority to use force "to deter, prevent or respond to aggression on other threats to U.S. interests." Therefore, modern presidents have articulated a constitutional power to send forces into combat whenever they detect threats to national security. This vision of commander-in-chief clause merges war and peace, offensive action and defensive conduct. If any threat to United States security around the world actives the executive's war powers, then the distinction between the executive emergency power to repel an attack and congressional power to authorize the introduction of U.S. forces into hostilities loses significance. As Judge Greene noted in *Dellums v. Bush*, such a reading of the Constitution would essentially write the Declare War Clause out of the Constitution. Moreover, it would be incredibly dangerous to allow the president alone to decide to attack Iraq, North Korea or any other nation he or she deems a serious threat to U.S. national security.

Finally, it is important to note that the president's commander-in-chief power to repel sudden attacks is an independent, but not preclusive emergency authority. The president has the independent constitutional authority to use American forces in self-defense until Congress can meet and decide what to do, but that independent power is not a sole, exclusive power which Congress cannot limit or restrict. Congress can limit the president's "repel attack" authority to a certain time period. Congress also could have prohibited the president from responding with nuclear weapons to a Soviet attack on American forces in Europe, or from attacking China in response to an attack on U.S. forces in Korea. The president's commander-in-chief power to repel attacks allows him to act in self-defense, independent of congressional authorization where Congress is silent, but not to act in disregard of affirmative restrictions that Congress enacts.

THE WAR POWERS RESOLUTION

The War Powers Resolution attempted to restore Congress's primacy over decisions to go to war. Nonetheless, virtually all observers recognize that the Resolution has failed. Every president since the enactment of the Act has considered it to be unconstitutional. Presidents have generally not filed a report starting the 60-day clock running, despite repeated executive introduction of armed forces into hostile situations in Indo-China, Iran, Lebanon, Central America, Grenada, Libya, Bosnia, Kosovo, or Somalia. Congress has usually not challenged this non-compliance. And the judiciary has persistently refused to adjudicate claims challenging executive action as violative of the Resolution, holding that members of Congress have no standing to seek relief, or that the claim presents non-justiciable political questions.

The War Powers Resolution was flawed in several key respects. The first flaw was that the Resolution imposed no operative, substantive limitations on the Executive's power to initiate warfare, but rather created a time limit on the president's use of troops in hostile situations of 60 days absent explicit congressional authorization.

This approach was a mistake, as some astute members of Congress such as Senator [Thomas] Eagleton (D-MO) and Congressman Dellums recognized at the time, because as a practical matter it recognized that the president could engage in unilateral war making for up to 60 days. But the Constitution requires that Congress provide authorization *prior to* initiating non-defensive war, not within 60 days *after* warfare is initiated. As history has demonstrated time and again, it is difficult to terminate warfare once begun; the key time therefore for Congress to weigh in is before hostilities are commenced, not within 60 days afterwards.

Second, the War Powers Resolution correctly recognized that congressional silence, inaction or even implicit authorization was insufficient to authorize the president to engage in warfare, but failed to provide an adequate mechanism to enforce that basic principle. The automatic termination provision in Section 5(c) requiring that the president terminate any use of United States forces in hostilities or imminent hostilities after 60 days unless Congress affirmatively declared war or specifically authorized warfare proved to be unenforceable. Presidents simply ignored it; Congress had an insufficient interest in enforcing it; and the courts responded by saying that if Congress did nothing, why should we?

Congressman Campbell's effort to enforce the War Powers Resolution during the Clinton Administration's air war against Yugoslavia in 1999 provides a vivid example of the resolution's unenforceability. Through tremendous persistence, Campbell managed to invoke the priority procedures of the resolution and force Congress to vote on whether to authorize the war. The House voted against declaring war by a lopsided margin, against requiring the president to withdraw troops, and, by a tie vote against authorizing the war. Moreover, both the House and Senate voted to appropriate funds for the war. Campbell and two dozen other members of Congress filed a complaint in Federal District Court seeking to enforce the Resolution. The president was in clear violation of the Resolution since more than 60 days had passed since United States warplanes had commenced hostilities against Yugoslavia. The House had refused to authorize hostilities, and the Resolution explicitly denied the president authority to continue hostilities based on congressional enactment of appropriations for the war unless such provision specifically authorized hostilities. Where Congress is too divided, conflicted, or unsure to affirmatively authorize warfare, both the Constitution and the War Powers Resolution require that the United States not go to war. What had in effect occurred was that Congress had not wanted to specifically authorize the war because many members disagreed with it, but neither did it want to be responsible for forcing the president to terminate it. That situation was contemplated by the Resolution, which required explicit, affirmative authorization.

Nonetheless, the judicial response to Campbell's claims was that congressional refusal to authorize the war was insufficient to invoke judicial enforcement because [the court said,] "Congress has a broad range of legislative authority it can use to stop a president's war making...." Congress could have passed a law forbidding the use of U.S. forces in the Yugoslav campaign, or Congress could have cut off funds for continuing the war. Indeed, every time I argued a case seeking to enforce the constitutional or statutory mandate that Congress affirmatively authorize war—in the Central American cases of the 1980s, the first Iraq War before Judge Greene in 1990 or the Kosovo case almost a decade later—judges said in effect "why should I enforce congressional war powers when Congress will not?" The answer I gave was that to require Congress to act affirmatively to stop a war reversed the Constitution's presumption that the president was required to obtain explicit, affirmative congressional authorization to go to war, not that he or she could go to war unless Congress could muster a majority to stop the war. Congressional silence is sufficient constitutionally to deny the president authority to go to war; nonetheless it was insufficient to force either the president to terminate warfare or to get the Courts to do so on behalf of members of Congress.

The difficulties of enforcing a congressional mandate requiring legislative action to review executive emergency action is not unique to the War Powers Resolution. The

1976 National Emergencies Act sought to ensure congressional review of any executive invocation of emergency power by mandating that within six months of the declaration of a national emergency, "each House of Congress *shall* meet" to consider terminating the emergency. Nonetheless, Congress has not considered and voted on whether to terminate the emergencies declared by the president since 1976, despite their continuation for years. When plaintiffs injured by a presidential invocation of emergency power sought relief in federal court, the First Circuit Court of Appeals held that there was no legal remedy for a congressional failure to comply with the statute.

REVISING THE WAR POWERS RESOLUTION

I believe that it is necessary and possible to reform the War Powers Resolution, and that H.R. Res. 53 is an excellent step in that direction. The first, crucial revision contained in the new statute is the language in Section 3 prohibiting the president from initiating warfare without clear authorization from Congress, unless he or she is acting to repel armed attacks on United States territories, troops or citizens.

Various administrations and commentators have argued that the situations in which the president requires independent authority to use American forces in an emergency cannot be limited to repelling or responding to an armed attack. The original Senate 1973 War Powers Legislation upon which Section 3 is modeled was criticized as being unduly restrictive of the president's power to use American armed forces abroad. The various attempts by Senator Biden and others in the late 1980s and early 1990s to reform the War Powers Resolution ran into difficulties in attempting to define exceptions to deal with a broad range of emergency situations. For example, Senator [Joseph] Biden's (D-DE) proposed 1988 Use of Force Act would have authorized the president to use U.S. troops "to respond to a foreign military threat that severely and directly jeopardizes the supreme national interests of the United States under extraordinary emergency conditions that do not permit sufficient time for Congress to consider statutory authorization," and "to participate in emergency actions undertaken pursuant to the approval of the United Nations Security Council." These exceptions would constitute enormous, and in my opinion unwarranted, loopholes in the legislation that would essentially eviscerate the prohibition on unilateral Executive use of force. In my opinion, H.R. Res. 53's approach is fundamentally sound in only allowing the Executive to use force without congressional approval to respond to attacks on U.S. territories, troops or citizens.

One could, of course, hypothesize a myriad of situations where the nation might want the Executive to use force to respond to an emergency which did not constitute an attack on U.S. territories, troops or citizens. But the actual Executive uses of armed force in the decades since 1973 do not support the exceptions that various Administrations have claimed are necessary to protect national security. Can one think of any case in the past several decades where the president launched an armed action against another nation or terrorist organization but had no time to secure advance authorization from Congress? The air strikes against Libya in 1986, Baghdad in 1993 and again in 1998, Afghanistan and Sudan in 1998 and Yugoslavia in 1999 all could have been authorized by Congress in a timely manner before they were initiated. Military effectiveness merely required that the details and timing of the operation be secret—but there was sufficient time for Congress to decide whether to authorize those actions. The Panamanian and Haitian invasions were threatened for months and involved long-standing tensions. The Panamanian and Libyan operations were discussed for many months before they were actually launched. The Grenada invasion was arguably time driven, but only if you accept the implausible and factually inaccurate proposition that the operation was a direct response to the threat that American medical students would be taken hostage. Both of our attacks on Iraq in 1991 and 2003 took place after many months of military buildup and threats to invade, and after congressional authorization. Moreover, launching a surprise attack against a nation that has not attacked us ought not be a reasonable justification for avoiding the constitutional process. The phrase "repel sudden attacks" simply cannot, with any rationality, be turned into a justification for "launching sudden attacks."

Today, as in 1787, the reality is that American national security can be adequately served if the president's power to use American forces in combat unilaterally is reserved to repelling attacks or imminent attacks on American troops or territories, and evacuating citizens under attack. And repelling means just that; it does not mean retaliating for an attack on an American citizen or soldier that took place several days, weeks or months before. The president can respond defensively to attacks that have been launched or are in the process of being launched, but not to rumors, reports, intuitions, or even informed intelligence warnings of attacks.

Moreover, Congress has demonstrated that where United States national security is seriously threatened, it can and will act quickly. On September 14, 2001, just three days after the September 11 attacks, Congress authorized the president to use military force against the perpetrators of those attacks. In all likelihood, congressional authorization could have been secured even earlier had the administration not initially sought an overbroad authorization. So, too, the Clinton Administration could have sought quick congressional authorization to use military force in 1998 against the perpetrators behind the August 7, 1998 bombings of the American embassies in Nairobi, Kenya, and Dar es Salaam, Tanzania, or the 1993 World Trade Center bombing.

It is true that many situations will be murky, complicated or divisive and therefore that quick congressional action will not be forthcoming. But in those cases, the United States should not use military force until a substantial consensus develops in Congress and the public that military force is necessary, appropriate and wise.

While there might be rare future emergencies not covered under the repel armed attack exception in which we might want a president to act unilaterally, the solution is not to accord the president broad emergency authority or to dilute the statute with a host of exceptions. For as Justice Jackson said in Youngstown, "emergency powers kindle emergencies." The better approach is to accept that in the rare situation where the force is really necessary and appropriate, and there is no time for Congress to meet to authorize warfare, the president should act openly and unconstitutionally and immediately seek congressional and public ratification of such action. That was what both President Jefferson and President Lincoln argued should be done when faced with such grave emergency crises.

From this constitutional perspective, section 3 of the Constitutional War Powers Amendments of 2007 correctly provides that the initiation of hostilities by the armed forces may only occur when authorized by Congress or in order to repel an armed attack upon the United States or its armed forces and citizens located outside the united States. I am troubled, however, by the language in Section 3(a), (3) and (4) that provides the president with the authority to use force "to the extent necessary" to repel such attacks. I realize that the probable intent of that language is to limit the president's use of armed force to *only* that force which is essential to repel an attack, but the phrase "to the extent necessary" seems vague, and could be read by future presidents to justify a preventive use of force where he or she believes it necessary to repel or prevent a future attack on the United States or troops. That is not what the drafters of this statute intended, but the language could be subject to misinterpretation. As then-congressman Abraham Lincoln argued in 1848,

> Allow the president to invade a neighboring nation, whenever *he* shall deem it necessary to repel an invasion…and you allow him to make war at pleasure. Study to see if you can fix *any limit* to his power in this respect.

I would therefore remove the words, "to the extent necessary," and substitute "to repel an armed attack or such an imminent attack that the president has no time to obtain congressional authorization." I would also remove 3(b) which permits the president to take necessary and appropriate retaliatory actions in the event of such an attack. This provision, which seems to me a Cold War vestige contained in the original Senate War Powers Bill, is not necessary because the president can use force to actually respond to an attack and Congress should fairly quickly authorize whatever force is necessary to defend against an ongoing attack and respond to the aggressor.

I would also like to comment on the enforcement measures contained in the bill. Sections 3(b) and 6(c) that prohibit the use of appropriated funds for any executive use of force that is unauthorized under the statute are a welcome strengthening of current law. Nonetheless, a president who claimed that the statute was unconstitutional and initiated hostilities in disregard of the statute would undoubtedly use appropriated funds to do so, forcing Congress into the difficult position of having to decide whether to authorize funds for troops engaged in combat.

The bill also tries to reverse the judiciary's past refusal to intervene to prevent presidential unilateral war making by providing that members of Congress have standing to challenge a violation of the law in federal court. I am doubtful that this provision will accomplish its objective. In *Raines v. Byrd* [1997], the Supreme Court held that members of Congress suffer no concrete injury sufficient to confer Article III standing in federal courts when they claim injuries not in any private capacity but solely because they are members of Congress. The Court so held despite a provision in the statute at issue that specifically provided that any member of Congress could bring an action in federal court. The Court noted that although Congress's decision to grant a particular plaintiff the right to challenge an act's constitutionality eliminates any prudential standing limitations, Congress cannot erase Article III's core, constitutional standing requirement that a plaintiff have suffered a concrete, particularized, personal injury. The Court did suggest that a narrow exception might exist allowing congressional standing when a member of Congress's vote is totally nullified, but the D.C. Circuit Court of Appeals seems to have foreclosed even that exception in *Campbell v. Clinton* [2000].

The statute should also direct the courts to not apply the various non-justiciability doctrines that courts have relied on to abstain from ruling on war powers challenges in the past. A provision should be added similar to that contained in Senator Biden's Use of Force bill providing that in any action brought by private plaintiffs or members of Congress seeking compliance with the provisions of this Act, the court shall not decline to make a determination on the merits based on the doctrine of political question or any other non-justiciability doctrine. The statute could also state that a presidential violation of the bill would create an impasse with Congress and that Congress's view was that separation of powers principles required the Court to decide the merits of any challenge brought against an alleged violation. In the two wars against Iraq, soldiers who did have standing challenged presidential violations in court, but their claims were dismissed as presenting nonjusticiable political questions. While Congress cannot override any core Article III requirement, it can negate the prudential judicial concerns that the resolution of the issue should be left to the political branches to determine.

Moreover, to ensure greater enforceability of the statute, I would define a privileged resolution in Section 7(a)(2) as one that is introduced after the president has submitted a written request *or was required by the statute to submit* such a report. Such a change would clarify that a privileged motion can be introduced even when the president is acting in violation of the statute and has not filed a report.

Finally, an important aspect of the statute is Sections 5's strengthening of the reporting provisions of the War Powers Resolution. Not only must Congress explicitly authorize non-defensive uses of force, but it ought to do so after searching, informed and independent review. I would therefore suggest that a subpart (8) be added to the statute which would require the president to report on why he or she believes that the use of force contemplated is consistent with international law and United States treaties, particularly the U.N. Charter. Hopefully, this requirement will help focus congressional attention on that issue, which in my opinion is critical to Congress's decision whether to authorize a non-defensive use of American forces.

In conclusion, the statute's revision of the War Powers Resolution to only permit Executive unilateral use of U.S. armed forces to repel an armed attack on American territories, troops or citizens is a welcome and excellent improvement on the current War Powers Resolution. Hopefully the statute will engender and encourage a debate on whether that position is correct and a bipartisan consensus will develop that it is.

The War Powers of the President: Leave As Is

STEPHEN G. RADEMAKER

THE VIEW FROM THE EXECUTIVE BRANCH

As you know, there are profound differences in opinion between the Executive branch and many Members of Congress about the proper allocation of powers between the Executive and legislative branches with respect the use of armed force. These differences are institutional rather than partisan in nature. President [Richard M.] Nixon vetoed the War Powers Resolution in 1973 because he believed it was unconstitutional, and every president since him has come to share his view of this law. It is a safe bet that our next president will be someone who is today a United States Senator, but it would defy experience to expect that former Senator's view of the War Powers Resolution to be any different than that of his or her predecessors in the White House.

There are two factors that, in my opinion, account for the consistent view of presidents that Congress need not give its prior approval to the use of armed force abroad. First, all presidents take very seriously their responsibility to protect the security of the American people, and more broadly to promote international peace and security. They quickly find that one of the most powerful tools at their disposal in seeking to influence crisis situations abroad is their ability to bring to bear, or threaten to bring to bear, armed force. As a result, they come to see congressional efforts to constrain their ability to use armed force as not just inconvenient, but potentially dangerous.

Second, there is within the Executive branch an entrenched view of the Constitution with regard to war powers that is at odds with the views of many Members of Congress. This is not the idiosyncratic view of a few extremist lawyers, but rather, so far as I am aware, the shared view of all the lawyers at the relevant Executive branch agencies, including the Departments of Justice, State, and Defense, as well as the White House.

I know you have devoted an entire hearing to the constitutional issues, and I will not seek to replow that ground today. But I do think it is worth pointing out some of the key legal precepts that are widely accepted within the Executive branch:

- Under the Constitution, the president is commander in chief of the Armed Forces. Congress does not have to give the president an army, but if it does, there are very serious limits on Congress's ability to tell him what he can do with it.

- The Constitution's grant of authority to Congress to declare war cannot be read as a grant of exclusive authority to Congress to authorize the use of military force. Historically declarations of war were one way that nations got themselves into a state of war, but by no means the only way. A state of war arises once a nation is attacked, for example, and in such a case there is no need under international law for the attacked nation to declare war. Moreover, there have always been many uses of force that take place outside a state of war. For all these reasons, the function of declaring war is easily distinguishable from the function of authorizing the use of force.

- The history of the "declare war" clause at the Constitutional Convention—in particular the switch to the term "declare war" from the original language which would have granted Congress the power to "make war"—leaves no doubt that the Founders wanted the president to be able to defend the nation from attack without first obtaining the approval of Congress. It therefore can be argued that "non-defensive" uses of force may require the prior approval of Congress—uses of force that in modern usage would be termed "acts of aggression." But defensive uses of force do not require prior congressional approval. Defensive uses of force include not only repelling attacks on the territory of the United States, but also defending our deployed land and naval forces abroad, our shipping, American citizens, American property, and also in some circumstances our vital national interests.

- As first articulated in President Nixon's veto message in 1973, the War Powers Resolution is constitutionally defective in at least two process-related respects. First, its requirement that the president withdraw U.S. Armed Forces from foreign deployments when so directed by a concurrent resolution of Congress denies the president his right to veto legislation set forth in the presentment clause of the Constitution. Second, the so-called "60-day clock," under which the president is required withdraw U.S. Armed Forces from foreign deployments after 60 days unless Congress has authorized the deployment, also effectively denies the president his right to presentment of legislation. The first of these constitutional objections appears to have been vindicated by the Supreme Court's 1983 decision in *INS v. Chadha*.

- Beyond these process-related objections, for all of the reasons set forth above, it is questionable whether Congress has the constitutional authority to order the president to terminate deployments of U.S. Armed Forces—at least defensive deployments. Could Congress constitutionally forbid the president to defend some part of the United States from attack? If not, there must be other defensive uses of force that are also beyond the authority of Congress to forbid.

THE EXECUTIVE BRANCH'S PERCEPTION OF CONGRESS

The Executive branch finds Congress to be a difficult partner on war powers questions. In part this is because Congress is not a rubber stamp, as all presidents wish it would be. But it is also because Congress can be a fickle institution, particularly on questions of war and peace. I saw first-hand as a congressional staffer how often members of Congress agonize over how to vote on whether to authorize particular military operations. For many members, this is the only time they are ever called on to make what amounts to life-or-death decisions, and they can be uncomfortable with the responsibility. Sometimes rather than give a clear "yes" or a clear "no," they look for a way to say "maybe."

This is an understandable human impulse, but when the Congress as a whole responds to a use of force question by saying "maybe," the Executive branch is left shaking its head. Not only is the question of legal authority for the use of force left ambiguous, but the political landscape is even more confused. When the Congress says "maybe," the Executive branch believes Congress is trying to have it both ways: Congress wants to be able to share in the credit if the operation turns out well, and condemn it as ill-conceived and illegal if it turns out poorly. Needless to say, the Executive branch regards this as an evasion of responsibility and a non-serious approach to what are in fact deadly serious questions.

Congress, of course, does not literally say "maybe" to proposed uses of force, but it has a number of ways of doing the functional equivalent. I would contend that this is the answer that Congress gave to all of the peacekeeping and peacemaking operations undertaken during the Clinton Administration—Somalia, Haiti, Bosnia, and Kosovo. The most important functional equivalent to saying "maybe" is permitting the sixty-day clock set forth in the War Powers Resolution to expire. According to the War Powers Resolution, this clock requires the president to terminate a use of force if Congress has not affirmatively authorized it within sixty days. It is, in other words, a default that kicks in if Congress does absolutely nothing. No president has ever curtailed a military operation because the sixty-day clock was about to expire, and Congress has never seriously sought to enforce it. It therefore serves in practice as a way of permitting a military operation to go forward, while reserving to Congress the right to disavow it should it go badly.

THE EXECUTIVE BRANCH AND CONGRESSIONAL AUTHORIZATION FOR THE USE OF FORCE

As you know, the Executive branch is not fond of the War Powers Resolution and would be happy to see it go away. But in the years since the resolution was enacted in 1973, the Executive branch has certainly learned how to live with it. In my testimony last month I described some of the ways the Executive branch has come to apply the resolution in order to minimize its impact. Most importantly, it has developed legal theories under which it does not report to Congress at all on foreign deployments of U.S. armed forces, or else reports that such deployments are not into situations where involvement in hostilities is imminent. In either case, the result is the same: the Executive branch satisfies itself that sixty-day clock of the War Powers Resolution has not been triggered. Some of the most extreme examples of this took place during the 1990s when the Clinton Administration was eager to extend U.S. participation in UN peacekeeping operations that had not been authorized by Congress.

This is not to say that the resolution has no effect on the actions of the Executive branch. The legal theories I have described are of little use in cases where U.S. forces are to be deployed into sustained combat that will likely last more than sixty days. In such cases, the president's lawyers may advise him that he has authority under the Constitution to proceed with the deployment irrespective of the War Powers Resolution, but they also have to warn him that after sixty days he will be unable to argue that he is in compliance with the letter of the resolution. In other words, after sixty days, he will be in clear noncompliance with the resolution, and the only legal justification for his actions will be his claim that the resolution is unconstitutional. As a former White House lawyer, I can assure you that this is the kind of situation that we tried mightily to avoid for our client.

We had precisely this sort of discussion during the administration of President George H.W. Bush with regard to his decision to liberate Kuwait from Saddam Hussein [in 1991]. President Bush was advised by his lawyers that he had the constitutional authority to order a military operation to liberate Kuwait even without advance approval from Congress. His lawyers went on to warn him, however, that he would likely be in violation of the letter of the War Powers Resolution if combat operations lasted longer than sixty days. I believe that in the end President Bush decided to seek congressional authorization for political rather than legal reasons, but certainly one of the political considerations in his mind was that domestic political opposition to his policy would be much stronger if his opponents were able to argue that he was breaking the law.

I had occasion to briefly discuss this with President Bush shortly after the successful conclusion of Operation Desert Storm. Recalling the enormous political pressure he came under not to commence ground operations following the air campaign against Saddam Hussein, he commented to me: "Thank God we got that authorization from Congress. Can you imagine the mess we would have had on our hands if we hadn't gotten that?" I can only imagine how many times our current president has had the same thought about his decision to seek authorization from Congress for the Second Persian Gulf War.

REFORMING THE WAR POWERS RESOLUTION

The current arrangement under the War Powers Resolution suits the Executive branch reasonably well. As a practical matter, the resolution does not stand in the way military operations that will be intense but short in duration (e.g., Grenada, Panama), nor operations of longer duration that arguably do not involve hostilities (e.g., the UN peacekeeping operations of the Clinton era). The resolution does discourage presidents from initiating much larger military operations without congressional authorization, but as demonstrated by the two Persian Gulf Wars, that generally serves the president's own political interests.

It follows that, short of repealing the War Powers Resolution as Congressman [Henry] Hyde (R-IL) tried to do in 1995, there are not many reforms in this area that the Executive branch would likely support. Needless to say, the Executive branch would not favor tightening the restrictions of the War Powers Resolution or removing any of the definitional flexibilities that it has developed over time.

[In earlier testimony,] I laid out my own thoughts about how Congress could reform the War Powers Resolution if it wishes to be a full partner with the president in national decision-making with respect to the use of force. I suggested that Congress could replace the sixty-day clock with a mechanism requiring Congress to vote under expedited procedures when U.S. forces are deployed into hostilities. Under this mechanism, an affirmative vote would be a vote to authorize the deployment and a negative vote would be a vote to order the withdrawal of U.S. forces.

The Executive branch would like this mechanism to the degree it induced Congress to authorize deployments ordered by the president. Certainly there would be many cases where it would have that effect. But the Executive branch would strongly dislike the mechanism to the degree it resulted in cases where Congress voted to order the president to withdraw U.S. forces. In such cases, the president either would have to comply with the wishes of Congress, or rely on the strength of his veto pen to carry forward with his policy. This means that, on balance, the Executive branch would not like the mechanism very much at all.

I doubt, however, that the Executive branch is worried my suggestion will become law. As I indicated earlier, the Executive branch does not believe that Congress wishes to fully share the responsibilities of national decision-making with respect to the use of force.

THE CONTINUING DEBATE:
The War Powers of the President

What Is New

President Bush's stance that he had the authority to act unilaterally as commander in chief against Afghanistan in 2001 and Iraq in 2003 reflects a view of presidential authority that he continued and expanded later in his years in office. When, for instance, critics objected to his plan in 2007 to "surge" a large number of extra troops into Iraq without congressional or public opinion support, Bush asserted, "I've made my decision, and we're going forward." Bush also relied on the commander-in-chief language to justify wiretaps and other electronic surveillance without a warrant to monitor Americans suspected of terrorist links. Attorney General Alberto Gonzales argued that the president could do so "based upon…his inherent role as commander in chief." Thus the war powers issue has come to include more than just the use of the military. Barack Obama had criticized Bush's expansive interpretation of his war powers. As president, though, Obama has followed policies that partly mirror Bush's both in the area of domestic and foreign clandestine operations and in the use of U.S. forces. For one, Obama did not feel the need to get congressional support to surge troops into Afghanistan in 2010. As Debate 17 indicates, some opponents of adding troops to Afghanistan believed Obama's order exceeded his legal authority.

Where to Find More

A review of the WPR's effectiveness is in the Congressional Research Service, *The War Powers Resolution: After Thirty-Six Years* (April, 2010) at opencrs.com/document/R41199/. A report of a commission co-chaired by two former secretaries of state that studied the war power and made recommendations about how to structure the relationship between the president and Congress is the *National War Powers Commission Report*, James A. Baker, III and Warren Christopher, co-chairman (Miller Center for Public Affairs of the University of Virginia, 2008). The report is online at www.millercenter.org/policy/commissions/warpowers/. For comments on Obama's use of the war powers see Ryan C. Hendrickson, "War Powers in the Obama Administration," *Contemporary Security Policy*, (August 2010).

What More to Do

Clear up more than 200 years of confusion about Congress' authority to declare war and the president's authority as commander in chief. Write and debate in class an amendment to the Constitution that will define as precisely as possible when (if ever) presidents can use military force or send U.S. forces into harm's way on their own authority and when (if ever) doing so would require a declaration of war or other form of congressional authorization.

BUREAUCRACY

POLICY POSITIONS OF FEDERAL AGENCIES:
Reflect the President's Position *or* Be Determined Independently?

REFLECT THE PRESIDENT'S POSITION

ADVOCATE: James L. Gattuso, Senior Research Fellow in Regulatory Policy, Thomas A. Roe Institute for Economic Policy Studies, Heritage Foundation

SOURCE: Testimony during hearings on "The Rulemaking Process and Unitary Executive Theory" before the U.S. House of Representatives, Committee on the Judiciary, Subcommittee on Commercial and Administrative Law, May 6, 2008

BE DETERMINED INDEPENDENTLY

ADVOCATE: Peter L. Strauss, Betts Professor of Law, Columbia University Law School

SOURCE: Testimony during hearings on "The Rulemaking Process and Unitary Executive Theory" before the U.S. House of Representatives, Committee on the Judiciary, Subcommittee on Commercial and Administrative Law, May 6, 2008

Article II of the Constitution begins with the words: "The executive power shall be vested in a president of the United States." Other phrases in the article give presidents the authority to appoint most executive branch officials and to have them report to him. Although limited and vague, this language implies extensive executive authority for the president.

Yet when presidents have been asked how much control they have over the executive branch, most have complained about their limited authority. Indeed, political leaders around the world frequently bemoan their inability to control their own governments. Once, during a joint press conference, President Vladimir Putin of Russia and President George W. Bush were professing a wish to cooperate but worried that their respective bureaucracies would not follow their lead. Bush fretted that his policy "sometimes…doesn't necessarily get translated throughout the levels of government [due to] bureaucratic intransigence." Putin agreed, "There is always a bureaucratic threat."

One reason that presidents find it hard to control the government is because career employees, civil servants, or bureaucrats overwhelmingly staff it. Moreover, the number of bureaucrats and their policy-making role have expanded considerably as the government has become larger and more complex. Bureaucratic authority also comes from the rulemaking authority that Congress has given bureaucratic agencies. As government has become larger and more complex, Congress has increasingly passed legislation that establishes general goals and delegates the authority to fill in the gaps to the executive branch. For example, the Americans with Disabilities Act (1990) requires employers to make a "reasonable accommodation" to avoid discriminating against handicapped workers unless doing so creates an "undue hardship." What reasonable accommodation and undue hardships are is left up to the agencies administering the law to work out. A third source of bureaucratic power is the laws that shield careerists from political interference. Beginning with job protection under the civil service acts, political officials are restrained from using political criteria when deciding whom to appoint to or fire from most government jobs. Similarly, civil servants are supposed to give advice and make decisions based on their professional opinions, rather than on political calculations. To advance the idea, Congress has created numerous independent regulatory agencies such as the Food and Drug Administration and provided them with various protections from political influence.

Presidents and others have been prone to claim that all these factors have made the bureaucracy too insulated and to look for ways to gain greater control over it. One of these methods is to require agencies to submit rules they wish to make, reports they want to issue, and even some speeches, congressional testimony and other views to the White House staff, the Office of Management and Budget, or some other oversight point. As this process has grown, a counterattack has been mounted. It charges that the president is subverting democracy by trying to politicize what should be unbiased administration and to subvert Congress' authority to establish agencies and procedures beyond political control. In recent times the term "unitary executive theory" has been used to denote the idea that the entire executive branch should be under the control of the president and that the policy positions and decisions of all agencies should be subject to presidential control.

The following two articles take up unitary executive theory. In the first reading, James L. Gattuso, a senior research fellow at the Heritage Foundation, a conservative think tank in Washington, D.C., argues that both the Constitution and democracy require that president, who is elected, be able to ensure that his views and priorities are reflected throughout the Executive branch where most officials are not answerable to the people. Columbia University Law School Professor Peter L. Strauss takes the opposite point of view and claims that in recent years and especially in the Bush administration, the effort to impose political control over agencies that Congress has tried to endow with independent authority reflects monarchical pretensions in the presidential office.

POINTS TO PONDER

➢ Notice that James Gattuso, like most who defend executive authority, cast the issue as a matter of long history on which presidents of both parties agree, while Peter L. Strauss, like most current critics, focuses on the presidencies of Ronald Reagan and, even more, George W. Bush.

➢ Is it always right or always wrong for public employees to openly oppose the policy stands of elected officials? If not "always" either way, then what is acceptable and when is it not?

➢ If you favor agency independence from the president, make sure you are comfortable with bureaucrats expressing views and making decisions against the president's wishes in cases when you agree with the president.

Policy Positions of Federal Agencies:
Reflect the President's Position

JAMES L. GATTUSO

"I agree with you, but I don't know if the government will," President John Kennedy is said to have once told a visitor. Kennedy's lament encapsulates in many ways the questions being discussed today. To what extent can—or should—a president be able to ensure that his views and priorities are reflected throughout the executive branch?

It's not just a matter of constitutional principle. Perhaps the greatest challenge faced by presidents in this regard is a practical one. Charged by the Constitution with "tak[ing] care that the laws be faithfully executed," they often find their efforts frustrated by the machinery of the executive branch that they head. Reflecting this frustration, Harry Truman predicted difficulties for his successor, the former general Dwight Eisenhower: "[H]e'll say, 'Do this! Do That!' And nothing will happen."

Nowhere has the challenge been greater than in the area of regulation. More than 50 agencies, ranging from the Animal and Plant Inspection Service to the Bureau of Customs and Border Protection, have a hand in federal regulatory policy. With nearly 250,000 employees, they produce over 4,000 new rules—and some 70,000 pages in the *Federal Register*—each year.

Managing this regulatory machinery in a way that not only reflects the president's priorities but faithfully executes the will of Congress and the mandates of the courts is no easy task. That is why, starting a generation ago, presidents began to establish systematic review processes for the promulgation of regulations.

The first such process was created in 1971, when President Richard Nixon required regulatory agencies to perform "quality of life" analyses of significant new regulations. Supervised by the Office of Management of Budget, the analyses were to outline regulatory analyses and their costs.

Gerald Ford expanded on this process, making control of regulatory growth part of his war on inflation, requiring agencies to prepare "Inflation Impact Statements," which were reviewed by the White House Council on Wage and Price Stability. Ford also set up a cabinet-level group to focus on other initiatives to control the cost of regulation.

Despite a different party affiliation, Jimmy Carter continued—and even expanded—regulatory review mechanisms during his Administration, continuing the practice of conducting economic analyses of proposed regulations and setting up a cabinet-level Regulatory Analysis Review Group to review proposed new rules. Upon taking office, [President Ronald W.] Reagan established a "Task Force on Regulatory Relief," chaired by Vice President George Bush, to oversee review of the regulatory process. In addition, he issued an executive order—E.O. 12291—detailing the review system. And perhaps most importantly from an institutional point of view, he charged the newly created Office of Information and Regulatory Affairs [OIRA] with oversight of that process.

The Reagan executive order on regulation continued in place during President George [H.W.] Bush's term, with a cabinet-level Council on Competitiveness headed by the Vice President taking the place of the Task Force on Regulatory Relief. OIRA continued to manage the review process, although no permanent OIRA chief was ever confirmed.

In 1993, President Bill Clinton replaced the Reagan-era Executive Order on regulatory review procedures with one of his own, E.O. 12866. Among the changes in the

Clinton order were greater transparency requirements and a limitation of review requirements to "significant" rules. But the basic structure of the review system was kept in place.

Further reflecting the continuing stability of the review system, President George W. Bush has kept the Clinton executive order in place. During his tenure, however, OIRA has issued a series of guidance documents for agencies—ranging from a "best practices" guide for regulatory impact analyses, to expanded requirements for peer review—to improve the consistency and quality of reviews under the executive order. Most recently, the Administration amended the executive order in several, relatively minor, ways—including expanding the role of agency "regulatory policy officers." Today—37 years after the first requirements were imposed, and 28 years after the creation of OIRA—centralized regulatory review is an almost universally accepted part of the regulatory landscape. Since the first review processes were established, seven Administrations—five Republican and two Democratic—have built upon them. Each changed the system in various ways, most improving upon that of its predecessor, but none has challenged its basic utility or legitimacy.

As six former OIRA Administrators—including Sally Katzen, the administrator under Bill Clinton—wrote in a 2006 joint letter: "All of us…recognize the importance of OIRA in ensuring that federal rules provide the greatest value to the American people. In our view, objective evaluation of regulatory benefits and costs, and open, transparent, and responsive regulatory procedures, are necessary to avert policy mistakes and undue influence of narrow groups."

And, despite early questions by some, the constitutionality of the idea of centralized White House review of rulemaking is today not seriously challenged. As early as 1981, in fact, the D.C. circuit [District of Columbia circuit of the U.S. Court of Appeals] recognized "the basic need of the President and his White House staff to monitor the consistency of agency regulations with Administration policy." Moreover, it could be argued that some type of review is constitutionally required in order for the president to reasonably meet his constitutional duty to "take care that the laws are faithfully executed."

To the extent there is any debate over the constitutional legitimacy of the process, it is when it conflicts with congressional assignments of responsibility or discretion to inferior officers within the executive branch. In such cases, some have argued, the president may not substitute his judgment for the judgment of the officer selected by Congress to perform a particular duty. As argued by Peter Strauss of Columbia Law School in previous testimony, the president is not "the decider," but merely the "overseer of decisions by others." While the chief executive oversees the performance of other executive branch officers, it is argued, he may not assume the decisional responsibility granted to them by Congress. Thus, in this view, the executive order's provision that disagreements between a regulatory agency head and the OIRA administrator be decided by the president is unconstitutional.

The problem is that this theory flies in the face of the principle that executive power under the Constitution is not shared—the concept of a "unitary executive." Article II of the Constitution flatly states that, "[t]he executive power is vested in a President of the United States of America." Not in plural "presidents," or "a president and other officers designated by Congress," but in "a president."

The unitary executive concept is not an exotic theory, but one of the most commonly held tenets of our constitutional system. As [legal scholars] Steven Calabresi and

Saikrishna Prakash have observed [in a *Yale Law School Journal* article]: "[T]hat the President must be able to control the execution of federal laws is easily understood and resonates strongly with the very earliest lessons we learn about our constitutional system." And, consistent with those lessons, the framers of the Constitution clearly rejected the idea of a shared executive—rejecting proposals for a multiple presidency and for a decision-sharing council.

In modern America, there are of course many examples of non-unitary executives. Most states, for example, have one or more elected statewide executive officers besides the governor, ranging from attorneys general to insurance commissioners. Christopher Berry and Jacob Gerson of the University of Chicago, in a forthcoming article, write in favor of a similar system for the federal government, suggesting the possibility of a "directly elected War Executive, Education Executive, or Agriculture Executive." However, even to outline the idea of an "unbundled executives" underscores the fact that that is not the system we currently have.

Of course, the differences between the sides in the current debate over the president's powers are not that stark. The unitary executive concept does not deny to Congress the assignment of duties to individual officers within the executive branch, as long as the president is able to exercise ultimate responsibility.

Conversely, few advocate a fully unbundled executive for the federal government. For the most part, even critics of the unitary executive concept recognize the president's power to articulate priorities and views, request adherence to them, and to dismiss those who do not help carry out his agenda.

This is important, since in practice the president almost never needs to issue an "order" to a regulatory officer make a particular decision. Even in cases where the president serves as the final arbiter in a dispute under regulatory review process, the officers involved—being appointees of the president—almost always accept the articulated priorities of the president. And when they do not, resignation or dismissal is the next likely option.

In this sense, the theoretical differences in the debate over the unitary executive may not come down to much in practical application. Under most any view, the president can legitimately exercise control over the rulemaking process.

And this is as it should be, for many reasons. The most important of these—perhaps counter-intuitively—is the check that clear responsibility provides over presidential power. Were authority shared among multiple persons in the executive branch, it would be relatively easy for the chief executive to avoid accountability for his actions. He would always be able to point his finger to some other officer, and mumble "my hands were tied." But with ultimate authority vested in the president, he is held to account for decisions, enabling voters—as well as other policymakers—to assign blame or credit.

It should also be noted that a strong system of centralized regulatory review, anchored in presidential authority, does not necessarily imply either more or less regulation. It simply means that the president's priorities—whatever they are—will be more accurately represented in decision making.

Lastly, none of this means that Congress has no role—or indeed does not have the primary role—in the regulatory policy. Just as the Constitution provides the president with executive power, Congress has ultimate legislative authority. If Congress disagrees with how the terms of a statute are applied in rules promulgated by the executive branch, it can simply make the statute more explicit (or even better, make its intent clear in the first instance).

Moreover, under the Congressional Review Act of 1996, a particular regulatory decision may be specifically "disapproved" by Congress. The statute—though so far rarely used—provides for expedited consideration by both Houses of a resolution of disapproval of a specific rulemaking. If approved by Congress, the resolution can take effect, even over a presidential veto, given sufficient support in Congress.

More generally, Congress's influence over regulatory policy could also be expanded through institutional changes within Congress, including the creation of a "Congressional Regulation Office." While Congress today receives detailed information from the Congressional Budget Office on the state of the budget and on proposals that would affect the budget, it has no similar source of information on regulatory programs. A Congressional Regulation Office would help to fill this gap. Such an office could review the regulatory impact of legislative proposals and report on the effects of rules adopted by agencies. In this way, it could act as both a complement to and a check on OIRA.

Lastly, to minimize the need for White House intervention in agency decision-making, policymakers should strengthen the ability of agencies themselves to evaluate the effects of their own regulations. Review and analysis need not be an adversarial process. Ideally, critical examination of the purpose and effects of proposed rules begins within the agency itself. To facilitate this, policymakers should ensure that each agency has sufficient analytical resources, and well as a well-designed internal review office to ensure that those resources are used meaningfully.

Systematic and centralized regulatory review of federal regulations is not only a legitimate use of presidential power, but—given the vast scope of rulemaking—virtually essential to taking care that the laws are faithfully executed. Congress nevertheless retains a primary role in regulatory policy—which can be exercised through more explicit legislation, review of specific rulemakings, and by expanding its own institutional capability to review and analyze the effects of rules.

Policy Positions of Federal Agencies:
Be Determined Independently

PETER L. STRAUSS

We all understand that the Constitution creates a single chief executive officer, the president, at the head of the government Congress defines to do the work its statutes detail. We do have a unitary executive. Disagreement arises over what the president's function entails. Once Congress has created a government agency and specified its responsibilities, we know both Congress and the courts are just to oversee the agency in its assigned work, not actually to perform that work. But is it the same for the president? When Congress authorizes the Environmental Protection Agency to regulate pollution, the Occupational Safety and Health Administration to regulate workplace safety, or the Food and Drug Administration to regulate the safety of food, drugs, and medical devices, what is the president's role? May he decide these matters, or is he, too, only to oversee the agencies' decision processes?

Our Constitution is very clear, in my judgment, in making the president the overseer of all the varied duties the Congress creates for government agencies to perform, including rulemaking. Yet our Constitution is equally clear in permitting Congress to assign duties to administrative agencies rather than the president. When it does, our president is not "the decider" of these matters, but the overseer of their decisions. As Attorney General [William] Wirt advised President [James] Monroe in 1823, when the president fails to honor that admittedly subtle distinction, he fails in his constitutional responsibility:

> [the president's role is to give] general superintendence [to those to whom Congress had assigned executive duties, as] it could never have been the intention of the constitution...that he should in person execute the laws himself....[W]ere the president to perform [a statutory duty assigned to another], he would not only be not taking care that the laws were faithfully executed, but he would be violating them himself."

That is, the assignment of decisional responsibility to others is a part of those laws to whose faithful execution the president must see. And when agency officials treat the president as the person entitled to decide matters Congress has committed uniquely to their judgment, they too fail in their obligations to the law. Consult with him they must; but at the end of the day, they are the ones responsible for deciding any matters placed uniquely in their charge.

Underlying today's inquiry, I imagine, are aspects of the Environmental Protection Agency's relationship with the White House and, in particular, the Office of Information and Regulatory Affairs [OIRA] over recent rulemaking, in particular the rulemaking concluded this past March setting primary and secondary national standards for ozone. From a variety of elements that have come to light—in good part, I must say, due to the welcome transparency of OIRA in its administration of Executive Order 128663—one can conclude that both the White House and the leadership of EPA regard the White House as having the final voice of decision on rulemakings statutorily committed to EPA's responsibility. Thus, in his recent confirmation hearings, the nominee to be General Counsel of the EPA resisted the suggestion that EPA should take an independent view, remarking that "ultimately, the [EPA] administrator works for the president of the United States." Recent writings, from Charlie Savage's brilliant account of the signing statement controversy, *Takeover: The Return of the Imperial Presidency and the Subversion of American Democracy* [Little, Brown, 2007], to Jack Goldsmith's chilling, *The Terror Presidency: Law and Judgment Inside the Bush Administration* [Norton, 2007], have made clear the strength of our president's claim to be "the Decider" across the breadth of government, and without regard to the particular assignments of authority that Congress may have enacted.

Internal and external communications that have come to public attention in the ozone rulemaking show how this attitude has prevailed. Within EPA, it is clear, scientific indicators from both inside and outside the agency pointed unequivocally in the direction of a secondary national standard for ozone that would differ from the primary standard. OIRA, it is equally clear, dug in its heels. The agency responded to OIRA's March 6 signal of unhappiness with a detailed memorandum on March 7 explaining the scientific basis for its preferred course and objecting to OIRA's apparent introduction of the cost concerns EPA is forbidden by law to rely upon in its decisionmaking. Not content, even after EPA's close consultation with the White House, to permit the agency to decide the matters Congress had left in its hands, OIRA then pushed the issue upstairs. The result was a remarkable letter from OIRA Administrator [Susan] Dudley: "The president has concluded that, consistent with Administration policy, added protection should be afforded to public welfare by strengthening the secondary ozone standard"—an outcome that was never in doubt, although even following EPA's preference the strengthening would have been less than its scientific advisors had counseled—"and setting it to be identical to the new primary standard...." This, Administrator Dudley continued, would avoid "setting a standard lower or higher than is necessary."

While Administrator Dudley's letter gives the appearance of recognizing that "you intend to render your determination," all parties understood that she was communicating a presidential decision with an expectation of obedience. Under the current administration's notoriously strong theory of a unitary presidency, EPA had no choice; its obligation was to implement the president's conclusion. The reported reaction of the solicitor general [the third ranking official in the U.S. Department of Justice], that what the White House was doing ran afoul of positions his office had recently taken in the Supreme Court, only underscores the hazards these developments pose to the rule of law. As the solicitor general had argued and the Court had agreed, EPA is forbidden to take costs into account in its Clean Air Act decisionmaking.

One gets the strong sense that the Supreme Court sustained EPA's extraordinary range of authority over air quality issues, in good part, precisely because it concluded Congress had authorized that agency to act only on the basis of science, and not a broader array of political factors such a economic cost or impact. This makes it possible to regard the decision as one governed by law, and within the ambit of judicial review that can assure its legality. But if the president, relying on his strong theory of a unitary presidency, is issuing commands, and he and his appointees regard it as his right to do so—and, consequently, their duty to obey—any assurance we might have about legality disappears. Transparently, concern with economic impact and not with EPA's reasoning from the scientific views in its rulemaking record underlay the president's reported conclusion. And that, to my mind, sharply illuminates the deep problems of confusing the president's legitimate, indeed essential role as overseer of all executive government, with a right to decide matters that Congress has delegated to particular agencies. When a decision is taken out of the hands of the agency equipped to be expert about the science and constrained by Congress's instructions, and delivered to a White House motivated by a much larger array of essentially political considerations reaching well beyond those factors Congress has authorized, legality disappears and is replaced simply by power politics.

I should be clear that the issues here are not simple ones. Our Constitution does make clear that we have but a single chief executive. The president's politics stand behind appointments to high office, and he properly claims opportunities to discuss his administration's policy preferences with his appointees. Indeed, the Constitution's text is explicit that he may demand consultation, in writing, on matters within the duties of their offices. In my judgment, that makes clear his right to discipline any appointee— even one to an independent regulatory commission—who refuses to consult with him and hear his views. Insofar as it creates a framework for consultation, Executive Order 12866 reflects a sound view of executive authority. It would do so even if it were fully extended to the independent regulatory commissions, that it now reaches only in part. The difficulties arise when a president reaches past consultation to demanding particular decisions. This is the subtle ground between hearing out the president and obeying him, and this is the issue that concerns me here.

In some contexts—for example, where Congress has empowered not one but two or three different agencies to deal with the same social issues—the government's practical need for coordination, for a view coherent across agency boundaries, can justify the president's assertion of authority to decide. When the Occupational Safety and Health Administration acted to limit worker exposure to atmospheric benzene, for example, its authority to protect gas station attendants overlapped with the EPA's responsibility to protect citizens from the same hazard. It was the EPA's authority to protect citizens who might be pumping their own gas from the same fumes. Resolving that kind of conflict requires a central voice. But in the case of ozone, we really do not see that. Setting the secondary air quality standard for ozone is indisputably EPA's business, and the very same phrase of the Constitution that recognizes the president's right to consult with EPA also recognizes that the duty of decision lies with EPA. The president's right to an opinion is the right to an opinion about a matter within the duty of the Department.

Finding the right balance between politics and law in our society, as any society, is achingly hard. I tell my administrative law students every year that this basically is what our subject is about. And clearly those who framed our Constitution understood that many of the constraints that operate on our government are properly those of politics, not law; yet where the constraints lie in politics, we ought to know politics is at work, not disguised as expertise. Moreover, law has its place, a place that is particularly important in the regulatory state with its enormous impacts on the economy and the public. Perhaps I can illustrate these points with two more vignettes from our early history.

The first is implicit in often-quoted passages from *Marbury v. Madison* [1803], Chief Justice [John] Marshall's opinion that famously established the place of the courts in the constitutional order. Distinguishing between those acts that a court might control by law, and those that were not subject to legal constraint, he denied any purpose to reach acts he was entitled to command from his subordinates. When an official:

is to conform precisely to the will of the president [h]e is the mere organ by whom that will is communicated. The acts of such an officer, as an officer, can never be examinable by the courts....The province of the court is, solely, to decide on the rights of individuals, not to enquire how the executive, or executive officers, perform duties in which they have a discretion. Questions, in their nature political, or which are, by the constitution and laws, submitted to the executive, can never be made in this court.

The thing to note is that we would never describe rulemaking decisions of the administrator of the EPA about air quality in the way Chief Justice Marshall describes decisions of the secretary of state about foreign affairs. The secretary of state is exercising discretion in its largest sense, cases in which there is no law to apply and which "can never be examinable by the courts." The great Chief Justice Marshall was not addressing the mixed questions of law and politics that are the everyday focus of administrative law and of judicial review for "abuse of discretion" under the APA. For those acts we actually depend on the possibility of effective judicial review to justify their legality; if standards did not exist permitting a court to assess the legality of the Administrator's acts, we would say an unconstitutional delegation had been made. These are not matters to be decided by politics, and they are questions examinable by the courts. And that brings us right back to the difficulty of having the president purport to decide them.

The second of my vignettes underscores the political constraints that operate on a president who better understands the importance of keeping politics and law apart. President Andrew Jackson had risked his reelection to a second term in office in 1832 with his successful veto of the bill that would have reauthorized the Bank of the United States. When he was then reelected by a wide margin, he took that as political vindication of his position on the Bank. He asked his Secretary of the Treasury, Louis McLane, to remove the government's funds from the Bank and deposit them in state Banks. But the Bank's authority ran until 1836, and the relevant statute provided that government funds were to be kept in it "unless the Secretary of the Treasury shall at any time otherwise order and direct." When Secretary McLane decided against removing the funds, Jackson removed him and appointed William Duane as his successor. Duane also proved resistant to Jackson's persistent demands, responding that "[i]n this particular case, Congress confers a discretionary power, and requires reasons if I exercise it. Surely this contemplates responsibility on my part." In September of 1833, after Duane had declined to remove the funds despite lengthy and fervent correspondence between them, Jackson removed him and appointed Roger Taney acting secretary. Almost immediately, Taney made the requested order. The result was a political furor. The Senate passed a Resolution of Censure and subsequently rejected Taney's nomination as secretary—the first time in American history it had rejected a presidential nomination to the cabinet. When, in 1835, President Jackson nominated Taney to a seat as associate justice of the Supreme Court, that nomination, too, failed. Changes in Senate membership finally permitted his renomination and confirmation as chief justice months later, in 1836, and the eventual expungement of the Resolution of Censure.

The president thus did prevail, but only at the political cost of an open fight with Congress, that reacted by tightening controls over his appointments. If the president removes the head of the EPA for not acting as he would prefer, that is likely to be a more public and politically costly act than having a subordinate write him "the president has concluded that…" with the expectation of obedience on both sides. President Jackson's recognition that the discretion involved lay with the Secretary of the Treasury, not himself, gave the events high political visibility and animated the machinery of checks and balances. Such visibility might lead a president simply to accept his official's contrary-to-advice decision. To underscore the legal understanding where authority over the bank funds lay, recall that Jackson was the president who at about the same time famously responded to the Supreme Court's decision in *Worcester v. Georgia* [1832] with "John Marshall has made his decision, now let him enforce it."

Twentieth century events reflect the same distinctions and concerns. Justice Hugo Black wrote for the Supreme Court, in assessing one of the century's most striking events of presidential overreaching, that "the president's power to see that the laws are faithfully executed refutes the idea that he is to be a lawmaker." Surely he knew how frequently executive agencies adopt regulations (currently about ten times as often as Congress enacts statutes). Strikingly, no one has drawn any connection between this holding and rulemaking; in my judgment, they have not drawn it precisely because they understand that agencies, and not the president, are the ones empowered to make rules. Agencies are lawmakers; except as Congress has authorized it, the president is not. Similarly, mid-century events emphasized the political constraints attached to the president's having to fire someone with whose actions he disagreed, rather than simply put his own decision in place. During the run-up to World War II, a time surely as testing as the present day, Attorney General Robert Jackson would advise President Franklin Roosevelt that it was his Secretary of the Interior, Harold Ickes, who had the legal authority to permit the sale of helium to Germany. Roosevelt earnestly wished to permit that sale while we were still formally a neutral country, prior to our entry into World War II. Ickes, following his own star, would not permit it In the end, Roosevelt preferred keeping Ickes in place, and the helium undelivered, to the alternative of replacing him.

Impressive recent contributions to the scholarly literature further underscore the importance for the integrity of rulemaking of keeping power politics out of it. Later this month two University of Texas Law School scholars, Thomas McGarity and Wendy Wagner, will be publishing *Bending Science* with Harvard University Press. It is a chilling account of the range of sophisticated legal and financial tactics political and corporate advocates use to discredit or suppress research on potential human health hazards. The economics-grounded political attack on the ozone regulation seems to fit right in. And it is hardly the only such episode in the newspapers today, as recent accounts about NOAA's efforts to secure protection for the right whale will attest; they portray the vice president's office delaying a final rule for more than a year by expressions of concern about the science involved. Of course the vice president's office has no scientific expertise and responsibilities; the questions raised were quickly and emphatically answered; and the delays continue. Lisa Bressman and Michael Vandenbergh interviewed top political officials at the EPA during the Bush I [George H. W.] and Clinton administrations and found what is perhaps not surprising, that political interventions from the White House in the president's name on high-profile or high-stakes matters come from multiple voices and often enough in varying tones. One cannot always be sure that "the president has concluded" refers to the incumbent's decision, rather than a subordinate's or internal cabal's belief about what it ought to be. "According to EPA respondents, OIRA review and other White House involvement are unsystematic… triggered in many cases not just by the need for centralized oversight of particular regulatory matters but also by the interest of the particular officials involved." Professors Bressman and Vanderbergh also express skepticism that "presidential control facilitates political accountability. EPA respondents believed that they were more transparent and responsive than the White House....We conclude, somewhat paradoxically, that agencies, though not comprising elected officials, may better promote political accountability than the White House....If the White House shapes high-level issues, it ought to reveal in what manner and through which office or offices it does so. For now, agencies appear to better represent public preferences and resist parochial pressures—the asserted aims of political accountability."

You will likely hear arguments that the president is, after all, our chief executive, that our Constitution embodies the judgment that we should have a unitary executive, and so even if the result of OIRA's interventions is to convert agency judgments about rulemaking into presidential judgments, that only accomplishes what the Constitution commands. In my judgment it is not only an erroneous argument, but one dangerous to our democracy. The president is commander in chief of the armed forces, but not of domestic government. In domestic government, the Constitution is explicit that Congress may create duties for heads of departments—that is, it is in the heads of departments that duties lie, and the president's prerogatives are only to consult with them about their performance of those duties, and to replace them, with senatorial approval required of their replacements, when their performance of those duties of theirs persuades him that he must do so. This allocation is terribly important to our preservation of the rule of law in this country. The heads of departments the president appoints and the Senate confirms must understand that their responsibility is to decide—after appropriate consultation to be sure—and not simply to obey. We cannot afford to see all the power of government over the many elements of the national economy concentrated in one office.

Professor Peter Shane, a highly respected scholar of the presidency and a former lawyer in the Office of Legal Counsel, [recently] put the matter this way:

> The [George W.] Bush administration has operated until recently against the backdrop of Republican-controlled Congresses and a Supreme Court highly deferential to executive power....Not only has it insisted, in theory, on a robust constitutional entitlement to operate free of legislative or judicial accountability, but it also has largely gotten away with this stance. And that success—the administration's unusual capacity to resist answering to Congress and to the courts—has fed, in turn, its sense of principled entitlement, its theory that the Constitution envisions a presidency answerable, in large measure, to no one....

What might Congress do about the simple affront President Bush's strong "unitary executive" theory appears to me to be to Congress's authority to confer organization and authority on elements of government by enacting statutes? You might enact by statute the judgment that EPA preferred; that would not only freeze matters probably best left to flexible administration, but also risk a presidential veto—the price you pay whenever you delegate authority to the executive branch. Politically, you hold the power of the purse. When the House attempted to exercise that power last summer, in connection with the president's remarkable amendments to Executive Order 12866 on which I have previously testified before you, I understand that OMB responded with the claim that a failure to appropriate funds for OIRA would be an unconstitutional intrusion on the president's constitutional authority—the power of the unitary executive. What a laughable claim that is! The president, like the king of England in his battles with Parliament, must rely on Congress for the funds he desires and if you find him abusing his authority you can withhold those funds. My late colleague Charles Black once wrote "My classes think I am trying to be funny when I say that, by simple majorities, the Congress could at the start of any fiscal biennium reduce the president's staff to one secretary for answering social correspondence…but I am not trying to be funny; these things are literally true." Why should Congress tolerate the expenditure of government moneys to fund politicized White House operations by which the president or the vice president purport to divert agencies from the tasks it has given them, to substitute power politics for law? This too, of course, is a political control—and it is precisely the kind of political control the framers of our Constitution put in place as a safeguard [among other things], against monarchical pretension in presidential office.

THE CONTINUING DEBATE:
Policy Positions of Federal Agencies

What Is New

Like Debate 12 on the president's war powers, this debate on the president's authority as chief executive arises in part from the brevity and frequent vagueness of the Constitution. Article III vests the "executive power" in the president, says he may "require the opinion" of the principle officers of the executive branch, and direct him to ensure that the country's laws are "faithfully executed." That is scant verbiage to decide what powers of the chief executive office of the world's most powerful country are or should be. Like a great deal of the current understanding of what the president's powers are, the scope of his executive authority is the product of the current president and Congress. Certainly President Bush pushed the notion of a unitary executive, but it is also not surprising that usually only Democrats in Congress condemned it. Then once Barack Obama became president, the Democrats in Congress became less intent on limiting the president's authority to control the bureaucracy, and it was the Republicans who grumbled. It is also worth noting that Obama came to office pledging not to interfere. However, it did not take long for complaints to begin. For example, Jeffrey Ruch, an attorney who represents scientific whistle-blowers to the press, "We are getting complaints from government scientists now [July 2010] at the same rate we were during the Bush administration."

Where to Find More

More on agency rulemaking and the idea of a unitary executive is in the statement of Curtis W. Copeland of the Congressional Research Service on "Federal Rulemaking and the Unitary Executive Principle" during hearings before the Subcommittee on Commercial and Administrative Law, Committee on the Judiciary, U.S. House of Representatives on May 6, 2008. It is available at www.judiciary.house.gov/judiciary/hearings/pdf/Copeland080506.pdf/. A study that traces the history of presidential executive authority and is sympathetic to a unitary executive is Steven G. Calabresi and Christopher S. Yoo, "The Unitary Executive During the First Half-Century," *Case Western Reserve Law Review* (1996). For the opposite take, go to Karl M. Manheim, and Allan Ides, "The Unitary Executive, Loyola-LA Legal Studies," Paper No. 2006–39 (2006), available at the Social Science Research Network site, www.ssrn.com/abstract=943046/. On the issue of bureaucracy in a democracy, read Willliam T. Cormley Jr. and Steven J. Balla, *Bureaucracy and Democracy: Accountabilitly and Performance* (CQ Press, 2004).

What More to Do

As you ponder this issue, focus on the principle and avoid deciding what you think based on the immediate case at hand. For example, many strongly criticized President Bush in 2007 for suppressing the worried views on global warming of scientists at the National Aeronautics and Space Administration because they differed from his more sanguine position. That might outrage you, but also consider how you feel about the controversy when President Harry S. Truman, who wanted to confine the Korean War to the Korean peninsula, fired the U.S. commander, General Douglas A. MacArthur, who wanted to attack China and lobbied Congress to support him. Was this one of Truman's finest moments, or was he abusing his power?

JUDICIARY

ELENA KAGAN'S NOMINATION TO THE SUPREME COURT:
Flawed *or* Worthy of Confirmation?

FLAWED

ADVOCATE: Charles Grassley, Republican U.S. Senator, Iowa

SOURCE: Debate on the floor of the U.S. Senate, *Congressional Record*, August 3, 2010

WORTHY OF CONFIRMATION

ADVOCATE: Lindsey Graham, Republican U.S. Senator, North Carolina

SOURCE: Debate on the floor of the U.S. Senate, *Congressional Record*, August 3, 2010

This debate is partly an extension of the controversy in Debate 1 over whether federal judges should decide constitutional issues solely by trying to determine what those who wrote it and its amendments meant, or go beyond original intent to apply the Constitution within the context of modern circumstances.

This controversy is important because each year the Supreme Court makes numerous decisions that are of major policy importance. Moreover, the court's ability to decide policy is nearly unchecked when it comes from constitutional interpretation. Thus there is a great degree of literal truth to what Chief Justice Charles Evans Hughes once observed: "We are under a Constitution, but the Constitution is what the judges say it is."

When deciding what the law is, no judge is a legal automaton who looks only at original intent and precedent (what earlier justices have ruled in similar cases). Instead, every justice brings a degree of personal/ideological perspective to the court. It is not surprising then that almost always Democratic presidents appoint Democratic judges and Republican presidents appoint Republicans to the bench. Given the ideologies of the respective parties, it is also not surprising that justices appointed by Democratic presidents tend to take liberal positions on the bench, and Republican-appointed judges most often make conservative rulings.

Under President George W. Bush, the Supreme Court moved at least somewhat rightward after he appointed two conservative justices, Chief Justice John G. Roberts, Jr. and Associate Justice Samuel A. Alito, Jr. They joined two other conservative justices, Antonin Scalia and Clarence Thomas. Of the remaining five justices, four (Stephen G. Breyer, John Paul Stevens, David H. Souter, and Ruth Bader Ginsburg) had somewhat liberal records. The ninth justice, Anthony M. Kennedy, had a moderate to slightly conservative voting record and became the "swing vote on the court." The measure of each justice's ideology is how the justices line up with one another on cases they decide by a 5-to-4 vote. These are often the most crucial cases with important constitutional implications. There were 59 such 5-to-4 decisions during the 2007, 2008, and 2009 terms of Supreme Court, and on 68% of those decisions the four conservative justices voted one way and the four liberal justices voted the other way, with Kennedy casting the deciding vote.

President Barack Obama got his first chance to nominate a justice when Justice Souter announced in April 2009 that he would retire. To replace him, Obama nominated Sonia Sotomayor. After a fairly contentious confirmation hearing and debate, the Senate confirmed Sotomayor on August 6, 2009, by a vote of 68 to 31. All 59 Democrats voting supported her; 31 of the 40 Senate Republican opposed her. During her first year, she clearly filled the liberal opening left by Souter's departure. Of 18 votes during the 2010 term that split 5 to 4, 61% had the conservative four justice (Roberts, Scalia, Thomas, and Alito) on one side and the four liberal justice (Stevens, Breyer, Ginsburg, and now Sotomayor) on the other, with Kennedy once again the deciding vote.

President Obama had another opportunity to name a new justice in 2010 when another liberal justice, John Paul Stevens retired. This time, Obama picked U.S. solicitor general Elana Kagan. The debate over her nomination in early August 2010 took place almost one year exactly after that of Justice Sotomayor. In the first reading, Republican Senator Charles Grassley of Iowa explains why he opposes Kagan's confirmation. In the second reading, South Carolina's Lindsey Graham indicates why he is one of the few Republican senators supporting Kagan. Senator Ben Nelson of Nebraska was the only Democrat to opposed Kagan, but unfortunately he did not explain his position.

POINTS TO PONDER

➤ What does it say about how politically neutral courts are that the votes of the liberal and conservative justices on contentious political issues can line up along political lines and, thus, are reasonably predictable?

➤ Unlike most members of his party, Senator Graham was willing to give the president considerable leeway in the ideological leanings of his nominee. Does this seem bravely nonpartisan or politically naïve?

➤ What do you make of the debate over Kagan's experiential qualifications?

Elena Kagan's Nomination to the Supreme Court: Flawed

Charles Grassley

I rise to take a few minutes to discuss the reasons why I am voting against Elena Kagan to be Associate Justice. An appointment to the Supreme Court is one of the most important positions an individual can hold under our Constitution. It is a lifetime position on the highest Court of the land. I take very seriously my constitutional role of advice and consent. The Senate's job is not only to provide advice and consent by confirming nominees who are intelligent and accomplished. Our job is to confirm nominees who will be fair and impartial judges, individuals who truly understand the proper role of a justice in our system of government. Our job, then, is to confirm nominees who will faithfully interpret the law and the Constitution without personal bias or prejudice.

When the Senate makes its determination, we must carefully assess the nominee's legal experiences, record of impartiality, and commitment to the Constitution and rule of law. We need to assess whether the nominee will be able to exercise what we call judicial restraint. We have to determine if the nominee can resist the siren call to overstep his or her bounds and encroach upon the duties of the legislative and executive branches. Fundamental to the U.S. Constitution are the concepts of these checks and balances and the principle of separation of powers. The preservation of our individual freedoms actually depends on restricting the role of policymaking to legislatures rather than allowing unelected judges with lifetime appointments to craft law and social policy from the judicial bench. The Constitution constrains the judiciary as much as it constrains the legislative branch and the executive branch under the president.

When President Obama spoke about the criteria by which he would select his judicial nominees, he placed a very high premium on a judge's ability to have, in his words, "empathy when deciding the hard cases." This empathy standard glorifies the use of a judge's heart and broader vision of what America should be in the judicial process. He said that individuals he would nominate to the Federal judiciary would have "a keen understanding of how the law affects the daily lives of American people."

So when President Obama nominated Elena Kagan to the Supreme Court, we have to assume he believed she met his "empathy" standard.

This empathy standard is a radical departure from our American tradition of blind, impartial justice. That is because empathy necessarily connotes a standard of partiality. A judge's impartiality is absolutely critical to his or her duty as an officer of an independent judiciary, so much so that it is actually mentioned three times in the oath of office that judges take.

Empathetic judges who choose to embrace their personal biases cannot uphold their sworn oath under our Constitution. Rather, judges must reject that standard and decide cases before them as the Constitution and the law requires, even if it compels a result that is at odds with their own political or ideological beliefs.

Justice is not an automatic or a mechanical process. Yet it should not be a process that permits inconsistent outcomes determined by a judge's personal predilections rather than from the Constitution and the law. An empathy standard set by the president that encourages a judge to pick winners and losers based on that judge's personal or political beliefs is contrary to the American tradition of justice.

That is why we should be very cautious in deferring to President Obama's choices for the judicial branch. He set that standard; we did not. We should carefully evaluate these nominees' ability to be faithful to the Constitution. Nominees should not pledge allegiance to the goals of a particular political party or outside interest groups that hope to implement their political and social agendas from the bench rather than getting it done through the legislative branch.

When she was nominated to the Supreme Court, meaning Ms. Elena Kagan, Vice President [Joe] Biden's Chief of Staff, Ron Klain, assured the leftwing groups that they had nothing to worry about in Elena Kagan because she is, in his words, "clearly a legal progressive." So it is pretty safe to say that President Obama was true to his promise to pick an individual who likely would rule in accordance with these groups' wishes. A justice should not be a member of someone's team working to achieve a preferred policy result on the Supreme Court. The only team a justice of the Supreme Court should be on is the team of the Constitution and the law.

I have said on prior occasions that I do not believe judicial experience is an absolute prerequisite for serving as a judge. There have been dozens of people, maybe close to 40, who have been appointed to the Supreme Court who have not had that experience. Solicitor General Kagan, however, has no judicial experience and has very limited experience as a practicing attorney.

Unlike with a judge or even a practicing lawyer, we do not have any concrete examples of her judicial method in action. Thus, the Senate's job of advice and consent is much more difficult. We do not have any clear substantive evidence to demonstrate Solicitor General Kagan's ability to transition from a legal academic and political operative to a fair and impartial jurist.

Solicitor General Kagan's record and her Judiciary Committee testimony failed to persuade me that she would be capable of making this crucial transformation. Her experience has primarily been in politics and academia. As has been pointed out, working in politics does not disqualify an individual from being a justice. However, what does disqualify an individual is an inability to put politics aside in order to rule based upon the Constitution and the law. In my opinion, General Kagan did not demonstrate that she could do that during her committee testimony. Moreover, throughout her hearings, she refused to provide us with details on her views on constitutional issues.

It was very unfortunate we were unable to elicit forthcoming answers to many of our questions in an attempt to assess her ability to wear the judicial robe. She was not forthright in discussing her views on basic principles of constitutional law, her opinions of important Supreme Court cases or personal beliefs on a number of legal issues. This was extremely disappointing.

Candid answers to our questions were essential for us as Senators to be able to ascertain whether she possesses the proper judicial philosophy for the Supreme Court. In fact, her unwillingness to directly answer questions about her judicial philosophy indicated a political approach throughout the hearing. I was left with no evidence that General Kagan would not advance her own political ideas if she is confirmed to the Federal bench.

General Kagan's refusal to engage in meaningful discussion with us was particularly disappointing because of her position in a 1995 Law Review Article entitled "Confirmation Messes, Old and New." In that article she wrote—and she was then Chicago Law Professor Kagan—that it was imperative that the Senate ask about, and the Supreme Court nominees discuss, their judicial philosophy and substantive views on issues of constitutional law. Specifically, then-Professor Kagan wrote:

> When the Senate ceases to engage nominees in meaningful discussion of legal issues, the confirmation process takes on an air of vacuity and farce, and the Senate becomes incapable of either properly evaluating nominees or appropriately educating the public.

That is in Professor Kagan's own words.

Bottom line, General Kagan did not live up to her own standard. She was nonresponsive to many of our questions. She backed away from prior positions and statements. She refused to discuss the judicial philosophy of sitting judges.

When asked about her opinions on constitutional issues or Supreme Court decisions, she either declined to answer or engaged in an overview of the status of the law rather than a discussion of her own personal views. Because of her shallow record on the issues, this approach to the hearing was extremely troubling.

At her confirmation hearing, General Kagan told us to "look to [her] whole life for indications of what kind of judge or justice [she] would be." Well, General Kagan's record has not been a model of impartiality, as we looked at her record and her life just as she asked us to. There is no question that throughout her career she has shown a strong commitment to far-left ideological beliefs. Solicitor General Kagan's upbringing steeped her in deeply held liberal principles that at one point she stated she had "retained...fairly intact to this date." Her jobs have generally never required her to put aside her political beliefs, and she has never seen fit to do so. Her first instinct and the instincts she has relied upon throughout her career are her liberal, progressive political instincts put to work for liberal, progressive political goals. I have no evidence that if Solicitor General Kagan were confirmed to the Supreme Court she would change her political ways or check her political instincts or goals at the courthouse door.

In fact, General Kagan gained her legal expertise by working in politics. She started out by working on Congresswoman Liz Holtzman's Senate campaign, hoping for, in her words, a "more leftist left." She also worked as a volunteer in Michael Dukakis's presidential run. The Dukakis campaign wisely put her to work at a task that is political to the core—opposition research. There she found a place where she was encouraged to use her political savvy and make decisions based upon her liberal, progressive ideology.

Moreover, while clerking for Justice [Thurgood] Marshall, General Kagan's liberal personal convictions—rather than the Constitution and the law—seemed to be her ultimate guide when analyzing cases. General Kagan consistently relied on her political instincts when advising Justice Marshall, channeling and ultimately completely embracing his philosophy of "do[ing] what you think is right and let[ting] the law catch up." Her Marshall memos clearly indicate a liberal and outcome-based approach to her legal analysis.

In several of her memos, it is apparent she had a difficult time separating her deeply held liberal views and political beliefs from the law. For example, in one case she advised Justice Marshall to deny certiorari because the Court might make "some very bad law on abortion." In another case, she was "not sympathetic" that an individual's constitutional right to keep and bear arms had been violated. In essence, her judicial philosophy was a very political one.

During her tenure at the White House, Solicitor General Kagan worked on a number of highly controversial issues, such as abortion, gun rights, campaign finance reform, and the Whitewater and Paula Jones scandals. She herself described her work for President Clinton as being primarily political in nature.

In a 2007 speech, she said, "During most of the time I spent at the White House, I did not serve as an attorney, I was instead a policy adviser....It was part of my job not to give legal advice, but to choose when and how to ask for it."

Her documents from the Clinton Library prove just that. She forcefully promoted far-left positions and offered analyses and recommendations that were far more political than legal in nature. For example, during the Clinton administration, General Kagan was instrumental in leading the fight to keep partial-birth abortion on the books. Documents show that she boldly inserted her own political beliefs in the place of science. Specifically, she redrafted language for a nonpartisan medical group to override scientific findings against partial-birth abortion in favor of her own extreme views. Despite the lack of scientific studies showing that partial-birth abortion was never necessary and her own knowledge that "there aren't many [cases] where use of the partial-birth abortion is the least risky, let alone the 'necessary,' approach," Solicitor General Kagan had no problem intervening with the American College of Obstetricians and Gynecologists to change their own policy statement.

After her intervention, this doctor group's statement no longer accurately reflected the medically supported position of the obstetricians and gynecologists. Rather, the group's statement now said that partial-birth abortions should be available if the procedure might affect the mother's physical, emotional or psychological well-being. The reality is that General Kagan's change was not a mere clarification. It was, in fact, a complete reversal of the medical community's original statement.

Other documents show that Solicitor General Kagan also lobbied the American Medical Association to change a statement it had issued on partial-birth abortion. These documents demonstrated her "willingness to manipulate medical science to fit the Democratic Party's political agenda on a hot button issue of abortion."

During her hearing, General Kagan refused to admit she participated in the decision-making process of what language the gynecologists would use in their statement on partial-birth abortion. The documents present a very different picture. Although she stated that there was "no way she could have intervened with the ACOG," she did exactly that. Instead of responding to a legitimate inquiry in an open and honest manner, she deflected the question and gave, at best, nonresponsive answers.

In addition, Solicitor General Kagan worked on a number of initiatives to undermine second amendment rights. She was front and center of the Clinton administration's anti-second amendment agenda. She collaborated closely with Jose Cerda on the administration's plan to ban guns by "taking the law and bending it as far as we can to capture a whole new class of guns." After the Supreme Court in *Printz v. U.S.* found parts of the Brady antigun law to be unconstitutional, she endeavored to find legislative and executive branch responses to deny citizens' second amendment rights.

Even in academia, Solicitor General Kagan took steps and positions that were based on her strongly held personal beliefs rather than an evenhanded reading of the law. As dean of Harvard Law School, she actively defied Federal law by banning military recruiters from campus while the Nation was at war. Prior to her appointment as dean, the Department of Defense had made clear to Harvard that the school's previous recruitment policy was not in compliance with the Solomon Amendment, so Harvard did what Harvard should have done: changed its policy to abide by the Federal law. But when the Third Circuit, which does not include Massachusetts, ruled on the issue, then-Dean Kagan immediately reinstituted the policy barring the military from the Harvard campus. She took this position because she personally believed the military's longstanding policy of don't ask, don't tell, in her words, was "a profound wrong—a moral injustice of the first order." She claimed her policy was equal treatment. However, the Air Force believed the policy was playing games with its ability to recruit. The Army believed the policy resulted in it being stonewalled. Then-Dean Kagan was entitled to her opinion, but—no different than anybody else in this country—she was not free to ignore the law. The Solomon Amendment required that military recruiters be allowed equal access to the university as any other recruiter.

The bottom line is that then-Dean Kagan refused to follow the law and instead interpreted that law in accordance with her personal beliefs. The Supreme Court unanimously rejected her legal position on the Solomon Amendment and upheld our military.

I am concerned that Solicitor General Kagan will continue to use her personal politics and ideology to drive her legal philosophy if she is confirmed to the Supreme Court, particularly since her record shows she has worked to bend the law to fit her political wishes.

Further, I am concerned with the praise Solicitor General Kagan has lavished on liberal jurors who promote activist philosophies such as those of Israeli Judge Aharon Barak. Judge Barak is a major proponent of judicial activism who believes judges should "bridge the gap between law and society." He also went on to say that we ought to use international law to advance a social and political agenda on the bench.

At a Harvard law event attended by then-Dean Kagan, Judge Barak noted with approval cases in which "a judge carries out his role properly by ignoring the prevalent social consensus and becoming a flag bearer of new social consensus." When I asked General Kagan if she endorsed such an activist judicial philosophy, she replied that Judge Barak's philosophy was something "so different from any that we would use or want to use in the United States." But that contradicts her previous statement about Judge Barak that he is a "great, great judge" who "presided over the development of one of the most principled legal systems in the world." I am not able to ascertain if Solicitor General Kagan agrees with Judge Barak or if she rebukes his positions, so I am left to believe she endorses the judicial method of what she calls her "judicial hero" and his views on judicial restraint or lack thereof. I cannot support a Supreme Court nominee whose judicial philosophy endorses judicial activism as opposed to judicial restraint.

With respect to the second amendment, General Kagan testified that the *Heller* and *McDonald* cases were binding precedent for the lower courts and due all the respect of precedent. However, I worry that, if confirmed, her deeply engrained personal belief will cause her to overturn this precedent because she does not personally agree with those decisions or the constitutional right to bear arms. At the hearing, Solicitor General Kagan was unwilling to discuss her personal views on the second amendment or whether she believes the right to bear arms is what it is today—a fundamental right. When I asked her about her thoughts on the issue, she simply replied that she "had never thought about it before." I also asked her whether she believed self-defense was at the core of the second amendment. She could only respond: "I have never had the occasion to look into the history of the matter." As a former constitutional law professor both at Chicago and Harvard, Solicitor General Kagan's response ought to be troubling to anybody who heard it.

A key theme in the U.S. Constitution reflects the important mandate of the Declaration of Independence. It is the recognition that the ultimate authority of a legitimate government depends on the consent of a free people, the "consent of the governed." As Thomas Jefferson wrote:

> We hold these truths to be self-evident, that all men are created equal, that they are endowed by their Creator with certain unalienable Rights, that among these are Life, Liberty, and the pursuit of Happiness. That to secure these rights, Governments are instituted among Men deriving their just powers from the consent of the governed.

As former Attorney General Edwin Meese explains:

> That all men are created equal means that they are equally endowed with unalienable rights....Fundamental rights exist by nature, prior to government and conventional laws. It is because these individual rights are left unsecured that governments are instituted among men.

So I am concerned that Elena Kagan refused to agree with my comments about the Declaration of Independence—that there are such things as inalienable rights and if government does not give, government cannot take away.

Similarly, Senator [Tom] Coburn (R-OK) asked General Kagan if she agreed with William Blackstone's assessment about the right to bear arms and use those arms in self-defense. She replied, "I don't have a view on what are natural rights, independent of the Constitution."

If you don't have a view about rights that existed before the Constitution was ever written, do you have the knowledge to be a Supreme Court justice?

Bottom line: The fact that General Kagan refused to answer our questions about her personal opinions on the right to bear arms leads me to conclude that she does not believe people have a natural right of self-preservation, unrelated to the Constitution.

I am concerned about Solicitor General Kagan's views on our constitutional right to bear arms not only because of her anti-second amendment work during the Clinton administration but also in light of her memo in the *Sandidge* case when she clerked for Justice Marshall. In her memo, she summarily dismissed the petitioner's contention that the District of Columbia's firearm statute violated his second amendment right to keep and bear arms. Instead of providing a serious basis for her recommendation to deny the certiorari, her entire legal analysis of this fundamental right consisted of one sentence: "I am not sympathetic."

A further basis for my concerns about whether she will protect or undermine the second amendment if she is confirmed is the decision of the Office of Solicitor General under her leadership not to even submit a brief in the second amendment *McDonald* case. Solicitor General Kagan's record clearly shows she is a supporter of restrictive gun laws and has worked on numerous initiatives to undercut second amendment fundamental rights. So, not surprisingly, as solicitor general, she could not find a compelling Federal interest for the United States to submit a brief in a case that dealt with fundamental rights and the second amendment of the Constitution. This was a case that everyone knew would have far-reaching effects. It is apparent that political calculations and personal beliefs played a role in Solicitor General Kagan's decision not to file a brief in this landmark case to ensure that constitutional rights of American citizens were protected before the Supreme Court.

With respect to the Constitution's commerce clause, Solicitor General Kagan was asked whether she believed there are any limits to the power of the Federal Government over the individual rights of American citizens.

Unfortunately, her response didn't assure me that, if confirmed, she would ensure that any law Congress creates does not infringe on the constitutional rights of our citizens. Specifically, Senator Coburn asked her whether she believed a law requiring individuals to eat three vegetables and three fruits a day violated the commerce clause. Though pressed on this and other lines of questioning on the commerce clause, she was unwilling to comment on what would represent appropriate limits on federal power under the Constitution—and probably the commerce clause has been used more than any specific power of Congress for greater control of the Federal Government over State and local governments or over the economy and probably depriving individual rights in the process.

I am not sure Solicitor General Kagan understands that ours—meaning our government—is a limited government and that the restraints on the Federal Government's power are provided by the Constitution and the concept of federalism upon which our Nation is founded. The powers of the Federal Government are explicitly enumerated in article I, section 8 of the Constitution. Further, the 10th amendment provides that the powers not expressly given to the Federal Government in the Constitution are reserved to the States.

The Founding Fathers envisioned that our government would be constitutionally limited in protecting the fundamental rights of life, liberty, and property and that the laws and policies created by the government would be subject to the limits established by the Constitution. As James Madison wrote in *Federalist* No. 45, "The powers delegated by the proposed Constitution to the federal government are few and defined. Those which are to remain in the State government are numerous and indefinite."

I am not convinced the solicitor general appreciates that there are express limits the Constitution places on the ability of Congress to pass laws. I am not persuaded by her nonanswers to our commerce clause questions that she won't be a rubberstamp for unconstitutional laws that threaten an individual's personal freedoms.

Elena Kagan's Nomination to the Supreme Court: Worthy of Confirmation

Lindsey Graham

My view of Elena Kagan is quite simple. I found her to be a good, decent person; well qualified in terms of her legal background to sit on the Court. The people who know her the best, who worked with her, have nothing but good things to say about her. She is not someone a Republican President would have picked—she is definitely in the liberal camp when it comes to judging—but I think within the mainstream of the left wing of the Court.

The Court has two wings to it. A lot of decisions are—not a lot, some decisions are 5–4. But you know who the conservatives on the Court are and you know who the liberals are. The one thing they have in common is that they are highly qualified, great Americans who happen to view the law a bit differently in terms of philosophy. But they have brought honor to the Court.

Justice [Ruth Bader] Ginsburg is definitely in the left wing of the Court. Justice [Antonin] Scalia is definitely in the right wing of the Court. From what I have been told, they have a deep personal friendship; that Justices Scalia and Ginsburg have become fast friends and admire each other even though they often cancel out each other's vote and they have some real good give and take in their opinions. In that regard I think they represent the best in judging and the best in our democracy, and that is two different philosophies competing on the battlefield of ideas but understanding that neither one of them is the enemy. They have a lot of respect for each other.

What brought me to the conclusion to vote for Solicitor General Kagan ? I believe the advise and consent clause of the Constitution had a very distinct purpose. Under our Constitution, article 2, it allows the President of the United States to appoint Supreme Court Justices and judges to the Federal bench in general. That is an authority and a privilege given to him by the Constitution. You have to earn that by getting elected President.

After having watched Senator [John] McCain (R-AZ) literally about kill himself to try to be president, I have a lot of admiration for those who will seek that office. It is very difficult to go through the process of getting nominated and winning the office. I daresay that Senator McCain would indicate it is one of the highlights of his life to be nominated by his party and to go out and fight for the vote of the American people.

Senator [Barack] Obama (D-IL) was a member of this body before being elected president. I can only imagine what he went through, going through the primary process, beating some very qualified, high-profile Democrats to get the nomination of his party. When it was all said and done, after about $1 billion and a lot of sweat and probably sleepless nights, he was elected by the people of the United States to be our president. I want to honor elections.

My job, as I see it—and I am just speaking for me—each Senator has to determine what they believe the advise and consent clause requires. From my point of view I will tell you what I think my job is in this process. No. 1, it is not to be a rubberstamp. Why would you even have the Senate involved if the president could pick whomever he or she chose? So there is a collaboration that goes on here. There is a check and balance in the Constitution where we have to advise and consent. So I do not expect myself or any other Senator to feel once the election is over, you have to vote for whomever they pick. You do not. There may be a time when I vote "no" to a President Obama nominee.

But my view of things is sort of defined by the *Federalist* Paper No. 76, Alexander Hamilton, who was one of our great minds of this country's history. He said, "The Senate should have special and strong reasons for denial of confirmation."

I think his comment to us is that, yes, you can say no, but you need to have a special and strong reason because the Constitution confers upon the president the right to pick. What would those strong and special reasons be? Whatever you want it to be. That is the fact of politics. Those strong and special reasons can literally be whatever you want it to be as a Senator. But here is what Alexander Hamilton had in mind as to strong and special reasons. He continued:

> To what purpose, then, require the cooperation of the Senate? I answer, that the necessity of their concurrence would have a powerful, though, in general, a silent operation.

I think that powerful and silent operation is meant to be a firm but not overly political check and balance; not a continuation of the campaign. Because the campaign is a loud experience. It is 50 plus 1, rah-rah-rah, build yourself up, tear your opponent down. So when Alexander Hamilton indicated to the Senate his view of the advise and consent clause, that it would be powerful, though in general a silent operation, I think he is telling us: The campaign is over. Now is the time to govern. So when this nominee comes your way from the person the Constitution confers the ability to pick and choose, you should have in mind a powerful but silent operation.

"It would be an excellent check upon a spirit of favoritism...." I think that is pretty self-evident, that one of the things we do not want to have with our judiciary is it becomes an award or prize for somebody who helped in the campaign, picking somebody who is close to you personally, related to you, so that the job of Federal judge becomes sort of political patronage. The Senate could be a good check and balance for that. I think that is one of the reasons we are involved in the process, to make sure that once the election is over, the President himself does not continue the campaign. The campaign is over and we have a silent operation in terms of how we deliver our advice and consent. So he is telling the president through the Senate that once the campaign is over, you should not pick someone who will help you politically or return a favor; you should pick someone who will be a good judge.

It "would tend greatly to prevent the appointment of unfit characters from State prejudice." That is another view that Alexander Hamilton had, as to how the Senate should use its advise and consent duties, to make sure that unfit characters do not go on the Court. I can imagine that has probably been used in the past.

"From family connection," that one is obviously self-evident. You don't want to pick someone from your family unless there is a good reason to do so. "[F]rom personal attachment or from a view to popularity."

When I add up all these things, I am looking at the necessity of their concurrence with a: "powerful, though, in general, silent operation. It would be an excellent check upon the spirit of favoritism...to prevent the appointment of unfit characters...from family connection, from personal attachment, or from a view to popularity."

In other words, we are trying to make sure the president, he or she, picks a good, qualified judge, not some unfit character, some person tied to him or her personally, not someone who would be a popular choice but would be a lousy judge.

When I apply that standard to Elena Kagan, I cannot find anything about her that makes her an unfit character to me. Frankly, what I know about her from listening to her for a couple of days and having people tell me about her is I think she is a very fine person with stellar character.

The letter that moved me the most about Elena Kagan the person, I wish to share with the Senate and read, if I may. This comes from Miguel Estrada. For those of you who may not remember, Miguel Estrada was chosen by President Bush to be on the court of appeals. For a variety of reasons—there is no use retrying the past—he never got a vote by the Senate. He never got out of committee. All I can say from my point of view is, it was one of the great mistakes. I am sure there have been times when Republicans have done the same thing or something like it to a well-qualified Democratic selection. But I happened to be here when Miguel Estrada was chosen by President Bush. So he had a very unpleasant experience when it came to getting confirmed as a judge. But here is what he wrote about Elena Kagan, a Republican conservative lawyer chosen by President Bush to be on the court of appeals, writing for Elena Kagan:

> I write in support of Elena Kagan's confirmation as an Associate Justice of the Supreme Court of the United States. I have known Elena for 27 years. We met as first year law students at Harvard, where we were assigned seats next to each other for our classes. We were later colleagues as editors of the Law Review and as law clerks to different Supreme Court Justices; and we have been friends since.
>
> Elena possesses a formidable intellect, an exemplary temperament, and a rare ability to disagree with others without being disagreeable. She is calm under fire and mature and deliberate in her judgments. Elena would also bring to the Court a wealth of experience at the highest level of our Government and of academia, including teaching at the University of Chicago, serving as the Dean of the Harvard Law School and experience at the White House and as the current Solicitor General of the United States. If such a person, who has demonstrated great intellect, high accomplishments and an upright life, is not easily confirmable, I fear we will have reached a point where no capable person will readily accept a nomination for judicial service.
>
> I appreciate that considerations of this type are frequently extolled but rarely honored by one side or the other when the opposing party holds the White House. I was dismayed to watch the confirmation hearings for then-Judge Alito, at the time one of our most distinguished appellate judges, and find that they range from the—

Well, I am not going to read it all.

> ...one could readily identify the members of the current Senate majority, including several who serve on the Judiciary Committee [and their partisan views].
>
> Lest my endorsement of Elena's nomination erode the support she would see from her own party, I should make it clear that I believe her views on the subjects

that are relevant to her pending nomination—including the scope of judicial role, interpretive approaches to the procedure and substantive law, and the balance of powers among the various institutions of government—are as firmly center-left as my own are center-right. If Elena is confirmed, I would expect her rulings to fall well within the mainstream of current legal thought, although on the side of what is popularly conceived as "progressive." This should come as a surprise to exactly no one. One of the prerogatives of the president under our Constitution is to nominate high federal officers, including judges, who share his (or her) governing philosophies. As has often been said, though rarely by senators whose party did not control the White House at the time, elections have consequences.

Elena Kagan is an impeccably qualified nominee. Like [Justices] Louis Brandeis, Felix Frankfurter, Robert Jackson, Byron White, Lewis Powell and William Rehnquist—none of whom arrived at the Court with prior judicial service—she could become one of our great Justices. I strongly urge you to confirm her nomination without delay.

I think that says a lot of Elena Kagan. I think it says a lot about Miguel Estrada. She wrote a letter basically—I asked her to—to tell me what she thought about Miguel Estrada. I will read that in a minute. But at the end of the day, those of us in the Senate have to understand that every branch of government includes human beings and there is a rule that stood the test of time. I didn't make this one up. It was somebody far wiser than I am, somebody far more gifted than I ever hope to be, somebody I put a lot of trust in.

It is called the Golden Rule. "Do unto others as you would have them do unto you." That is probably one of the most powerful statements ever made. It is divine in its orientation, and it is probably something that would serve us all well if we thought about it at moments such as this.

I am going to vote for Elena Kagan because I believe constitutionally she meets the test the Framers envisioned for someone to serve on the Court. I don't think the Framers ever envisioned Lindsey Graham from South Carolina voting no because President Obama picked someone who is clearly different than I would have chosen. Because if that were the case, the campaign never ended. It would undercut the president's ability to pick someone of like philosophy. My job is to make sure the person he chose is qualified, of fit character, not chosen for favoritism or close connection but chosen based on merit.

I have no problem with Elena Kagan as a person. I have no problem with her academic background. I have no problem with her experience as a lawyer. Even though she has worked for Justices whom I would not have ruled like, even though she has taken up political causes I oppose, that is part of democracy.

Her time as solicitor general, where she represents the United States before the Supreme Court, was reassuring to me. She has had frontline experience in the war on terror. She has argued before the Supreme Court that terrorist suspects should be viewed under the law of war. She supports the idea that someone who joins al-Qaida has not committed a crime. They have taken up arms against the United States, and they can be held indefinitely without trial if, under proper procedures, they have been found to be part of the enemy force. She understands detainees held at Bagram Airfield in Afghanistan should not be subject to judicial review in the United States because they are prisoners of war in an active theater of combat. If she gets on the Court—and I am certain she will—

she will be able to bring to the Court some frontline, real-world experience in the war on terror. She has had an opportunity to represent the United States before the Supreme Court, arguing that this Nation is at war, and the people who attacked us on 9/11 and who continue to join al-Qaida are not some common criminals but people subject to the law of armed conflict. Her testimony when she was confirmed as solicitor general was reassuring to me that she understood that very important concept.

How she rules, I don't know. I expect she will be more similar to Justice [John Paul] Stevens in the way she decides cases. The person she is replacing is one of the giants of the Court from the progressive side. I expect she will follow his lead most of the time. I do believe she is an independent-minded person. When it comes to war on terror issues, she will be a valuable member of the Court and may provide a perspective other judges would not possess. That is my hope.

I don't vote for her expecting her to do anything other than what she thinks is right, ruling with the Court most of the time in a way a Republican nominee would not have ruled. It gets back to my point of a minute ago. If I can't vote for her, then how can I ask someone on the other side to vote for that conservative lawyer, maybe judge, who has lived their life on the conservative side of the aisle, fighting for conservative causes, fighting for the pro-life movement, standing for the conservative causes I believe in, a strong advocate of a second amendment right for every American? That day will come. I hope sooner. But one day that day will come. What I hope we can do from this experience is remember that when that day does come, the Constitution has not changed at all. The only thing changed was the American people chose a conservative Republican president. I ask my colleagues to honor that choice, when that conservative president, whoever he or she may be, picks someone whom my colleagues on the other side would not have chosen. But that has been the way it has been for a couple hundred years now.

Justice Ginsburg, the ACLU general counsel, got 96 votes. Justice Scalia got 96 or 97 votes. Senator [Strom] Thurmond, my predecessor, voted for Justice Ginsburg. There is no way on God's green Earth [that] Strom Thurmond would have voted for Justice Ginsburg if he believed his job was to pick the nominee. There is no way many of my colleagues on the other side would have ever voted for Justice Scalia if they thought it was their job or they had the ability to make a selection in line with their philosophy. No one could have been more polar opposite than Ginsburg and Scalia. But not that long ago, in the 1990s, this body, without a whole lot of fussing and fighting, was able to put on the Court two people who could not be more different but chose to be good friends.

The history of confirming nominees to the Supreme Court is being lost. Seventy-three of the 123 Justices who served on the Supreme Court were confirmed without even having a roll-call vote. Something is going on. It is on the left, and it is on the right. I hope this body will understand one thing: The judiciary is the most fragile branch of government. They can't go on cable TV and argue with us as to why they are qualified. They cannot send out mailings advocating their positions. They have no army. All they have is the force of the Constitution, the respect of the other branches and, hopefully, the support of the American people.

Having gone to Iraq and Afghanistan many times, the one thing I can tell my colleagues that is missing in most countries that are having difficult times is the rule of law. What is it? To me, the rule of law is a simple but powerful concept. If you ever find yourself in a courtroom or before a magistrate or a judge, you will be judged based not on what tribe you came from. You will be judged based on what you did, not who you are.

The one thing we don't want to lose in this country is an independent judiciary. We are putting the men and women who are willing to serve in these jobs sometimes through hell. Judge Alito was poorly treated. I am very proud of what Senator Sessions was able to do as ranking member. We had a good, spirited contest with Sotomayor and Kagan . I thought the minority performed their role in an admirable fashion. I appreciate what Senator Leahy did working with Senator Sessions. I thought these two hearings were conducted in the best traditions of the Senate.

The votes will be in soon. She is going to get a handful of votes on our side. I have chosen to be one of those handful. From a conservative point of view, there are 100 things one can find at fault in terms of philosophy and judicial viewpoint with Elena Kagan . I have chosen not to go down that road. I have chosen to go down a different path, a path that was cleared and marked for me long before I got here, a path that has a very strong lineage, a path that I believe leads back to the Constitution, where the advice and consent clause is used in a way not to extend the election that is now over but as a reasonable, powerful but silent check on a president who chose a judge for all the wrong reasons. Choosing a liberal lawyer from a president who campaigned and governs from the left is not a wrong reason. Choosing a conservative lawyer or judge once you campaign for the job running right of center, in my view, is not the wrong reason. The wrong reason would be if the person you chose was not worthy of the job, did not have the background or the moral character to administer justice. I cannot find fault with Elena Kagan using that standard.

I will vote for her. I will say to anybody in South Carolina and throughout the country who is listening: She is not someone I would have chosen, but it is not my job to choose. It is President's Obama's job. He earned that right. I have no problem with Elena Kagan as a person. I think she will do a good job, consistent with her judicial philosophy. I hope and pray that the body over time will get back to the way we used to do business. If we don't watch it, we are going to wake one day, and we will politicize the judiciary to the point that good men and women, such as Sam Alito, Justice [John] Roberts, and Elena Kagan, will not want to come before this body and be a judge. If that ever happened, it would be a great loss to this country.

THE CONTINUING DEBATE:
Elena Kagan's Nomination to the Supreme Court

What Is New

On August 5, 2010, the Senate confirmed Elena Kagan as the Supreme Court's 112th justice. The 63–37 vote was mostly along party lines. All but one Democrat voted for her; all but five of the Senate's Republicans voting against her. At age 50 when she was confirmed, Justice Kagan may well be on the court and exercise an important influence over law and policy until 2040 or later. Although Kagan will probably vote mostly with the liberal blue on the Court, it will be difficult to begin to assess how she will vote on the Court and otherwise perform before the end of its 2011 term (October 2010–June 2011). She will almost certainly play a large role in deciding some of cases such as *United States v. Arizona* (Debate 2) and *Perry v. Schwarzenegger* (Debate 4) that are discussed in this volume and that are working their way through the federal court system.

Where to Find More

For current court information, including voting patterns, go to the Supreme Court of the United States blog (SCOTUSBLOG) at www.scotusblog.com/. *The Harvard Law Review* also publishes annual data on cases, voting, and other matters, usually in its November issue. Visit the Supreme Court's Web site at www.supremecourtus.gov/, especially for the cases on its docket for the current term that begins each year October. Another good site, one which contains visual and audio material as well, is www.oyez.org/. For the selection of justices, read Christine L. Nemacheck, *Strategic Selection: Presidential Nomination of Supreme Court Justices from Herbert Hoover through George W. Bush* (University of Virginia Press, 2007). For attitudinal influence on the votes of justices, see Issac Unah and Ange-Marie Hancock, "U.S. Supreme Court Decision Making, Case Salience, and the Attitudinal Model," *Law & Policy* (2006). For more on Sotomayor, go to her confirmation hearings on the Web site of the Senate Judiciary Committee at www.judiciary.senate.gov/.

What More to Do

Check to see how Justice Kagan is voting and how those votes line up with other justices. Most analysts, including Senator Graham in the second reading, expect that on 5 to 4 votes she will align herself with the liberal justices: Breyer, Ginsburg, and Sotomayor. But justices sometimes befuddle predictions. Also read up about current cases and see if you can predict how Justice Kagan will vote given your appraisal of her approach to the law.

15 STATE AND LOCAL GOVERNMENT

ALLOWING STATES TO COLLECT SALES TAXES ON INTERSTATE COMMERCE:
Leveling the Playing Field *or* A Threat to Electronic Commerce?

LEVELING THE PLAYING FIELD

ADVOCATE: Steven Rauschenberger, past President, National Conference of State Legislatures

SOURCE: Testimony during hearings on "H.R. 3396—The Sales Tax Fairness and Simplification Act" before the House of Representatives, Committee on the Judiciary, Subcommittee on Administrative and Commercial Law, December 6, 2007

A THREAT TO ELECTRONIC COMMERCE

ADVOCATE: George S. Isaacson, Tax Counsel for the Direct Marketing Association

SOURCE: Testimony during hearings on "H.R. 3396—The Sales Tax Fairness and Simplification Act" before the House of Representatives, Committee on the Judiciary, Subcommittee on Administrative and Commercial Law, December 6, 2007

Under the first U.S. Constitution, the Articles of Confederation (in force 1781–1788), the United States was more a league than a country. Those who drafted the Articles were so anxious to avoid the excesses of British rule that they created a document that gave the central government very little power beyond foreign affairs and reserved for the states all other aspects of government power. As a result, the central government could not function effectively. Among other weakness, the central government could not regulate commerce either among the states or between them and foreign countries. As such, the individual states could and did establish and apply tariffs, embargoes, and other trade regulations against each other as well as internationally.

With no central economic authority, the country floundered during the 1780s. Rampant inflation, plummeting foreign and domestic commerce, and other economic hardships burdened the land. Economic woes created turmoil, and it is not too strong to say that the survival of the United States as a united country was in doubt by the mid-1780s.

To meet this peril, delegates from the 13 states met in 1787 at the Constitutional Convention in Philadelphia, drafted a new Constitution, and sent it to the states for ratification. When in June 1788 New Hampshire became the ninth state to ratify the Constitution, it went into force. The new Constitution significantly increased the power of the central government and diminished the power of the states. Two clauses in Article I are particularly important to this debate about states levying a sales tax on items moving between states. The "interstate commerce clause" in section 8 gave Congress the authority to regulate commerce among the states and with foreign countries. And section 9 declared that, "no tax or duty shall be laid on articles exported from any state." "Exported" in the meaning of the time meant sent to another state as well as to another country. For most of U.S. history, cases arising under the interstate commerce clause were the most numerous to reach the Supreme Court. However, the legal battle over whether a state can charge a sales tax on items leaving it or arriving in it is relatively new. One reason is that sales taxes are relatively new. The first enacted was by Alabama in 1921. Currently, 45 of the 50 states have a sales tax. Another reason is that despite the advent of catalog sales in the late 1880s by Richard Sears and Alvah C. Roebuck, the amount of goods being purchased by consumers in one state remotely (by mail, phone, or now the Internet) was limited.

As such interstate sales began to grow, however, the states moved to tax them by requiring that vendors collect taxes on items being sent into the state or to supply to the state records of everyone in a state who had purchased an item out-of-state. Frequently these taxes were called "use taxes" because a state cannot apply a sales tax in another state. The legality of this practice was decided by two Supreme Court cases in the 1960s. The first ruled that a vendor that had a "substantial physical presence" such as a store in a state could be required to collect a sales tax on items shipped into the state even if the items bypassed the store and went directly to the consumer. But in the second case, the Supreme Court denied to states the power to tax remote sales if the only connection is that the vendor had with the buyer was by mail or another form of interstate communications. The court reaffirmed this decision in *Quill v. North Dakota* (1992), specifically noting the burden on interstate commerce of complying with the varying sales taxes that are or could be levied by the more than 29,000 state, country, and local governments. Also in that decision, though, the court noted that Congress has the authority to require vendors to collect sales taxes on goods moving in interstate commerce and to devise a formula for passing those on to the states.

In an effort to persuade Congress to allow the taxation of interstate sales, the states have been working to formulate a common program called the Streamlined Sales and Use Tax Agreement to tax online and other remote sales. Hearings on legislation in Congress to allow that brought the countervailing testimony of Steven Rauschenberger, past President of the National Conference of State Legislatures, and George S. Isaacson, Tax Counsel for the Direct Marketing Association. Rauschenberger argues in the first reading that states are losing over $33 billion in possible revenue from taxes on remote sales. He believes there needs to be a change in a tax system that was designed for an economy that existed almost 80 years ago and that creates tax discrimination depending on where a consumer makes a transaction. Isaacson disagrees, arguing that Congress should avoid removing the constitutional barrier to the tax of interstate sales which, he says, have served the nation well for two centuries and created the largest and most vibrant economy in the history of the world.

POINTS TO PONDER

➢ What is the main issue, whether all states agree to the Streamlined Sales and Use Tax Agreement or whether there should be new tax?

➢ If Congress decides to allow a remote-sales tax, should the revenues be divided among the states or used by the federal government for its own purposes?

➢ Is there a "fairness" issue involved, or is this issue simply a matter of money?

Allowing States to Collect Sales Taxes on Interstate Commerce: Leveling the Playing Field

STEVEN RAUSCHENBERGER

Ever since 2002, state legislators through the National Conference of State Legislatures (NCSL) have adopted resolutions calling upon the Congress of the United States to consider and approve federal legislation that would give a state authority to require all sellers (except those qualifying for the small business exception) to collect the state's sales taxes if that state is in compliance with the Streamlined Sales and Use Tax Agreement. The National Conference of State Legislatures is the bi-partisan national organization representing every state legislator from all fifty states and our nation's commonwealths, territories, possessions and the District of Columbia. Let me make this very clear, state legislators are not advocating any new or discriminatory taxes on electronic commerce. We desire, however, to establish a streamlined sales and use tax collection system that is seamless for sellers in the new economy and respects the sovereignty of state borders. [A use tax is a sales tax applied to something purchased in another state or country.]

The new economy or if you prefer, electronic commerce, which is not bound by state and local borders makes it critical to simplify and reform state and local taxes to ensure a level playing field for all sellers, to enhance economic development, and to avoid discrimination based upon how a sale may be transacted. Government cannot allow a tax system that was designed for an economy that existed almost 80 years ago to be the deciding factor as to where our constituents make a transaction.

SALES TAX POPULARITY

As we all know, taxes are never popular. However, if state and local governments are to provide necessary services, such as education and public safety, then we need to maintain our ability to levy taxes. In surveys of taxpayers as to which tax of all the major federal, state and local taxes they dislike the least, the surprising answer has consistently been the sales tax.

Voters all over the country have approved local sales taxes to pay for sports stadiums, added police protection, land acquisition for open space, and transportation improvements. The taxpayers of the state of Michigan overwhelmingly voted to use the sales tax as opposed to property tax as the major source of revenue for education, and then in following years they have voted to increase the sales tax in order to provide additional funding for education.

The general sales and use tax is the primary consumption tax for state and local governments. In 2005, sales taxes accounted for one-third of state revenues—over $311 billion—with the largest percentage of the funds used to finance K—12 education.

SALES TAX AND ELECTRONIC COMMERCE

The problem states have with the sales tax is that the tax base keeps shrinking. In the 1930s, when the sales tax was first imposed, consumers bought goods from the local merchant and it was not that difficult for the merchant to collect a few cents on the dollar. Also, most Americans spent very little on services—they spent most of their money on taxable goods. And there were very few "remote sellers."

In the 1970s and 1980s, the share of personal consumption expenditures began to shift from taxable goods to services—things like medical care, health clubs, legal and accounting services. So the sales tax was applied on a smaller and smaller share of tangible products. This was compounded on the goods side by mail order outlets selling goods without collecting sales taxes from their customers—a practice sanctioned by the U.S. Supreme Court in the *National Bellas Hess* case in 1967 and reaffirmed in the *Quill* decision in 1992.

Today, states face a new threat to sales tax revenue, electronic commerce, with the potential to dramatically expand the volume of goods sold to customers without collection of a sales or use tax. The combined weight of the shift to a service-based economy and the erosion of sales tax revenues due to electronic commerce threatens the future viability of the sales tax and the ability of state governments to fund essential services such as education, homeland security and public safety.

According to the Center for Business and Economic Research at the University of Tennessee, in 2003, the estimated combined state and local revenue loss due to remote sales was between $15.5 billion and $16.1 billion. [Remote sales would include items purchased out-of-state personally, by mail, or by some other non-electronic means and shipped to one's home or business, thus avoiding the sales tax in either state.] For electronic commerce sales alone, the estimated revenue loss was between $8.2 billion and $8.5 billion. The report from the University of Tennessee further estimates that the revenue loss will grow and that by 2008, the revenue loss for state and local governments could be as high as $33.6 billion, of which it is estimated that $17.8 billion would be from sales over the Internet. (See Table 1.)

TABLE 1

Combined State & Local Revenue Losses from E-Commerce
and All Remote Commerce—2008

State	E-Commerce Loss ($ millions)	All Remote Sales ($ millions)
Alabama	238.7	449.7
Arkansas	190.6	359.2
Arizona	435.7	821.1
California	2452.0	4620.4
Colorado	287.8	542.4
Connecticut	266.0	501.2
District of Columbia	48.8	91.9
Florida	1248.2	2351.1
Georgia	600.0	1130.5
Hawaii	130.3	245.5
Iowa	141.4	266.4
Idaho	66.3	125.0
Illinois	582.2	1097.0
Indiana	323.6	609.7
Kansas	178.8	336.9
Kentucky	214.6	404.3
Louisiana	409.8	772.2

TABLE 1   (continued)

Combined State & Local Revenue Losses from E-Commerce and All Remote Commerce—2008

State	E-Commerce Loss ($ millions)	All Remote Sales ($ millions)
Massachusetts	286.4	539.6
Maryland	265.9	501.1
Maine	67.2	126.6
Michigan	587.3	1106.6
Minnesota	381.2	718.3
Missouri	313.9	591.5
Mississippi	191.9	361.6
North Carolina	405.9	764.9
North Dakota	34.3	64.6
Nebraska	123.4	232.4
New Jersey	469.9	885.5
New Mexico	140.4	264.6
Nevada	186.6	351.5
New York	1288.4	2427.7
Ohio	608.6	1146.8
Oklahoma	185.4	349.3
Pennsylvania	585.6	1103.4
Rhode Island	58.5	110.3
South Carolina	209.4	394.5
South Dakota	47.0	88.6
Tennessee	508.3	957.9
Texas	1634.5	3079.9
Utah	150.7	284.0
Virginia	294.8	555.4
Vermont	29.1	54.8
Washington	574.6	1082.7
Wisconsin	303.4	571.7
West Virginia	86.6	163.2
Wyoming	38.9	73.3
United States	17,872.9	33,677.8

Source: Dr. Donald Bruce & Dr. William Fox, Center for Business & Economic Research, University of Tennessee

State legislators recognize that they have been part of this problem. Over the last 80 years, state and local policymakers have created a confusing, administratively burdensome tax system with very little regard for the compliance burden placed on multi-state businesses. In 1999, NCSL passed a resolution, written by NCSL's Task Force on State and Local Taxation of Telecommunications and Electronic Commerce that acknowledged that states need to simplify their sales and use taxes and telecommunications taxes for the 21st century. We recognized that we have been a key part of the problem and we accepted the fact that it was our problem to solve.

In our resolution, we formulated a set of seven principles that we used to develop a proposal for simplifying and streamlining state and local sales and use tax collection systems. The overriding theme of those seven principles is competitive neutrality. State legislators from across the country unanimously approved this resolution that declared that "State and local tax systems should treat transactions involving goods and services, including telecommunications and electronic commerce, in a competitively neutral manner." The resolution further stipulated that "a simplified sales and use tax system that treats all transactions in a competitively neutral manner will strengthen and preserve the sales and use tax as vital state and local revenue sources and preserve state fiscal sovereignty.

THE COST OF COLLECTION FOR SELLERS

As you are aware, the sales tax is imposed on the customer, not the seller. Sellers determine the sales tax to be collected, collect the tax and remit the tax collected to the state (in four states, Alabama, Arizona, Colorado and Louisiana, sellers also must remit the local portion of the sales tax directly to the local government). Under the current sales tax system, the seller also is liable for any mistakes that might occur due to misinformation from the buyer or even the state. This means that the seller is liable for any uncollected sales tax plus interest and penalties.

A recent national survey commissioned by the Joint Cost of Collection Study, a public/private sector group, and conducted by PricewaterhouseCoopers LLP, has shown that in fiscal year 2003 the total cost to sellers to collect state and local sales taxes was $6.8 billion. This amount was calculated after subtractions for state vendor discounts and retailer float on the sales tax revenues.

The study showed that for fiscal year 2003, for retailers selling between $150,000 and $1 million, the average cost was 13.47 percent of the sales taxes collected or approximately $2,386; for mid-size retailer, between $1 million and $10 million in sales, the average cost was 5.2 percent or approximately $5,279; and for the larger retailers, over $10 million in sales, the average cost of collection was 2.17 percent or approximately $18,233. It is important to remember that these amounts, including the total cost for all retailers of $6.8 billion, are not reimbursed to the retailer by the state or local government, these costs come out of the retailer's own pocket.

The burden on retailers to comply with 46 different sales tax systems and the monetary cost to retailers for compliance resulted in the two Supreme Court decisions, cited above, that prohibited a state from requiring an out-of-state seller from collecting sales tax on a purchase made by a resident of the state.

SOLUTION: STREAMLINED SALES AND USE TAX AGREEMENT

Beginning in 2000, state legislators, governors and tax administrators, along with representatives of retailers and others in the private sector, started the process to develop a simpler, uniform and fairer system of sales and use taxation, that removes the burden imposed on retailers, preserves state sovereignty, levels the playing field for all retailers, and enhances the ability of U.S. companies to compete in the global economy. The urgency to develop such a system caused NCSL's Executive Committee to set aside NCSL's rule of non-interference in state legislation and to endorse model legislation committing sales tax states to multistate discussions on developing a fairer and simplified system. By 2002, 35 states had enacted this legislation, sending delegations composed of legislators, tax administrators, local government officials and representatives of the private sector to monthly meetings that resulted in the formulation and approval of the Streamlined Sales and Use Tax Agreement. As of today, all of the sales tax states, except for Colorado, are participating in the ongoing process to simplify sales tax collections.

The key features of the agreement are simplification of sales and use tax laws and administration; the use of technology for calculating, collecting, reporting and/or remitting the tax; and, state assumption of the costs of collection for remote sellers. The key simplifications contained in the agreement as adopted by the states are:

- Uniform product definitions, from food and related items to digital products
- Uniform state and local tax base
- Reductions in the number of tax rates
- Requirements for state/central administration
- Central seller registration
- Uniform returns and remittances
- Simplified exemption administration
- Uniform audit procedures/reduction of the number of audits
- Uniform privacy protections
- Notice requirements for rate changes
- Uniform sourcing
- Uniform telecommunications sourcing
- Uniform administrative definitions
- Eliminations of caps and thresholds on rates
- Standardization for sales tax holidays
- Uniform rounding rule

Since the agreement was ratified in November 2002, 22 states have enacted legislation to bring their sales tax statutes and administrative rulings into compliance with the agreement. On October 1, 2005, thirteen states with a population of over 55 million residents were certified to be fully in compliance with the agreement. It is expected that on January 1, 2008, the states of Arkansas, Nevada, Washington and Wyoming will be in full compliance with the agreement as their statutes become effective.

SALES TAX FAIRNESS AND SIMPLIFICATION ACT

The Streamlined Sales and Use Tax Agreement is voluntary for states as well as for remote sellers. Since October 1, 2005, over 1,100 retailers have volunteered to begin collecting sales taxes for the member states, and these states have started to receive previously uncollected revenues for sales tax on transactions made through out-of-state retailers.

I believe that you will agree that this effort to streamline sales tax collection has been unprecedented in our history. In less than six years, the states working together with the support and assistance of the private sector, developed a new sales tax system that was fairer, simpler, more uniform and is technologically applicable; 22 states, almost half of all the states with a sales tax, enacted legislation to comply with these changes; and, the system is working. It is operational! However, our work to establish a truly seamless system is only half done. It is now Congress' turn to act. The states through the Streamlined Sales and Use Tax Agreement have provided Congress with the justification to allow states that have complied with the agreement to require remote sellers to collect those sales taxes as was intended in the Quill decision.

The Sales Tax Fairness and Simplification Act, H.R. 3396 embodies all the simplification requirements of the Streamlined Sales and Use Tax Agreement and provides certainty for taxpayers, retailers and other businesses that the states cannot backtrack on simplifications but if we do, the prohibition of the Quill decision will be reinstated.

NCSL supports H.R. 3396 because the legislation:

- provides for a national small business exception so that sellers with less than $5 million in taxable remote sales would be exempt from collection requirements;

- ensures reasonable and adequate compensation for all sellers for the cost of collection;

- provides certainty to taxpayers and sellers by allowing for an appeals process that includes review of the decisions of the Governing Board of the Streamlined Sales Tax System by the United States Court of Federal Claims;

- ensures that any filings by sellers in the course of registering, calculating, collecting and/or remitting sales and use taxes collected cannot be used as a criterion for determining nexus for any other tax responsibilities, including state business activity taxes; and

- ensures that the agreement simplifications are applied to the administration and collection of transactional taxes on telecommunications services.

MISCONCEPTIONS AND MISSTATEMENTS

Over the last six years, as we have worked to develop a simplified and fairer sales tax system, we have heard criticisms and arguments against streamlining and against Congress setting aside the *Bellas Hess* and *Quill* decisions. I would like to take a few moments to correct some of the misconceptions that our opponents have made, some of which I am sure will be expressed this morning.

Myth: "The Streamlined Sales Tax Agreement does not simplify tax compliance for retailers."

Fact: Even if states did nothing more than adopt the proposed administrative changes contained in the Streamlined Sales and Use Tax Agreement, all retailers will benefit from reduced complexity. Opponents contend that rates are the biggest complication, but even Robert Comfort, Vice President for Tax Policy at Amazon.com, told a congressional hearing in 2001, "...rates are not a problem for Amazon.com." Sellers have testified over and over that the real burdens with collection are not sales tax rates but the different product definitions from state to state, different state and local tax bases and the different rules and administrative procedures for registering, collecting, filing and remittance of sales taxes.

Under the agreement, the certified automated system calculates the sales tax to be collected not the merchant, based upon the delivery address submitted by the consumer. All merchants that collect sales taxes using the state certified automated technology would be held harmless for any miscalculations. The state assumes the liability from the merchant, who under the current collection system bears total liability. The merchant would only be held liable for under-collection, if the merchant tampered with the certified technology or fraudulently failed to remit the sales taxes collected.

Myth: "The agreement will pose a threat to consumer privacy."

Fact: The Streamlined Sales and Use Tax Agreement has strong provisions that will protect the privacy of all consumers. The agreement provides that a certified service provider "shall perform its tax calculation, remittance, and reporting functions without retaining the personally identifiable information of consumers." The only time that a certified service provider is allowed to retain personally identifiable information is if the buyer claims an exemption from taxation.

The agreement requires the certified service providers to retain less information than is currently captured by VISA, MasterCard, American Express, Discover, or any other credit card company when a consumer makes a purchase and these companies can use this information for marketing purposes. If certified providers use or sell any information gathered from calculating sales taxes, they would lose certification to be a collector.

Let me set the record straight; the only information maintained by the vendor or third party collector for sales tax calculation are product, price, zip code, and sales tax collected. Unless the consumer is the only person living in the zip code, no one would know who the consumer is!

Myth: "The agreement will force states to forfeit sovereignty over tax policy to out-of-state bureaucrats."

Fact: No, the Streamlined Sales and Use Tax Agreement does not force any state to forfeit its sovereignty. Compliance to the agreement is always optional for a state. The decision to comply with the agreement can only be made by the state legislature and governor—and they can withdraw at any time.

Each state that complies with the agreement will have one vote on the Governing Board of the agreement. Each state that complies with the agreement can have a delegation of up to four people with the state legislature in each state deciding who represents the state. In many cases, state legislators and tax administrators have been designated to serve on the Governing Board. The agreement protects the sovereignty of each state to decide who represents them.

The agreement also requires a 60-day notice on amendments that must be sent to the governor and the legislative leaders of each member state; the same governor and legislative leaders who have appointed the delegates to the Governing Board. The Streamlined Sales Tax Governing Board cannot change any state's sales tax statute, only the state legislature and the governor have that authority and nothing in the agreement abrogates that authority.

Myth: "The agreement and federal legislation to require remote sales tax collection would violate the Constitutional doctrine of federalism. It would force businesses in states where the legislatures have chosen not to join the system or do not have a sales tax to collect sales taxes for other states."

Fact: The Streamlined Sales and Use Tax Agreement does not in any way violate the Constitution and is actually a vibrant example of federalism. The agreement is voluntary for states and for merchants; this is not a mandatory compact or violation of the Commerce Clause of the Constitution. The states voluntarily participated in the process to formulate the Streamlined Sales and Use Tax Agreement by enacting legislation by the people's elected representatives in each state, signed by the governor. The agreement ratified by the states' delegates, responds to the challenges raised by the Supreme Court in two decisions, *Bellas Hess* and *Quill*, and provides a blueprint for Congress to overturn these decisions.

Should Congress grant states remote sales tax collection authority if they comply with the agreement, then businesses that are located in a state that chooses not to comply with the agreement or that has no sales tax would only be subject to collection requirements under the agreement if that seller chooses to sell into a state in which the legislature has decided to comply with the agreement. Opponents exclaim fear that "This implicates profound practical and theoretical federalism concerns." However, no seller is forced to sell into states that comply with the agreement. Out-of-state sellers make that decision and in doing so, they also make themselves liable to the other state's non-sales taxes statutes and regulations protecting consumers and conducting business. An insurance company domiciled in Illinois must follow New Hampshire's insurance laws when doing business in New Hampshire, the same for banks and many other interstate businesses.

Myth: "The agreement will reduce tax policy competition between the states."

Fact: No. As I have stated many times, the state legislature in each state that complies with the Streamlined Sales and Use Tax Agreement will still decide what is taxed, who is exempt and at what rate it wants to tax transactions. How is tax competition eliminated by simplified administrative efficiency or even uniform product definitions? In fact, the competitive strength of America's businesses would be enhanced by reducing the regulatory complexity, costs and burden of the current state sales tax collection system on businesses. Who could oppose reducing or eliminating the current $6.8 billion a year it costs American retailers to collect our sales taxes?

The Streamlined Sales and Use Tax Agreement is a prime example that states are "laboratories of democracy." States working together have developed a solution to ensure the viability of a major revenue stream while eliminating the burden, complexity and cost on retailers to collect the states' sales taxes and maintain state sovereignty for tax policy. State legislators and governors are finding ways to maintain vital government services such as education, health care, public safety and homeland security while ensuring the viability of America's businesses in a global marketplace.

Myth: "The agreement will impede the success of electronic commerce. Collecting sales taxes on electronic commerce transactions is a new tax."

Fact: Under the Streamlined Sales and Use Tax Agreement, the buyer making a transaction will not need to fill out any additional forms in order for the sales tax to be calculated or collected. The tax is determined by the delivery address, and anyone who is buying a tangible product online wants to make sure that the product is delivered to the right address. The consumer fills out only one address field. In cases of digital products like online books or movies, the online seller wants to be paid and they will not accept a credit card payment without address verification. Once again, no additional tax form would be required.

A study released by Jupiter Research in January 2003, "Sales Tax Avoidance Is Imperative to Few Online Retailers and Ultimately Futile for All," found most people are unaware that they are not paying sales taxes when they make a purchase over the Internet. In the same study by Jupiter, only 4 percent of online buyers said that the collection of sales and use taxes would always affect their decision to buy online.

The effort to streamline sales tax collection is not a new tax on electronic commerce. Online sellers already collect sales taxes where they have nexus. The effort of states to streamline sales tax collection will only remove the burden from all sellers in collecting a tax already levied by state and local governments.

Myth: "The University of Tennessee's study on revenue loss for states due to remote sale transactions is not accurate. The estimates of revenue loss are too high."

Fact: The Business and Research Center at the University of Tennessee issued its first study on potential revenue loss due to transactions that occur through remote sellers, including electronic commerce in 2001. This study was updated in July 2004 at the request of the National Conference of State Legislatures and the National Governors Association. The updated study shows that the estimates of potential revenue loss was not as high as first predicted. The authors of both studies, Dr. Donald Bruce and Dr. William Fox, provided the following explanation for the difference in estimates between 2001 and 2004: "The experience of the last several years indicates that e-commerce has been a less robust channel for transacting goods and services than was anticipated when we prepared the earlier estimates. The findings provided here are based on lower estimates of e-commerce, and the result is a smaller revenue loss than we previously indicated. Our loss estimates are also lower because many more vendors have begun to collect sales and use taxes on their remote sales. Still, the Census Bureau reports a combined $1.6 trillion in 2002 in e-commerce transactions by manufacturers, wholesalers, service providers, and retailers, and Forrester Research, Inc.'s expectations continue to be for a strong growth in e-commerce in coming years. Thus the revenue erosion continues to represent a significant loss to state and local government."

Myth: "The agreement will widen the digital divide, because it will disproportionately impact rural, low income, disabled or even elderly buyers."

Fact: If brick and mortar stores are not as accessible in rural areas as they were say, ten years ago, perhaps they no longer can afford to compete with the price advantage enjoyed by online/remote sellers that do not collect sales taxes. When brick and mortar stores in rural areas are forced out of business that means the rural farmer will have to pay higher property taxes on his farm or increased state income taxes. Higher property or income taxes, just so that one can buy a book or CD on-line sales tax free?

Opponents imply that the streamlined sales tax effort will have the effect of widening the so-called "digital divide." Unfortunately, they fail to show an equal concern for those hard working Americans who may lack the credit or the ability to shop on-line because of a lack of access to the Internet or even a computer. These Americans are paying the sales tax every time they make a purchase in a local brick and mortar store. However, those consumers who have sufficient credit, home computers and access to the Internet are able to avoid the sales tax with almost every online purchase. In truth, if the states fail to simplify their sales tax systems and Congress fails to give states that comply with the agreement remote sales tax collection authority, the consequences will be the greatest for low income Americans who do not have the resources to shop out of state.

Myth: "The agreement is a good concept but it can never really work."

Fact: Since the Streamlined Sales Tax System became operational on October 1, 2005, over 1,100 remote sellers have volunteered to begin collecting sales taxes for those states that have complied with the agreement. The certified service providers were approved in May of 2006 and even before the certified automated system was online and available to sellers, these sellers had started to collect sales tax and remit those taxes to the states. The Streamlined Sales Tax System is so much simpler that without even the software in place, remote sellers could begin collecting sales taxes on transactions made by residents of these states.

CONCLUSION

In closing, I would like to reiterate for the members of this Subcommittee that twenty-two states have enacted compliance legislation and many others have enacted some of the changes needed to comply with the agreement. I believe we are at a point that if Congress fails to act soon on the federal legislation as envisioned in the Sales Tax Fairness and Simplification Act, the momentum in the remaining states will slow. In some of these states, compliance to the agreement may require politically difficult changes to the sales tax statutes. Congressional approval of this legislation will help the legislatures in those states make the necessary changes. As I stated previously, states have made unprecedented progress to eliminate the burdens and costs to retailers that the *Quill* decision outlined. It is now Congress' opportunity to ensure that the simplified system that the states have developed for the seamless collection of transactional taxes in the new economy is not impeded by those who merely are trying to avoid paying legally imposed taxes.

Allowing States to Collect Sales Taxes on Interstate Commerce: A Threat to Electronic Commerce

GEORGE S. ISAACSON

I want to thank you for the opportunity to testify today. The DMA is the largest trade association for businesses interested in direct marketing to consumers and businesses via catalogs and the Internet. Founded in 1917, the DMA today has over 4,700 member companies in the United States and 53 foreign countries.

As both an attorney practicing in the area of sales and use tax law for more than 25 years and an instructor in Constitutional Law at Bowdoin College, I welcome the opportunity to discuss with you the important public policy implications associated with H.R. 3396, the so-called "Sales Tax Fairness and Simplification Act," and the threat it presents to core constitutional principles and America's ability to maintain its preeminent position in the field of electronic commerce.

H.R. 3396 presents a critical policy choice for Congress. Advocates of expanded state tax jurisdiction argue that the need for additional state revenue outweighs the constitutional protections for interstate commerce. Congress should be loathe, however, to set aside these constitutional standards, which have served the nation well for two centuries and created the largest and most vibrant economy in the history of the world. Expanded and overlapping state tax jurisdictions would seriously jeopardize the continued growth of electronic commerce in the United States and it would impede the access of small and medium-sized companies to a nation-wide market. Indeed, the Internet has been an incubator for start-up companies and small businesses that have the entrepreneurial ambition and talent to market their goods and services throughout the country. Erecting a tax compliance barricade across the electronic highway is no way to spur economic growth or encourage small and medium-sized companies to expand their markets.

IF ENACTED, H.R 3396 WOULD RESULT IN AN UNPRECEDENTED EXPANSION OF STATE TAXING AUTHORITY

The Streamlined Sales and Use Tax Agreement (SSUTA) was drafted by state tax administrators for the express purpose of expanding the jurisdictional reach of state tax systems. H.R. 3396 now seeks congressional complicity in this effort. The peculiar process by which the SSUTA came into being is a troubling one. Unlike the procedure customarily employed for the development of uniform state laws, which follows the time-tested route of hearings, deliberations, and drafting by the Commissioners on Uniform State Laws in the case of the SSUTA, state tax administrators in this instance chose to bypass altogether the Uniform Law Commission, whose membership consists of distinguished jurists, law school professors, government officials, and lawyers. Instead state tax officials chose to confer almost exclusively among themselves, sometimes even in closed sessions, to produce an agreement that contains scant contribution from the academic community and, most significantly, a rejection of almost all of the suggestions from that portion of the business community that would be most affected by the agreement, *i.e.*, the direct marketing industry.

The Commissioners on Uniform State Laws have successfully produced over 200 uniform state laws in addition to their landmark work—the Uniform Commercial Code. A number of these uniform state laws deal with multi-state taxes (such as the Uniform Division of Income for Tax Purposes Act—UDITPA) and with electronic commerce (such as the Uniform Electronic Transactions Act). If state tax officials had truly been interested in streamlining, simplifying, and making more uniform the crazy quilt of existing state and local sales and use tax laws, they would have requested that the Uniform Law Commission develop draft legislation for consideration and adoption by state legislatures. The fact that this traditional approach to developing uniform state laws was not employed is revealing of the true motives of state tax administrators. Their goal was neither simplicity nor uniformity, rather their objective was to obtain authority to export their tax systems across state borders and impose tax obligations on businesses that currently are constitutionally protected from over-reaching state tax laws.

The SSUTA is a document drafted by tax administrators for tax administrators, and, as might be expected, it resulted in little in the way of tax simplification. It has not reduced the number of sales/use tax jurisdictions in the United States, which currently number over 7,500. It has not reduced the number of state and local tax rates; indeed, it has authorized an increase in the number of such rates. It has not reduced the number of audits to which an interstate marketer would be subject (each state revenue department would still conduct its own independent audit). It has not produced a one stop/one form tax return and remittance system. It has not halted the explosion of confusing and totally discrepant sales tax holidays, which create mini-tax systems with separate rules of only several days' length. In fact, in certain respects, the SSUTA makes sales/use tax compliance more complex and confusing for both consumers and retailers.

Put simply, Congress should not endorse this misnamed exercise in state tax reform. Instead, this subcommittee should urge state governors and the direct marketing industry to work together in a genuine and collaborative effort, under the auspices of the Uniform Law Commission, to standardize the administration of state tax laws. The Direct Marketing Association would be a willing and active participant in that process.

STATE TAX ADMINISTRATORS HAVE GROSSLY OVER-ESTIMATED LOST SALES/USE TAX REVENUES

The alleged tax revenue benefits of the SSUTA are illusory. SSUTA advocates have grossly exaggerated, by as much as 400 percent, the revenue "losses" states and localities have incurred as a result of the constitutional limitation on their ability to impose tax collection obligations on catalog companies and electronic merchants beyond their borders. The true figure is, in fact, only a fraction of one percent of total state sales and use tax collections. Recent analysis shows that the "lost" revenue for all current SSUTA full member states for 2006 totals only $145 million, not the billions of dollars claimed by state tax officials.

The claims of state government officials of enormous revenue "losses" because of uncollected sales and use taxes on electronic commerce are simply not supported by currently available data. Advocates of the SSUTA rely almost exclusively on predictions of lost tax revenue reported by two researchers affiliated with the University of Tennessee ("UT Study"). Their report, first issued in 2000, and then updated in 2001 and reviewed in 2004, is based on non-validated data collected by a private research firm. Actual data from the U.S. Department of Commerce Census Bureau's 2007 E-Commerce Report analyzed by DMA Senior Economist Dr. Peter Johnson ("Johnson Study"), however, shows that on-line consumer sales growth has been much more modest than predicted in the UT Study, so that untaxed sales are (and will continue in the foreseeable future to be) much lower than assumed by state tax administrators.

Even more to the point, the UT Study also was founded on a number of faulty assumptions. The Johnson Study is illuminating in this regard. First, the vast majority of e-commerce—well in excess of 90 percent—is comprised of business-to-business ("B-to-B") transactions on which transaction taxes are either collected by vendors or remitted by companies that self-report the use tax. Most B-to-B transactions (88%) are conducted via electronic data interchange ("EDI"), for which the sales/use remittance rate is effectively 100 percent. Even for the much smaller portion of B-to-B sales conducted over the Internet, a recent study by the Department of Revenue for Washington State indicates a sales/use tax remittance rate of 85 percent. Thus, the implication that states are "losing" a substantial portion of their sales tax revenues to electronic commerce is simply false, because the vast majority of e-commerce transactions are not consumer sales.

Furthermore, even as to business-to-consumer ("B-to-C") Internet transactions, state estimates of uncollected tax revenues are grossly inflated. Again, the UT Study over-estimated both total e-commerce growth and B-to-C growth, so state projections of gross revenue potentially subject to tax are far off the mark. Moreover, as the authors of the UT Study conceded in 2004, there are many more multi-channel retailers (*i.e.*, retailers with both retail stores, Internet websites, and, in some cases, catalog operations) that have commenced collection of sales/use tax on their Internet and other remote sales than originally estimated by the UT Study. In this regard, the perceived "problem" of catalog and Internet vendors not collecting use tax has proven to be largely self-correcting. As remote sellers grow, most of them embark on a multi-channel sales strategy, which includes opening retail stores and a corresponding decision to begin collecting state sales/use taxes voluntarily on all sales (including Internet sales) to residents in states where their stores are located.

Correcting for these and other flaws in the UT Study and relying on actual data from the U.S. Commerce Department, the Johnson Study shows that the amount of sales/use tax which remote e-commerce retailers could not be compelled to collect for all states is a mere fraction of the amount predicted in the UT Study. In total, combining B-to-C with B-to-B transaction data, "uncollected" sales and use taxes on online sales is best estimated to be only 0.2 percent of all state and local tax revenues for 2006. For the 15 states that are currently full members of the SSUTA, this translates into $145 million in total, not the many billions of dollars claimed by SSUTA advocates. (In fact, SSUTA member states have probably experienced somewhat higher tax collections than indicated above, as a result of voluntary participation in the SSUTA by some retailers that might otherwise not have decided to collect use tax.)

In light of these figures, I would hope that members of this Committee would question whether forsaking long-standing constitutional standards is the proper response to the greatly exaggerated, and largely self-correcting, problem of lost use tax revenue claimed by state tax officials.

JURISDICTIONAL LIMITATIONS ON STATE TAXING AUTHORITY ARE NOT A LEGAL "LOOPHOLE" EXPLOITED BY RETAILERS, BUT RATHER DERIVE FROM CORE CONSTITUTIONAL PRINCIPLES

The stated purpose of H.R. 3396 is to authorize member states of the SSUTA to subject businesses not located within their borders—*i.e.*, companies lacking "nexus"—to tax collection and remittance obligations. This is no trivial matter. Determining the appropriate reach of the sovereign authority of state and local governments is central to the American system of government. Indeed, the Constitutional Convention of 1787 was initially called to address the problem of individual state legislatures imposing taxes and duties on trade with other states, a practice that was pushing the young country into a depression. The solution devised by the Constitution's Framers was a federal system of dual national and state sovereignty, the genius of which is that *each state is sovereign within its own borders* and can adopt those policies that best suit its particular needs and reflect the political preferences of its citizens. Needless to say, this plan has worked remarkably well for more than 200 years.

Of necessity, federalism restricts the ability of a state (or locality) to export its tax system across state borders. Permitting each state to visit its unique tax system on businesses that have no nexus with the taxing state would be chaotic as a matter of both tax administration and compliance (involving fifty state governments, and the more than 7,500 local taxing districts in the United States, imposing their vastly different tax regimes on businesses in each of the forty-nine other states). Moreover, out-of-state companies would have no way to influence the very state tax systems that are newly imposed on them. In the most real sense, allowing the expansion of tax authority beyond state borders is "taxation without representation."

The constitutional limitations on the territorial scope of state and local taxing jurisdiction also has enormous economic importance. The United States Constitution—and the Commerce Clause in particular—has been the guardian of this nation's open market economy. A central purpose of the Commerce Clause was to prevent states from suppressing the free flow of interstate commerce by imposition of taxes, duties, tariffs, and other levies. Indeed, more than two centuries before the establishment of the European Union, the framers of the United States Constitution created a common market on this continent through the Commerce Clause, and their foresight powered the greatest economic engine mankind has ever known.

In this era of electronic commerce and increased international competition, it is imperative that Congress not abandon, or undermine, the core Commerce Clause principle of a single, free-flowing national marketplace. In the last two decades, U.S. companies have been dominant in the field of electronic commerce; but abandoning constitutional ideals in favor of short-sighted efforts to increase state tax revenues could undermine the position of American companies in this crucial, but still fledgling, sector of the world's economy. The vitality of e-commerce should not be curbed by federal legislation that saddles American businesses with the burdens of disparate state tax laws whose authority extends far beyond traditional jurisdictional borders.

With record high energy prices threatening the nation's economy, now is certainly not the time for Congress to abandon the original intent of the Commerce Clause. Moreover, debate over the wisdom of a federal law to expand state and federal tax jurisdiction cannot be divorced from consideration of the impact such legislation would have on the competitiveness of American companies. Forcing new tax collection obligations on U.S.-based companies would have the undesirable (and undoubtedly unintended) effect of advantaging their foreign competitors, on whom state and local tax collection obligations could never be effectively imposed.

Congress should be skeptical of arguments that the Commerce Clause is outdated and its restriction on state taxing authority is nothing more than a constitutional loophole exploited by business. As a professor of constitutional law, I respectfully disagree. In my view, the Supreme Court's consistent application of long-standing constitutional principles should not be viewed as a "problem" in need of correction. Rather, the inter-related ideals of federalism and unfettered interstate commerce have made America both the greatest experiment in representational democracy and the most successful economy the world has ever known.

H.R. 3396 WOULD UNFAIRLY BURDEN BUSINESSES IN A MAJORITY OF STATES TO SATISFY THE DEMANDS OF A MINORITY OF STATES THAT ARE MEMBERS OF THE SSUTA

The proposed legislation being considered by this subcommittee would be unfair to the great majority of states—including California, Texas, New York, Florida, Illinois, Pennsylvania, and Massachusetts—which have elected not to become members of the SSUTA. The burdens of H.R. 3396 would fall primarily on businesses in those states that will realize no reciprocating benefit. The legislation grants favored treatment to the minority of states that are full members of the SSUTA (only 17 states, representing approximately 25 percent of the nation's population). The bill would allow those few states to impose tax collection, reporting and remittance duties on *retailers in every other state in the nation*, regardless of whether a state is a member or not a member of the SSUTA.

Most states that participated in the Streamlined Sales Tax Project have decided not to become members of the Streamlined Sales and Use Tax Agreement for a variety of different reasons. The most common reason is that these states (primarily larger states) do not want to surrender their tax sovereignty to the dictates of the SSUTA Governing Board. Consequently, most states have concluded that membership in the SSUTA would be detrimental to their best interests.

H.R. 3396 would, nonetheless, force non-participating states to tolerate the incongruous situation in which companies headquartered in their states are required to collect sales/use taxes for SSUTA member states, but there would be no similar and reciprocal obligation on the part of retailers located in the SSUTA member states. To put the issue in more specific terms, under this bill, an Internet retailer based solely in California or Massachusetts (neither of which are SSUTA members) would be subject to tax collection, reporting and remittance obligations for its sales to residents of Nebraska, North Carolina, Wyoming, and every other SSUTA state, but neither California nor Massachusetts would receive any additional tax revenue from an Internet retailer with operations solely in any of the SSUTA member states. In this regard, H.R. 3396 is hardly a bill promoting sales tax fairness for retailers, consumers, and states through the country.

Supporters of H.R. 3396 argue that the legislation would encourage additional states to bring their sales/use tax laws into compliance with the SSUTA. But this is faulty and self-flattering reasoning. If the SSUTA were attractive on its own merits, more states would have already joined. Instead, the reality is that the legislatures in the vast majority of states, making up more than 70 percent of the United States population and including each of the six largest states in the nation—California, Texas, New York, Florida, Illinois, Pennsylvania—have chosen not to adopt the SSUTA for good reasons. Legislative leaders in those states have concluded that the SSUTA is simply not consistent with their state's tax scheme (*e.g.*, sourcing requirements) or otherwise is not in the state's best interest. Large states are also skeptical of handing over authority to an SSUTA Governing Board dominated by tax administrators from smaller states. Moreover, because the SSUTA has been so frequently amended by the Governing Board despite the short life of the agreement, these larger states are concerned over what future requirements might be imposed upon them by the Governing Board in the event they were to become full members.

In fact, it is this inherent tension between the insistence of states on maintaining sovereignty, pitted against the desire to expand their taxing jurisdiction, that has made the SSUTA fatally flawed and doomed to fail in achieving real simplification and uniformity in state and local sales and use tax systems.

THE SSUTA ADOPTED "LOW BAR" REFORM FROM THE OUTSET AND HAS PROVEN TO BE A MOVING TARGET OF INCREASING COMPLEXITY AND DECREASING UNIFORMITY

Although nominally a bold reform initiative to simplify, harmonize and modernize state and local sales and use tax laws, the Streamlined Sales Tax Project has never promoted true simplification or uniformity. Instead, state tax administrators, from the outset of the Project, and at every turn since, have sacrificed real reform to accommodate the peculiarities of individual states tax systems. The goal of the Project's organizers was not to maximize uniformity among state laws, but rather to maximize the number of states willing to sign on to SSUTA full membership.

The inevitable result of this recruitment-at-all-costs strategy has been the progressive dilution of the Project's stated uniformity objectives. Successive compromises of the SSUTA's stated principles have produced a lowest-common-denominator standard for sales/use tax reform. Moreover, these on-going revisions have made the SSUTA a moving target for affected businesses, as they confront frequent amendments, illogical interpretive rulings and a burgeoning number of complex rules. Having closely followed and contributed to the SSTP process over the past 7 years, I find the contrast between the SSUTA process and the more conventional drafting process for uniform state legislation developed by the Commission on Uniform States Laws (such as UDITPA) a most striking one.

THE SSUTA FAILED TO ADOPT FUNDAMENTAL REQUIREMENTS OF SIMPLICITY AND UNIFORMITY

To understand the dissolution of the SSUTA process, it is instructive to consider its history. The Streamlined Sales Tax Project was launched in 2000 on the heels of two earlier joint government/industry initiatives (the National Tax Association [NTA] Communications and Electronic Commerce Tax Project, and the congressionally established Advisory Commission on Electronic Commerce), both of which had concluded that the existing state sales and use tax system was one of daunting complexity, and that true simplification would require sweeping reforms. To this end, in August 2000, the Direct Marketing Association set forth in a letter to Streamlined Sales Tax Project leaders a comprehensive list of reform proposals, a copy of which is attached to my written testimony. The fate of DMA's proposals is telling: of more than 30 specific reform recommendations offered by the DMA, the SSUTA fully adopted only two, centralized registration and uniform bad debt provisions, and the latter provision has not been honored by most of the member states.

Perhaps most emblematic of the SSUTA's failure to achieve genuine sales/use tax reform was the early demise of the single most important step toward simplification: the adoption of a single sales and use tax rate per state for all commerce ("one rate per state"), which would have eliminated the problem of merchant compliance with thousands of local tax jurisdictions with different tax rates. The United States is the only economically developed country in the world with a system of sub-state transaction taxes not only for municipalities and counties, but also for school districts, transportation districts, sanitation districts, sports arena districts, and other local tax jurisdictions. In light of this wildly complex system, the adoption of a "one rate per state" standard was the unanimous recommendation of the NTA's E-Commerce Project (which included delegates from the National Conference of State Legislatures, National Governors Association, and the U.S. Conference of Mayors) and was also the majority report recommendation of the Congressional Advisory Commission.

Despite this background, the SSTP abandoned the "one rate per state" standard early in its deliberations, and instead decided to permit (a) two state-level rates (one of which only applies to food, food ingredients, and drugs) and (b) additional separate rates as chosen by each local taxing jurisdiction in the state. The effect of this decision was to allow an increase, rather than require a decrease, in the number of sales/use tax rates to which an interstate merchant might be subject in collecting and remitting taxes.

How could such a fundamental goal of sales/use tax reform be forsaken so early in the SSTP process? State tax administrators associated with the SSUTA now freely admit that the "one rate per state" proposal was dead on arrival, because they quickly were informed that it was unacceptable to most states and localities who clearly prized their unique taxing prerogatives over the uniformity and simplification recommendations of the prior commissions.

I have had the opportunity, in testimony before this subcommittee (in October 2003) and last year (July 2006) before the Senate Finance Committee, to explain in detail numerous other ways that the SSUTA disregarded broadly recognized principles of sales/use tax simplification and standardization, and I would be happy to provide copies of such testimony to the subcommittee members. In brief, a few of these glaring shortcomings include:

- **The failure to establish uniformity in the tax base:** The SSUTA rejected from the outset adopting a uniform tax base, instead insisting that uniform definitions among states for taxable and exempt products would be adequate simplification for retailers. But the number of product definitions in the SSUTA to which member states must adhere is very limited, and states can choose to exempt or tax any product or service not specifically defined. The agreement has no definitions that would cover many everyday consumer items, from cookware to holiday decorations to home and garden items.

- **There is no uniformity in the measure of tax for like transactions:** The SSUTA also does not simplify the way retailers must measure the dollar amount (transaction value) subject to tax. Instead, the SSUTA's definition of "sales price" allows states to include, or exclude, multiple components, resulting in a dizzying array of state-specific alternatives, with no uniform measure of tax among states for identical transactions. In fact, as explained later, the SSUTA has recently made the determination of "sales price" even more complex.

• **There is no meaningful reduction in the burdens of tax collection, reporting, remittance and audits for interstate marketers:** State tax administrators refused to adopt a proposal for joint audits (i.e., one audit for all member states). As a result, the number of tax audits to which an interstate marketer would be subject under H.R. 3396 would substantially increase over current practice, since non-nexus companies would become subject to audit not only by the state revenue department in their home state, but by tax auditors from each of the member states, at considerable additional administrative burden and expense to America's retailers.

• **The SSUTA failed to seek independent testing of tax compliance software:** While SSUTA officials rely heavily on computer technology as the "silver bullet" to address the increased tax compliance burdens that would result from passage of H.R. 3396, the Project never sought independent testing of the software systems put forward by service providers (none of which were originally developed for the purpose of SSUTA compliance), and instead conducted the certification process internally. To date, the SSUTA has certified 3 private companies, but many retailers, after investigating the available providers, have concluded that using their software would be prohibitively expensive without any real guarantee of accuracy. Moreover, despite the fact that private service providers will have access to highly confidential personal consumer information, the SSUTA has no articulated standards for assuring the security and privacy of such information.

• **The failure to guarantee fundamental fairness with respect to vendor compensation for tax collection:** On its face, the SSUTA, since its adoption in 2002, has required states to compensate both third party service providers and self-reporting vendors for the considerable costs of serving as the states' collection agents, but five years later the Governing Board has only approved compensation for the certified providers (who would not, of course, have sought certification otherwise), and has reneged on its promise of compensation to retailers.

THE SSUTA HAS BEEN STEADILY WEAKENED SINCE ITS ADOPTION THROUGH A MYRIAD OF AMENDMENTS AND INTERPRETIVE RULINGS THAT LESSEN ITS UNIFORMITY REQUIREMENTS AND INCREASE ITS COMPLEXITY

Regrettably, the SSUTA has suffered a further "lowering of the bar" since its initial adoption. Again, in stark contrast to a truly Uniform Act, such as the Uniform Division of Income for Tax Purposes Act, which was promulgated 50 years ago and has remained remarkably stable over time, the SSUTA has already been subject to more than 70 amendments during its short life span. Not surprisingly, there are nearly 20 additional proposed amendments on the agenda for the Governing Board's meeting next week. Dozens of the agreement's provisions have been materially modified; whole sections have been repealed or replaced; and new sections have been added. At the same time, the Governing Board has issued numerous interpretive rulings which, rather than requiring member states to conform strictly to the agreement's provisions, have instead tolerated widely disparate practices by member state revenue departments. The result has been to increase, rather than reduce, variations in the administration of state tax laws. In a very real sense, the SSUTA is a moving target, adding new uncertainties for

businesses and increasing both their compliance costs and their exposure to unantici-
pated tax assessments.

THE SSUTA HAS OPENLY AUTHORIZED STATES TO ADOPT REPLACEMENT TAXES

Many of the recent amendments to the SSUTA, as well as those currently under consideration by the Governing Board, represent a further degradation of even the modest uniformity provisions contained in the agreement when it was first adopted. The enactment
by member states of "replacement taxes," and the now infamous example of the "fur
clothing tax," has become emblematic of the Governing Board's refusal to stand firm and
of member states' refusal to abide by the agreement's requirements. Instead, the
Governing Board has tolerated, at times even encouraged, blatant departures from the
substance and spirit of the SSUTA on the part of state governments in order to avoid
member states from withdrawing, or being disqualified, from membership in the SSUTA.

The replacement tax issue came to the fore in the following way. SSUTA advocates
proudly point to the list of product definitions as the Project's central accomplishment
in achieving greater uniformity. Member states are required to adopt the definitions, and
must then either tax, or exempt, all items that fall within each product definition.
Among the defined products is "clothing," defined as "all human wearing apparel suitable for general use," with a lengthy, non-exclusive list of examples within the definition that includes furs. Observers, I among them, noted that the full member state of
Minnesota exempted "clothing" from sales and use tax, but separately imposed an excise
tax on fur clothing, in apparent violation of the agreement.

In 2006, I submitted a request to the SSUTA Governing Board for a determination
whether the fur clothing tax imposed by Minnesota violated the agreement. In
response, the SSUTA's Compliance and Review Committee determined, and the
Governing Board agreed, that because the fur clothing tax was denominated in
Minnesota's statute as a gross revenues excise tax separate from its general sales and use
tax, it was not subject to the agreement's requirements. In other words, simply re-naming a sales tax as an excise tax frees a state from the requirements of the SSUTA. The
ruling clearly signaled to all states (current SSUTA members and those states that had
reservations about surrendering tax sovereignty to the SSUTA) that they were free to
game-the-system simply by re-naming transaction taxes to take them outside the scope
of the agreement.

This message was readily received by other states. For example, the legislature in
New Jersey, another "Full" SSUTA Member, soon followed suit, enacting in its 2006
legislative session its own version of the fur tax. The New Jersey law creates a new gross
receipts tax on fur clothing, despite the fact that New Jersey otherwise exempts "clothing" (as defined in the SSUTA) from its sales tax. Moreover, the New Jersey fur tax
applies at a rate of 6 percent, despite the fact that New Jersey in 2006 raised its general sales and use tax rate to 7 percent. As a result, the New Jersey fur tax flaunts not only
the definitional requirements of the SSUTA, but also the requirements that members
have only one state-level sales tax rate (other than for food and drugs).

Following the enactment of the New Jersey tax, there was an outcry among
observers, and even some supporters, of the SSUTA. Such "replacement taxes," *i.e.*,
sales and use taxes re-named to avoid the agreement, undermined the integrity of the
entire SSUTA process. The SSUTA's Business Advisory Committee, comprised of

industry supporters of the agreement, was highly critical of the enactment of replacement taxes. Proposals were presented to the Governing Board to prohibit the practice. To date, however, these proposals have not been acted upon, and the SSUTA Governing Board has failed to pass an amendment, or even a resolution, that would prohibit state legislatures from making an end-run around the SSUTA by adopting replacement taxes.

Rather than punish states that have enacted replacement taxes, the Governing Board has instead chosen the path of least resistance. Its approach has been: "If a state violates the agreement, we will simply change the agreement." With the fur clothing tax, rather than disciplining New Jersey, the SSUTA in December 2006 amended the agreement to remove fur from the general "clothing" definition and approved a new, separate definition of "fur clothing," thus allowing separate tax treatment for fur clothing and glossing over the non-conformity of both New Jersey and Minnesota.

THE SSUTA HAS ELIMINATED UNIFORMITY IN THE TREATMENT OF DELIVERY CHARGES

The SSUTA Governing Board's willingness to bend and amend the agreement to accommodate state-specific tax practices has taken a decidedly disturbing turn in connection with the treatment of delivery charges. Consumers need to know whether sales tax will be computed before or after inclusion of "shipping and handling charges." Early in the streamlining project, the Direct Marketing Association urged uniformity on this subject for the benefit of consumers and retailers alike. Not only did the SSUTA not incorporate DMA's original proposal, but recently it has taken a giant step backward from the position taken at the time of the agreement's original adoption.

A little background on this subject may be useful in understanding direct marketers' concerns. The tax treatment of charges to consumers for delivery of products has long been an area of considerable complexity. Some states impose tax on all delivery charges; others exempt all delivery charges so long as they are separately stated on the invoice; some states tax handling charges, but not common carrier freight charges; most, but not all, states exempt postage charges for direct mail paid to the USPS, even if the state taxes freight charges by a private carrier; some exempt "shipping" charges only if they represent the actual cost of shipping a particular product, but not if the charge is based on average shipping costs; and the list goes on.

Initially, the SSUTA sought to simplify the definition of "delivery charges" to include all charges related to delivery of product to a purchaser, which meant not only shipping costs, but also handling and other charges (including postage, a decision which allowed some member states to impose new taxes on postage they had not previously levied). At the same time, however, the SSUTA protected state tax prerogatives (at the expense of uniformity) by listing delivery charges among those items that a state could elect to include, or exclude, from the taxable "sales price" of the product.

Under political pressure from a number of quarters, including states that previously separated the tax treatment of shipping from other charges, the Governing Board in September 2007 approved an amendment that modifies the definition of "delivery charges" under the agreement to allow member states to treat "shipping" separately from "handling," undoing any simplification that had previously been achieved. Beginning in 2008, SSUTA member states may elect to tax both shipping and handling, may tax neither, may tax only shipping and not handling, or vice-versa. As a result, the number of possible permutations of the taxable "sales price" that consumers and retailers may encounter has greatly increased.

THE SSUTA HAS INTERPRETED SOME DEFINITIONS, IN PARTICULAR "DIRECT MAIL," TO APPLY ONLY FOR ADMINISTRATIVE PURPOSES, LEAVING STATES FREE TO TAX OR EXEMPT MULTIPLE ADDITIONAL PRODUCTS

In addition to amendments to the agreement, the official Interpretations issued by the SSUTA Governing Board and its committees have further degraded any claim to uniformity. For example, the SSUTA contains a definition for "direct mail," *i.e.*, printed material delivered at no charge via U.S. Mail or by another delivery service to a mass audience or persons identified on a mailing list. This is an area of great importance to the direct marketing industry. In October 2006, the SSUTA received a seemingly innocuous request "[w]hether billing invoices, return envelopes and any additional marketing materials are included in the definition" of direct mail. Although on its face this was a question about the definition, the answer had additional significance because member states are authorized to allow a different tax treatment for "delivery charges" on direct mail transactions, *i.e.*, to include or exclude such charges on direct mail in a manner different from the state's treatment of delivery charges for most products.

The SSUTA's Interpretations Committee found that the invoices, envelopes and other items met the SSUTA's definition of direct mail, but then went on to state that the definition of "direct mail" in the agreement applies only for the purpose of determining proper "sourcing" of sales transactions, and *not* for determining whether "delivery charges" are included in the taxable price! The Governing Board subsequently approved the ruling in December 2006.

The direct marketing industry was left totally confused. As a strained rationale, the SSUTA stated that the "direct mail" definition appears in the agreement's "Administrative Definitions" and not its "Product Definitions," so that the agreement does not purport to define, at all, what categories of printed material are subject to tax in a member state, and what categories are not subject to tax. In other words, states could have conflicting definitions and categorization of direct mail for different tax purposes. Indeed, several SSUTA member states have chosen to tax and exempt different categories of printed materials, all of which appear to meet the uniform definition of "direct mail" under the agreement. The result is that even though the SSUTA purports to define "direct mail," sellers and buyers cannot look to the agreement to determine whether their products and services are subject to tax or not, or what taxable measure applies to the transaction.

The Interpretive Ruling that the SSUTA's "Administrative Definitions" cannot be relied upon to determine which types of "direct mail" are taxable and which are not, is disturbing, yet there are now proposed amendments pending before the Governing Board that would formalize and extend that understanding to all Administrative Definitions in the agreement. Currently, the "Administrative Definitions" include such terms as "bundled transaction," "delivery charges," "telecommunications non-recurring charges," none of which apparently can be relied upon anymore by retailers for guidance except in regard to the "administration" of taxes under the agreement. Perhaps most incredibly, the Administrative Definitions include the SSUTA's definition of "tangible personal property," the bedrock definition of every sales and use tax system. On even this point, the SSUTA has implicitly disavowed uniformity among the member states.

SALES TAX HOLIDAYS DEFEAT UNIFORMITY, AND THE SSUTA FAILS TO RESOLVE THIS PROBLEM

One of the myriad ways the SSUTA has bowed to parochial state concerns is through its preservation of sales tax "holidays," the temporary suspension of sales and use taxes on particular products or classes of products, such as clothing, computers or school supplies. Sales tax holidays are increasingly attractive to state legislatures as (a) a form of consumer tax relief, (b) a way to encourage purchases that will promote certain state government policy objectives, and (c) a means of stimulating the economy around specific seasonal events, such as the start of the school year. Although this form of short-term tax incentive is very popular with the public, and always focused around local events, sales tax holidays present enormous complexity to interstate retailers, who need to publish tax instructions on their websites and in their catalogs. The SSUTA currently permits members to implement such tax holidays only with respect to product categories specifically delineated in the agreement (such as clothing or school supplies). The agreement, however, imposes no limit on the duration of such holidays, and allows states to impose eligibility thresholds, so that the temporary exemption applies to purchases only above a minimum dollar amount, increasing the complexity for retailers to administer tax holidays.

The popularity of sales tax holidays among state legislatures means that new proposals for such holidays are frequent. Now before the Governing Board is an amendment proposed by North Carolina, a full member state, to allow a sales tax holiday for all products that qualify for "Energy Star" designation under guidelines set by the U.S. Department of Environmental Protection. According to the EPA, products in more than 50 categories qualify for the Energy Star label. Authorizing a sales tax holiday based on such a designation would have the effect of creating a new mini-tax system of limited duration. Moreover, every SSUTA member state would be free to choose whether, when and for how long to implement such a holiday, imposing enormous burdens on retailers. It is precisely the pursuit of such state-specific tax policy objectives that generate the overwhelming complexity in sales and use tax systems.

Even more complex proposals for sales tax holidays are being considered by state legislatures. This year, the State of Florida (not currently a member of the SSUTA) adopted a "Hurricane Preparedness Sales Tax Holiday" running for 10 days in late May 2007 designed to encourage residents to prepare for the hurricane season. The holiday applied to dozens of types of products in multiple categories, such as candles and flashlights, coolers and ice chests, cell phone batteries, radios, tarpaulins, and window shutter materials. Moreover, the exemptions for different types of products applied only *below* a specified dollar cap, such as $20 for gas-powered lanterns, $50 for bungee cords, and $75 for carbon monoxide detectors. This may be laudable tax policy, but allowing such a system to be exported across state lines would require retailers across the country to comply with the unique policy prerogatives of distant states. Such a system would place crushing burdens on interstate commerce.

THE SSUTA IS POISED TO COMPROMISE ITS ADOPTION OF UNIFORM, DESTINATION-BASED SOURCING

The one rate per state proposal has recently re-surfaced in the debate among SSUTA members concerning the "sourcing" of transactions for sales and use tax purposes. "Sourcing" is the term used by tax analysts to describe the mechanism for determining which jurisdiction will have the opportunity to tax a particular transaction. The issue of sourcing would be far less controversial under a "one rate per state" rule, because the absence in variation among tax rates within a state would make sales tax compliance straightforward. However, when local rates differ widely, the issue of which jurisdiction gets to tax the transaction becomes very confusing. Does a merchant who delivers product from one jurisdiction to another charge sales tax at the merchant's home district rate ("origin sourcing") or must the retailer "source" the sale to the location where the product is received and collect tax based on the recipient's jurisdiction ("destination sourcing")?

The SSUTA originally committed itself, for reasons of simplicity and uniformity, to destination sourcing for all transactions. This meant that a retailer would collect tax for the state and local jurisdiction where the consumer—not the retailer—is located. This effort at uniformity has not gone down well, however, with a number of states and localities that permit or require origin sourcing for in-state vendors. Consequently, the SSUTA Governing Board has been asked to abandon its commitment to destination sourcing and accommodate states that want to have destination sourcing at the state level but origin sourcing at the local level. Such a change in the SSUTA would hardly serve the interests of consistency, simplicity, and uniformity. But those concerns have not deterred the Governing Board from amending the agreement in the past.

If a state allows origin sourcing for in-state businesses, while demanding destination sourcing for out-of-state businesses (as some of the proposed amendments would permit), there is an obvious issue of fairness. Moreover, if the combined state and local tax rate applicable to an in-state seller is lower than the combined rate applicable to an out-of-state seller for a comparable transaction, the Supreme Court has ruled that such a tax scheme violates the Commerce Clause and is unconstitutional in *Associated Industries of Missouri, Inc. v. Lohman* (1993).

An obvious question is: "Why would the Governing Board consider abandoning its straightforward commitment to destination sourcing for all transactions and, instead, create a complex set of rules that would differentiate between state and local taxes on the one hand, and in-state and out-of-state sellers on the other hand?" The answer is that the Governing Board is willing to abandon principle to attract new member states.

Instead of insisting on state conformity with the original requirements of the SSUTA as a condition of full membership, the Governing Board is trying to broker a "compromise" that would permit states to retain their origin sourcing rules. Interestingly, Indiana, one of the states represented on the Governing Board, has proposed an amendment that would, in effect, allow a member state to adopt a separate single rate for delivery sales (in contrast to over-the-counter sales). This would have the effect of keeping compliance burdens on in-state sellers light, but it would also eliminate much of the unfairness of disparate sourcing rules for out-of-state sellers. Thus, under the Indiana proposal, states with origin sourcing could join the SSUTA without adopting destination sourcing, if they would adopt one rate per state. Although the Indiana proposal is on the agenda for the meeting of the SSUTA Governing Board next week, and has considerable support among the business community, Governing Board officials have indicated in public meetings that they feel the proposal does not even merit discussion, because states with origin sourcing will never accept the "one rate per state" alternative, showing again that real reform under the auspices of the SSUTA is impossible.

The DMA has expressed its concerns regarding multiple sourcing provisions for a single state in a letter to the Governing Board.

THE SSUTA HAS REPEATEDLY COMPROMISED CONFORMITY STANDARDS IN ORDER TO INCREASE OR MAINTAIN MEMBERSHIP

The SSUTA has repeatedly demonstrated a willingness to descend to the lowest common denominator of uniformity in order to accommodate members and potential members, and it has likewise repeatedly bent and even changed its rules regarding compliance requirements. The purpose behind this progressive lowering of the bar has been to enlist and retain member states that are unable or unwilling to bring their laws in line with the agreement's requirements.

A Weak Compliance Standard. To become and remain a member of the SSUTA, a state must only certify to the Governing Board that the "effect" of its laws, rules, regulations and policies is "substantially compliant" with each of the requirements of the agreement. This weak standard of compliance means that there is no guarantee that any member state's laws are fully compliant with the terms of the agreement to begin with. This is only one way that the SSUTA has enabled states to circumvent its compliance requirements.

The SSUTA Began by Creating a Class of Not Fully Compliant "Associate Members." Initially, the agreement, by its terms, was only to take effect when at least ten states comprising at least twenty percent of the total population of all states imposing a state sales tax were determined to be in conformity. The participating states set a deadline for themselves of October 1, 2005, to achieve this level of conformity.

The SSUTA Governing Board was so concerned, however, in April 2005 that it would not secure the membership of enough states to meet their self-imposed threshold, that it quickly adopted a new provision allowing for so-called "associate" members, which were states that the Project participants acknowledged had not yet conformed their laws to the agreement, but which states would, nonetheless, be counted toward the critical mass necessary for the SSUTA to become effective. State representatives to the SSUTA have publicly acknowledged that the provisions regarding associate members were adopted in haste in 2005, without careful consideration of all of the ramifications of creating this second class of members on other parts of the agreement, in order to "meet the quota" necessary for the SSUTA to take effect.

When this new category of membership was created in April 2005, associate members were given more than three-and-a-half years, until December 31, 2007, to bring their laws into full conformity with the agreement, or they would forfeit their associate membership status. At the time the participating states declared success in meeting the membership threshold on October 1, 2005, there were six states granted associate membership status: Arkansas, Nevada, Ohio, Tennessee, Utah, and Wyoming. Together with the thirteen states granted full membership, the SSUTA claimed to have enlisted states comprising a little more than 29 percent of the population as of October 1, 2005.

The SSUTA Next Refused to Expel Utah After Its Legislature Repealed Conformity Legislation. After creating the associate member category, SSUTA officials have shown themselves ready to take any measures necessary to prolong the membership of associate members. The first such compromise came in 2006, when the legislature in Utah, one of the associate member states, repealed a large number of laws that had originally been enacted to bring the state into SSUTA conformity. There was no question that Utah's tax code was no longer in compliance with multiple SSUTA requirements and that the state did not, after the repeal legislation, meet the standard for associate membership.

Rather than take steps to terminate Utah's SSUTA membership, the Governing Board determined that it was not required to expel Utah on the theory that, under the agreement, the status of associate members did not need to be reviewed until the December 31, 2007 deadline for full conformity. The Governing Board simply declined to take up the matter of Utah's non-compliance and, as of this date, Utah remains an associate member, accepting SSUTA vendor registrations, participating on SSUTA committees, and voting on matters with other associate member states.

The SSUTA Created a New Category of Associate Member to Accommodate Tennessee. While some states originally granted associate member status have subsequently petitioned for and been granted full membership, the two largest of the states initially granted associate member status in 2005, Ohio and Tennessee, have remained associate members. In Tennessee, a number of the changes in its laws that have proven most controversial within the state were adopted with effective dates pushed off well into the future for political reasons. The proposed effective date for many such laws had been July 1, 2007, in time for the December 31, 2007 deadline for associate member states to come into full compliance. But in the 2007 legislative session, the Tennessee legislature pushed back the effective date on many provisions until July 1, 2009, delaying the date for the state's possible conformity until after the SSUTA's previously set deadline.

Rather than Tennessee losing its membership status, the SSUTA in June 2007 promptly enacted an amendment to the agreement which created a new category of associate members, described as states petitioning for membership after January 1, 2007. Such states are qualified for associate membership status if they are found to be in compliance with the agreement's requirements except that the effective date of their conformity is delayed for not more than twelve months, or with Governing Board approval, eighteen months, beyond their proposed entry date into the agreement.

Although Tennessee was already an associate member prior to January 1, 2007, it was nevertheless permitted to petition for associate member status under the new provision for associate members petitioning after January 1, 2007. The Governing Board promptly approved Tennessee's associate member status under the new provision, based on its proposed new conformity date of July 1, 2009. These machinations are little more than smoke and mirrors.

The SSUTA Is Poised to Make Concessions on Origin Sourcing to Extend the Deadline for Ohio. Of considerable concern now to SSUTA officials is the impending failure of Ohio, the largest state with membership status in the SSUTA, to gain full membership status by December 31. For Ohio, the central issue of non-conformity is its system of in-state origin sourcing. With Ohio's deadline to conform to the SSUTA approaching, the Ohio legislature in the 2007 legislative session not only declined to adopt destination sourcing, but affirmed its system of origin sourcing. As a result, Ohio will not meet the December 31, 2007 deadline for conformity, and will be required under the current language of the agreement to forfeit its membership.

SSUTA officials desperately want Ohio to retain its membership and, indeed, to attain full member status. Indeed, the possibility of Ohio falling out of the SSUTA, together with the desire to attract other states that have origin-based sourcing, is driving the Governing Board's push to amend the agreement and depart altogether from a uniform destination-based sourcing standard.

At the same time, separate amendments have been proposed regarding associate member status that would prolong Ohio's membership. One such measure would simply extend the current conformity deadline by an additional six months, to July 1, 2008. Another would allow the Governing Board to approve associate membership for a state whose only area of non-conformity is with SSUTA sourcing rules. The proposed amendments will be voted upon at next week's Governing Board meeting. Given the SSUTA's track record to date, it will come as no surprise if Ohio is granted some form of reprieve and remains an associate member for some additional period of time. When it comes to membership status, SSUTA rules are meant to be waived—not enforced.

The Governing Board Amended the Agreement to Approve New Jersey's Non-Conforming Fur Tax. The SSUTA's weak stance on conformity has also benefited at least one full member state. As I explained earlier, the New Jersey legislature in 2006 enacted a replacement "fur tax" which most observers believed was not in conformity with the agreement's requirement that a state [either] tax or exempt all products for which the agreement has a formal definition. After New Jersey enacted the fur tax, the SSUTA, rather than disciplining or even expelling the state in its annual re-certification process, simply amended the agreement to adopt a definition for fur clothing, thus bringing New Jersey's fur tax into *post-hoc* conformity.

DESPITE REPEATEDLY DILUTING ITS STANDARDS, THE SSUTA HAS NOT ATTRACTED MANY NEW MEMBERS, AND NOW FACES DECLINING MEMBERSHIP

The contortions the Governing Board has gone through to retain members is probably best explained by its inability to attract additional participation by states. The SSUTA has proven unattractive to most states, and the largest states have been most averse to membership. A number of state legislatures, including Florida and Virginia, have outright rejected conformity legislation. Upon the agreement's effective date in October 2005, the SSUTA had 13 full member states; on January 1, 2008, it will have 17. The only states to join as full members in the past three years have been Arkansas, Rhode Island, Vermont and Wyoming. The SSUTA is clearly a minority system.

In fact, the SSUTA is losing membership. With Ohio and Utah due to fall out of the SSUTA, the percentage of population will likely fall below the 29 percent level claimed by the SSUTA in October 2005. In fact, if the SSUTA were vigilant regarding compliance and excluded both Tennessee and New Jersey, the percentage of the population represented by full and associate member states participation would fall dangerously close to the 20 percent threshold necessary for the agreement to remain in effect under its own terms.

It is now time for the Streamlined Sales Tax Project to confront the painful reality that the terms of the SSUTA and its governance procedures are fundamentally flawed, that it has not achieved meaningful sales and use reform, and that is not attractive to the great majority of states. It is time, instead, to re-assess the process that brought the SSUTA to this point and initiate a new process, perhaps through the Commissioners on Uniform State Laws, to craft a truly uniform act whose hallmark is real simplification of state sales and use tax regimes. On behalf of the DMA, I want to thank you again for the opportunity to offer my comments on this important issue.

THE CONTINUING DEBATE:
Allowing States to Collect Sales Taxes
on Interstate Commerce

What Is New

The bill, "H.R. 3396, The Sales Tax Fairness and Simplification Act," discussed in the readings, did not make it out of committee and to the floor for debate and a vote. One reason that allowing states to collect sales taxes on remote interstate sales has not received more support in Congress is that 52% of Americans oppose the idea, with only 38% in favor, and 10% unsure. Still, many states continue to find a way to tax remote sales. In 2008, New York State passed legislation to tax the sales of vendors like Amazon whose only physical presence in the state is affiliate vendors that advertise through Amazon. Whether this is sufficient to meet the Supreme Court "substantial physical presence" standard for such taxation remains to be determined by the courts in the suits that have been filed by Amazon and others.

Where to Find More

Congressional Research Service, *State and Local Sales and Use Taxes and Internet Commerce,* Report RL31252 (March 9, 2006). A related CRS report that is helpful is, *The Streamlined Sales and Use Tax Agreement: A Brief Description,* Report RS22387 (February 22, 2006). The University of Tennessee study discussed in the readings with updated data including 2008 is Donald Bruce and William F. Fox, "State and Local Sales Tax Revenue Losses from E-Commerce: Estimates as of July 2004." It is available on the Web site of the university's College for Business Administration at www.cber.utk.edu/ecomm.htm/. U.S. government data on e-commerce can be found at www.census.gov/mrts/www/ecomm.html/. For the Web site of the NCSL's Executive Committee Task Force on State and Local Taxation of Telecommunications and Electronic Commerce go to www.ncsl.org/programs/fiscal/tctelcom.htm/. The opposing view of the Direct Marketing Association is on the Internet at www.the-dma.org/taxation/. An argument opposed to an interstate sales tax on the grounds that sales taxes are regressive and extending them to new areas would compound that problem is made by Christopher G. Reddick in "Electronic Commerce and the State Sales Tax System: An Issue of Tax Fairness," *Journal of Electronic Commerce in Organizations* (2006). The taxation of e-commerce is a global, as well as a U.S. issue, as evident in Subhajit Basu, *Global Perspectives on E-commerce Taxation Law* (Ashgate, 2007).

What More to Do

Formulate a proposal to tax remote sales. Consider letting each state collect the taxes based on its own rates or having a single national tax rate with the federal government distributing the revenue. If each state gets tax from commerce within it, should the sales tax apply to the state where the item is shipped from, where the vendor's corporate headquarters is located, or where the purchaser is located? Would you tax all items sold in interstate commerce or would you exempt some, such as children's clothing and medicine? Should the government compensate vendors for the new burden of tax administration? How would you deal with goods going to/arriving from overseas?

BUDGETARY POLICY

REDUCING FEDERAL BUDGET DEFICITS:
Focus on Increasing Revenue *or* Focus on Reducing Spending?

FOCUS ON INCREASING REVENUE

ADVOCATE: Leonard E. Burman, Daniel Patrick Moynihan Professor of Public Affairs. Maxwell School, Syracuse University

SOURCE: Testimony during hearings on "Taxes and the Budget" before the Subcommittee on Select Revenue Measures, Committee on Ways and Means, U.S. House of Representatives, March 23, 2010

FOCUS ON REDUCING SPENDING

ADVOCATE: Douglas Holtz-Eakin, President, American Action Forum

SOURCE: Testimony during hearings on "Taxes and the Budget" before the Subcommittee on Select Revenue Measures, Committee on Ways and Means, U.S. House of Representatives, March 23, 2010

During fiscal year 2010 (FY2010, which was from October 1, 2009 through September 30, 2010), the U.S. government collected revenues of $2.17 trillion but spent $3.72 trillion, creating a budget deficit for the year of $1.55 trillion. Such numbers are immense by any standard. FY2010 spending, for example, came to about $12,000 for every U.S. resident or, by another measure, about $10.2 billion a day. Such numbers are so large that they lead to a sort of disconnect with any empirical reality that most of us can truly grasp. Even as far back as the mid-1960s, when federal spending was only about $130 billion (less than 4% of FY2010 spending), its enormity led Senator Everett Dirkson (R-IL) to reputedly quip about this effort to reduce spending, "A billion here, a billion there—sooner or later it adds up to real money." Another revealing statement came in the early 1980s from David Stockman, President Ronald Reagan's budget director. Spending was up to about $750 billion (less that 25% of FY2010 spending), but even at that point Stockman bemoaned the "internal mysteries of the budget" and confessed, "None of us really understands what's going on with all these numbers."

Given the budget's "internal mysteries," it is important to specify how the budget is discussed here. First, the figures for the budget include both its parts. This includes "on-budget" amounts, the bulk of revenue raised by income and most other taxes, and the bulk of annual spending authorized and appropriated by Congress. The second part of the budget is made up of "off-budget" revenues and spending. Currently this includes the budgets of the Social Security Administration and Postal Service, which Congress for political reasons have established in this second category. For FY2010, the off-budget amounts were 29% of revenue and 15% of spending. Because the off budget had a surplus of $78 billion, it helped reduce the overall deficit. However, the off-budget surplus comes entirely from the Social Security Administration (SSA), and it is expected to have a persistent deficit beginning as early as 2014.

Two other sometimes-confusing budget terms are the "discretionary budget" and the "mandatory budget." The discretionary budget includes those expenditures specifically established by Congress through an appropriation or other act for a specific year. The funding of the Defense Department is an example. The mandatory budget is based on formulas and contractual obligations. For instance, Congress creates certain standards for who can get Medicare and then authorizes spending whatever it takes to pay for the care. In the short-term, such spending is mandatory because contractual relations between, for example, hospitals and the government occur. In the longer term, though, such programs are not mandatory because Congress has the authority to alter formulas or even terminate a program.

It is also important to be aware of different ways of measuring the budget. For example, federal budget spending has grown, but that growth can be calculated in two ways. Most commonly, the budget is measured in "current dollars," the amount spent in any given year. In FY1991, spending in current dollars was $1.32 trillion, and in FY2010 it was $3.72 trillion. One could say that spending grew 182% during the two decades. But inflation eroded the value of the dollar over the twenty years, and it is arguably better to measure growth in terms of "real dollars," those adjusted for inflation. Doing that shows the spending of $1.32 trillion in FY1991 was equal to $2.94 trillion in 1991 real dollars. By this calculation, the increase between FY1991 and FY2010 was 123% in real dollars compared to 192% in current dollars.

The federal budget has had a deficit in every year since FY1969 except of a brief stint, FY1998–FY2000. By FY1991 the deficit was $269 billion, and during the next two decades it increased 476% to $ 1.55 trillion. However, in real dollars, the increase was a less-daunting 255%. It is also worthwhile to measure the deficit it in terms of national wealth. That is because a debt of say $100,000 is much more manageable for someone making $250,000 a year than for someone making $25,000 a year. One measure of national wealth is gross domestic product (GDP, the value of all productive activity within the country). The FY1991 deficit was 4.5% of that year's GDP ($5.93 trillion). In FY2010, the deficit was 10.6% of the GDP ($14.62 trillion).

There have been periods of alarm over the federal budget deficits, and the United States has been experiencing one of those periods in the last few years. The only ways to cut a budget deficit are by (1) increasing taxes and over revenues, (2) decreasing spending, or (3) some combination of the first two. Like virtually everyone, Professor Leonard E. Burman from Syracuse University and Douglas Holtz-Eakin, president of the American Action Forum, advocate option 3 in the following two readings, but Burman emphasizes increasing taxes and Holtz-Eakin emphasizes cutting spending.

POINTS TO PONDER

➤ Including all three (federal, state, and local) levels of government, revenue for FY2009 was $3.53 trillion, and spending was $5.14 trillion, for a government-wide deficit of $1.61 trillion.

➤ Is it good or bad that U.S. total taxes (federal, state, and local), at 28% of GDP in 2008, were the lowest (tied with Japan) among the world's major industrialized countries, whose taxes averaged 45% percent of GDP?

➤ Is it good or bad that U.S. total government spending, at 39% of GDP in 2008, was much lower than the average of 46% of GDP among the world's major industrialized countries?

Reducing Federal Budget Deficits:
Focus on Increasing Revenue

Leonard E. Burman

AVOIDING CATASTROPHIC BUDGET FAILURE

It has become a cliché to say that current budget trends are unsustainable, and to cite [noted economist] Herb Stein's dictum that if something can't go on forever, it will stop. Stein was clearly correct, but *how* our debt stops growing matters. The best outcome is that it stops growing because policymakers make the hard choice of cutting programs and raising taxes before the economy has suffered any real damage.

A slightly more painful option is that interest rates start to increase to reflect the increasing riskiness of government securities—because higher debt brings with it a risk that the US will either default on some of its debt or be forced to print money to avoid a default, triggering inflation or even hyperinflation. Higher interest rates would bring increasing political pressure to reduce the deficit from businesses that can't afford to invest and consumers who can't afford to borrow to buy a home or car. The downside is that the higher interest rates would also increase government's debt service costs, making the required fiscal adjustments even more painful. And higher interest rates could precipitate a recession (or stifle a nascent recovery).

The worst outcome is that interest rates show no perceptible effect from the US borrowing binge for a long time. Rates may stay low because our foreign lenders have an incentive to keep enabling our borrowing habit. The money they lend us fuels our giant trade deficit, which in turn props up their economies. If they pulled the plug, the dollar would collapse in value and US demand for foreign goods would slow to a trickle. So, in part, our debt habit simply reflects a very dangerous codependency between us and our foreign enablers.

We might hope that financial markets would save us from catastrophe by demanding higher interest rates on Treasuries, but that would require a degree of foresight that we haven't seen lately. Despite some saber rattling from bond rating agencies, our lenders have clearly calculated that Treasuries are a safe investment at low interest rates because as long as we can roll over maturing debt at low rates, we can easily pay the interest our lenders demand.

This dynamic is eerily similar to the bubble logic that overtook the housing market. Lenders concluded that as long as housing prices were growing at double digit rates, almost any borrower was worthy of a mortgage because, under the worst case scenario, the lender could foreclose and sell the house at a profit. Cheap and easy credit boosted demand for homes and kept prices soaring, fulfilling the expectations of lenders—for a while. The problem was that prices couldn't rise forever, and when they stopped, the bubble burst.

The analogy in the government bond market is that at some point investors will decide that lending to the US government is risky and demand a higher interest rate. The higher rate increases default risk as debt service becomes more burdensome, and the higher risk pushes the required interest rate up further. This vicious cycle pushes interest rates ever higher. When the dust settles, the government may only be able to borrow at exorbitant interest rates—or possibly not at all.

That is, the market for government bonds might be a classic bubble. But when this bubble bursts, the government won't have the option to borrow to prop up financial markets if its borrowing caused the crisis.

Unable to borrow, the government will have to cut spending to the bone—including potentially devastating cuts in Social Security, Medicare, and Medicaid—and have to raise taxes to levels never before seen in this country. And even that may not be enough for forestall default. In October 2009, more than $2.5 trillion of debt had a maturity of less than one year. If the government could not roll over that debt, there is no way that it could cut spending or raise taxes fast enough to avoid default. (CBO [the Congressional Budget Office] projected total income tax revenues in 2010 to be about $1.1 trillion, so doubling the income tax—which is neither feasible nor desirable—would not close even half the gap.) As the debt grows, the amount of debt coming due each year—and the size of the potential crisis—will grow as well.

Thus, the Federal Reserve would have to serve as the "lender of last resort" for the US government, massively expanding the money supply. If the bubble burst tomorrow, the Fed might be able to plausibly commit to tightening the money supply in the near future as the federal government ran surpluses to buy back the debt. If investors believed this, we might avoid hyperinflation. But even in this case, investors might be skeptical of any promise of fiscal responsibility from the government that precipitated the crisis. And if the debt were twice as big when the bubble bursts, the government would have no credibility at all.

The consequence would likely involve a long and severe recession or depression and hyperinflation. In their survey of financial crises through the ages, [economists] Carmen Reinhart and Ken Rogoff reported that the average debt crisis of the sort we're likely to experience came with inflation of 9000 percent. That is, after the crisis, a dollar might be worth a little more than a penny.

Bottom line: catastrophic budget failure would involve hyperinflation, an eviscerated public sector, taxes that would make a Scandinavian revolt, and a crippled economy. Avoiding that fate should be your highest priority.

TAX INCREASES ARE INEVITABLE

Nobody likes to pay taxes, but there is no practical way to tame the debt without higher taxes unless you are willing to renege on promises made to seniors. There are currently about 4.7 working age individuals (ages 20–64) for every person of retirement age (65 and older). But, as the baby boomers reach retirement age, that number plummets to 4.0 in 2018 and just 3.0 in 2028. Some refer to the inverse of this ratio as the "dependency ratio"—a measure of how many retirees depend on Social Security and Medicare for each person working and paying into the system. Even if health care costs weren't growing faster than the rest of the economy, the swelling dependency ratio would require the dwindling share of workers to shoulder larger burdens.

The consequence is that either taxes must increase significantly above historic levels to prevent enormous accumulations of public debt, or that government services, especially those benefiting the elderly, must be cut substantially below current levels. The data indicated that even if health care costs grew at the same rate as the economy from 2009 on (rather than the historical average of 2.5 percent per year faster than GDP), primary spending—excluding interest on the debt—would still escalate rapidly from 20 percent of GDP in 2012 because of the demands of aging baby boomers. By 2030, spending would reach 23 percent of GDP. If revenues were kept at their post-war average level of 18.3 percent of GDP, deficits, the debt, and interest payments on the debt would soar.

In reality, healthcare spending has grown much faster than GDP for decades—by an average of 2.5 percentage points. If it continues to follow that path, spending will increase dramatically. CBO projects that total federal primary spending will exceed 25 percent of GDP by 2030 and top 27 percent by 2040. Clearly, healthcare spending will have to slow or households and governments at all levels will be bankrupted. It is highly unlikely, however, that we can hold the rate of growth of health costs below that of the economy. One reason is that a significant share of healthcare spending has paid for valuable innovations that have improved the quality and length of life. Artificial joint replacements that preserve pain-free mobility for older people are the classic example. [One study] argues that, given the potential benefits, we are not spending enough on healthcare. [Other scholars] argue that spending on preventive care is far below optimum, and [still other scholars] explain why human foibles (procrastination and the tendency to undervalue future benefits relative to current costs) lead people to consume too little healthcare.

Thus, while it is essential that healthcare costs be restrained over the long term, it may be neither feasible nor desirable to shrink healthcare spending as a share of the economy. Furthermore, tremendous uncertainty exists about future health technology and spending patterns, but past experience is not encouraging. It is highly likely that health spending will compound the long-term budget problem.

It is tempting to wish that we will grow out of the problem, but that is implausible. Most of the factors that have boosted output over the past few decades are unlikely to repeat. For example, the tremendous increase in women's labor force participation was a one-time event.

The greater risk is that swelling national debt will slow economic growth. [Two scholars have recently] calculated that countries with debt above 90 percent of GDP grow by an average of 1.3 percentage points per year slower than less debt-ridden countries. (The debt-to-GDP ratio is currently about 60 percent of GDP; CBO projects it will reach 90 percent around 2020 under current policies.) If growth slows, all of the economic challenges that we face will worsen.

TAXES AND ECONOMIC GROWTH

With few exceptions, taxes entail economic costs. Some supply-siders have even contended that cuts in marginal tax rates could pay for themselves because the economy would grow faster and generate more tax revenues. Serious analyses of supply-side tax cuts, even by those very sympathetic to the premise that tax cuts can boost economic growth, have all concluded that deficit-financed tax cuts do not pay for themselves over the long run. In fact, if the resulting deficits are ultimately offset by higher tax rates, the ultimate effect is likely to be lower GDP.

This occurs because the cost of taxation grows disproportionately with the tax rate. Thus, if top tax rates are cut from 40 percent to 35 percent for a while, but then raised to 45 percent to pay back the resulting debt, the 5 percentage point increase in rates reduces growth by much more than the temporary 5 percentage point rate cut boosted it.

As a general rule, stable tax rates impose less economic cost than volatile ones. For that reason, it would be far better to raise taxes soon to reduce or eliminate the deficit (after the economy has recovered from the economic downturn) than to postpone action for many years. The longer we wait, the higher tax rates would have to be to restore balance. And income tax rates of 50 or 60 or 70 percent would entail huge economic costs compared with a 40 percent rate.

TAXING THE RICH WON'T BE ENOUGH

While supply-siders hold out hope that tax cuts can somehow pay for themselves, liberals also cling to their own version of wishful thinking—that tax increases on the rich would suffice. President Obama has repeatedly promised not to raise taxes on households earning less than $250,000 per year. [This year economists] at the Tax Policy Center estimated how much income tax rates would have to increase—assuming the rest of the Obama budget were enacted—to get the deficit down to an average of 2 percent of GDP from 2015 to 2019. They concluded that rates would have to increase by almost half: the 10-percent bracket would increase to almost 15 percent and the top bracket would increase to 52 percent—a level not seen since enactment of the Tax Reform Act of 1986.

Table 1.
Rates Required to Reduce Deficit to Two Percent of GDP from 2015 to 2019

Current Tax Rates	Raise All Rates	Raise Top Three Rates	Raise Top Two Rates
10.0	14.9	10.0	10.0
15.0	22.3	15.0	15.0
25.0	37.2	25.0	25.0
28.0	41.7	60.8	28.0
33.0	49.1	71.7	85.7
35.0	52.1	76.1	90.9

If tax increases are limited to those with higher incomes, the top rates would have to become truly exorbitant to hit the 2-percent deficit target. Raising only the top 3 rates would require a top rate of 76 percent; and raising only the top 2 rates—the policy most consistent with the President's promise to spare the middle class—would require a top rate of almost 91 percent, a level not seen since the Kennedy Administration.

As [the Tax Policy Center study] points out, those estimates do not account for the increased tax avoidance that high rates would engender. Accounting for such behavioral responses would require even higher rates. It is thus infeasible that the deficit target could be met with tax increases on the rich alone. And, given that the deficit grows ever larger, the target would grow more elusive over time.

BASE BROADENING AND DEFICIT REDUCTION

Tax rate increases harm the economy and cannot, by themselves, close the budget gap. In contrast, base broadening can boost tax revenues and make the income tax more efficient, fair, and comprehensible. Loopholes and preferences in the income tax complicate tax preparation and create opportunities for tax avoidance and evasion. For example, long-term capital gains face a 15-percent top rate compared with a 35-percent rate for ordinary income. The capital gains preference has created a whole tax shelter industry designed to convert highly taxed ordinary income into lightly taxed capital gains. The lower rate can distort investment and occupation choices. For example, finance experts who work in the private equity arena are taxed at less than half the rate of bond traders who may work down the hall and do very similar work. Taxing capital gains at the same rate as other income would eliminate those distortions.

The numerous tax preferences in the Code reduce tax revenues by an enormous amount—over $1 trillion a year. Like healthcare expenditures, they are growing faster than the rest of the economy. Over the next 5 years, so-called "tax expenditures" will reduce federal revenues by over $9 trillion, or 74 percent of income tax revenues. Subjecting tax expenditures to the same level of scrutiny we apply to direct spending programs could improve the efficiency of the government and help tame the budget deficit. And, arguably, since tax expenditures are really just spending programs in disguise, limiting tax expenditures could be seen as consistent with the President's promise to spare the middle class from tax increases. Indeed, the President has proposed to limit cap the growth of discretionary spending. It would make sense to apply the same budget discipline to the far larger category of spending programs run through the tax system.

The concept of tax expenditures is controversial, but it has been around for decades, since Treasury Assistant Secretary Stanley Surrey proposed that deviations from the normal tax rules that serve to benefit a particular group or activity should be considered spending. The basic notion is that a $100 tax reduction for undertaking a particular activity is identical to a $100 cash grant for the subsidized activity in terms of its effect on the deficit and resource allocation.

Conservatives have objected to the notion of a tax expenditure since long before Surrey coined the term. William Gladstone, a Tory member of the British parliament, argued in 1863 that the government should monitor the uses of the charitable deduction allowed under the income tax, just as it would any other spending program. The rebuttal from Sir Strafford Northcote could be lifted from the modern ultraconservative's critique of tax expenditures: "The right hon. Gentleman, if he took £5 [£ is the symbol for the British pound] out of the pocket of a man with £100, put the case as if he gave the man £95…"

For some reason, modern conservatives find this talking point compelling, but I have a hard time understanding why. Virtually any spending program could be converted into a tax expenditure. Why does that sleight of hand inoculate a spending program from scrutiny? The late Princeton economist David Bradford—one of the intellectual forebears of the "flat tax"—used to quip that he could fund the Pentagon with tax expenditures (by, for example, providing refundable tax credits in lieu of cash to arms manufacturers), reducing the size of the recorded defense budget without hurting national security one bit.

To take another example, suppose we offered individuals eligible for Medicare the option of buying their insurance for an actuarially fair premium from the government, in exchange for a tax credit equal to 110% of the premium. Higher-income seniors with sufficient tax liability to use the credit would presumably take advantage of this great deal. It would cut Medicare spending, and cut taxes by even more. Government would appear to be smaller and taxes lower, but in reality, we'd only have complicated tax compliance for seniors and increased the deficit.

The growth of tax expenditures has been fueled by a political environment that favors "tax cuts" over spending, even when a spending program might be more effective. But tax expenditures strongly resemble entitlement programs and can be just as detrimental to the budget over the long term. And they often make the tax system more complex.

Monitoring tax expenditures would require a significant change in the budgeting process [because] most tax subsidies are now virtual entitlements, continuing (and growing) unless Congress legislates change or repeal. Former JCT [Joint Committee on Taxation] chief of staff George Yin (2009) has proposed sunsetting [establishing an end date unless reauthorized by Congress] all tax expenditures and requiring periodic reauthorization as for discretionary programs. A less radical approach would be to include the value of tax expenditures with direct expenditures and subject the totals to caps as part of the congressional budget process. This obviously would create some jurisdictional challenges for Congress (between appropriating committees and the tax-writing committees), but it is, in my view, the only way to get total spending under control. It makes no sense to exempt more than $1 trillion of spending from budget scrutiny.

I'm certainly not proposing to eliminate all tax expenditures. It makes sense to run some programs through the tax system instead of setting up another bureaucracy. I just think we ought to subject these expenditures to the same fiscal constraint and scrutiny that the president wants to apply to other domestic spending programs.

CONCLUSIONS AND RECOMMENDATIONS

Taming the budget will require both spending cuts and new tax revenues. The best way to raise revenues would be to broaden the base—eliminate or reform tax expenditures that are not serving their purpose with the goal of making the tax system simpler, fairer and more conducive to economic growth. As part of that process, other more efficient sources of revenue such as a VAT should be considered.

The President has signaled that his deficit reduction panel may consider tax reform as part of a package of revenue increases and spending cuts. That's a good idea. However, if Congress makes most of the [President George W.] Bush and [President Barack] Obama tax cuts permanent, as the president proposes, tax reform would become much more difficult. A better approach would be to extend the tax cuts for two or three years and commit to a real process of tax and expenditure reforms to eliminate the primary deficit by a certain date.

Reducing Federal Budget Deficits:
Focus on Reducing Spending

DOUGLAS HOLTZ-EAKIN

The federal government faces daunting fiscal challenges, as the budgetary outlook is a threat to the very foundations of the U.S. economy and the tradition of leaving to the next generation a promise of prosperity that is greater then that which was inherited. In these circumstances, one can only hope that the business of this hearing would translate quickly into actual legislation, congressional passage, and a reversal of the trajectory upon which federal government finds itself.

In my testimony, I hope to make three major points: (1) that the budgetary outlook is a threat to the economic future of the United States, (2) that the budget outlook is driven by excessive spending, not a paucity of revenues, and (3) that the top tax priority should be reform, not revenue increases.

THE PROBLEM

The core, long-term issue has been outlined in successive versions of the Congressional Budget Office's Long-Term Budget Outlook. In broad terms, over the next 30 years, the inexorable dynamics of current law will raise federal outlays from about 20 percent of gross domestic product (GDP) to anywhere from 30 to 40 percent of GDP. Any attempt to keep taxes at their post-war norm of 18 percent of GDP will generate an unmanageable federal debt spiral. In contrast, a strategy of ratcheting up taxes to match the federal spending appetite would be self-defeating and result in a crushing blow to economic growth.

The policy problem is that spending rises above any reasonable metric of taxation for the indefinite future. Period. There is a mini-industry devoted to producing alternative numerical estimates of this mismatch, but diagnosis of the basic problem is not complicated. The diagnosis leads as well to the prescription for action. Over the long-term, the budget problem is primarily a spending problem and correcting it requires reductions in the growth of large mandatory spending programs and the appetite for federal outlays, in general.

Just as some would mistakenly believe that we can easily "tax our way out" of this budgetary box there is an equally misguided notion in other quarters that we can "grow our way out." The pace of spending growth simply must be reduced.

This depiction of the federal budgetary future has been unchanged for a decade or more. The diagnosis and prescription have remained unchanged. The only thing missing has been action; well, at least action in the right direction.

Those were the good old days. Now the problem is dramatically worse and happens more quickly. The federal government ran a 2009 deficit of $1.4 trillion—the highest since World War II—as spending reached nearly 25 percent of GDP and receipts fell below 15 percent of GDP. In each case, the results are unlike those experienced in over 50 years.

Going forward, there is no relief in sight. Each year the federal budget is projected to be in enormous deficit. Over the next 10 years, according to the CBO's [Congressional Budget Office] preliminary analysis of the president's budget, the deficit will never fall below $700 billion dollars. In 2020, the deficit will be 5.6 percent of

GDP, roughly $1.3 trillion, of which over $900 billion will be devoted to servicing debt on previous borrowing.

The budget outlook is not starved of revenues. The CBO projects that over the next decade the economy will fully recover and revenues will be 19.6 percent of GDP—over $300 billion more than the historic norm. Instead, the problem is that spending. Federal outlays in 2020 are expected to be 25.2 percent of GDP—about $1.2 trillion higher than the 20 percent that has been business as usual in the postwar era.

As a result of the spending binge, in 2020 debt in the hands of the public will have more than doubled from its 2008 level to 90 percent of GDP and will be on an upward trajectory. Measured in nominal [current] dollars, by 2008 our republic had amassed a debt of $5.8 trillion. The debt is expected to relentlessly expand. In 10 years, it will be $20.3 trillion—nearly $60,000 per American.

In short, what used to be a problem that would take 30 years to mature is now upon us in the next decade. The diagnosis is the same—too much spending and too much debt—and the prescription is the same. But there is less time to waste.

THE RISKS

Deficits have economic consequences that impact both fairness and growth. At the most basic level, they force our children and grandchildren to pay the bill for our over-consumption. Often it is argued that it is "fair" to do so because the debt-financed spending confers a corresponding benefit to those generations, but the debts contemplated in the near future cannot pass any reasonable test of equity.

Federal deficits can crowd out domestic investment in physical capital, human capital, and technologies that increase potential GDP and the standard of living. Financing deficits may require net capital inflows that crowd out exports and harm our international competitiveness. We should worry about large borrowing from competitors like China limiting the United States' range of economic and diplomatic options.

In addition to these continued, corrosive effects of budget deficits, analysts have long worried about more dramatic fallout from the budgetary outlook. At what point do rating agencies downgrade the United States? When do lenders price additional risk and charge higher interest rates to federal borrowing, leading to a damaging spike in interest rates? How quickly will international investors flee the dollar for a new reserve currency? If so, how will the resulting higher interest rates, diminished dollar, higher inflation, and economic distress manifest itself? How quickly could such a tsunami of debt-related economic weakness arise? And when could it happen?

Since the basic outlook has been around for a quite some time, one explanation of why such events have yet to transpire is that the same financial market analysts who understand the weak state of the U.S. books also believe that they will be rectified before serious distress arrives. That is, they are counting on the U.S. to put its house in order.

If so, the marked deterioration in the next 10 years raises the urgency of action. Put bluntly, the U.S. is relying on the faith of others in its ability to undertake serious budgetary reforms, and time is getting short.

The obvious problem is that movement in the other direction is hard—lower spending—and requires sacrifice. Will it be worth it? There is no way to know for certain. However, if Congress does take action and it turns out that there was never a risk of being punished by international capital markets or otherwise suffering economic disruption, then all that will happen is that national saving will be higher, productivity and wages will grow, international competitiveness will be enhanced, and the federal budget will have maneuvering room in the event of a future crisis. If, on the other hand, it does not and these threats are real the Nation will be demonstrably weakened.

In thinking about these risks, it is useful to note that we are in an era unlike the past. While there have been nations whose debt approached or exceeded U.S. levels, it has never been in a situation in which nearly every part of the developed world faces a debt problem comparable (or worse) to that of the United States. We simply have no experience with massive debt management on this global scale, raising the risks associated with inaction.

THE NEED TO CONTROL SPENDING

This hearing is intended to discuss the tax code, the central purpose of which is to raise revenue to finance federal outlays. As noted above, in the years to come mandatory spending programs will grow quite rapidly. The rising fiscal pressures emanating from spending on Social Security and health programs, if left unchecked, will threaten the three pillars of U.S. post-war economic success. First, the successful U.S. economic strategy has been to rely largely on the private sector; the mirror image of this approach being a government sector that is relatively small (granted, "small" is in the eye of the beholder) and contained. Growth in spending of the magnitude promised by current laws guarantees a much larger government.

Second, the small U.S. government has been financed by taxes that are relatively low by international standards and interfere relatively little with economic performance. Spending increases of the type currently projected would entail taxes higher by 50 percent or more to unprecedented levels. Such a policy would impair economic growth and reduce living standards for future generations.

Finally, a hallmark of the U.S. economy has been its ability to flexibly respond to new demands and disruptive shocks. In an environment where old-age programs consume nearly every budget dollar, to address other policy goals future politicians may resort to mandates, regulations, and the type of economic handcuffs that guarantee lost flexibility.

In sum, the ability of the tax code to meet its primary objective is most threatened by the absence of reforms to mandatory spending programs. This raises the specter of a generational injustice: bequeathing to our children and grandchildren a rising burden of taxation, a less robust economy, or both. The most pressing issue of fairness cannot be addressed by raising taxes, but rather requires a reducing the growth of spending.

THE NEED FOR TAX REFORM

As noted above, the central budgetary challenge is to control the rise in federal spending. However, even assuming that Congress rises to this challenge, it will be desirable to undertake reforms of the federal revenue system.

1. Objectives of Tax Policy

Keeping the burden of taxes low. The importance of keeping federal spending contained to national priorities and thus permitting taxes to be as low as possible is straightforward: taxes directly reduce the ability of families to pay their bills and save for the future. However, even the best tax system impairs market incentives, imposes obstacles for households and firms alike, and undermines economic performance. A goal of tax policy should be to keep such interference and waste a small as possible. This interference is sometimes referred to as the "efficiency cost," "deadweight loss," or "excess burden" of the tax system and captures the reality that there is a loss to households above and beyond the amount of tax revenue collected.

In this regard, unfortunately, our tax code is in need of a major overhaul. Tax-based distortions permeate our daily economic lives. Decisions on saving, retirement, education, investment, debt and equity finance are driven by tax-based planning to the detriment of our ability to meet pressing national needs. The tax code is a basic impediment to the United States' ability to grow robustly and compete on global markets.

The loss in economic performance is exacerbated by the sheer cost of complying with an overly complex tax code. According to the recent President's Advisory Panel on Federal Tax Reform, If the money spent every year on tax preparation and compliance was collected—about $140 billion each year or over $1,000 per family—it could fund a substantial part of the federal government, including the Department of Homeland Security, the Department of State, NASA, the Department of Housing and Urban Development, the Environmental Protection Agency, the Department of Transportation, the United States Congress, our federal courts, and all of the federal government's foreign aid.

Supporting economic mobility. The tax code should not unnecessarily impair the ability of lower-income families lacking insurance to climb up the ladder of American prosperity. Recent legislative efforts such as the stimulus bill and the Senate health care bill raise to shocking levels the effective marginal tax rates (EMTR) on lower and middle-income singles and families—with the government taking up to 41 percent of each additional dollar.

The effective marginal tax rate is the answer to the question: "If I earn $1 more, how much less than $1 do I get to save or spend?" If you can keep that full dollar for your disposal, the effective marginal tax rate is zero. If earning another dollar does not raise your disposable income by even a penny, the effective marginal tax rate is 100 percent.

Obviously, neither extreme is realistic. But exactly where federal policies come down in between has dramatic implications for the ability of families to rise from the ranks of the poor, or to ascend toward the upper end of the middle class. This mobility is the heart of the American dream that has made the United States a beacon of economic light for centuries.

How can a family be expected to get ahead when taking an extra shift, finding a way for a second parent to work, or investing in night school courses to qualify for a raise means handing the government as much as 41 percent of the additional income earned? Parents already juggle the tough trade-off between working more to build their family's future and spending time at home with their children. The bigger the EMTR, the tougher that tradeoff becomes.

Every "phase-out" of a tax credit or subsidy program is an EMTR in disguise. The cumulative impact is a cruel twist on "targeting," as families are anchored near the bottom of the income distribution by layers of fiscal cement. Excessive EMTRs damage these incentives, discourage the taxed, and threaten to rob America of a vitality that is its signature.

Fairness. A final objective is to raise taxes in a fair fashion. Unfortunately, there are two major obstacles to an easy evaluation of the success in meeting this standard. The first is figuring out who really pays a tax. For example, in 2012 the CBO projects that the federal government will raise over $300 billion from the corporation income tax. However, corporations will not "pay" the tax in any meaningful sense—they merely send in the check. In the process of meeting their tax obligation, however, firms could raise prices, cut back on wages, reduce fringe benefits, slow replacement of equipment or scale back expansion plans, cut dividends, or many combinations of their options to alter their revenues and cost structures. The result is that the corporation tax is "paid" by customers, workers, or investors. Indeed, recent evidence suggests that the relatively high U.S. corporation income is ultimately paid by workers in the form of lower wages.

A second difficulty is the absence of an ethical consensus on distributional fairness. In the absence of such benchmark, two guidelines prove useful. The first is to note that individuals view market transactions as a "fair deal" when they get back value equal to what they paid. By analogy, a benchmark for judging the tax system is whether a tax-payer's liability is equal to benefits received from the federal budget—a neutral system. If benefits received exceed taxes, the household is a net beneficiary of the tax system and vice versa.

This perspective differs from two other metrics that are commonly employed—effective tax rates and tax shares. Effective tax rates are the ratio of taxes paid to income—roughly the share of income taken by taxes. A drawback to evaluating fairness using effective tax rates is that the rates may change because of movements in the denomina-tor—families' incomes—that have nothing to do with tax policy. Incomes are influenced by taxes, but also are determined by skills, education, effort, risk-taking and innovation, regulations, and other factors. Tax shares—the fraction of the overall taxes that each individual pays—have the drawback that they ignore the spending side of the equation. Given that taxes are necessary only because of spending, this omission is striking.

Viewed from this perspective, the U.S. tax code is highly progressive—lower income individuals receive much more than they pay in taxes. According to the CBO, over the bottom 40 percent of the income distribution paid no federal income tax in 2006. Of course there are other taxes. In particular, payroll taxes are the largest tax for a majori-ty of households. But examining the payroll tax is ultimately a reminder of the need for social security reform. The progressivity of this program will depend upon the scale of the benefits individuals receive in the future.

A second perspective on fairness stems from the fact that the tax code assigns tax-payers with the same income, number of children, and other factors different tax bur-dens. As noted above, taxes will differ depending on whether a family purchases health insurance or receives it as part of an employer compensation package. Two families with the same income will pay different taxes because they reside in different states, and some families receive state-provided services for which they can deduct income and property taxes. A person who saves more of their earnings in taxable accounts will pay more in taxes than a non-saver who has the exact same earnings year by year. Indeed, some inequality may stem from the sheer complexity of the tax code and the inability of individuals to take advantage of tax benefits for which they are eligible. These dif-ferences between otherwise similar taxpayers are at odds with basic fairness and under-mine faith in the fairness of the tax code.

Summary. The most pressing tax fairness issue facing the United States is the poten-tial for dramatic tax increases, slower income growth, and reduced standards of living for future generations if the spending growth profile of the federal government is not reduced. All other fairness issues pale by comparison.

As the economy recovers, the federal tax system will roughly achieving its goal of providing financing for federal spending. However, there is little else to defend in the current tax code. It is overly complex and burdensome, interferes too much with commerce and economic competitiveness, and is riddled with uneven treatment. Far-reaching reforms are merited; more modest efforts will not succeed in raising federal revenues in a pro-growth and fair fashion.

2. Objectives for Tax Reform

Consumption-based taxation. A consumption tax is just what it sounds like: a tax applied to consumption spending. However, under that deceptively simple umbrella resides a vast array of potential variants. Consumption taxes can be flat or contain multiple rates; can be applied to households, firms, or both; and can be viewed as "direct" or "indirect" taxes.

For purposes of my remarks today, let me focus on a few identities that give the flavor of the issues. For a household—or the country as a whole—all income (Y) is either consumed (C) or saved (S): Y=C+S. This suggests two broad strategies for taxing consumption. One is to tax consumption (C) as in a national sales tax. The alternative is to tax it "indirectly" by levying the tax on "consumed income"—income after deducting saving or investment: (Y–S). This is the strategy taken by a value-added tax (VAT), the Hall-Rabushka flat tax, or the "X-tax," a more progressive variant of the Hall-Rabushka tax developed by the late David Bradford.

Interest in a U.S. consumption tax is not new. Advocates have touted the potential benefits from moving to a consumption tax for many years. However, I wish to separate my support from some of the more overreaching arguments. In particular, my support for a consumption-based tax reform is not about:

1. Simplicity. Some consumption taxes—notably the original Hall-Rabushka flat tax—have been publicized on the basis of their "simplicity." Who can forget (admittedly tax economists have a limited reservoir of thrills) the first time they saw the Hall-Rabushka postcard tax return? Similar simplicity arguments have been made about a national retail sales tax, where advocates tend to argue that there is little to do except piggyback on existing state efforts.

But this really misses the point for three reasons. First, no tax system will be that simple. For any household, the goal is to legally minimize its tax liability. The innate craftiness of the American populace will dictate that any tax system will acquire a growth of rulemaking that delimits the boundaries of acceptable behavior. That is, a certain amount of complex rule-making will be necessary. A common complaint of income-tax defenders is that consumption tax folks compare an ideal consumption tax with the actual income tax. This is truly unfair and no way to decide between the two. Second, as noted above, for many there is nothing simpler than the current income tax—they don't pay it. As is becoming more widely appreciated, the current income tax is not your father's income tax. Complexity of the income tax is the curse of those who pay it. Third, postcards are obsolete. Today your taxes are "done"—that is computed—by tax-preparation software and filed on-line.

2. Making taxes more or less visible. A common argument supporting a national sales tax is that it would make more visible the cost of government. Perhaps, but the ultimate measure of the size of government is its spending. Once the dollars have been committed, the taxpayer will pay one way or the other. Either taxes will be levied to match the spending, or there will be borrowing to cover the federal deficit. It may be important to raise the visibility of congressional decisions, but putting taxes on your register receipt does not display spending. Indeed, if a national sales tax did produce pressure to keep taxes low, it may do nothing to address the tsunami of future Medicare spending and lead to larger deficits.

3. Raising the national saving rate. A consumption tax would remove the tax-bias in favor of current consumption, and many believe that this would raise the private saving rate. If so, then good. The main idea is to eliminate tax-based financial decisions and have households choose based more on the economic fundamentals. However, I suspect that the scope for dramatic changes is a somewhat limited. Instead, the most rapid improvement in the national saving rate will come from controlling federal spending and thus reducing government borrowing.

Instead, a consumption tax meets the following needs of the tax system:

1. The philosophical foundation of the tax code. Public policies should mean something. As I have stressed, the tax code exists for a single purpose: it exists to finance the costs of public programs. The powerful behavioral effects of taxation are real, and a tribute to the power of market incentives as the mechanism by which taxes influence behavior is to change prices. Since the purpose of the tax code is to raise revenue, it has as its core mission the reducing the resources of some households. The central question is why choose those who consume over those with income. Consumption is the spending that extracts resources from the economy. In contrast, saving is economic activity necessary to contribute to a growing economy. Recall the identity: $Y=C+S$. An income tax treats identically those high-income individuals who live frugally and plow their resources back into the economy and those that spend every night drinking champagne in a limousine while hopping from club to club. Taxing consumption reduces the burden on the former, while focusing it on the latter.

2. Economic efficiency. A consumption tax would reduce the extent to which economic activity is dictated strictly by reducing taxes (an unproductive use of time and money). First, it broadens the tax base to include all consumption. The essential recipe in any tax reform is to broaden the tax base and lower tax rates. Specifically, the base would include the consumption of employer-provided health insurance (currently entirely untaxed) thereby correcting a major inefficiency that feeds health spending pressures. In addition, it would eliminate the current deduction for state and local taxes, thereby including consumption provided by sub-federal governments. Thus, it would improve the allocation of consumption spending across sectors.

A consumption tax would not distort household choices in the timing of consumption—after all you would either pay the tax now or pay it later. In contrast, under an income tax households pay at both times if they choose to save and consume later. A consumption tax would equalize the tax treatment of investments in physical capital, human capital, and intangible capital. At present, the firm purchases of the latter two types of investment are "expensed" (immediately deducted), while physical capital expenditures are depreciated. Moreover, by eliminating the deduction for mortgage interest, the allocation of physical capital would be improved as business investments would compete on a level playing field with the construction of housing.

A desirable feature that is difficult to quantify is the impact on entrepreneurs. Entrepreneurial forces are widely acknowledged to be important to the success of the United States, but tax policy is rarely formulated with an eye to their incentives. For example, entrepreneurial ventures develop a scale and financial structure dictated by market conditions. In contrast, the tax code interferes with these incentives—extracting a double tax on equity in "C corporations," subsidizing leverage, and thus distorting the choices of business form and financing. The flat business-level tax does not depend on financial structure—it is focused on "real" business transactions—and yields the same liability regardless of legal organization.

3. Acknowledgment of reality. Our current income tax is an exercise in fantasy. An important part of its administration is the taxation of the return to capital. To be successful, this requires that capital income—interest, dividends, capital gains, rents, royalties—be comprehensively measured and adjusted for depreciation and inflation. There is no reason to believe that the U.S. is even moderately successful in this effort, or that the continuing maturation of global financial markets will make it anything but less successful in the future. A consumption tax focuses the tax base on real economic activity—not financial transactions. This is an important difference in a world in which global financial markets have made if virtually impossible to tax capital income, and an excessive regulatory and enforcement regime has grown up around attempts to do so. Instead, the consumption tax focuses on "taxing at the source" before business income enters into financial markets and ultimately is paid to investors.

Specifically, the X-tax (along with the VAT or flat tax) would impose a single-rate business-level tax on a base that consisted of total receipts minus the sum of purchases from other firms and employee compensation. Implicit in those receipts is the contribution of capital, which is taxed prior to distributions in the form of dividends or interest.

4. Fairness. Because a consumption tax is neutral regarding the timing of consumption, it does not penalize those patient households that save their income for a greater lifestyle later in life. That is, two households with the same lifetime income will pay the same lifetime taxes. More generally, consumption taxes may be designed to achieve conventional distributional goals. To begin, under the X-tax, households are taxed on the basis of comprehensive employee compensation. However, such a system would include a generous exemption for a basic standard of consumption and a progressive rate structure.

A concern often raised is that taxing compensation permits high-income individuals to "avoid" tax on their capital income. However, an appropriately-designed consumption tax includes the vast majority of such earnings in its base. In the X-tax, saving and investment is immediately tax-deductible or expensed, but all principle and interest is taxed in the form of revenues at the entity level. Mechanically, this differs from an income tax only by the fact that under an income tax the saving and investment would be depreciated and not expensed. That is, the two approaches differ only by the timing of tax receipts to the U.S. Treasury—less up front for the consumption tax because of expensing, but more in later years because there is no ongoing stream of depreciation. Accordingly, the two tax bases differ only by the return to Treasury securities—the least risky and lowest rate of return. All additional returns—accruing from risk, monopoly power, luck, and other sources—are included in the tax base of both tax systems. Since these types of capital returns are responsible for the largest differences in incomes and consumption tax would capture these in the base, the distributional consequences of such a consumption tax would be in accord with U.S. tradition.

Tax policy and the distribution of economic well-being. Concern has arisen that economic growth no longer translates into acceptable increases in standards of living for too many American households. This has generated a further concern that pro-growth tax policy per se is responsible. The facts, however, suggest otherwise. The dominant source of change in the income distribution is a long-term trend in the wage structure in the U.S., and not recent changes in tax policy. To the extent that policymakers wish to address this issue, the most fruitful approaches involve improving K–12 educational outcomes, thereby equipping future workers with better skills and the ability to be successful in college.

A large literature in labor economics documents a substantial widening of the U.S. wage structure during the 1980s. Wage differentials by education, by occupation, and by age and experience group all rose substantially. The growth of wage inequality was reinforced by changes in non-wage compensation leading to a large increase in total compensation inequality. These wage structure changes translated into a rise in household income inequality. The trend to wage inequality in the 1990s was considerably slower than in the 1980s, with the key feature being that the highest earners (the 90th percentile of the wage and earnings distribution) continuing to grow faster than the median, but no noticeable decline for low earners. The more recent labor market data suggests a continuation of this pattern.

THE CONTINUING DEBATE:
Reducing Federal Budget Deficits

What Is New

In its proposed FY2011 budget, the Obama administration projected that during the next five years revenues would increase faster than spending and that by FY2015 the budget deficit would be $752 billion or about half the FY2010 deficit. Such estimates are always based on assumptions about variable economic conditions and resulting revenues. With the U.S. economy continuing to lag in late 2010, with some analysts worried about a "double dip" recession, and with even optimistic projections predicting only a slow economic recovery, it is unlikely that the deficits will drop as far as the White House has suggested. An August 2010 survey found 92% of Americans saying it was important to reduce the deficit. Despite this consensus, there has been no serious movement in Congress or the White House to take decisive action. One reason is that moving too far too fast to decrease spending or increase taxes might seriously disrupt an already weak economy. The other reason that moving closer to a balanced budget is hard is because most Americans oppose any cuts in programs that benefit them, and also oppose any increase in the taxes that they, rather than someone else, pay. There is also no broad agreement on the topic of this debate. When asked about the balance of spending cuts and tax increases, a thin majority (52%) favored emphasizing reduced spending, 12% preferred to focus on tax increases, 29% wanted the two approaches to be about equal, and 7% were unsure.

Where to Find More

A first-rate book urging restoration of fiscal responsibility is David M. Walter, *Comeback America: Turning the Country Around and Restoring Fiscal Responsibility* (Random House, 2010). You can learn a lot about the U.S. budget at www.gpoaccess.gov/usbudget/. Under "browse" the current budget, especially look at the category "historical tables." The budget rests on the economy to a substantial degree, and to look at it and future projects, access the annual *Economic Report to the President* by the Council of Economic Advisors at http://fraser.stlouisfed.org/publications/ERP. A third invaluable source is the Congressional Budget Office at www.cbo.gov/. A readable and valuable look at the budget is Scott Bittle and Jean Johnson, *Where Does the Money Go?: Your Guided Tour to the Federal Budget Crisis* (Harper, 2009).

What More to Do

A good perspective on the problems of reducing the budget deficits will be to have the class propose tax hikes and spending cuts, but only those that clearly would impact at least a few members of the class. Watch the conflict between the theory of fiscal responsibility and the reality of pragmatic self-interest collide.

CREDITS

Asian American Legal Foundation. Amicus curiae brief to the U.S. Supreme Court in *Parents Involved in Community Schools v. Seattle School District No. 1* (2007).

Attorneys representing Arizona and its governor, Janice K. Brewer, seeking to block a petition by the U.S. government to enjoin the enforcement of Arizona's S.B. 1070 in *The United States of America, Plaintiff, v. The State of Arizona; and Janice K. Brewer, Governor of the State of Arizona, in her Official Capacity, Defendants,* Case 2:10-cv-01413, U.S. District Court for the District of Arizona, July 6, 2010.

Attorneys representing plaintiffs Kristen M. Perry, et al. seeking to have California's constitutional clause barring gay marriage declared a violation of the U.S. Constitution in *Kristin M. Perry, et al., Plaintiffs, v. Arnold Schwarzenegger, et al., Defendants, and Proposition 8 Official Proponents Dennis Hollingsworth, et al., Defendant-Intervenors*; Case3:09-cv-02292-VRW; U.S. District Court for the Northern District Of California; Responses to Court's Questions for Closing Arguments, June 15, 2010.

Attorneys representing Proposition 8 official proponents Dennis Hollingsworth, *et al.*, seeking to have California's constitutional clause barring gay marriage upheld in *Kristin M. Perry, et al., Plaintiffs, v. Arnold Schwarzenegger, et al., Defendants, and Proposition 8 Official Proponents Dennis Hollingsworth, et al., Defendant-Intervenors*; Case3:09-cv-02292-VRW; U.S. District Court for the Northern District Of California; Responses to Court's Questions for Closing Arguments, June 15, 2010.

Attorneys representing the U.S. government seeking to enjoin the enforcement of Arizona's S.B. 1070 in *The United States of America, Plaintiff, v. The State of Arizona; and Janice K. Brewer, Governor of the State of Arizona, in her Official Capacity, Defendants,* Case 2:10-cv-01413, U.S. District Court for the District of Arizona, July 6, 2010.

Brady, David W. From "The 2008 Democratic Shift," by David W. Brady, Policy Review, December 2008. Reprinted with permission.

Bright, Stephen B. Testimony during hearings on "An Examination of the Death Penalty in the United States" before the U.S. Senate, Committee on the Judiciary, Subcommittee on the Constitution, February 1, 2006.

Brown, Barbara Berish. Testimony during hearings on the "Paycheck Fairness Act" before the U.S. Senate, Committee on Health, Education, Labor & Pensions, April 12, 2007.

Burman, Leonard E. Testimony during hearings on "Taxes and the Budget" before the Subcommittee on Select Revenue Measures, Committee on Ways and Means, U.S. House of Representatives, March 23, 2010.

Chemerinsky, Erwin. "Constitutional Interpretation for the Twenty-first Century," *Advance: The Journal of the American Constitution Society Issues Groups*, Fall 2007. Reprinted with permission from The American Constitution Society for Law and Policy, Copyright © The American Constitution Society for Law and Policy, 1333 H St, NW, 11th Floor, Washington, DC 20005. Telephone: (202) 393-6181 Fax: (202) 393-6189. Web site: www.acslaw.org/.

Cheney, Richard B. From "Remarks by Richard B. Cheney", by Richard B. Cheney, American Enterprise Institute, Washington, D.C. May 20, 2009. Reprinted with permission.

Cost, Jay. "The 'Enduring Majority'—Again: No, the Democrats Will Not Be in Power Forever," National Review (June 8, 2009). © 2009 by National Review, Inc., 215 Lexington Avenue, New York, NY 10016. Reprinted by permission.

Flint, Alex. Testimony during hearings on before the U.S. House of Representative, Select Committee on Energy Independence and Global Warming, March 12, 2008.

Flournoy, Michèle P. Testimony during hearings on "Developments in Afghanistan" before the Committee on Armed Services, U.S. Senate, June 15, 2010.

Fonte, John. Testimony during hearings on "Comprehensive Immigration Reform: Becoming Americans—U.S. Immigrant Integration," U.S. House of Representatives, Committee on the Judiciary, Subcommittee on Immigration Citizenship, Refugees, Border Security, and International Law, May 16, 2007.

Gattuso, James L. Testimony during hearings on "The Rulemaking Process and Unitary Executive Theory" before the U.S. House of Representatives, Committee on the Judiciary, Subcommittee on Commercial and Administrative Law, May 6, 2008.

Gerstle, Gary. Testimony during hearings on "Comprehensive Immigration Reform: Becoming Americans—U.S. Immigrant Integration" before the U.S. House of Representatives, Committee on the Judiciary, Subcommittee on Immigration Citizenship, Refugees, Border Security, and International Law, May 16, 2007.

Greenberger, Marcia. Testimony during hearings on the "Paycheck Fairness Act" before the U.S. House of Representatives, Committee on Education and Labor, Subcommittee on Workforce Protection, July 11, 2007.

Graham, Lindsey. Remarks on the floor of the U.S. Senate, *Congressional Record*, August 3, 2010.

Grassley, Charles. Remarks on the floor of the U.S. Senate, *Congressional Record*, August 3, 2010.

Hayduk, Ron. "The Case for Immigrant Voting Rights," an original essay, 2009.

Henderson, M. Todd. "Citizens United: A Defense," Faculty Blog, University of Chicago Law School. March 12, 2010. Reprinted with permission.

Holtz-Eakin, Douglas. Testimony during hearings on "Taxes and the Budget" before the Subcommittee on Select Revenue Measures, Committee on Ways and Means, U.S. House of Representatives, March 23, 2010.

Huffington, Arianna. Testimony during hearings on Senate Subcommittee on "The Future of Journalism" before the U.S. Senate, Committee on Commerce, Science, and Transportation; Subcommittee on Communications, Technology, and the Internet, May 6, 2009.

Isaacson, George S. Testimony during hearings on "H.R. 3396—The Sales Tax Fairness and Simplification Act," U.S. House of Representatives, Committee on the Judiciary, Subcommittee on Administrative and Commercial Law, December 6, 2007.

Laycock, Douglas. From a discussion of the topic "Under God? Pledge of Allegiance Constitutionality," sponsored by the Pew Forum on Religion & Public Life, March 19, 2004. Reprinted with the permission of the Pew Forum on Religion & Public Life. For more information on this issue, please visit www.pewforum.org. Copyright © 2006 Pew Research Center.

Lee, Shirley Jackson. Remarks on the floor of the House of Representatives, *Congressional Record,* March 10, 2010

Lobel, Jules. Testimony during hearings on "War Powers for the 21st Century: The Constitutional Perspective" before the U.S. House of Representatives, Committee on Foreign Affairs, Subcommittee on International Organizations, Human Rights, and Oversight, April 24, 2008.

McAdams, John. Testimony during hearings on "An Examination of the Death Penalty in the United States" before the U.S. Senate, Committee on the Judiciary, Subcommittee on the Constitution, February 1, 2006.

Mann, Thomas E. Testimony during hearings on "Examining the Filibuster: Legislative Proposals to Change Senate Procedures" before the Committee on Rules and Administration, U.S. Senate, June 23, 2010.

National Education Association, et al. Amicus curiae brief to the U.S. Supreme Court in *Parents Involved in Community Schools v. Seattle School District No. 1* (2007).

National Popular Vote. From "Agreement Among the States to Elect the President by National Popular Vote," National Popular Vote, April 29, 2009. Reprinted with permission.

Obama, Barack. Speech delivered at the National Archives Museum, Washington, D.C., May 21, 2009.

Podesta, John. Testimony during hearings on "Economic Opportunity and Poverty in America" before U.S. House of Representatives, Committee on Ways & Means, Subcommittee on Income Security and Family Support, April 26, 2007.

Rademaker, Stephen G. Testimony during hearings on "War Powers for the 21st Century: The Executive Branch Perspective" before the U.S. House of Representatives, Committee on Foreign Affairs, Subcommittee on International Organizations, Human Rights, and Oversight, April 24, 2008.

Rauschenberger, Steven. Testimony during hearings on "H.R. 3396—The Sales Tax Fairness and Simplification Act" before the U.S. House of Representatives, Committee on the Judiciary, Subcommittee on Administrative and Commercial Law, December 6, 2007.

Rawls, Lee. Testimony during hearings on "Examining the Filibuster: Legislative Proposals to Change Senate Procedures" before the Committee on Rules and Administration, U.S. Senate, June 23, 2010.

Rector, Robert. Testimony during hearings on "Economic Opportunity and Poverty in America" before U.S. House of Representatives, Committee on Ways & Means, Subcommittee on Income Security and Family Support, April 26, 2007.

Renshon, Stanley. "The Debate Over Non-Citizen Voting: A Primer," on the Web site of the Center for Immigration Studies, April 2008.

Samples, John. "A Critique of the National Popular Vote Plan for Electing the President," *Policy Analysis*, No. 622 (October 13, 2008). Reprinted with permission of The Cato Institute.

Sekulow, Jay Alan. From a discussion of the topic "Under God? Pledge of Allegiance Constitutionality," sponsored by the Pew Forum on Religion & Public Life, March 19, 2004. Reprinted with the permission of the Pew Forum on Religion & Public Life. For more information on this issue, please visit www.pewforum.org. Copyright © 2006 Pew Research Center.

Simon, David. Testimony during hearings on Senate Subcommittee on "The Future of Journalism" before the U.S. Senate, Committee on Commerce, Science, and Transportation; Subcommittee on Communications, Technology, and the Internet, May 6, 2009.

Squassoni Sharon A. Testimony during hearings on "Nuclear Power in a Warming World: Solution or Illusion?" before House of Representative, Select Committee on Energy Independence and Global Warming, March 12, 2008.

Strauss, Peter L. Testimony during hearings on "The Rulemaking Process and Unitary Executive Theory" before the U.S. House of Representatives, Committee on the Judiciary, Subcommittee on Commercial and Administrative Law, May 6, 2008.

Whittington, Keith E. "Originalism Within the Living Constitution," *Advance: The Journal of the American Constitution Society Issues Groups*, Fall 2007. Reprinted with permission from The American Constitution Society for Law and Policy, Copyright © The American Constitution Society for Law and Policy, 1333 H St, NW, 11th Floor Washington, DC 20005. Telephone: (202) 393-6181 Fax: (202) 393-6189. Web site: www.acslaw.org/.

Youn, Monica. Testimony during hearings on the "First Amendment and Campaign Finance Reform After *Citizens United*," before the Committee on the Judiciary, U.S. House of Representatives, February 3, 2010.